The Dream of an Absolute Language

The Dream of an Absolute Language

Emanuel Swedenborg
and French Literary Culture

Lynn R. Wilkinson

State University of New York Press

Published by
State University of New York Press, Albany

Portions of the text are reprinted with permission of the Modern Language Association of America from "*Le cousin Pons* and the Invention of Ideology," *PMLA* 107:2
(1992): 274-89.

Portions of an article entitled "Embodying the Crowd: Balzac's *l'Envers de l'histoire
contemporaine* and the Languages of Class Consciousness" taken from *Symposium*
43:2 (Summer 1989): 127-37. Reprinted with permission of the Helen Dwight Reid
Educational Foundation. Published by Haldref Publications, 1319 Eighteenth
Street, N.W., Washington, D.C. 20036-1802. Copyright © 1989.

For information, address State University of New York Press,
State University Plaza, Albany, N.Y., 12246

Production by Diane Ganeles
Marketing by Bernadette LaManna

Library of Congress Cataloging-in-Publication Data

Wilkinson, Lynn R.
    The dream of an absolute language : Emanuel Swedenborg and French
literary culture / Lynn R. Wilkinson.
        p.   cm.
    Includes bibliographical references and index.
    ISBN 0-7914-2926-1 (PB : acid free). —ISBN 0-7914-2925-3 (CH : acid free)
    1. Swedenborg, Emanuel, 1688–1772—Contributions in philosophy of
language.   2. Swedenborg, Emanuel, 1688–1772—Influence.   3. Language
and languages—Philosophy.   4. French literature—19th century—History and
criticism.   5. France—Intellectual life—18th century.   6. France—Intellectual
life—19th century.   7. Language Universal.   I. Title.
    P85.S9W55   1996
    840.9'384—dc20   95-30210
                                                                               CIP

10 9 8 7 6 5 4 3 2 1

For my parents

Contents

Preface

This book began with a series of questions concerning the similarities between Swedenborg's theories of language and those of Balzac and Baudelaire. My point of departure was recent work on language theory and intellectual history, notably Michel Foucault's *Les mots et les choses* and several very suggestive studies on Swedenborg by a Swedish literary and intellectual historian, Inge Jonsson. The latter's study of the origins and evolution of Swedenborg's doctrine of correspondences, which showed the concept to be embedded in rationalist notions of language and consciousness, suggested that there was much to be said on the subject of the French reception of the doctrine of correspondences, especially since references to it appear in the writings of Balzac and Baudelaire. Why, I asked, would two major writers—major, at least, from our standpoint—refer to the work of an apparently obscure Swedish scientist and visionary? And why in connection with significant formal and theoretical innovations in their work?

It became clear to me, as I worked on the project, that my original conception entailed several problems. First and foremost was the issue of transmission. Few people in France seem actually to have read Swedenborg, and, in addition, Jonsson's study had emphasized his debt to seventeenth-century philosophy to the extent that later interest in Swedenborg could only seem an anachronism—at least in what might be called elite culture. Swedenborgianism, it turned out, was transmitted in the context of the doctrines of Mesmerism and freemasonry, and the evolution of a myth of Swedenborg and a notion of an absolute language identified with his doctrine of correspondences involves complex interactions between popular and elite culture. Robert Darnton's *Mesmerism and the Enlightenment in France* brought home to me the importance of political dreams and fantasies in the image of Swedenborg that was transmitted in French popular culture in the first half of the nineteenth century.

Second, Foucault's categories of "correspondences" and "representation," which had originally seemed so suggestive for the study of Sweden-

borg, who uses both words in his discussion of language and consciousness, seemed to reduce the most disparate works to a single category:
instead of marking out a clear division between *epistemes* or scientific or
cultural paradigms, they pointed to two aspects of every written text, what
Jakobson had called its "metaphoric and metonymic axes." In the works of
Swedenborg, Balzac, and Baudelaire, one finds juxtaposed a concern both
with classification and representation, on the one hand, and with resemblances among individual words and things, on the other. Foucault, I con-
cluded, had attempted to make historical distinctions on the basis of a
theory of language that was itself historical. I came to see that Swedenborgianism was intimately linked to a theory of language, the theoretical
underpinnings of which were worked out in the late seventeenth and eighteenth centuries, but which came to exercise widespread fascination over
many aspects of French culture in the nineteenth. Here, I found much
help in the nuanced studies collected in Hans Aarsleff's *From Locke to
Saussure*. These emphasized the continuing importance of rationalist
thought for many nineteenth-century linguists and pointed to the connections between Adamic theories of language of the late seventeenth century
and the revival of interest in eighteenth-century language theory that
formed the context for Saussure's ground-breaking work at the end of the
nineteenth. It appeared, however, that this revival entailed more than a
turning back on the part of professional linguists and philosophers; indeed,
that there had been a widespread fascination with the notion of a universal
language in other areas of French culture, including not only literature,
but also social theory and aesthetics. And, I thought that tracing the reception of Swedenborg's work in France would be an excellent point of departure for understanding just how—and why—ideas of a universal language
evolved there in the late eighteenth and nineteenth centuries.

I shall argue here that it was precisely the rationalist aspects of
Swedenborg's doctrine of correspondences that nineteenth-century French
writers found attractive. In France, as in England and Germany, the notion
of a language of nature played an important role in late-eighteenth- and
early-nineteenth-century philosophy and aesthetics, with the important
difference that French writers tended to view this language as ahistorical,
akin to the unchanging structures of logic and mathematics, and not immediately apparent to common sense or the naked eye. Swedenborg's doctrine of correspondences appeared to be one version of a language of nature that mediated between science and theology, on the one hand, and
suggested an inner logic hidden beneath the surfaces of a corrupt world,
on the other.

It is true, as Hans Aarsleff has pointed out, that historians often over-
emphasize the influence of Herder on the development of language theory

in Germany—and, one might add, England and German *poets* most often associate the notion of a language of nature to a spirit of place and the particular history of a poet. In the work of Balzac, Baudelaire, and many other French writers, in contrast, the evocation of a language of nature carries with it universalizing associations in line, partly, with the aims of the Catholic Church. But to derive the differences between French poetry and that of Germany and English-speaking countries merely on the basis of religious differences would be misleading. One of the major thinkers whom French writers invoke as an authority on a universal language of nature is Leibniz. And to insist exclusively on religious differences is to overlook the central importance of a group of thinkers who denied the importance of any kind of historical religion and who had utmost importance for the interpretation and transmission of a notion of a language of nature in French culture in the nineteenth century. For it was the Idéologues who made the crucial link between a *quest* for a universal language not yet found in any particular time and place and the future establishment of a utopian social order.

In the work of the Idéologues, language itself, rather than particular rituals or symbolic systems, becomes a basis for what cultural historians such as Lynn Hunt have recently called a reinvention of politics and authority after the French Revolution. The work of the Idéologues, like other attempts during the decades following the Revolution to develop rituals and symbols to replace those of the monarchy and Catholic Church, grows out of parallel efforts in the eighteenth century, especially the rites and symbols associated with freemasonry. The role of this movement in educating individuals in the practices of democratic participation has only begun to be explored. The work of Margaret Jacob, especially, suggests that the notion of a symbolic reinterpretation of the world, secret but with universal aims, could go hand in hand with desires for a radical transformation of the social order. So if the Idéologues' work often seems to have been more cited than read—and here the parallel with Swedenborg is striking—the associations between the notions of a universal symbolism or language and a reordering of society according to rational precepts gave at least one aspect of their works a special prominence in French culture in the first half of the nineteenth century. One would be hard pressed, for example, to attribute Fourier's fanciful interpretations of a universal language of nature to a careful reading of anyone, and yet the intended correspondence between language and a utopian social order resembles a plausible interpretation of this central aspect of the Idéologues' work. And Fourier's work, in turn, was crucial for emphasizing the connection between notions of linguistic and social order. Moreover, one ambiguity in his thought, i.e., the potential for his universal system, in which, as in Plato's *Republic*, every individual is assigned a place, to be interpreted as a blueprint for a totalitarian social order, was to be particularly troubling—or inspiring—for other nineteenth-century French writers.

If the novelist Stendhal, who seems to have read extensively in the work of the Idéologues, sees in their exposition of a universal language a justification for individual freedom, Balzac, who never mentions the Idéologues, but invokes Swedenborg as the exponent of a very similar theory of language, interprets this notion very differently. Like the conservative social theorists Louis de Bonald and Joseph de Maistre, Balzac in his prefaces argues that a language of nature points to the necessity for a return to the authority of the Catholic Church. In his novels, however, Swedenborg and Swedenborgianism most often appear as a kind of fiction. It is highly improbable that Balzac was a Swedenborgian believer, and there was no Swedenborgian Church in France. The references to Swedenborgianism suggest, especially in the later works of *La comédie humaine*, that Balzac is aware of the extent to which he is bound to write within a notion of a totality that may very well be a fiction. In very late novels, especially *Le cousin Pons*, it even seems that he has reached the conclusion that the totalizing structures that inform his attempt to represent the whole of contemporary French society themselves represent a kind of ideology, an ideology that is bound up with the very language he is using. To say this, of course, is to use the term "ideology" in a very different sense from that intended by the Idéologues. But, as I shall argue in my chapter on Balzac's late works, such a shift is justified by transformations in the style and subject matter of Balzac's late novels.

Balzac's knowledge of Swedenborgianism appears to have derived from a few popularizing handbooks, *abrégés* of the Swedish theosopher's doctrines. But his works, in turn, seem to have informed many popularizing accounts of Swedenborg in the mid-nineteenth century, as well as Baudelaire's understanding of the literary importance of Swedenborg. Successive interpretations of Swedenborgianism, especially the theory of language known as the doctrine of correspondences, provide a red thread through a complicated context. The pattern that emerges indicates shifting attitudes towards the shape of language and the nature and aims of the French Revolution, whose universal aims tended to be abandoned, or at least viewed with considerable ambivalence, by groups who became enfranchised. Unlike many of the less talented or successful writers who interpreted Swedenborg and his language theory, Balzac and Baudelaire invoke Swedenborgianism in connection with their questioning of the aims and limits of a notion of a language of nature that might serve as the basis not only for the criticism of a corrupt social order but also for the justification of an order that denies a voice to any of its subjects. For both writers, the discovery of the oppressive or distorting aspects of apparently utopian language schemes occurred in the context of disillusionment with political platforms and agendas. The years surrounding 1830 and 1848 proved crucial in this respect.

Reading Balzac's and Baudelaire's subtle explorations of the limits of of an unchanging language of nature suggested to me that one reason Foucault's linguistic intellectual history fails to capture them is that it is itself caught up in the paradigm of a universal language—a paradigm that can spill over into the potentially totalitarian belief that individuals have nothing to say and have only to obey. At the end of *Les mots et les choses*, Foucault suggests—hopefully, perhaps—that a time is coming when, as Nietzsche predicted, "man" will disappear from the world as we know it. But such an event, I argue here, already occurred in mid-nineteenth-century French literature. Turning back to Balzac and Baudelaire may well tell us something about the conditions under which one may be persuaded to believe that one is not the subject of one's discourse, that one has no voice.

This book has a long history. Parts of chapters 3, 4, and 5 originated in my doctoral dissertation in Comparative Literature at Berkeley, and I would like to thank my director, Professor Denis Hollier, for his readings of my work in its early stages, and the University of California for two grants enabling me to research Swedenborg and his popularizers in Sweden, London, and Paris. The final version was completed during a year at Harvard, and I thank members of the Department of Germanic Languages for their hospitality and the teaching schedule that made my work possible. At Texas, ongoing conversations with colleagues, particularly the participants in the assistant professors' reading group, have been a constant reminder of the interdisciplinary nature of this study.

Thanks are also due to those who took the time to read and comment on my manuscript: Professors Hans Aarsleff, Frank Paul Bowman, and especially Inge Jonsson, whose work on Swedenborg has been a major impetus for my own. My readers, of course, are not responsible for the demons—Swedenborgian or otherwise—which I suspect still lurk in my text.

More generally, this study owes much to Professor Hanna Pitkin, who had nothing to do with it specifically, but whose generosity and gift for bringing things to life helped make it possible.

I am also grateful for permission to reproduce portions of articles that appeared in *PMLA* and *Symposium*.

Introduction:
Swedenborg, French Culture, and the
Dream of an Absolute Language

"Le beau nom SVEDENBORG sonne étrangement aux oreilles françaises," wrote the French poet Paul Valéry with characteristic wryness. His words appear at the beginning of an essay on a recent translation of an intellectual biography of Swedenborg by the eminent Swedish literary historian, Martin Lamm. This study follows the career of Emanuel Swedenborg (1688–1772) through its many stages, noting his many interests in the natural sciences and rationalist philosophy, before turning to Lamm's main focus: those works Swedenborg wrote in the early 1740s, which may provide clues to why he chose to abandon the natural sciences in order to shut himself up in his garden house for decades and produce tract after tract detailing life in other worlds, invisible, but parallel to our own. For Lamm, Swedenborg's change of direction coincided with the beginnings of preromanticism in Sweden and elsewhere in Europe: his appeal to posterity lies in his apparent rejection of reason during the last decades of his life.[1]

For Valéry, writing as an inheritor of a modernist tradition in French poetry that includes the works of Baudelaire and Mallarmé, the connection between Swedenborg and posterity seemed less clear. What he learned from Lamm's biography contrasted peculiarly with the little he had known before it came into his hands. "*Séraphitus-Séraphitâ* de Balzac et un chapitre de Gérard de Nerval avaient été jadis mes seules sources," he writes. Moreover, their allusions to Swedenborg served more to evoke a general context than a personality or set of works or doctrines:

> J'imagine que cette époque fut l'une des plus brillantes et des plus complètes que des hommes aient pu connaître. On y trouve l'étincelante fin d'un monde et les puissants efforts d'un autre qui veut naître, un art des plus raffinés, des formes et des égards encore très mesurés, toutes les

1

forces et toutes les graces de l'esprit. Il y a de la magie et du calcul
différentiel; autant d'athées que de mystiques; les plus cyniques des cyniques et les plus bizarres des rêveurs. (1:867)

Reading Lamm's biography did not appear to have significantly changed
Valéry's assessment of Swedenborg's importance for the development of
French literature or culture; this has little to do with the personality or
even specific works of the man, but rather lies in the heritage of one aspect
of Enlightenment culture and the transmission of theories of language
that united mathematical precision with the evocativeness of music. "Le
beau nom SVEDENBORG *sonne* . . ."

Had he been more interested in the subject, Valéry might have located
a significant number of French texts citing Swedenborg and even expounding his works. It is curious, for example, that he omitted Baudelaire in his
citation of "sources," for Baudelaire not only wrote a sonnet, "Correspondances," that has traditionally been associated with Swedenborg's doctrine
by the same name, but he also referred to Swedenborg and to *correspondances* in several other works. Valéry might also have found a respectable
intellectual biography of Swedenborg in French written by the religious
historian, Jacques Matter, and published in 1863. Similarly, he might have
unearthed such finds as a summary of Swedenborg's doctrines, one of
many translations into French of his works, tracts showing the intimate
connections between Mesmerism, somnambulism, and Swedenborgianism,
or a work of eclectic theosophy citing Swedenborg written by one of the
many writers we now classify as minor, such as Guillaume Oegger (c.
1790–c. 1853)[2] or Alphonse-Louis Constant (1810–1875), also known as
Eliphas Lévi. Valéry might have noted that these writers, too, linked
Swedenborg to French culture in the late eighteenth century, although
nineteenth-century writers emphasize the revolutionary heritage of this
context to a far greater extent than Valéry. On one point, however, he
would have agreed with the earlier writers: whatever else it calls up, the
name of Swedenborg is inextricably linked to the question of language.
And it is precisely because of this link that the relation of Swedenborg, his
doctrines, and work, to French literature and culture in the late eighteenth and nineteenth centuries, is of particular interest. For the reception
of Swedenborg and his doctrine of correspondences in France not only
provides a red thread through the intricate context of late eighteenth-
century and early nineteenth-century pseudoscience and esotericism; it
also suggests how and why the theory of a universal or absolute language,
displaced among professional linguists and philosophers by the historical
study of language, was kept alive in popular culture and avant-garde literature at this time. I intend this study of French interpretations of Sweden-

borg to provide an approach to the cultural history of a theory of language that purports to be universal and ahistorical.

In the late eighteenth and early nineteenth centuries, the notion of a language of nature exerted a widespread appeal in European culture, among poets and literary writers, as well as philosophers. Within this context, the question of origins played a central but ambiguous role, for it was understood in two, fundamentally opposed, ways. The first follows a general tendency in Enlightenment thought to view the question in fundamentally ahistorical terms; in other words, to use the word to evoke an analogy or unchanging relationship between, for example, language and consciousness, or language and a state of nature. The second, which takes after Herder's emphasis on the importance of the specific historical development of individual languages, ties language to the fortunes of particular people in particular places. This interpretation was especially important for the development of nationalism, but such an emphasis on the organic development of individuals and languages appears in the work of many poets, especially in Germany and England.[3] While it also appears in the work of some French writers, I argue here that the first interpretation of language origins is of greater importance in France, appearing, in connection with the notion of a universal or absolute language that cannot be identified with any historically existing language, in the works of such disparate writers as the Idéologues, Fourier, Stendhal, Balzac, and Baudelaire. The notion of a universal language is not always tied to theology, orthodox or heterodox. Sometimes, as in the work of the Idéologues and Stendhal, the theory of a universal language underlying appearances is linked to an anti-clerical and anti-religious point of view. At other times, in the works of Balzac and Baudelaire or the conservative social theorists Louis de Bonald and Joseph de Maistre, it appears in connection with the name of Swedenborg and the universalizing aims of the Catholic Church, although for both French writers, the extent to which this link is intended to be taken seriously is open to doubt. I argue that, despite the apparent religious differences, there is significant common ground among these theories of a universal language, which sometimes comes to be identified with a language of nature. All suggest that language possesses a certain utopian potential, although they differ on whether the state of perfection is to be expected in the future or in a return to a past golden age (or, similarly, whether the ideal universal language is to be discovered or recovered).[4] The notion of a hidden but absolute order seems inevitably to carry with it the potential for criticizing the corrupt institutions of society. And a belief in a universal language that corresponds both to the structures of human consciousness and the world provides a means for individuals, however isolated, to imagine themselves as part of a whole, or what Marxist historians often call a totality.[5] Finally, the very link between language and totality entails an ambiguous attitude towards human freedom. For if it makes it impossible to imagine oneself apart from a social world or group, it also suggests that obedience, rather than autonomy, is what counts in the maintenance of order.

Why was the notion of a universal language of such importance for the development of French literature, or at least of a certain modernist literary tradition that develops through the work of Balzac, Stendhal, Baudelaire, and Mallarmé? It is impossible to adduce influence here, especially the influence of Swedenborg. Instead, to bring in a hopelessly vague but indispensable term of Raymond Williams's, I think one has to do with a structure of feeling, a longing for wholeness, and a radical transformation of what is perceived to be a degenerate world that is both recognized as a wish-fulfillment dream *and* transposed into a theory of an *invisible* absolute language.[6] In their evocation of this hidden order, artists turn to the doctrines of men such as Swedenborg, Mesmer, and other pseudoscientific and esoteric writers and practitioners. These doctrines both purported to map out the contours of a whole world that extended beyond the boundaries of the senses and suggested the dream-like nature of such an enterprise. In this respect, the frequent linking of Swedenborg with the doctrines and practices of Mesmer and animal magnetists is significant, for Mesmer and his followers focused on the relation of the invisible to dreams and to desires. And in popular culture, Mesmerist doctrines very often suggested, especially in the last decades of the eighteenth century, a politics of fulfillment in which individual desires and the perfecting of society might be reconciled.

There are several excellent studies of the context of French esotericism and pseudoscience in the late eighteenth and early nineteenth centuries. Apart from the many important monographs on individual writers that point to the importance of the contemporary movements for their subjects, several general works are indispensible. First and foremost, in a series of studies, Auguste Viatte mapped out the development of French esoteric and pseudoscientific thought during this period, emphasizing the importance of minor writers, and the increased interest in these theories after each transformation in French politics. Viatte also notes the peculiarity of the French interest in Swedenborg, who, he writes, "n'avait rien d'un enthousiaste."[7] More recently, Karl-Erik Sjödén has traced in great detail the fortunes of French Swedenborgians in the late eighteenth and early nineteenth centuries, showing both the striking isolation and lack of success of this sect and the continuing link, even in the most apparently isolated cases, between French Swedenborgianism and revolutionary politics.[8] Most studies of Swedenborg's influence and reception, however, overlook the complexity both of his work and of the context of French esotericism and pseudoscience at this time, characterizing Swedenborg and his doctrines as preromantic and attributing his apparent influence to parallels in eighteenth- and nineteenth-century attitudes towards reason and religion.[9] Recent work in two different areas, the history of language and European cultural history, suggests a more interesting approach.

Martin Lamm's thesis that Swedenborg's work coincided with a widespread questioning and rejection of rationalist science and philosophy fails to hold up under closer scrutiny either of his work or of the reception of his works—at least in France. In a series of monographs published in the 1960s and 1970s, the Swedish literary and intellectual historian Inge Jonsson took a closer look at aspects of Swedenborg's work, focusing especially on the importance of rationalist psychology and language theory in Swedenborg's work as a whole. In a study of the origins and evolution of the doctrine of correspondences, Jonsson found that the most important precedents for the doctrine were Leibniz's attempt to construct an ars combinatoria, a system of symbols that could be combined with mathematical precision to investigate the unknown, and the psychology of Nicolas Malebranche, who used the terms *correspondance* and *représentation* in ways quite similar to Swedenborg: to indicate the mirror-like relationship of the mind's perceptions to the world.[10] Swedenborg drew on both these models in his own speculative works on human psychology, especially in a very difficult unpublished text which probably dates to the early 1740s, *Clavis hieroglyphica*. However, in other transitional works written at about this time, Swedenborg also turned to neoclassical literary forms in order to think through physiological problems he was working on: a Latin creation epic links the story of Adam and Eve to the hatching of a world egg. For Jonsson, Swedenborg's work, far from pointing forward to the antiscientific spirit of some Romantic poets and philosophers, reflects the divergent interests of Swedish scholars of the preceding century, who, like latter-day Renaissance men, inhabited an intellectual world unmarked by what T. S. Eliot called a "dissociation of sensibility."[11] Jonsson's work raises, but never directly addresses, the important question of why anyone would be interested in the work of such an anachronism. But his very careful contextual readings do provide a point of departure for answering it.

Swedenborg's works of speculative psychology are probably less idiosyncratic—or original—than most students of his work have claimed. The kinds of questions he posed could only be addressed speculatively, through precisely the kinds of analogies and fictions he proposed. The breadth of Swedenborg's knowledge—even though, as Jonsson notes, it is sometimes overestimated[12]—allowed him to explore the limits of the rationalist underpinnings of other speculative psychologies of the time. This aspect of Swedenborg's work, I argue here, presents striking parallels to the theories and practices of Mesmer.[13] That the doctrines of the two men were often associated in the late eighteenth and early nineteenth centuries points to a widespread perception of certain broadly based similarities. Moreover, Mesmerism was only one contemporary or near-contemporary intellectual and cultural movement that informed the reception of Swedenborg; indeed, some of the earliest Swedenborgians were associated with masonic communities that claimed his doctrines as the origin and justification of their rites. Some also claimed that Swedenborg himself had been a mason.[14] What is at stake in the association, however, is not the transmission of masonic symbolism from one context to another, but rather a general tendency to construct idiosyncratic symbolic systems that not only assumed cosmological proportions, but also provided a language for an individual's initiation into and understanding of his—and very occasionally, her—place within a community of equals.

Two excellent works in cultural history have mapped out the development of Mesmerism and freemasonry, emphasizing the relation of these two cultural movements to the politics of the French Revolution. In his *Mesmerism and the End of the Enlightenment in France*, published in 1968, Robert Darnton considered the role of Mesmerist iconography within French popular culture from the 1780s to the 1850s. References to Mesmerism during the years surrounding the French Revolution of 1789, he found, were intimately bound up with popular beliefs concerning the ability of science to perfect the social world. Interpretations of Mesmerism in the first part of the nineteenth century carry associations to the revolutionary iconography of 1789, but with increasing pessimism. For Darnton, the frequent association of Mesmerism with Swedenborgianism and other spiritualist doctrines in the nineteenth century is a sign of a widespread disillusionment with political agendas, utopianism, and even reason in general. Infusions of Swedenborgianism into a Mesmerist-tinged popular culture, it seems, mark out "the end of the Enlightenment," or at least of a certain kind of Enlightenment politics, in France.

Mesmerism and the End of the Enlightenment in France was Darnton's first book and also one of the first American studies to focus on French popular culture. His argument parallels that of Jürgen Habermas in his *The Structural Transformation of the Public Sphere*, first published in German in 1962. Habermas argues that during the century preceding the French Revolution there developed in France a reading public capable of articulating and evaluating complex social issues. Paradoxically, perhaps, the Revolution of 1789 put an end to the progressive print culture of the Enlightenment, by shifting the forum for debates to the streets and by allowing the less educated to participate. Although he does not discuss them directly, Habermas would count the minor writers who expounded Swedenborg and Mesmer, often together, in the 1840s and 1850s, as participants in a mass political culture incapable of debating political issues rationally or serenely. Like Marx in his *Eighteenth Brumaire*, both Habermas's and Darnton's studies of the 1960s consider the iconography of mid-nineteenth-century popular politics as parodies of 1789, unintentionally farcical imitations of a bourgeois model. Ironically, however, later works by Darnton have focused on Enlightenment writers who failed to make it into the bourgeoisie, a grub street which he sees as an "other Enlightenment."[15] These and other recent studies of print culture in France suggest that Habermas's original formulation is too narrowly based on class identity. Is print culture inherently bourgeois? It may depend on who is speaking or writing.[16]

It would be difficult to argue that the writers Auguste Viatte discusses in his *Victor Hugo et les Illuminés de son temps* did not provide elements of Hugo's own politically charged poetic symbolism. Or that the writers themselves did not see their work as closely related to politics, even when it was conceived as an alternative to social revolution. The "petit romantique" Alphonse-Louis Constant, for example, who was imprisoned for his early *La Bible de la liberté* (1841) and participated in the events of 1848, later renounced politics, but changed his name to Eliphas Lévi and spent the rest of his life writing about magical systems he believed were more powerful than ordinary politics.[17] It is clear that the relation of the language and symbolism of popular political culture in France in the 1840s and 1850s to the culture of the Ancien Régime is more complex than either Habermas or Darnton suggested in the 1960s. In *Work and Revolution: The Language of Labor and the Ancien Régime*, for example, William H. Sewell argued that artisans in mid-nineteenth-century Paris transformed elements of the symbolism of guild corporatism into a language expressing class solidarity.[18] Mid-nineteenth-century Swedenborgianism often reflects a similar development, but reaches back to a bourgeois "corporative" symbolism, that of the freemasons.

In several recent studies, Margaret Jacob has reconsidered the old question of the relation of freemasonry to the French Revolution. If some conservative thinkers at the end of the eighteenth century saw freemasonry as an international revolutionary conspiracy, Jacobs gives a more nuanced portrait of freemasonry as embodying a potentially democratic political culture. The societies, for example, gave bourgeois individuals, almost always men, the opportunity to experience a kind of "ennoblement" as they passed through the various grades of freemasonry and to participate in a democratic community in which values often associated with the bourgeoisie, honesty and work, were recognized as paramount.[19] It is difficult not to see in Swedenborg's construction of a personal symbolism a parallel wish for ennoblement and recognition based on work; if he had been ennobled in 1719, his sympathies were often republican, rather than monarchical, and he remained throughout his life somewhat of an outsider in the European scientific community, although he was a successful public official in Sweden. Many nineteenth-century French writers draw on guild traditions, the language of corporatism, and Swedenborgianism, but the implications of the latter often depend on the writers' class origins. For most of them, as for Swedenborg, the exposition of a cosmic symbolism becomes a means for conferring legitimacy both on the utterances of the individual and his or her activity *as a writer*. In the work of marginal writers, then, Swedenborgianism thus accompanies a claim to the right to participate in a public sphere that embraces both political participation and publication.

In the texts of bourgeois writers, the function of references to Swedenborgianism is less clear. In the writings of men who aimed mainly at proselytizing for the sect, Swedenborgianism is often associated with a political agenda, usually, but not always, that of the left.[20] In *literary* texts, however, the politics of allusions to Swedenborg and his doctrine of correspondences is ambiguous at best. Drawing on the popularizing writings of French Swedenborgians and specialists in esoteric traditions, writers such as Balzac and Baudelaire allude to Swedenborg and his doctrine of correspondences in contexts which suggest that their primary function is literary: Swedenborgian doctrines refer to aspects of a system that is above all fictional or poetic. In this sense, what is most important about references to Swedenborg in the work of Balzac and Baudelaire is their connection to a theory—perhaps theories—of language. For Baudelaire, as well as Balzac, the notion of a totality is central for the evocation of contemporary French society. In the earliest preface to a work included in *La comédie humaine*, Balzac compares this totality to Leibniz's monad, a "miroir concentrique du monde." For Baudelaire, it is more nebulous: his friend, Barbey d'Aurévilly, wrote of the "architecture secrète" of *Les fleurs du mal.*[21] But their brief and often ironic allusions to Swedenborgianism also entail a distance to the struggle for enfranchisement of more marginal writers who invoked esoteric doctrines in order to be heard as Bearers of the Word.

In nineteenth-century French culture, Swedenborgianism is an important vehicle for the transmission of a concept of structure associated with the universal language theory of the seventeenth and eighteenth centuries. In his collection of essays, *From Locke to Saussure*, Hans Aarsleff has argued the continuing importance of structural theories of language in nineteenth-century linguistic and philosophical circles. His argument provides a frame for mine, for I believe that the transmission and transformation of esoteric doctrines, especially Swedenborgianism, in French literature and popular culture also played an important role in establishing this sort of continuity, and that, moreover, literary and popular texts point to some of the ideological connotations this structure can assume; indeed, its fundamental complicity with notions of ideology in the nineteenth century. For in the works of Balzac and Baudelaire, as well as those of Fourier, Bonald, and Maistre, the notion of a language of nature was inextricably bound up with concepts of an ideal social order.

In his introduction to *From Locke to Saussure*, Aarsleff takes issue with Michel Foucault's linguistic categories in his structuralist study of European science and philosophy from the Renaissance to the present, *Les mots et les choses*. Foucault's insistence on breaks in modes of thought or what he calls *epistemes*—between the Renaissance and the late seventeenth century or the Enlightenment and nineteenth-century European thought—just does not hold up under scrutiny. (22) Moreover, Aarsleff argues, "the re-emergence of the eighteenth century after 1850 is much too powerful to ignore." (23) And why, considering that his divisions are not unusual, does he not take into consideration the French Revolution? I cite Aarsleff's criticisms at length, because I began this study with the idea that apparent "correspondences" among the works of Balzac, Baudelaire, and Swedenborg represented an anachronistic and anomalous continuity between eighteenth- and nineteenth-century writing. What I came to see was that both contexts were far more complex than either Foucault or conventional intellectual history had acknowledged, and that a schematic system that failed to distinguish between competing cultural voices—or to recognize the importance of voices, at all—was inadequate for my purposes. And finally, I came to see that Foucault's schema was itself based on a theory of a universal language that was historically determined. It is true that the conclusion of *Les mots et les choses* looks forward to the disappearance of "man," as well as the mutations of Enlightenment discourse that produced "him." But it is by no means certain that the only alternative to Foucault's notion of a universal linguistic structure is no structure at all. And, furthermore, one already sees many instances of a parallel disappearance in nineteenth-century writing, especially among participants and partisans in the revolutions of 1830, 1848, and 1871. Such works point to the circumstances that teach writers the limits of subjectivity.

In a wide-ranging discussion of French structuralism and its aftermath, the German philosopher and literary historian Manfred Frank has argued that the very notion of a total structure that underlies the work of

Claude Lévi-Strauss and many other French intellectuals is itself theological in origin and implications. And yet, Frank argues, the problem of how
one knows such a structure—or even whether it exists—is never directly
addressed in most French theoretical texts based either on the acceptance
of Lévi-Strauss's linguistic paradigm or its rejection. Although I do not
agree with Frank that German hermeneutics provides the only way to address these problems, his criticisms of structuralism and other subsequent
isms based on it seem well taken. The theological implications of the
structuralist model of language, however, have a history, above all in nineteenth-century French literature and culture, that suggests that this view
of language not only carries with it a host of ideological connotations, but
is fundamentally caught up with the development of notions of ideology. I
hope that this study of the reception of Swedenborg and his theory of
language in France will contribute toward an understanding of a theory of
language that defines itself as universal and ahistorical, but is never to be
grasped in the moment at hand.

This study is divided into two sections. Part I, "Swedenborgianism,
Popular Culture, and the Ends of the Enlightenment in France," opens
with a chapter on a minor French writer, Alphonse-Louis Constant, who
was also known as abbé Constant and as Eliphas Lévi, a name he adopted
in 1853. Constant/Lévi not only published a poem entitled "Les correspondances," but also included expositions of Swedenborg's doctrines in
various historical surveys of religious and esoteric tradition. The son of a
cobbler, Constant/Lévi was a prolific writer whose works were known, if
not always respected or admired. Imprisoned several times for his political
views and writings, after 1848 he turned from socialist politics to the study
and practice of esoteric lore; Constant/Lévi's career and writing help situate the reception of Swedenborgian doctrines in nineteenth-century
France in the context of politics and culture.

Chapter 2 turns back to the career and two representative works of
Swedenborg himself, his most widely read book, the popularization
Heaven and Hell, which contains an often-quoted definition of correspondences, and his journal of 1743–44, sometimes called *The Dream Book* or
The Journal of Dreams, which was not published until 1859, but which
links the doctrine of correspondences to the interpretation of dreams and
suggests, more clearly than any other work, the parallels between Swedenborg's work and that of Mesmer and his followers. Although this chapter
takes the work of Inge Jonsson and Martin Lamm as its point of departure,
its main focus is the parallels between Swedenborg's work and eighteenth-
century culture. The doctrine of 'correspondences', I argue, has much in
common with some of Rousseau's writings, especially his *Essai sur l'ori-*

gine des langues, as well as Mesmerism and freemasonry. Swedenborg's emphasis on language, moreover, points to the importance of print culture in the career of this talented but isolated scientist, who pursued his interests during extended study journeys abroad, reading and producing summaries of what he had read in highly speculative treatises that were, with the notable exception of the self-analysis he undertook in his journal of 1743–44, almost never based on data or experiments.

Chapter 3 turns to the general context of Swedenborg's reception among minor writers in France between 1780 and 1865. Its point of departure—like the title of this section of the book as a whole—is Robert Darnton's contention that Swedenborgianism represented an infusion of irrationalism into the materialistic doctrines of Mesmerism that turned them from a vehicle that had expressed an optimistic view of the ability of reason and science to improve every aspect of the world, including social institutions, into dogma that emphasized the existence of evil and the powerlessness of the individual. French interpretations of Swedenborgianism, this chapter argues, *are* highly eccentric and almost always inaccurate, but like Mesmerism, they are closely bound up with revolutionary politics, and are most often called into service by the marginal or disenfranchised to justify their claims to participation both in politics and in contemporary print culture. None of these writers, however, puts forward a claim to participate in public discourse as a "popular" or second-rate writer. What is it, this chapter asks in its conclusion, that allows us to classify a writer or a body of doctrines as belonging to popular culture? It is a particularly difficult and important question to pose, especially because the distinction between elite and popular culture was highly contested in post-revolutionary French society.

The division of this study into two parts, then, should not be taken as an affirmation that the writers discussed in the second part, Balzac and Baudelaire, belong to an unchanging canon of classical literary texts. Rather, the second section, "Fictions of Wholeness: Balzac and Baudelaire," focuses on two related issues in these writers' incorporation of aspects of Swedenborgianism into their texts. How is it, I ask here, that Balzac and Baudelaire define themselves and their writings against and within the context of the work of writers no longer read except by specialists and which I have—provisionally—characterized as popular culture? And to what extent can we identify their work with that of later writers—Mallarmé and Symbolist and Surrealist poets and writers—we often see as "avant-garde"? The second is an important question, because it is in this context that we most often find bandied about allusions to a notion of language as an impersonal and absolute system that transcends the will and desires of any individual.

Literary historians have often pointed to Swedenborgianism, as well as the general context of western esotericism, as possible sources for the aesthetics of Mallarmé and other turn-of-the-century writers, but they rarely do more than that: point. In a series of perceptive overviews of turn-of-the-century poetics, for example, the comparatist Anna Balakian notes the importance of Swedenborgianism for the development of both Symbolism and Surrealism, but comments: "*Swedenborg* is the patron saint of too many ideologies, philosophies, and literary trends to qualify as the special property of symbolism."[22] Other studies of nineteenth-century poetics, notably Albert Béguin's remarkable *L'âme romantique et le rêve*, suggest that the emphasis on dreams one notices in the writings of Swedenborg's French interpreters finds its place in a general reaction against reason and a turning towards Germanic models that pioneered the investigation of the irrational. What I hope to show in my discussion of Balzac and Baudelaire is that the work of these writers must be read in the general context of the French reception of Swedenborgianism, a context that includes the work of other nineteenth-century writers no longer widely read today and that is closely bound up with the politics of these writers. Drawing to a more or less limited extent on Swedenborgianism and other esoteric and pseudo-scientific doctrines, moreover, Balzac and Baudelaire fashioned a poetics that not only justified the separateness of one kind of literature from others they viewed as more deservedly fleeting, but that would also be widely influential in late-nineteenth- and early-twentieth-century French and European aesthetics. The notion of the literary text as a total system that evokes the whole of the world figures prominently in the work of both men, especially in connection with the representation of the metropolis as meaningful to a writer who plays the role of a perpetual outsider, a *flâneur* through its streets.

Not entirely intentionally, I believe, the German critic Walter Benjamin, always highly ambivalent on the subject of popular culture, provides us with a set of concepts that bring into focus the similar ambivalence of major nineteenth-century writers and their texts.[23] For Benjamin, an *aura* of the authenticity and uniqueness that characterize art produced in connection with religion and in homogeneous societies is precisely what art in an age of mechanical reproduction has lost and pretends to have recaptured. The citations of Swedenborgianism in Balzac and Baudelaire, I shall argue, have more to do with their attempts to distinguish their art as authentic and unique, however, than to reproduce the conditions of theological belief that Benjamin—and other theorists—have said are necessary for the production of one kind of art. Benjamin, moreover, ties the structures of nineteenth-century literature, especially the poetry of Baudelaire, to the architecture of Paris at this time. The *interior* figures particularly

prominently in his discussion of what he sees as the illusions of subjectivity and autonomy the poet evokes in his work. Swedenborg's doctrine of
correspondences and his interpretation of dreams draw explicitly on the
architecture and landscape of contemporary Europe, as do the interpretations of his doctrines of nineteenth-century French writers. Moreover, the
continuity between his representation of the city and that of nineteenth-
century writers sheds light on one prominent facet of modernist poetics:
the representation of the city as psychological, which, as Carl E. Schorske
has shown in his magisterial study of turn-of-the-century Vienna, in turn
suggests the importance of the city in the development of psychology and
psychoanalysis in nineteenth- and early-twentieth-century Europe.[24] If
critics and historians such as Jean Starobinski and Henri Ellenberger have
emphasized the importance of Mesmerism as a forerunner of psychoanalysis, the reception of Swedenborg's doctrine of correspondences in the
work of writers whose work draws on and shapes experience in a modern
city points to the equal importance of notions of language and narrative in
this line of development.[25]

Finally, Benjamin places at the center of his discussion of the utopian
potential of nineteenth-century literature a concept he calls the *dialectical
image*. What is it the *flâneur* sees as he (and almost always *he*) strolls
through the artificial streets of the city? How is it he is able to unify the
disparate items displayed in shop windows and strewn about the streets
into a unified whole that appears to situate him as a subject in an alien
world? It would be false, Benjamin suggests, to accept the totalizing systems of nineteenth-century French writers at face value. The city is no
unproblematic reproduction of the natural world, no "second nature."
Rather each of its elements has a history that reminds us of the distance
from nature, the suffering, that life in the city entails. And yet to focus on
this distance is to begin to understand the work that remains to be done,
not to return the city to a harmonious state of nature that, Benjamin
argues, never existed, but rather to rethink the city in terms of a utopia
that, like the dream of a blissful state of nature, can never really be named.

The secularization and aestheticization of Swedenborgianism, particularly the doctrine of correspondences, in the work of Balzac and Baudelaire goes hand in hand with a nostalgic evocation of a kind of pre-
revolutionary paradise in which human beings lived in a natural order.
Correspondances, however, suggest a temporal allegory in which original
meanings, like an impossible notion of an unmediated experience of nature, withdraw towards an infinitely receding vanishing point. The vanishing point of origin may be construed in various ways: as the founder of a
cult that never really took hold in France; as the possibility of a politics
capable of completely transforming the world, an ambivalent possibility at

best; or as the subjectivity of the reader or writer, the face or faces in the mirror Michel Foucault evokes in the opening pages on Velasquez in *Les mots et les choses*. In this study, I shall attempt to show how these three possibilities come together in the work of writers who turn in part to the doctrines of an obscure and eccentric Swede in order to construct an aesthetics capable of evoking—and perhaps also denying—the utopian promises of the cultures of the Enlightenment and its aftermath.

PART I

*Swedenborgianism, Popular Culture, and the
Ends of the Enlightenment in France*

In *Balzac's* Le cousin Pons *(1847), one of the principal characters, a concierge then known as Mme Cibot, visits a fortuneteller in a Parisian slum to find out whether or not she should go through with her plan to murder her tenant, Pons, in order to take possession of his art collection. The account of her visit is preceded by an essayistic passage, a digression on the nature of what Balzac calls the "occult sciences" and their fortunes in mid-nineteenth-century France. These "sciences," the narrator laments, have come down in the world:*

> Mais il en est des sciences occultes comme de tant d'effets naturels re-poussés par les esprits forts ou par les philosophes matérialistes, c'est à dire ceux qui s'en tiennent uniquement aux faits visibles, solides, aux résultats de la cornue ou des balances de la physique et de la chimie modernes; ces sciences subsistent, elles continuent leur marche, sans progrès d'ailleurs, car depuis environ deux siècles la culture en est aban-donnée par les esprits d'élite. (5:584)

The narrator's lament forms part of an argument for the establishment of a university chair in this subject, which, presumably, would rescue these doctrines from their degradation.

Yet if the digression on the occult maintains that the beliefs and practices of the fortuneteller and her clients represent a kind of science, the narrative portrays them very differently. In Le cousin Pons, *the occult has come to be identified with the interests of classes the narrator sees as alien, clients of the fortuneteller, such as the inhabitants of the Passage Bordin or the petit-bourgeois concierge, Mme Cibot, and in their hands, it certainly does not represent science or a transcendent truth. Despite the extended argument that the occult is scientific, the predictions of the for-tuneteller simply do not come true.*

Balzac's novel registers the change in status of the occult in the first half of the nineteenth century, a change documented by Robert Darnton in his Mesmerism and the End of the Enlightenment in France. *As Darnton has shown, at the end of the eighteenth century, Mesmer's doctrines figured prominently in elite as well as popular culture; Mesmerism, it seemed, promised to become a new science. In popular culture, Mesmerist doctrines reflected the mood of optimism in the years leading up to and immediately following the Revolution of 1789, suggesting the infinite potential of science and reason to transform all aspects of human existence. In the nineteenth century, however, academies refused to accept these doctrines as scientific. Mesmerism was relegated to the status of a pseudoscience, and its practitioners splintered into a number of competing sects. The fortunes of Swedenborgianism and Martinism followed a similar pattern. By the 1840s, theosophical and Mesmerist doctrines were often found together in the eclectic systems of working-class and petit-bourgeois thinkers who were far more interested in politics than in science.*

*For Darnton, as for Balzac, the fortunes of Mesmerism and the occult in France during the decades following the Revolution of 1789 illustrate the degeneration of a progressive revolutionary culture. Swedenborgianism, in particular, represents an infusion of the irrational into this context. (*Mesmerism, *127) Yet it is difficult to believe that the working-class or petit-bourgeois adherents of these doctrines, would have agreed with this characterization. Their works suggest that they were very aware of the political connotations of these doctrines and used them for the expression of interests that not only differed from, but also threatened, those of the bourgeoisie who had benefited in 1789.*

Balzac and later historians of the popularization and politicization of occult and pseudoscientific doctrines often represent nineteenth-century interpretations of these doctrines as if they were an ideology—in the sense that they cannot be identified with science or transcendent truth, but, instead, express the misguided beliefs and practices of people and classes who are perceived as other. This is an interpretation that Balzac's novel seems to invite, with its discussion of the relation of occult doctrines and popular cultures to elite science. Yet it is also one that deserves further examination. For it is precisely in the first half of the nineteenth-century that the word "ideology" came into circulation, often with very contradictory meanings. Balzac's novels, which evoke very different notions of ideology, have much to tell us about the fortunes of the occult in relation to French politics and society in the first half of the nineteenth century. The texts of writers now mostly unread and forgotten may say even more. And certainly, they tell the story from a very different perspective.

CHAPTER ONE

*Politics, Magic, and Language: Swedenborgianism in the
Works of Alphonse-Louis Constant, a.k.a. Eliphas Lévi*

In Europe and North America, the fortunes of Swedenborgianism in
the secular world are above all bound up with the semantics of a single
word, "correspondences." Although, as Inge Jonsson has shown, the term
has a complicated history both in Swedenborg's own intellectual development and in English and French tradition, in nineteenth-century everyday
and literary English and French, "correspondences" took on a new sense:
the word came to designate potential meanings suggested by the existence
of an allegorical language of nature which, it was believed, Swedenborg
had explained in a series of exegetical works.[1] And yet it seems that few
people actually read the works of Swedenborg, which makes the association of "correspondences" with allegory something of a paradox: for conventional notions of allegory presuppose a one-to-one relationship among
signs and referents that presupposes a kind of key.[2] The widespread association of "correspondences" with allegory and with a cult about which
most people knew very little suggests a kind of impossible figure, an allegory in which the necessary key had been lost or at least shunted to one
side.

French interpretations of the word often focus on the work of the
poet Charles Baudelaire, whose uses of the term in his prose works appear
in connection with references to the work of Fourier, Hugo, Delacroix, and
Wagner and seem to tie it to major developments in French and European
aesthetics. Discussions of the aesthetic significance of the word in the
poet's work, however, most often take as their subject a sonnet which—
fortunately—names no sources, but bears the name "Correspondances."
(The poem is reproduced in the appendix.)

What could Baudelaire have meant by this title? What is its significance for the development of his or Symbolist poetics in general?

Clearly, the poem makes no doctrinal references, and even its evocation of an allegorical temple of nature is problematic, for the temple emits
only occasionally "de confuses paroles."[3] Readings of the poem most often

situate Baudelaire's use of the term between tradition and innovation: if the poem harks back to Romantic notions of an allegory of nature, it uses this context in order to suggest how language might function to *evoke* meanings that are sensuous and resonant.[4] Although some interpretations of the sonnet "Correspondances" make passing reference to a much longer poem published in the 1840s and entitled "Les correspondances," none attempts to link Baudelaire's use of the word "correspondances" or references to Swedenborg to the context of contemporary esotericism. Critics claim quite rightly that "Les correspondances" is aesthetically inferior to Baudelaire's work.[5] The poem, they argue, has more to do with the outmoded aesthetics of Romanticism than with the innovative aspects of Baudelaire's work. And yet the longer poem and its author, who called himself abbé Constant at the time of its publication in the 1840s, but changed his name to Eliphas Lévi at the beginning of the next decade, belonged to a flourishing popular culture in which Swedenborgianism, Mesmerism, and other esoteric cults played important roles.

Recent work in French cultural history has focused on this context and its importance in transformation of French politics and culture during the decade following the French Revolution. If, in the late eighteenth century, political outsiders often turned to the doctrines of Swedenborg and Mesmer in order to imagine new, more inclusive, social orders, their attempts were echoed in the years surrounding 1830 and 1848 by successive groups who were also eager for enfranchisement. Some historians—notably Robert Darnton—have emphasized the element of repetition in the transmission of esoteric and pseudoscientific ideas in nineteenth-century France; for Darnton, references to Mesmer and Swedenborg in the 1840s and 1850s represent a degeneration of the faith in reason and progress that made the Revolution of 1789 possible. Other historians, however, have noted how Parisian artisans and workers transformed elements of the popular culture of the Ancien Régime so that it became a vehicle for the creation and expression of class solidarity.[6] But however they view the class affiliations of the popular pseudoscience and esotericism in mid-nineteenth-century Paris, historians generally agree that, in this context, the theories and practices of French occultists were almost always charged with political meanings and agendas.

The author of "Les correspondances," Alphonse-Louis Constant or Eliphas Lévi, played a particularly important role within the context of French popular esotericism and pseudoscience, for he published widely on both esotericism and politics during the decades surrounding 1848. Moreover, his work is of particular interest in suggesting some of the cultural resonances of the word, because, in addition to this poem, Constant/Lévi included summaries of some of Swedenborg's doctrines in more general considerations of magic and occultism.

In turning to the little-known poem, "Les correspondances," and situating it in the work of its author, who transformed himself from the religious socialist, abbé Constant, into a specialist on magic and occult traditions, *mage*, Eliphas Lévi, we can see a missing dimension of the meaning of the title of Baudelaire's sonnet, "Correspondances." For during the decades surrounding 1848, the word played a key role in the increasingly stratified contexts of popular and elite cultures in France. Before 1848, it pointed to the utopian desires of those who would take to the barricades, desires which seemed to conform to the dreams of the most isolated individuals. After 1848, it suggested a universal language underlying all aspects of experience, a language that designated the collective and universal elements in apparently idiosyncratic dreams and that was both all-engulfing and open-ended in its evocation of a future that could not be named.

1. Two Names, One Career: From Alphonse-Louis Constant to Eliphas Lévi

Who was Alphonse-Louis Constant, or Eliphas Lévi as he later called himself? Historians have often taken him at his word and presented two very different interpretations of his work and its significance. One focuses on the eclectic synthesis of Christian and socialist doctrines in the works he wrote in the 1840s and signed as Constant. The other presents him as the historian of magic and esoteric tradition, Eliphas Lévi.[7] Despite his change of name and apparent direction in his work, however, there is a fundamental continuity in Constant/Lévi's production, a continuity he had good reasons to deny during the years following 1848. For this reason, I shall use the combination of both names when referring either to his career as a whole or to his activities after he changed his name in 1853.

Born in 1810, Alphonse-Louis Constant was 35 when "Les correspondances" was published as part of a collection of poems and songs entitled *Les trois harmonies*.[8] Sent to school at a seminary by his father, a shoemaker who could not afford to educate his son in any other way, Constant studied to become a priest, but was forced to leave the seminary in 1836, after he had become involved with a young female student. Having no other means of earning a living, however, Constant was forced to beg the Church for some sort of employment, and it accorded him a humiliating position as a school monitor. The incident was to leave a lasting mark on Constant's emotional life and work, for he was to speak out time and again against the Church's insistence on celibacy for the clergy and its denigration of women; one sees, even in works written after 1848 in which he emphatically affirmed the importance of the authority of the Catholic Church, marks of a profound ambivalence that seems to have its roots in an education he detested and a calling that forced him to choose between a relatively comfortable life and his erotic and emotional needs.

In 1841–42, Constant had spent eight months in the prison at St. Pélagie for what the court found to be the incendiary politics of his book, *La Bible de la liberté*, published in 1841. And it was here, he tells us, that he first read Swedenborg. His first impressions, he writes in a work published in 1845, were less than enthusiastic:

> Cette lecture ne fit pas d'abord sur moi toute l'impression qu'elle devait faire par la suite; je le trouvais obscure, diffus et singulier, pour ne pas dire davantage. Ce n'est que par une connaissance plus approfondie de son système et surtout de sa base philosophique, que j'ai pu en apprécier l'immense sagesse. (*Le livre des larmes* 60)

During the 1840s, he published several more books which attempted to merge his eclectic socialist ideas with his unorthodox Christianity. One of these publications was *L'émancipation de la femme*, generally attributed to his friend Flora Tristan although the extent of Constant's authorship is unknown.[9] At the end of the decade, however, a second imprisonment convinced him to abandon writing about politics, a decision he announced in his *Le testament de la liberté* of 1848, which concludes:

> Maintenant notre oeuvre sociale est terminée, et nous ne demanderons pour elle ni indulgence ni sévérité. Nous avons écrit ce que nous dictaient notre intelligence et notre coeur; nous avons accompli un devoir, et nous trouvons que c'est pour nous une récompense suffisante. (219)

Earlier, in a song which Constant had published in *Les trois harmonies*, the writer points to the experiences that prompted his decision. Set to the music of "De la treille de sincérité," this work describes the author's imprisonment, but ends with the evocation of a double betrayal:

> Comme de cette illustre engeance
> Je prenais les affronts gaîment,
> Bientôt leur sublime vengeance
> M'en punit assez noblement.
> De mes lettres interprétées
> La police leur a fait part;
> Mes phrases sont interceptées
> Et je suis déclaré mouchard.

Je renonce à la politique
Et je dénonce à la chanson

La république
Et la prison.

Pour leur conter mon infortune,
Lorsqu'enfin je m'en vis sorti,
Je vais retrouver sur la Brume
Les gens de mon ancien parti.
Mais quelqu'un me dit à l'oreille
Que les deux meneurs principaux
Venaient de s'engager la veille
Dans les gardes municipaux,

Je renonce, etc.

Moreover, in 1853, Constant took on the *nom de plume* Eliphas Lévi or Eliphas Lévi Zahed, which, he claims, in a note tucked away in chapter 13 of the first part of *Dogme et rituel de la haute magie*, is the Hebrew translation of Alphonse-Louis Constant. This claim certainly suggests that the author saw the two names and the identities they suggested as continuous—and wanted to make this intention clear to readers persistent enough to read past the introduction and opening chapters.[10] Perhaps the name change also reflects Constant/Lévi's desire to assume a new identity after his wife left him that year. Whatever the reasons for the change of name and apparent direction in his writing, it is misleading to take Constant/Lévi at his word that his writing after 1848 marked a distinct break with that preceding the revolution. For although he had good reasons— above all, fear of reimprisonment—to hope that certain people would believe that he had abjured politics for good, he not only continued to produce a few works on explicitly political themes, but he also scattered significant references to contemporary society in his later esoteric works, references that link occult practices to the political beliefs and desires of the apparently isolated and unworldly author.

In 1855, for example, Constant/Lévi, an admirer of Béranger, composed an unflattering musical portrait of the emperor, which he called "Caligula."[11] The song landed him in prison a third time. He was able to extricate himself by composing a second song, "L'Anti-Caligula," which convinced Louis Napoléon that the first version, however insulting, was not sufficient reason to imprison its author.

Constant/Lévi lived until 1876, eking out a meagre existence in a series of rented rooms in Paris. Never achieving the kind of public literary success he desired, he did have a devoted following that included some more successful Parisian artists and writers, as well as those interested in occult matters. The exact nature of Constant/Lévi's political and religious beliefs and allegiances is difficult to ascertain. Although he was never able to make a complete break with the Church that had treated him so harshly during his youth or, after 1848, to speak or write directly concerning his political views, remarks scattered throughout all his writings suggest that he maintained a critical stance to the religious and political status quo. Eliphas Lévi Zahed, in other words, is a translation in more than words of Alphonse-Louis Constant.

2. Constant/Lévi's "Les correspondances"

Constant's most often quoted work, "Les correspondances," was first published in 1845 in a collection of poems and songs entitled *Les trois harmonies*.

It is significant that Constant/Lévi was a songwriter and admirer of the tradition of French revolutionary songs. While "Les correspondances" is not listed as a song, many of the other works in the collection were; it is at any rate a poem which lends itself to being read aloud and which, unlike many poems that followed in the tradition of Baudelaire's "Correspondances," could be understood when read aloud.[12]

In contrast to Baudelaire's sonnet, Constant's "Les correspondances" is a long and diffuse poem, one hundred octosyllables divided into ten stanzas of ten lines. The "correspondances" of the title refer to a divinely inspired language of nature we are aware of in dreams, reveries, and moments of faith and inspiration. Thus the poem opens with an evocation of sleep:

> Quand succombent nos sens débiles
> Aux enchantements du sommeil,
> Le pinceau des songes mobiles
> Présentent à l'âme un faux réveil.

And goes on to compare waking experience, in turn, to a kind of dream:

> En dormant nous rêvons la vie,
> Mais la veille, au temps asservie,
> N'est qu'un rêve d'éternité.

But the concluding stanza asserts that any believing individual is capable of perceiving both the Word of God and the unchanging mirroring relationship between nature and heaven:

> Mais que l'âme simple et fidèle
> En attendant l'agneau vainqueur,
> Ecoute, active sentinelle,
> Le verbe de Dieu dans son coeur:
> Car toute pensée extatique
> Est comme une onde sympathique,
> Où se reflète l'univers;
> Et l'âme, à soi-même attentive,
> Comme le pêcheur sur la rive
> Peut contempler les cieux ouverts.

If the "âme humble et fidèle" echoes the Christian commonplace that the meek are especially close to God, the characterization of isolated consciousness as "une onde sympathique,/ où se réflète l'univers" evokes a more sophisticated conception of the relation of consciousness to the world. In his unpublished "Avertissement du *Gars*" of 1828, for example, which is often regarded as a sketch for *Louis Lambert*, Balzac had depicted the consciousness of his isolated and uneducated novelist as a Leibnizean "miroir concentrique de l'univers." (8:1675) Although Constant could not have known this particular text, his characterization of Swedenborg's work elsewhere does seem to lean extensively on Balzac's work, and his presentation of Swedenborg in his *Histoire de la magie* is preceded by a discussion of Leibniz.[13]

The middle stanzas of the poem, however, point beyond the ordinary dreamer's intuitions to an imagined history in which originally transparent relations between earthly phenomena and their cosmic meanings were lost, only to be partially restored through the coming of the Messiah. The third stanza, for example, explains:

> Formé d'invisibles paroles,
> Ce monde est le songe de Dieu;
> Son verbe en choisit les symboles,
> L'esprit les remplit de son feu.
> C'est cette écriture vivante,
> D'amour, de gloire et d'épouvante,
> Que pour nous Jésus retrouva;
> Car toute science cachée

N'est qu'une lettre détachée
Du nom sacré de Jéhova.

Constant's characterization of "correspondances" as a language of nature, the significance of which was lost when humankind fell from grace, repeats a widespread Romantic commonplace. Allusions to such a lost language, often called a "hieroglyphic" language, occur in the work of many European writers in the late eighteenth and early nineteenth centuries. In French literature, such references are often tied to a vision of the ideal organization of society. For the conservative political theorists Bonald and Maistre, for example, the opacity of contemporary everyday language represents a corruption as inevitable as the social decadence they see everywhere in post-Revolutionary French society: only a return to the authoritarian structures of the past, including the Church, can restore order and coherence to human institutions. In the work of writers sympathetic to the Revolution, on the other hand, the notions that nature had a history and could be understood as a kind of language pointed towards the invention of a society based on a kind of natural culture.[14]

References in nineteenth-century French writings to a language of nature are so widespread and so tied to the political beliefs of writers that it is absurd to pretend that they originate in the work of any one individual. In the first half of the nineteenth century, however, many writers do credit eighteenth-century esotericism for refocusing attention on the social significance of a language of nature.[15] Within this context, an allusion to "correspondences" would almost certainly refer back to Swedenborg as one of many eighteenth-century visionaries whose work called attention to a kind of hieroglyphic language of nature whose meaning had been lost, but might be restored again through a program of individual and general reform. For, as we shall see in chapters 2 and 3, this was the one doctrine that was consistently emphasized in popularizations of Swedenborg's work, both by Swedenborg himself and by others.

In choosing as the title of his poem the term *correspondances*, then, Constant points to the continuing importance of the notion of a language of nature in the 1840s in France. Moreover, to a far greater extent than Baudelaire's sonnet, "Les correspondances" echoes earlier works in French literature—poems by Vigny and Lamartine, as well as Balzac's evocation of a Swedenborgian language of nature in *Louis Lambert* (1832–35). But if the poem's "lateness" marks it as a popularizing imitation of earlier models, "Les correspondances" also bears witness to the fact that by the 1840s the notion of a language of nature had come to play an important role in the formulation of the interests and desires of people who would take to the barricades in 1848.

3. Echoes of "Les correspondances" in Constant/Lévi's prose

Like Baudelaire's "Correspondances," Constant/Lévi's poem makes no direct reference to Swedenborg or to any specific set of esoteric, pseudo-scientific, or theological doctrines. He did, however, discuss Swedenborg and his doctrines in a work published the same year, *Le livre des larmes*, as well as in the entries on allegory and mysticism in his *Dictionnaire de la littérature chrétienne* of 1851 and his *Dogme et rituel de la haute magie*, first published in 1856 and 1857, and his *Histoire de la magie*, first published in 1860.

Significantly, Constant quotes "Les correspondances" in its entirety in the entry on allegory in his compendious *Dictionnaire de la littérature chrétienne*, published in 1851, still under the name Alphonse-Louis Constant.[16] In this eclectic and ambitious work, articles on literary genres and concepts, such as allegory, the marvellous, and style, stand side-by-side with entries on recognized French Catholic writers: Maistre, of whom he writes with ambivalent respect; Chateaubriand, who receives a generally favorable notice; and Lamartine, who is the object of the author's scorn. There is no entry for Balzac, although he is mentioned in connection with Swedenborg in the entry on "Les mystiques" and the entry on the novel, which discusses the dangers inherent in novel reading: it destroys one's faith in authority. There is, however, a long entry on the historical Faust and his literary progeny, which harks back to the tradition that the original Faust was a printer, a model, perhaps, for Constant, who was to self-consciously attempt to transform himself into a magician of the printed word in the years following the publication of the *Dictionnaire de la littérature chrétienne*.

The section of "Allégorie" which discusses "Les correspondances" and the term *correspondances* in relation to the allegorical tradition is, then, one of two passages which discuss Swedenborg or his doctrine of correspondences at some length. It is significant that there is no entry under his name. Discussion of the unorthodox Christian and his doctrines are inserted into entries on more orthodox matters.

The entry "Allégorie," which draws on an unnamed source or sources, traces the history of allegory from the beginnings of western culture through the present. The discussion of *correspondances*, however, forms part of a psychological explanation of the origins of allegory in the individual's perceptions of the harmonies of nature.

> Il existe donc dans la nature, entre les pensées et les formes, entre les choses visibles et les choses invisibles, entre les relations physiques et les relations morales d'abord, puis entre les choses corporelles elles-

mêmes, à divers degrés de lumières et de beauté, ainsi qu'entre les choses spirituelles prises séparément à divers degrés d'élévation vers Dieu, selon l'ordre hiérarchique, il existe, disons-nous, des harmonies réelles et des correspondances essentielles antérieurement à toute poésie, la poésie n'étant d'ailleurs que le sentiment de ces correspondances et de ces harmonies, dont la prophétie supérieure à la poésie sera la révélation.

And then, after quoting his poem in its entirety, Constant proceeds to compare *correspondances* to the hieroglyphics of the Egyptians, to which we might turn for a better understanding of the nature of allegory than the traditions of Christianity are able to provide:

> Ce symbolisme naturel de tous les êtres créés paraît avoir été la pensée dominante des anciens Egyptiens, et avoir présidé à l'invention de l'écriture hiéroglyphique. Les Egyptiens se piquaient aussi, comme on sait, d'expliquer les songes en y appliquant les règles d'allégorie, et supposaient par là ces règles tellement peu arbitraires, qu'elles agissaient d'elles-mêmes sur nous comme les nombres vivants de Pythagore. (61)

The association of Swedenborgianism and the doctrine of correspondences with a universal language which can be intuited by the most isolated of minds but which was first discovered by the Egyptians and other non-western cultures figures throughout Constant/Lévi's works, from *Le livre des larmes* on. In his writings of the 1850s, the role of the Egyptians is eclipsed by that of the cabalists and other occult traditions, but the general significance of the notion of a universal language of nature remains unchanged.

The discussion of Swedenborg inserted in the entry entitled "Les mystiques" also emphasizes the importance of *correspondances*: it even provides a short glossary of the Swedenborgian meanings of some phenomena. But this passage also suggests the emotional attraction of Swedenborgianism for Constant, who had been excluded from the Church and the living it provided by the vow of celibacy it demanded, for Swedenborgianism affirmed the importance of sexual love—on earth, as well as in heaven.

> Le mysticisme de la philosophie moderne est emprunté surtout aux livres du Suédois Swedenborg, visionnaire célèbre, dont la doctrine forme un vaste et complet sytème [sic] assez analogue à ceux de l'école d'Alexandrie. Swedenborg est ennemi de la virginité, et affirme qu'il n'y a de chasteté possible que dans le mariage; il nie que l'homme puisse mériter et démériter, et veut que chaque âme, après la mort, se fasse un ciel ou un enfer de la sphère de son amour. Il ne reconnaît pas d'autres anges que

les âmes des justes; mais les âmes, selon lui, ayant été créées par couples, doivent se réunir dans le ciel où, contre l'enseignement exprès de Notre-Seigneur, il permet encore des mariages et une génération spirituelle à la vérité, mais faite à l'image et à la ressemblance de nos générations de la terre. Il parle de trois mondes superposés: le divin, le spirituel et le naturel, et fait consister la révélation en une communication perpétuelle entre ces trois mondes, dont toutes les formes expriment la parole du Verbe, selon ses trois mondes, dont toutes les formes expriment la parole du Verbe, selon ses trois degrés de signification divine, spirituelle et humaine. Le bien, c'est l'harmonie entre les trois mondes; la parole de Dieu, c'est l'expression de cette harmonie. Ainsi le vrai exprime le bien, parce que le bien c'est le vrai manifesté dans l'ordre, etc., etc.

Aux yeux de Swedenborg, toutes les formes visibles ont des significations spirituelles et divines, et cette analogie, qui se reproduit de monde en monde, est ce qu'il appelle les correspondances. Nous en signalerons ici quelques-unes prises au hasard soit dans les *Arcanes célestes*, soit dans la *Clef Hiéroglyphique des arcanes*. (895–96)

This summary leads directly to a kind of glossary, a long list of "correspondences," of which I reproduce the beginning:

Correspondances ou analogies
Les animaux signifient les affections: Jardin et paradis, l'intelligence et la sagesse; les arbres, les perceptions et les connaissances; les aliments, les choses qui nourissent la vie spirituelle; le pain, toute bonté qui nourrit la vie spirituelle de l'homme. (895–96)

Constant's closing comments indicate both his impatience with this kind of "hieroglyphic key" and his sense of the limitations of Swedenborg's doctrines:

Nous n'en finirons pas, si nous voulions indiquer toutes les autres. Les ouvrages de Swedenborg offrent un singulier mélange de raison et de folie, de poésie et de pauvreté. Son système est parfaitement lié; il a des idées qui éblouissent et qui séduisent au premier abord, mais ses visions fatiguent le bon sens des lecteurs, et il semble mystifier souvent la curiosité naturelle de l'esprit humain. C'est un savant ridicule et un fou sublime.

M. de Balzac, celui de tous les écrivains modernes qui a possédé au plus haut degré la faculté de l'analyse, a résumé assez complètement, dans les trois nouvelles qui composent son livre mystique, le système de Swedenborg, auquel il ajoute un peu du sien.

Jacob Boemh [sic], Pascalis Martinès [sic] et Saint-Martin ont été, après Swedenborg, les illuminés les plus célèbres. (898)

The entries in the *Dictionnaire de la littérature chrétienne* are not the last texts by Constant/Lévi to hark back to "Les correspondances." A curious passage in Constant/Lévi's late work, *La science des esprits* (1865), also echoes the poem, as well as the author's interpretations of its linguistic context. Several of the texts included in this somewhat hotchpotch collection hark back to Constant's works of the 1840s, especially his *La dernière incarnation: légendes évangéliques du XIXe siècle* of 1846, which contains a *"légende"* entitled "Le poëte mourant,"[17] but the section in question, entitled "La mort d'un poëte," suggests a melancholy distance to the earlier affirmation of the value of the intuitions of the solitary individual. The opening of this section captures the sermon-like tone of much of this collection:

La mort d'un poëte

Il y avait donc en ce temps-là un jeune homme qui, de bonne heure, avait écouté dans son âme l'écho des harmonies universelles.

Or, cette musique intérieure avait distrait son attention de toutes les choses de la vie mortelle, parce qu'il vivait dans une société encore sans harmonie.

. . .

Ses jours passait dans un long silence et dans une profonde rêverie; il contemplait avec d'étranges extases le ciel, les eaux, les arbres, les campagnes verdoyantes; puis ses regards devenaient fixes, des magnificences intérieures se déployaient dans sa pensée et l'emportaient encore sur le spectacle de la nature. Des larmes alors coulaient à son insu le long de ses joues pâles d'émotion, et si l'on venait lui parler, il n'entendait pas. (474–75)

The young man, contemplating suicide, encounters a stranger who preaches to him the true meaning of poetic revery, which must be joined to a life of service and social responsibility:

Sache que l'esprit d'harmonie, c'est l'esprit d'amour que j'annonçais au monde sous le nom du consolateur.

. . .

Jusqu'à présent tu n'as fait de la poésie qu'en rêves et en paroles, mais le temps est venu de faire de la poésie en actions! Car tout ce qui se fait par amour de l'humanité, tout ce qui est dévouement, sacrifice, patience, courage et persévérance, tout cela est sublime d'harmonie, c'est la poésie des martyrs! (479)

This work makes a solitary reference to Swedenborg, linking his work to the kind of contemplative reverie that almost caused the downfall of the young man. If this passage is less preachy, its characterization of the visions of Swedenborg and other mystics and utopians as hallucinations implies a critical distance to their works:

> Goethe avait étudié la Kabbale, et l'épopée de Faust est sortie des doctrines du Sohar. Swedenborg, Saint-Simon et Fourier semblent avoir vu la divine synthèse kabbalistique à travers les ombres et les hallucinations d'un cauchemar plus ou moins étrange, suivant les différents caractères de ces rêveurs. Cette synthèse est en réalité ce que la pensée humaine peut aborder de plus complet et de plus beau. (125–26)

La science des esprits was published after the triptych of works on magic for which "Eliphas Lévi" is best known: *Dogme et rituel de la haute magie, L'histoire de la magie,* and *La clef des grands mystères.* In its affirmation of the importance of action, this work turns back to the works of the 1840s, the years before Constant renounced politics and changed his name. The parables recounted in this late and uneven work suggest that a preoccupation with language and contemplation can only lead one astray, that the individual should use them as points of departure for a life that is oriented towards the community.

The works on magic, however, tell a somewhat different story.

4. Magic, Politics, and Duplicity: Constant/Lévi's *Dogme et rituel de la haute magie*

Constant/Lévi's three most famous books on magic were published between 1856 and 1861. *Dogme et rituel de la haute magie* first appeared in two volumes in 1856 and 1857, and was subsequently reissued in 1861 with a new preface. The second work in the series, *L'histoire de la magie,* was first published in 1860, and the third, *La clef des grands mystères,* in 1861. In all three books, Constant/Lévi elaborates the theory and practice of a highly personal magical system based, he says, on the cabala, and he consistently represents the theories of other writers, including Swedenborg, as inferior to those of the Jewish mystical tradition. Moreover, references to Swedenborg and his doctrines do not suggest that Constant/Lévi had read more of his works: they are schematic and often inaccurate. The Swedenborgianism of the books on magic serves the author's own interests; a few key elements are incorporated into what looks like a highly personal, eclectic, magical system designed to justify the empowerment of the author as a magus whose words are not only true, but also capable of transforming the world. But one might question whether Constant/Lévi did more with *any* of the esoteric theories he cites.

A. E. Waite notes that he seems to have known relatively little of the work of Guillaume Postel, whom he often cites in these books, and argues that the errors in the Hebrew quotations indicate that Constant/Lévi's knowledge of the cabala was similarly limited. (*Transcendental Magic*, xiv) I would suggest that Constant/Lévi, living an isolated and marginal existence in rented rooms in Paris and lacking the livelihood and access to research facilities of an academic scholar, drew on a somewhat superficial and unscholarly familiarity with a wide variety of esoteric texts in order to work out his own magical system, a system based, like the late work of Swedenborg or the cabala, on the notion of an absolute language. In contrast to the poem "Les correspondances" and its echoes in the *Dictionnaire de la littérature chrétienne* and *La science des esprits*, however, Constant/Lévi's interest in language has shifted away from its relation to traditional allegory, from the potential of the meekest and most isolated individual to intuit harmonies in nature and tradition *that are already there*, to the ability of the initiate to control and manipulate language in such a way that it might transform the world around him.

There are echoes of Constant/Lévi's earlier work in the three books on magic which suggest that his reading of Swedenborg may have influenced his understanding of magic and language in some fundamental way. A passage, for example, in *Dogme et rituel* sets forth a theory of three worlds that is highly reminiscent of popularizations of Swedenborgianism, although triadic structures were so common in nineteenth-century culture that it would be impossible to trace the origins of this passage with any certainty. Constant/Lévi himself emphasizes the parallel between the theories of Swedenborg and his own triadic notion of the structure of experience, for he introduces his theory of corresponding worlds with a reference to Swedenborg:

> L'empereur Julien, dans son hymne au roi Soleil, donne une théorie du ternaire qui est presque identiquement la même que celle de l'illu-miné Swedenborg. (1:142)

Moreover, the link between Constant/Lévi's system and the doctrines of Swedenborg seems to be reinforced by the use of the verb *correspondre* in the passage that follows:

> Les trois mondes *correspondent* ensemble par les trente-deux voies de lumière qui sont les échelons de l'échelle sainte; toute pensée vraie *correspond* à une grâce divine dans le ciel, et à une oeuvre utile sur la terre. Toute grâce de Dieu suscite une vérité et produit un ou plusieurs

actes, et réciproquement tout acte remue dans les cieux une vérité ou un mensonge, une grâce ou un châtiment. Lorsqu'un homme prononce le tétragramme, écrivent les cabalistes, les neuf cieux reçoivent une secousse, et tous les esprits se crient les uns aux autres: Qui donc trouble ainsi le royaume du ciel? Alors la terre révèle au premier ciel les péchés du téméraire qui prend le nom de l'éternel en vain, et le verbe accusateur est transmis de cercle en cercle, d'étoile en étoile et de hiérarchie en hiérarchie.

Toute parole a trois sens, toute action une triple portée, toute forme une triple idée, car l'absolu correspond de monde en monde avec ses formes. . . . (1:144; my emphasis)

The use of *correspondre* in this passage echoes "Les correspondances" and its interpretations elsewhere in Constant/Lévi's work. Here, as well, the word points to a static series of vertical analogies or relationships hidden beneath the surfaces of appearances. But in the books on magic, this series is presented as only the point of departure for the magician's rituals, for his own manipulations of the absolute language hidden in nature. In Constant/Lévi's own words, it forms part of the dogma, rather than the ritual, of magic. But even the first, theoretical, volume of *Dogme et rituel de la haute magie* indicates that Constant/Lévi's view of the relationship of the absolute language of the magician or visionary to ordinary language and experience has changed since the mid-1840s. The situation of the solitary individual in "Les correspondances" suggests that visionary harmonies repeat the structures of the visible world, that *correspondances* are fundamentally representational. In *Dogme et rituel de la haute magie*, the relationships among language, visionary experiences, and the world are called into question. The words of the dreamer or visionary may be, as Constant/Lévi writes concerning Swedenborg, mere hallucinations, and the doctrines based on them, absurdities.

Constant/Lévi seems unaware of the attempts to establish a Swedenborgian Church in France or even perhaps of the English Swedenborgian Church. He cannot imagine what a Swedenborgian liturgy would be like:

Dans l'école d'Alexandrie, la magie et le christianisme se donnent presque la main sous les auspices d'Ammonius Saccas et de Platon. Le dogme d'Hermès se trouve presque tout entier dans les écrits attribués à Denis l'Aréopagite. Synésius trace le plan d'un traité des songes, qui devait plus tard être commenté par Cardan, et *composé d'hymnes qui pourraient servir à la liturgie de l'église de Swedenborg, si une église d'illuminés pouvait avoir une liturgie.* (1:71; my emphasis)

The Swedenborg of *Dogme et rituel de la haute magie* is fundamentally misguided. If his theories parallel those of other, sounder, mystical or esoteric traditions, such as the cabala (1:95) or the work of Jacob Boehme or Saint-Martin (1:95), or even the Emperor Julian (1:142), they are based on hallucinations, as one passage, which may well draw on the representation of *Erdgeister* (literally "earth spirits") in Goethe's *Faust*, suggests:[18]

> Les esprits élémentaires sont comme les enfants: ils tourmentent davantage ceux qui s'occupent d'eux, à moins qu'on ne les domine par une haute raison et une grande sévérité.
>
> Ce sont ces esprits que nous désignons sous le nom d'éléments occultes.
>
> Ce sont eux qui déterminent souvent pour nous les songes inquiétants ou bizarres, ce sont eux qui produisent les mouvements de la baguette divinatoire et les coups frappés contre les murailles ou contre les meubles; mais ils ne peuvent jamais manifester une autre pensée que la nôtre, et si nous ne pensons pas, ils nous parlent avec toute l'incohérence des rêves. Ils reproduisent indifféremment le bien et le mal, parce qu'ils sont sans libre arbitre et par conséquent n'ont point de responsabilité; ils se montrent aux extatiques et aux somnambules sous des formes incomplètes et fugitives. *C'est ce qui a donné lieu aux cauchemars de saint Antoine et très probablement aux visions de Swedenborg; ils ne sont ni damnés ni coupables, ils sont curieux et innocents.* (2:76; my emphasis)

Moreover, Constant/Lévi's understanding of Swedenborg's visions implies that, even when they are true, they are somewhat grotesque. Two passages present Swedenborg as a visionary who perceived human beings in animal shapes that represented their true nature:

> La forme de notre corps sidéral est conforme à l'état habituel de nos pensées, et modifie, à la longue, les traits du corps matériel. C'est pour cela que Swedenborg, dans ses intuitions somnambuliques, voyait souvent des esprits en forme de divers animaux. (1:278)

More specifically, he was apt to see them as sheep:

> Or, la métempsycose, qui a été souvent mal comprise, a un côté parfaitement vrai: les formes animales communiquent leurs empreintes sympathiques au corps astral de l'homme, et se reflètent bientôt sur ses traits, suivant la force de ses habitudes. L'homme d'une douceur intelligente et passive prend les allures et la physionomie inerte d'un mouton; *mais, dans le somnambulisme, ce n'est plus un homme à physionomie moutonne, c'est un mouton qu'on aperçoit, comme l'a mille fois expérimenté l'extatique et savant Swedenborg.* Ce mystère est exprimé dans le livre cabalistique du voyant Daniel par la légende de Nabuchodonosor changé en bête, qu'on a eu le tort de prendre pour une histoire réelle

comme il est arrivé de presque toutes les allégories magiques. (2:200; my emphasis)

And like the legend of Nebuchadnezzar's transformation, the writings of Swedenborg need to be interpreted by someone initiated into the secrets of magic and its lore: the uninformed are likely to take hallucinations literally.

The introduction to the 1856 edition of *Dogme et rituel de la haute magie* divides the work into two parts which only partly correspond to the two volumes of the work. The first, Constant/Lévi writes, presents the dogma or the *clavicule* of magic; and the second, its *grimoire*. Although, as the scattered references to Swedenborg suggest, discussions of the theory of magic and language occur in both volumes, the second volume is distinguished from the first by its inclusion of a series of rituals or spells the properly initiated magician might cast. It is here that Constant/Lévi puts into practice a theory of language that is performative, rather than representational, a theory that is only intimated in his discussions of esoteric and mystical doctrines elsewhere in *Dogme et rituel de la haute magie*.

If almost all the references to Swedenborg and Swedenborgianism tie these doctrines to interests in allegory and representation that Constant/Lévi had moved away from by 1856, one remarkable passage does link Swedenborg to a new aesthetic in French poetry. A section of the original introduction to *Dogme et rituel de la haute magie* cites Swedenborg as one of the ancestors of the concept of a "Book with unbound leaves," a Book that would capture the totality of nature in a language as precise as mathematics:

> Un autre livre existe encore; mais celui-là, bien qu'il soit en quelque sorte populaire et qu'on puisse le trouver partout, est le plus occulte et le plus inconnu de tous, parce qu'il contient la clef de tous les autres; il est dans la publicité sans être connu du public; on ne s'avise pas de le trouver où il est, et l'on perdrait mille fois son temps à le chercher où il n'est pas si l'on en soupçonnait l'existence. Ce livre, plus ancien peut-être que celui d'Hénoc, n'a jamais été traduit, et il est écrit encore tout entier en caractères primitifs et sur des pages détachées comme les tablettes des anciens. Un savant distingué en a révélé, sans qu'on l'ait remarqué, non pas précisément le secret, mais l'antiquité et la conservation singulière; un autre savant, mais d'un esprit plus fantastique que judicieux, a passé trente ans à étudier ce livre, et en a seulement soupçonné toute l'importance. C'est, en effet, un ouvrage monumental et singulier, simple et fort comme l'architecture des pyramides, durable par conséquent comme elles; livre qui résume toutes les sciences, et dont les combinaisons infinies peuvent ré-

soudre tous les problèmes; livre qui parle en faisant penser; inspirateur et régulateur de toutes les conceptions possibles; le chef-d'oeuvre peut-être de l'esprit humain, et à coup sûr l'une des plus belles choses que nous ait laissées l'antiquité; clavicule universelle, dont le nom n'a été compris et expliqué que par le savant illuminé Guillaume Postel; texte unique, dont les premiers caractères seulement ont ravi en extase l'esprit religieux de Saint-Martin, et eussent rendu la raison au sublime et infortuné Swedenborg. Ce livre, nous en parlerons plus tard, et son explication mathématique et rigoureuse sera le complément et la couronne de notre consciencieux travail. (1:68–69)

This is one of several passages in *Dogme et rituel de la haute magie* that points strikingly forward to aspects of Mallarmé's poetic system, most obviously to his formulation of the project of a total Book with detachable pages.[19] Elsewhere, too, Constant/Lévi's evocation of the situation of the poet as god-like—both conjure up the stars—suggests the thematic structure of some of Mallarmé's most famous poems.[20] Most significant, however, I think, is the parallel between the situations of the two men and their views of language: both were isolated individuals able to imagine themselves as transforming their small worlds, the interiors of rented rooms in Paris, through their manipulations of a language viewed as absolute, as precise in its harmonies as mathematics or a finely tuned musical instrument, and fundamentally evocative, or, to use an anachronistic term, performative.

This passage, which links the doctrines of Swedenborg to the project of a total Book based on an absolute language, suggests the tenuous but important link between the reception of Swedenborgianism in France and the development of a new poetics there in the second half of the nineteenth century. Swedenborg appears as a distant ancestor to a theory of language that might renew and transform a social world characterized by injustice, censorship, and the isolation and suppression of writers of genius. Moreover, as Constant/Lévi's later writings on magic, his *Histoire de la magie* and the second, 1861, preface to *Dogme et rituel de la haute magie*, show, Swedenborgian doctrines were also important for the associations they carried with the French revolutionary tradition.

There is much in the two later books on magic, *L'histoire de la magie* and *La clef des grands mystères*, that repeats material developed in the far more original *Dogme et rituel de la haute magie*. Yet between 1856, when volume one of *Dogme et rituel* first appeared, and 1861, which saw the publication of the last work in the series, *La clef des grands mystères*, as well as a second edition of *Dogme et rituel de la haute magie*, Constant/Lévi's views changed and developed in at least two respects. One biographer notes that in 1859 he began to frequent the French spiritualists, Henri Delaage and a Doctor Rozier.[21] In fact, the works Constant/Lévi published in 1860 and 1861 reflect recent developments in French spiritualism: the passages in *L'histoire de la magie* on nineteenth-century magic, the descriptions of séances in *La clef des grands mystères*, and even the new preface to the second 1861 edition of *Dogme et rituel de la haute magie* suggest a greater interest in, as well as knowledge of, this context.

At least two of the later works, *L'histoire de la magie* and the new preface to *Dogme et rituel de la haute magie*, also bear witness to an increased awareness of the political history and implications of magical doctrines. Since the 1861 preface to *Dogme et rituel* suggests how Constant/Lévi has developed some of the implications of the earlier work, I turn first to this text before discussing the far longer and more complex *Histoire de la magie*.

5. Language, Mesmerism, and Charisma: The Preface to the 1861 Edition of *Dogme et rituel de la haute magie* and *L'histoire de la magie*

In his introduction to his English translation of *L'histoire de la magie*, A. E. Waite writes of a kind of double agenda in Constant/Lévi's works on magic.[22] Nowhere does that double agenda seem more evident than in the 1861 preface to *Dogme et rituel de la haute magie*, although, unfortunately, Waite chooses not to include it in his translation, because he feels it is superfluous.[23] The opening paragraph notes the increased importance of spiritualism in the contemporary world of magic:

> Depuis que la première édition de ce livre a été publiée, de grands événements se sont accomplis dans le monde, et d'autres plus grands peut-être encore sont à la veille de s'accomplir.
> Ces événements nous avaient été annoncés comme d'ordinaire par des prodiges: les tables avaient parlé, des voix étaient sorties des murs, des mains sans corps avaient écrit des mots mystérieux, comme au festin de Balthasar. (1)

This is, however, the sole reference to spiritualism in the new introduction. Constant/Lévi proceeds to develop, more clearly than in the body of the text itself, his notion that language (*le Verbe*) is action. His argument begins in terms that echo the opening of Goethe's *Faust*, the proclamation of the protagonist that "Im Anfang war die Tat," which, in turn replays a controversy regarding the translation of the Biblical Hebrew.[24] Constant/

Lévi's extended and often very wordy argument opens in sermon-like terms:

> Jésus, dit l'Evangile, était puissant en oeuvres et en paroles; les oeuvres avant la parole: c'est ainsi que s'établit et se prouve le droit de parler. Jésus se mit à faire et à parler, dit ailleurs un évangéliste, et souvent, dans le langage primitif de l'écriture sainte, une action est appellée *un verbe*. Dans toutes les langues, d'ailleurs, on nomme VERBE ce qui exprime à la fois l'être et l'action, et il n'est pas de verbe qui ne puisse être suppléé par le verbe *faire*, en diversifiant le régime. *Dans le principe était le Verbe*, dit l'évangéliste saint Jean, Dans quel principe? Dans le premier principe; dans le principe absolu qui est avant toute chose. Dans ce principe donc était le Verbe, c'est-à-dire l'action. (5)

But if the beginning of the argument seems merely to develop and clarify some of the implications of the rituals of magic for the isolated individual discussed in the edition of 1856 and 1856, its ending ties the identification of language and action to questions of solidarity and recent French politics:

> Le Verbe divin et le Verbe humain, conçus séparément, mais sous une notion de solidarité qui les rendait inséparables, avaient dès le commencement fondé la papauté et l'empire: les luttes de la papauté pour prévaloir seule avaient été l'affirmation absolue du Verbe divin; à cette affirmation, pour rétablir l'équilibre du dogme de l'Incarnation, devait correspondre dans l'empire une affirmation absolue du Verbe humain. Telle fut l'origine de la Réforme, qui aboutit AUX DROITS DE L'HOMME. (19)

Yet Constant/Lévi proceeds immediately to identify the tradition of the rights of man with Napoleon, as well as the Reformation. (19) And then eventually with the authority of the Catholic Church. (40)

To speak of duplicity here would be to understate the net of contradictions Constant/Lévi weaves. For not only does Napoléon stand as the inheritor of the revolutionary tradition of the Reformation, but he also represents the right of universal suffrage, and, even more significantly, is on several occasions set in opposition to both anarchy and the anarchism of Proudhon:

> L'instinct des peuples se conforme en cela même à la logique des idées, et deux fois le suffrage universel, placé entre l'obscurantisme et l'anarchie, a deviné la conciliation de l'ordre avec le progrès, et a nommé Napoléon. (27)

Napoleon, in Constant/Lévi's somewhat suspect eulogy, represents the antithesis of forms of illegitimate authority that are allied with contemporary anarchism:

> Néron représente pour nous la personnification la plus complète de l'idéalisme sans autorité et de la licence du pouvoir: c'est l'*anarchie* de M. Proudhon résumée en un seul homme et placée sur la trône de l'univers; c'est l'*absolu* des matérialistes en voluptés, en audace, en énergie et en puissance. Jamais nature plus désordonnée n'effraya le monde de ses écarts; et voilà ce que les révolutionnaires de l'école de M. Proudhon entendent par *de la poésie*; mais nous ne pensons pas comme eux. (51)

The paragraph which follows further undermines this somewhat unconvincing alignment of Nero and Proudhon, for it affirms the God-like powers of the individual artist. What could be less susceptible to secular authority? And yet, here, too, Constant/Lévi's language seems deliberately contradictory, for if he begins by affirming the ultimate authority of the poet, he ends by apparently denying the poet's right to create, to represent the world other than it already is:

> Etre poëte, c'est créer; ce n'est pas rêver ni mentir. Dieu a été poëte lorsqu'il a fait le monde, et son immortelle épopée est écrite avec des étoiles. Les sciences ont reçu de lui les secrets de la poésie, parce que les clefs de l'harmonie ont été remises entre leurs mains. Les nombres sont poëtes, car ils chantent avec ces notes toujours justes, qui donnaient des ravissements au génie de Pythagore. La poésie qui n'accepte pas le monde tel que Dieu l'a fait, et qui cherche à en inventer un autre, n'est que le délire des esprits des ténèbres: c'est celle-là qui aime le mystère et qui nie les progrès de l'intelligence humaine. (51)

What to make of Constant/Lévi's apparent waffling, of his incongruous admiration for Napoléon as a champion of universal suffrage? It would be difficult not to read beneath Constant/Lévi's unconvincing affirmations of authority allusions to the other Napoléon, Victor Hugo's Napoléon le petit, who had come to power on the basis of a universal suffrage he had later denied—and who had also had Constant thrown into prison for a satirical song which compared him, not to Nero, but to another cruel and perverse Roman emperor, Caligula. Within this context, the allusions to anarchism and the God-given authority of the poet, who, if he is not allowed to create, will go underground, stand in a positive light. In fact, the parallels between Constant/Lévi's views and those of anarchism seem to have been recognized in Symbolist circles and to have formed a considerable part of the basis for his popularity there.[25]

Turning back from the Discours préliminaire of 1861 to the body of the text, one is struck by the engravings, provided by Constant/Lévi himself, who was also active as a painter and engraver. One in particular, an engraving of a hand, which is held in the position of a benediction, but which casts the shadow of a gargoyle-like demon, suggests that we read the entire text as a demonic allegory.

But an allegory of what, one might ask? Of the displacement onto language and magic of the political and erotic desires of the former socialist, recently separated from his wife? Of the possibility that language and magic might form the basis for a new solidarity developed in the underground world of French occultism during the Second Empire? Constant/Lévi, of course, never answers this question. And his refusal seems to reflect more than the conditions of censorship under Napoleon III, for it is also in line with his invention, in *Dogme et rituel de la haute magie* as a whole, of a theory of language as magical, evocative, and open-ended.

In *L'histoire de la magie*, Constant/Lévi turns back more specifically to the magical traditions he had drawn upon in his earlier work. The nearly six hundred pages of this volume, however, scarcely provide a sense that he had deepened his knowledge of the traditions in a scholarly way. But they do suggest Constant's ongoing concern with the historical significance of magical doctrines, especially in relation to the French revolutionary tradition.

Of the three works on magic, *L'histoire de la magie* is probably the most accessible, and, although it purports to trace the evolution of magic from Egyptian times to the middle of the nineteenth century, it is best on the subject of the spread and significance of esoteric and pseudoscientific doctrines in late-eighteenth- and nineteenth-century France. References to Swedenborg compare his doctrines—unfavorably—to those of the cabala. It seems likely that Constant/Lévi had read Adolphe Franck's pioneering study of this subject, first published in 1843, for the cabala has become his principal model for a magical universal language. For both the cabala and Swedenborgianism, however, Constant/Lévi's enthusiasm surpassed his interest in detail: his discussions of the actual doctrines of the cabala are as schematic as those of Swedenborg. In both cases, it seems, the French writer found what he was looking for in his explorations of esoteric and pseudoscientific tradition.

Brief references to Swedenborg in *L'histoire de la magie* also mention his doctrines in connection with a Swiss visionary by the name of Naündorff (453), the cabalistic doctrine of the macrocosm as a giant man, Adam Kadmon (54), a choirmaster of Notre Dame—probably the Swedenborgian, Guillaume Oegger—who, the text maintains, read too much Swedenborg (473–76); and, most significantly, Fourier (470). The discussion of the latter, moreover, suggests that the author harbors a Faustian project of his own, a utopian system that would replace not only the fantastical whimsies of Fourier but also traditional Christianity:

> La négation du dogme fondamental de la religion catholique, si poétiquement formulée dans le poëme de Faust, avait porté ses fruits dans le monde. La morale privée de sa sanction éternelle devenait douteuse et chancelante. Un mystique matérialiste retourna le système de Swedenborg pour créer sur la terre le paradis des attractions proportionnelles aux destinées. Par les attractions, Fourier entendait les passions sensuelles, auxquelles il promettait une expansion intégrale et absolue. Dieu, qui est la suprême raison, marqua d'un sceau terrible ces doctrines reprouvées: les disciples de Fourier avaient commencé par l'absurdité, ils finirent par la folie. (470)

The book's most extended discussion of Swedenborg occurs in the first chapter of book 6, which is entitled "Magic and the Revolution." Here four very general paragraphs link Swedenborgianism to the German Illuminati and to rumors of their revolutionary activity and compare his doctrines to the cabala and the theories of Mesmer and his followers—all to the detriment of Swedenborg's reputation:

> Pendant qu'on disputait ainsi à la religion ses conquêtes en Asie, une immense inquiétude agitait l'Europe. La foi chrétienne semblait prête à s'y éteindre et il n'était bruit de tous côtés que de révélations nouvelles et de miracles. Un homme sérieusement posé dans la science et dans le monde, *Emmanuel Swedenborg*, étonnait la Suède par ses visions et l'Allemagne était pleine de nouveaux illuminés; le mysticisme dissident conspirait pour remplacer les mystères de la religion hiérarchique par les mystères de l'anarchie; une imminente catastrophe se préparait.
>
> Swedenborg, le plus honnête et le plus doux des prophètes du faux illuminisme, n'était pas pour cela moins dangereux que les autres. Prétendre, en effet, que tous les hommes sont appelés à communiquer directement avec le ciel, c'est remplacer l'enseignement religieux régulier et l'initiation progressive par toutes les divagations de l'enthousiasme et toutes les folies de l'imagination et des rêves. Les illuminés intelligents sentaient bien que la religion étant un des grands besoins de l'humanité, on ne la détruira jamais; aussi voulaient-ils se faire de la religion même et du fanatisme qu'elle entraîne par une conséquence fatale de l'enthousiasme inspiré à l'ignorance, des armes pour détruire l'autorité hiérarchique de l'Eglise, comptant bien voir sortir des conflits du fanatisme une hiérarchie nouvelle dont ils espéraient être les fondateurs et les chefs.
>
> "Vous serez comme des dieux, connaissant tout sans avoir eu la

peine de rien apprendre; vous serez comme des rois, possédant tout sans avoir eu la peine de rien acquérir."

Telles sont en résumé les promesses de l'esprit révolutionnaire aux multitudes envieuses. L'esprit révolutionnaire, c'est l'esprit de mort, c'est l'ancien serpent de la *Genèse*, et cependant c'est le père du mouvement et du progrès, puisque les générations ne se renouvellent que par la mort; c'est pour cela que les Indiens adoraient Schiva, l'impitoyable destructeur, dont la forme symbolique était celle de l'amour physique et de la génération matérielle. (411–13)

Constant/Lévi goes on to affirm, once more, his belief that Swedenborgianism was similar but inferior to the cabala:

Le système de Swedenborg n'est autre chose que la kabbale, moins le principe de la hiérarchie; c'est le temple sans clef de voûte et sans fondement; c'est un immense édifice, heureusement tout fantastique et aérien, car si l'on avait jamais tenté de réaliser sur la terre, il tomberait sur la tête du premier enfant qui essayerait, nous ne dirons pas de l'ébranler, mais de s'appuyer seulement contre une de ses principales colonnes. (413)

Curiously, Constant/Lévi ties what he believes to be the flimsiness of this "system" to social anarchy, for these remarks follow the characterization of Swedenborgianism as a temple a child might tumble, merely by leaning up against one of its pillars. He notes:

Organiser l'anarchie, tel est le problème que les révolutionnaires ont et auront éternellement à résoudre; c'est le rocher de Sisyphe qui retombera toujours sur eux; pour exister un seul instant ils sont et seront toujours fatalement réduits à improviser un despotisme sans autre raison d'être que la nécessité, et qui, par conséquent, est violent et aveugle comme elle. On n'échappe à la monarchie harmonieuse de la raison, que pour tomber sous la dictature désordonée de la folie. (413)

The most suggestive aspects of Swedenborgianism, moreover, are better developed in the work of Mesmer, which, one presumes, provides a superior guide to former revolutionaries:

Le moyen proposé indirectement par Swedenborg, pour communiquer avec le monde surnaturel, était un état intermédiaire qui tient du rêve, de l'extase et de la catalepsie. L'illuminé suédois affirmait la possibilité de cet état, mais il ne donnait pas la théorie des pratiques nécessaires pour y arriver; peut-être ses disciples, pour combler cette lacune,

eussent-ils recouru au rituel magique de l'Inde, lorsqu'un homme de génie vint compléter par une thaumaturgie naturelle les intuitions prophétiques et kabbalistiques de Swedenborg. Cet homme était un médecin
allemand, nommé *Mesmer*. (413–14)

Constant/Lévi's remarks are most interesting for what they say about
the context of the reception of Swedenborgianism in mid-nineteenth-century France. His remarks on the actual doctrines themselves, however, are
very general. There is little in Constant/Lévi's actual discussion of Swedenborg that he could not have found in a few works by Balzac—*Louis Lambert*, *Séraphîta*, or the Avant-propos to *La comédie humaine*, which refers
to Swedenborg as a "Bouddha chrétien." (1:16) And Balzac, as well, had
tied Swedenborg to notions of a hieroglyphic language of nature, to Leibniz's monadology, and to the theories of Mesmer and his followers. What is
new in Constant/Lévi's discussion is the emphasis on the cabala as a model
for a magical universal language, as well as the disavowal of Swedenborg's
originality and importance. If the schematic discussion of the cabala can
be traced back to Adolphe Franck's 1843 study, the references to Jewish
mysticism nonetheless mark a shift in Constant/Lévi's notion of what language is and what it can do.

Constant/Lévi's skeptical presentation of Swedenborg and his doctrines in *L'histoire de la magie* echoes a long line of commentators who
expressed puzzlement over the attraction of these ideas in France, a line
that goes back at least to Henri Grégoire (1750–1831), who in his *Histoire
des sectes religieuses*, published in 1828, characterized French Swedenborgianism as "des révélations chimériques adoptées par quelques hommes
abondamment pourvus de crédulité." (5:109)

In the 1840s and 1850s, in fact, there were few Swedenborgian believers in Paris or France. Although the leader of the sect, J.-F.-E. Le Boys
des Guays translated many of Swedenborg's works at this time and started
a Swedenborgian journal, his energetic efforts did not succeed in gaining
many new converts or even spreading the doctrines of the sect. Nor do
Constant/Lévi's remarks on Swedenborg suggest that he had read or been
impressed by the interpretations of Le Boys des Guays or his predecessors:
rather they suggest an awareness that Swedenborg and his doctrines had
played a role in revolutionary culture and social thought in France from
the late eighteenth century to the middle of the nineteenth, a culture
whose implications or importance had yet to be fully explored.

What is significant about Constant/Lévi's brief and schematic discussion of Swedenborg is its context, for within the chapter "Auteurs remar-
quables du XVIIIe siècle," Swedenborg and his doctrines mediate between

the language theory of Leibniz and Mesmerism. The doctrines of all three, moreover, point to the hope that the discovery of a universal language or substance underlying the apparent chaos of everyday life might offer an objective means for resolving disputes of a religious or political nature. Constant/Lévi's reference to Leibniz and his language theory occurs in the context of his very general discussion of the European discovery of Chinese culture, especially the radically different system of writing, which was interpreted as a system of hieroglyphs. Leibniz, Constant/Lévi writes,

> croyait voir dans l'y Kim sa propre invention de l'arithmétique binaire, et dans la ligne droite et la ligne brisée de Fo-hi, il retrouvait les caractères 1 0, employés par lui-même dans ses calculs; il était bien près de la vérité, mais il ne l'entrevoyait que dans un de ses détails, il ne pouvait en embrasser l'ensemble. (411)

But if Leibniz and the Jesuit missionaries who were sent to China recognized the potential of a universal language to resolve religious disputes, they failed to apply these insights wisely. For Constant/Lévi, a better understanding of the way in which such a universal language might lead to peace and understanding was set forth by Swedenborg. But Swedenborg's doctrines, especially as understood by his isolated followers, were also lacking in clarity and scientific validity. Their imperfections, however, were corrected by Mesmer, whom Constant/Lévi describes as an "homme de génie [qui] vint compléter par une thaumaturgie naturelle les intuitions prophétiques et kabbalistiques de Swedenborg." (413–14)

The interpretation of Mesmer's doctrines in *L'histoire de la magie* is as schematic as those of Leibniz and Swedenborg. Instead of a universal language, Mesmer was able to point to a universal substance coursing through living and nonliving matter, a substance that enabled the Mesmerist not only to understand, but also to improve and cure, patients and world alike. The universal substance, moreover, functions like a Leibnizean universal language, based on the study both of other human languages and of mathematics:

> Les phénomènes de cohésion, d'élasticité, de densité ou de subtilité des corps, sont produits par les diverses combinaisons des deux propriétés du fluide universel ou de la matière première.
>
> La maladie, comme tous les désordres physiques, vient d'un dérangement de l'équilibre normal de la matière première dans un corps organisé.
>
> Les corps organisés sont ou sympathiques ou antipathiques les uns aux autres, par suite de leur équilibre spécial.

> Les corps sympathiques peuvent se guérir les uns les autres, en ré-
> tablissant mutuellement leur équilibre.
> Cette propriété des corps de s'équilibrer les uns les autres par l'at-
> traction ou la projection de la matière première, Mesmer la nomme mag-
> nétisme, et comme elle se spécifie suivant les spécialités des êtres,
> lorsqu'il en étudie les phénomènes dans les êtres animés, il la nomme
> magnétisme animal. (415)

For Constant/Lévi, Mesmerism was the most important contribution of the
eighteenth century to nineteenth-century culture, and subsequent chapters in *L'histoire de la magie* trace its fortunes in France to the decade
following 1848. As presented here, however, nineteenth-century Mesmerists such as du Potet failed to live up to the promises of Mesmer, perhaps
because they, like Constant/Lévi himself, had been reduced to the private
practice of doctrines which, at the end of the eighteenth century, had
seemed to hold out the promise of a more general, perhaps universal,
regeneration of the human condition. Constant/Lévi's criticisms of contemporary Mesmerists apply equally to his own work, but his views both of
du Potet and contemporary Mesmerism point to an important development in the interpretation of these marginal doctrines in mid-nineteenth-
century France.

What Constant/Lévi's remarks on contemporary Mesmerists betray is
above all his own awareness that these doctrines might serve, and, in fact,
often did serve, to buttress the authority of the practitioner, and that,
moreover, they had something to say about the nature of authority itself.
Despite their vagueness and many inaccuracies, the pages on Mesmerism
in *L'histoire de la magie* represent a noteworthy attempt to come to terms
with the mysterious power of some individuals over others. Constant/Lévi,
of course, is no sociologist, but what his own quest to understand and
attain this power seems to have led him to is the intuition that the authority of some individuals draws on irrational elements in human consciousness and that doctrines such as Mesmerism provide a language for the
understanding and exercise of these powers. Later writers would express
the link between Mesmerism and authority far more clearly, often in terms
related to the Weberian concept of charisma, but Constant/Lévi's remarks
suggest that mid-nineteenth-century writers were already aware of the
connection.[26]

To what extent was Constant/Lévi's awareness that Mesmerism and
other occult doctrines might explain or contribute to the irrational power
of one individual over others linked to a criticism of contemporary society,
of the power of the Emperor, for example? It would be wrong, I think, to
see Constant/Lévi as a kind of "emperor-worshiper," as at least one of his

critics has done.[27] Such an interpretation overlooks the critical remarks scattered throughout the works he published in the Second Empire. It is probably equally misleading to assume that Mesmerism or even Sweden-borgianism pointed merely to a program of tolerance or quietistic accep-tance, as some passages suggest.

Constant/Lévi suggests that Mesmerism and—to some extent—Swedenborgianism demonstrate the unity of science and magic, and that a correct understanding of the objective structures to which these doctrines point might lead to a better world. This argument, however, is double edged. It is true that the final paragraphs in the book appear to argue for mere tolerance and understanding:

> Notre *Histoire de la magie* a eu pour but de démontrer que, dans le principe, les grands symboles de la religion ont été en même temps ceux de la science alors cachée.
> Que la religion et la science, réunies dans l'avenir, s'entr'aident donc et s'aiment comme deux soeurs, puisqu'elles ont eu le même berceau! (559–60)

But the concluding paragraph of the chapter preceding the final "Résumé et Conclusion" and entitled "Les Sciences occultes," is far more radical. In esoteric doctrines and especially the cabala, the author writes:

> Voilà ce que le Sauveur du monde appelle le *royaume de Dieu*! C'est le *sanctum regnum* de la sainte kabbale. C'est la couronne et l'anneau de Salomon, c'est le sceptre de Joseph devant lequel s'inclinent les étoiles du ciel et les moissons de la terre.
> Cette toute-puissance nous l'avons retrouvée, et nous ne la vendons pas, mais si Dieu nous avait chargé de la vendre, nous ne trouverions pas que ce soit assez de toute la fortune des acheteurs; nous leur deman-derions encore, non pas pour nous, mais pour elle toute leur âme et leur vie! (528)

In contrast to the rather insipid reference to a "sisterhood" of science and magic at the end of the conclusion, the final paragraph of "Les sciences occultes," a chapter general enough to serve very well as a conclusion, suggests that the language theory and magical interests described in *L'his-toire de la magie* are intimately bound up with a Faustian project to trans-form the world through the initiation of a group of conspirators who un-derstand the significance—and the power—of the magical tradition.

This concluding paragraph—occult in that it hides behind the apparent conclusion—places the references to eighteenth- and nineteenth-century esotericism in a more politicized light than the wording of the passages seems to allow. The allusion to the oath demanded of would-be initiates—"nous leur demanderions encore, non pas pour nous, mais pour elle toute leur âme et toute leur vie!"—echoes the rituals of eighteenth-century freemasonry, including their radical offshoots in the allegedly conspiratorial orders of the Illuminati. The hidden conclusion also harks back to and places in a new light the earlier comparison of Fourier's utopian fantasies to Swedenborg's visions and to a project of negating or replacing Catholicism that the writer sees as Faustian: "La négation du dogme fondamental de la religion catholique, si poétiquement formulée dans le poëme de Faust, avait porté ses fruits dans le monde," (470) he writes at the beginning of Book VII, going on to note Swedenborgianism and Fourierism as two misguided attempts at replacements. At its mildest then, the knowledge Constant/Lévi believes that he has attained permits him to discern the follies inherent in other utopian projects. One wonders, however, about the violent overtones of the price exacted of would-be initiates. Does the passage allude to a possible revolutionary conspiracy, whose rituals, like those of the freemasons or the Illuminati, drew on and reworked elements of esoteric tradition? It is impossible to say. What is clear, however, is that, although *L'histoire de la magie* looks back upon and subsumes many esoteric and political traditions, the synthesis it presents is essentially linguistic. Language itself, Constant/Lévi argues in his many references to Swedenborg, the cabala, and other universal language theories, possesses a secret power that transcends the actions of individuals or specific historical events of the past.

Despite Constant/Lévi's apparent preference for the theories of Mesmer to the universal language schemes of Leibniz or Swedenborg, this is a power and a project that depend on language and writing, on the books in which he expounded his own universal system. Swedenborg and Leibniz erred in particulars. That Constant/Lévi realized the far-reaching importance of universal language theories is suggested by his attempts during the last decades of his life, to work out his principles of a universal language in a work on the cabala first published in 1920.[28]

The eclectic synthesis of pseudoscientific and esoteric doctrines, of Swedenborgianism and Mesmerism, set forth in *L'histoire de la magie*, then, offered an explanation of the relation of individuals and their desires to the totality of the social and natural worlds, an explanation of and perhaps a key for understanding and controlling dreams and their realization. As it is portrayed here, however, this process is far less individualistic than in the poem "Les correspondances," in which "correspondences" among consciousness, nature, and the supernatural are perceived in a dream state. If the emphasis in "Les correspondances" was on the ability of the humblest and most isolated dreamer to intuit divine correspondences underlying the surfaces of everyday life, in *L'histoire de la magie* what matters is the ability of the visionary individual to understand the systematic nature of these intuitions and to communicate them to other potential participants in the collective Faustian project of transforming the social world.

These are curious subjects to crop up in a *history* of magic, and, indeed, *L'histoire de la magie* is not always clear or accurate. Scholars such as Arthur Edward Waite have found fault with its presentation of many individual doctrines.[29] But it seems to me that, although because of its range and scope the work can serve as a history, that is not its primary purpose; nor is history the genre to which it properly belongs.

Recent work on the history of freemasonry and its reception in European culture in the last three centuries has emphasized the extent to which the masons plundered esoteric traditions in order to construct rituals of initiation and participation in a closed, egalitarian world, almost always a brotherhood.[30] As Scott Abbott has argued in a study of masonic imagery in the German novel, this process itself echoes the evolution or concoction of a Rosicrucian Enlightenment, a movement that seems to be much more than its ever-vanishing origins.[31] It seems to me that Constant/Lévi's *Histoire de la magie* harks back to precisely this kind of initiatory and participatory myth-making, and it does so from the point of view of a writer of non-bourgeois origins, once an outspoken partisan of socialism, who sees himself and the political culture in which he lives as the inheritors of the revolutionary culture of the eighteenth century. Like the Illuminati and the freemasons, Constant/Lévi looks back—or pretends to look back—over the entirety of esoteric traditions, but he also looks back and repeats the activity of constructing a participatory mythology that could lead to the revolutionary establishment of a juster social order. Constant/Lévi's actions as a writer, in other words, parallelled those of the artisans that William H. Sewell described in *The Language of Labor and the Ancien Régime*: from the vocabulary of the guilds and other associations of the Ancien Régime, Constant/Lévi and some Parisian workers were able to forge a new language of class solidarity.

Did subsequent writers understand this aspect of his work? There is a tradition in French Symbolism which associates a secret power of language with revolutionary violence, the poetry of Mallarmé, say, with the practices of his friend, Félix Fénéon. Some writers may well have been aware of and attempted to exploit this web of potential meanings. But throughout the nineteenth century, the notion of a universal language played into the hands of writers on both left and right. Later readers and

riters had no reason to see in Constant/Lévi's work only what he in-
nded.

From his very general references to Swedenborg and his doctrines, it
; impossible to tell which texts by or about Swedenborg Constant/Lévi had
ead. Did he become acquainted with Swedenborg's doctrines through one
f the popularizing handbooks by Daillant de la Touche or Robert Hin-
lmarsh that circulated in France in the late eighteenth and nineteenth
:enturies? Or had he read some of Swedenborg's theological and visionary
vorks, *Heaven and Hell*, perhaps? In the 1840s, the spiritualist Alphonse
Cahagnet summoned up and proceeded to interrogate a spirit he recognized as Swedenborg during his seances. (See especially his *Magnétisme*,
168–95) Did Constant/Lévi have or believe he had a similar source? At
times, the vagueness of his discussions of Swedenborg and his doctrines
make one want to believe so.

Whatever his sources, Constant/Lévi did incorporate some very general features of Swedenborg's doctrines. The French writer's books on
magic insist on the unity of science and reason, and Swedenborgianism
seems to have served as one model for the reconciliation of apparently
disparate tendencies in modern culture. Swedenborg's emphasis on the
importance of sexuality—even in heaven—seems, as well, to have exerted
a strong attraction for the former priest, who had been forced to leave the
Church because of his involvement with a young woman. And, although
triadic patterns are very common in nineteenth-century French thought,
Constant/Lévi seems to have associated a notion of allegorical relationships
among three levels of experiences with Swedenborg and his doctrine of
correspondences.

All of Constant/Lévi's works show a greater awareness of the intellectual context of the theological and visionary doctrines of Swedenborg and
their French reception than of the details of the Swede's writings themselves. He repeats the fairly common associations of Swedenborg's doctrines with those of Fourier and Mesmer, and, more remarkably, situates
Swedenborg's theory of language in the context of seventeenth-century
universal language schemes, especially that of Leibniz. Swedenborgianism,
however, figures in a minor way in Constant/Lévi's work. In the books on
magic, its importance has been all but eclipsed by Constant/Lévi's interest
in the cabala, although the French writer never falls into the trap of claim-
ing that the visionary was *influenced* by the Jewish mystical tradition.

If Constant/Lévi's evaluation of the intellectual context of Swedenborg's work is better than that of many literary historians, who see it as
part of a preromantic rejection of reason, the French writer's discussions
of the visionary—limited as they are—are most interesting for the story

they tell. Constant/Lévi's Swedenborgianism replays the plot of Balzac's *Louis Lambert*, whose visionary protagonist died very young because he was not strong enough to survive the intensity of his genius or to communicate his insights with his fellow human beings: the solitary poet of "Les correspondances" recalls Louis Lambert as a child or the isolated genius of Balzac's early preface, the "Avertissement du *Gars*," while Constant/Lévi's references to Swedenborgianism after he changed his name deny the possiblity that an individual can safely contemplate the totality of nature; but if the chapter of *La science des esprits* entitled "La mort du poëte" suggests the unhappy end of Louis Lambert himself, Constant/Lévi's works on magic, with their emphasis on the role of the exceptional and initiated individual, recall later works by Balzac in which only the man of exceptional will can survive on his own in a corrupt society.

Few twentieth-century interpretations of Constant/Lévi's works on magic recognize their literary complexity. For side by side with the evocation of an allegorical language of nature based partly on Swedenborg's doctrine of correspondences, the French writer's works also point to a different, much more practical, set of textual analogies. Their only partly hidden agenda suggests the repression of the Second Empire, the desirability of universal suffrage, and the hope that language might begin to bring about a social transformation that fighting on the barricades had failed to produce.

Constant/Lévi's compendious overviews of occult and pseudoscientific traditions find their place among many such reconsiderations in mid-nineteenth-century France: from Alexandre Erdan's scornful *La France mistique* [sic] (1855) to Jacques Matter's scholarly biographies of Saint-Martin and Swedenborg in the early 1860s. These works pose a problem for literary and cultural historians, for if both subject matter and style seem to relegate most of them to the margins of literary and cultural history, can we be so sure that they were so marginal to nineteenth-century readers? And where does one draw the line? Anyone familiar with the works of Fourier, Saint-Simon, and their followers will recognize the importance of occult and pseudoscientific ideas in French political theory in the first half of the century. Yet few scholars would classify their works as popular or marginal.[32]

In the 1840s and 1850s, a host of French writers, many but not all of them from the "other" classes, produced writings expounding systems that looked very much like those of the French utopians. The very number of these systems itself asks for interpretation. Why were there so many of them? What does one make of the range of writers engaged in producing individual versions or interpretations of utopian or occult systems?

In his ground-breaking survey of mid-nineteenth-century occultism, Auguste Viatte points to the importance both of 1848 and of the breakdown of belief in the utopian systems of the first half of the century. About this time, for example, the cosmology of Saint-Simon provided the point of departure for the development of a welter of personal neo-saint-simonian systems:

> Ainsi le saint-simonisme s'était couronné par une véritable superstructure—ici l'expression marxiste convient tout à fait—d'essence religieuse ou tout au moins métapsychique. Elle avait un moment fait illusion, et ses traces sur la mentalité générale sont durables. Mais, après une dizaine d'années, elle était tombée en morceaux, et ces morceaux, entre les mains de théoriciens divers, servent à bâtir de nouveaux systèmes. (*Victor Hugo*, 61)

And these systems, more often than not, presented an eclectic mixture of the doctrines of Swedenborgianism, Mesmerism, spiritism, and other occult and magical traditions. It would be wrong, however, to identify the cosmologies of the 1840s and 1850s with the interests of the left or right, however, for there seems to be a world system to accommodate every political position during these decades—despite each writer's claim to knowledge of the Absolute.

Certainly the producers of these tracts can only have been dismayed by the competition, which suggests perspectivism rather than a direct pathway to Absolute knowledge (and power). But the number of these texts also raises questions concerning the distinction—if there *is* a distinction—between elite and popular culture. None of these writers—including, if not especially, Constant/Lévi—aimed to produce second-rate, unsuccessful texts, even if they were forced to publish their works in cheap editions. But it does seem that a number of them were automatically relegated by their contemporaries to something like a culture for the uninformed masses: Constant/Lévi does seem, in many respects, to belong to this group. And such relegations often carry with them assumptions concerning the quality and complexity of the writer's work, assumptions that may have little to do with the texts themselves, because they are never read.

Consider, for example, a journalistic article about Constant, rediscovered by a Baudelaire scholar and published in the most recent Pléiade edition of his works because it is likely that Baudelaire wrote it. The article, which bears the title "L'abbé Constant, et un peu l'abbé Olivier, évêque d'Evreux," begins:

> Il y avait une fois, messieurs et dames, un gros petit abbé qui avait, disait-il, beaucoup de génie, peu de dévotion, disaient ses confrères, et

assez d'orgueil, à ce que prétendent tous ceux qui l'ont connu. . . Mais à
propos, l'avez-vous connu? Savez-vous ce que c'est que l'abbé Constant?
(2:1007)

If Baudelaire did write the essay, these words scarcely suggest that the poet
would consciously have borrowed from Constant. What the article does
attest to is considerable knowledge of Constant's life and work in the
1840s: his imprisonment for his *La Bible de la liberté*, which the author of
the essay judges to be "une oeuvre de la folie," rather than a politically
dangerous work; his association with Flora Tristan; and the rumors surrounding his relations with female pupils. What it does not attest to is
knowledge of—or interest in—his writing. Could it not be that even the
authors of hack journalism such as this refused to accept Constant or his
writing on the basis of his class origins and affiliations? What criteria distinguished those writers worthy of a hearing or reading among the educated public and those who were not?

    In *The Structural Transformation of the Public Sphere*, Jürgen Ha-
bermas argues that eighteenth-century France saw the rise of a print culture in which ideas circulated freely among an educated reading public,
who were free to reflect upon and debate them at their leisure. Events at
the end of the century, however, especially the Revolution of 1789 and the
inclusion of uneducated and unpropertied individuals in political events
and discussion, skewed this process, for many of the new writers and
readers lacked the distance and disinterested perspective that made the
reasonable evaluation and discussion of printed texts possible. Many cultural historians have questioned aspects of Habermas's argument, pointing, for example, to the class- and sex-bound aspects of his argument. The
German social theorist does seem to identify print culture with the interests of the bourgeoisie and to represent the expression of the needs of
those considered as outsiders as emotional and irrational. It is, perhaps,
too easy to fault a work published in 1962 for its classist and sexist perspectives. Habermas's work is extremely suggestive for the reconsideration
of writers such as Constant/Lévi, not least because it points to many of the
assumptions at play in his relegation to the status of a "minor" or "popular" writer.

    These assumptions also govern Robert Darnton's work on French pop-
ular culture, although his later studies call them increasingly into question. In his *Mesmerism and the End of the Enlightenment in France*,
published in 1968, Darnton characterized the work of Constant and other
producers of occult pseudo-systems of the mid-century as betrayers of the
Enlightenment revolutionary tradition, which, he argues, had been able to
incorporate Mesmerism's strange fusion of science and occultism, but dis-
solved when "irrational" doctrines such as those of Swedenborg were

added.[33] Darnton's later work on eighteenth-century hack journalism, however, provides a different perspective on the nature of Enlightenment print culture and the relation of marginal writers to a bourgeois public sphere. In contrast to officially recognized and remunerated writers, many of whom were not better writers, the grub-street journalists Darnton discusses in *The Literary Underground of the Old Regime* eked out a hand-to-mouth existence writing whatever and however they could for whoever would pay them. The texts produced by these writers of what Darnton calls the "other Enlightenment" were anything but disinterested. *The Literary Underground* suggests both that the print culture of the French Enlightenment was more multifarious than Habermas (or Darnton) had argued in the 1960s and that the nature and classification of a writer's works often reflect factors that have very little to do with quality.

How, then, should one read the works of a writer such as Constant? In his introduction to his anthology of Constant's works of the 1840s, Frank Paul Bowman argues that the works of this writer have a particular significance, a significance tied to the nature and status of the writings of a whole group of writers in nineteenth-century France he calls "petits romantiques":

> Ces "petits romantiques"—et l'Abbé Constant en fut un—révèlent mieux que les grands les tendances de l'époque les plus profondes comme les plus durables, celles qui allaient s'épanouir avec Baudelaire, avec le Victor Hugo des *Contemplations* et de *La Légende des siècles*. (6)[34]

Certainly, in this and other studies on religious aspects of French Romanticism, Bowman has shown the importance of an indigenous French occult and pseudoscientific tradition, a tradition at least as important as German Romantic philosophy and aesthetics for the development of French literature in the first half of the nineteenth century. But if he has emphasized the importance of the works of these writers in their own right, one wonders about the temporal relationship implied in his suggestion that what appears *in nuce* in the works of Constant and other minor romantics blossoms in those of the now-canonical Baudelaire and Hugo. The careers of Constant and Baudelaire ran parallel to each other in the 1840s and 1850s, and Constant/Lévi's writings of the 1850s and early 1860s, if less self-consciously literary than those of Baudelaire, are no less complex. The works of both men reveal an intense preoccupation with self-cultivation and -preservation as an artist in the politically repressive Second Empire. And in the work of both, elements from the systems of occult, pseudoscientific, and political traditions play an important role in the exploration of this and related subjects.

By emphasizing the parallels between the work of Constant/Lévi and

Baudelaire, I do not mean to suggest that Constant/Lévi's work is the aesthetic or literary equal of that of Baudelaire. I do mean to emphasize that one cannot be derived from the other, but that, as Bowman has suggested in his work as a whole, they are mutually illuminating. I have focused on the work of Constant/Lévi and its references to Swedenborg and uses of the term *correspondances* because it so well illustrates the kinds of questions posed by the study of language and culture in mid-nineteenth-century France, as well as the importance of contemporary contexts for the transmission and transformation of Swedenborgianism and its doctrines in that country during the decade following the Revolution of 1789.

I shall return to the question of Baudelaire and the cultural significance of *his* poetic *correspondances* in a later chapter. However, before I do so, I now turn back, first to the work of Swedenborg, and then to some of his earlier interpreters in France, including the canonical works of the novelist Balzac, as well as some texts by writers at least as marginal as Constant/Lévi. These works, I hope, will further suggest what is at stake in the French reception of Swedenborgianism in the late eighteenth and early nineteenth centuries.

CHAPTER TWO

Swedenborg's Correspondences and the Cultures of the Enlightenment

For Constant/Lévi and many of his contemporaries, Swedenborg and his doctrine of correspondences had come to seem little more than shimmering names among a constellation of others that also suggested notions of a language of nature allied both with ideology and magic. But what of Swedenborg himself? Can one find a more precise definition of "correspondences" in his work? And does it have any relation to later interpretations of it, especially in France?

The question calls for a more complex response than most historians have been willing to give it. Swedenborg was an enormously productive writer, who published in many fields in the natural sciences, as well as theology and what has come to be called theosophy, but most of his work falls through the net of traditional intellectual history that emphasizes the relations among canonical texts. He was an erudite (although, perhaps, not always as erudite as he liked to seem[1]) and extremely prolific writer, but his works, even his many, well-informed, and suggestive treatises in the natural sciences, exerted virtually no influence on elite culture during his lifetime. Although his interests ran parallel to those of many contemporary European scientists and philosophers, few of Swedenborg's scientific treatises were read by his contemporaries, and as he turned from cosmology to anatomy and physiology and eventually to dream analysis and the depiction of other "parallel" worlds, his work diverged increasingly from the mainstream of European intellectual life.

Understandably enough, intellectual and literary historians have had difficulty placing his work. Some interpretations see Swedenborg romantically, as an isolated and misunderstood genius, whose work points forward to a later age's questioning of the limits of Enlightenment rationality, others as a fraud or a madman, still others as the producer of unreadable mystical texts. Studies by members of the Swedenborgian church emphasize the close ties between Swedenborg's early scientific work and his later theological doctrines, arguing that both are equally reasonable and scientific—certainly a view that Swedenborg himself would have endorsed. The work of two fine Swedish intellectual historians, Martin Lamm and Inge Jonsson, has also emphasized the close connections between the scientific and religious or visionary phases of his career: from somewhat different points of view, both have stressed the importance of seventeenth-century intellectual models for Swedenborg's overall production. Both Lamm and Jonsson, moreover, have pointed to the literary merits of some of Swedenborg's writings, and have done much to situate his production in the context of early modern Swedish science and intellectual life, a rich and fascinating context, even if it is little known outside of Scandinavia. One of Jonsson's monographs, which traces the origins of the term correspondences back from Swedenborg's theosophical and theological works through his scientific writings and European intellectual history, points to the close connections between Swedenborg's writing and the universal language schemes of the late seventeenth and eighteenth centuries, suggesting that the question of the relation of his work to nineteenth-century French poetics might be redefined to focus on issues of literary structure, rather than religious or mystical origins. But if Lamm and Jonsson cast much light on the writings of Swedenborg himself, the studies of both historians emphasize the idiosyncratic nature of these texts. Although Lamm characterizes Swedenborg as a "preromantic," neither he nor Jonsson can account for later apparent interpretations of his work. To echo the puzzled words of another intellectual historian, Auguste Viatte, who has mapped out the French reception of Swedenborgian and other sectarian and pseudoscientific doctrines in the early and mid-nineteenth century: Swedenborg "n'avait rien d'un enthousiaste." (*Sources occultes*, 72)

Swedenborg's main influence on European culture—if one must speak of influences—occurred in the realm of religion, and even there it was quite limited, especially in relation to established churches. Although Swedenborg probably never intended to found a new religion and died a Lutheran, after his death a number of his followers established a new branch of Christianity based on his works, and churches were set up in England, Scandinavia, the United States, and other countries. Even in Protestant countries, however, Swedenborgians failed to gain many converts. In nineteenth-century France, they remained an extremely isolated group which never managed to establish more than a chapel on the rue Thouin in the Latin Quarter in Paris. Although some literary critics refer to writers who cite Swedenborg or refer to *correspondances* in a possibly mystical context in their works as "Swedenborgian," it is extremely unlikely that these quotations denote a religious affiliation. They point, instead, to the secular importance of Swedenborgianism and other religious and pseudoscientific cults in the late eighteenth and nineteenth centuries.

In late-eighteenth- and early-nineteenth-century Europe, Sweden-borgian doctrines were most often transmitted in the context of a group of mildly contestatory practices that emphasized the cultivation of the individual and his (occasionally her) desires in connection with the formation of new kinds of communities based on the precepts of freemasonry, Mesmerism, and utopianism. Studies by Margaret Jacob and Robert Darnton have focused on the ways in which the practices and iconography of free-masonry and Mesmerism were embedded in the larger political culture of the Enlightenment. Jacob suggests that freemasonry provided a space in which men—and occasionally women—could meet and work out ways in which all could participate as equals in a community based on honesty, self-improvement, and work. Darnton emphasizes the importance of Mesmerism both as an alternative scientific community capable of absorbing and exalting ambitious outsiders and as a popular movement whose symbols served as a vehicle for the representation of political and social fantasies in the late eighteenth and early nineteenth centuries. Despite the prominence of theories of language in Swedenborg's work and in that of later writers who quote him, no study has considered his reception from the perspective of recent work in cultural history—perhaps because the prospect of looking at a body of texts written mostly in Latin from the point of view of popular culture does seem at first heretical.

And yet, despite this—not very ominous—possibility, no consideration of Swedenborg's reception can afford to ignore his texts. One of the persistent flaws in studies of Swedenborg is the tendency to apply labels all too freely to either his entire work or his later, theological and theosophical production. If Lamm portrayed Swedenborg very generally as a preromantic, Robert Kirven sees him and his work as participating in a general European "revolt against Deism." Swedenborg was, however, an enormously productive writer, and the sheer volume of his works makes the possibility of simply applying a label or labels and moving on very attractive.

In this chapter, then, I shall first survey Swedenborg's life and work, focusing on recent work in intellectual and cultural history that sheds new light on its significance, before turning to two texts by Swedenborg that, I believe, are of crucial importance for understanding the relation of his work to both his own and later cultural contexts.

The first is a work that exerted no influence whatsoever, at least not until it was published in 1859: Swedenborg's journal of 1743–44 is a record of dreams and visions that may be read both as an account of a transforming religious experience and as an extended self-analysis undertaken by an intellectual who had spent the previous decade mulling over the nature of the relationship between mind and body. More than any other work by Swedenborg, however, the diary links the development of the author's notion of parallel worlds and his doctrine of correspondences to the world in which he lived.

The second text is a relatively short work Swedenborg produced almost at the midpoint of the theological and theosophical phase of his career, *Heaven and Hell*, first published in 1758 and intended to serve as a popularizing summary of doctrines he had expounded at far greater length in his multi-volume exegesis of the Bible, *Arcana coelestia*. It is Swedenborg's most translated, quoted, and probably most read work. *Heaven and Hell*, I shall argue, maps out not only invisible realms inhabited by angels, demons, and the spirits of the recently dead, but also a utopian world in which personal merit forms the basis for social standing, and the desire for transparency and sincerity can be reconciled with a right to privacy and property.

These two works tie Swedenborg's doctrine of correspondences and his later visionary texts to some of the most significant tendencies in popular culture of the time—to Mesmerism and to the utopian and mystical ideals associated not only with the work of Rousseau, but also with the spread of freemasonry and other communitarian movements during the decades preceding the French Revolution.

1. The Worlds of Emanuel Swedenborg

The life of Emanuel Swedenborg (1688–1772) spanned an age of rapid transformation in Swedish culture and society.[2] Born into an upwardly mobile Swedish family at the end of the seventeenth century, Swedenborg witnessed the end of one form of Swedish absolutism, with the defeat and death of Charles XII (1682–1718), whom he served during his youth, and, as a member of the House of Nobles, actively participated in the political life of the decades that followed, the so-called Age of Freedom in Sweden. This was a period that saw the evolution of two political parties and the imposition of restrictions on the power of the monarchy. The year before Swedenborg's death, however, marked the ascension to the throne of Gustav III, who would curtail the power of the nobility and reinstitute absolutism in Sweden, although it did not survive his assassination in 1792. As Assessor on the Board of Mines and as a natural scientist, Swedenborg both participated in the upsurge of interest in the natural sciences in Sweden in the eighteenth century, and helped bring about practical reforms that modernized a country which, at the time of his birth, lagged far behind the more southern regions of Europe, both culturally and economically. If most of his life was spent in practical and worldly pursuits, however, during the last years of his life and certainly after his death, Swedenborg came to be known as a kind of visionary or seer who spent decades peering into and recording what he saw in invisible worlds he believed were parallel to our own.[3] He was the third of nine children of an ambitious and outspoken clergyman, Bishop Jesper Swedberg (1656–1735) and his first wife, Sara Behm (d. 1696). Jesper Swedberg's family had grown prosperous in the mining trade, his father had been able to send him to university to study theology, and he rose rapidly, marrying well and becoming Bishop of Skara in 1703. As a boy and young man, Swedenborg, too, was known by the surname of Swedberg; the name Swedenborg was bestowed when Jesper Swedberg's family was ennobled in 1719. The ennoblement gave the younger man not only a new name, but also the right to vote in the Swedish House of Nobles, a right he exercised for most of his life. In a more general sense, the two names can be seen as part of a pattern of doubling in Swedenborg's life. In his autobiographical *Journal of Dreams*, he writes of a dream in which the bestowal of a new name, the curiously double *Nicolai Nicolaiter*, seems to suggest a kind of rebirth or at least spiritual ennoblement that eventually led the writer/dreamer to see himself as a privileged inhabitant of two worlds, one visible, one not. The tendency to experience things in two's, however, probably goes back to an event far more tragic than a young man's conflicted social identity; Swedenborg's mother died when he was eight years old, and he and his siblings were raised by Jesper Swedberg's second wife, called, like his first, Sara, a woman whom Swedenborg said on numerous occasions proved an excellent mother, a fine replacement for the first.

In a letter that sketches out his life, Swedenborg said that, as a child, he was accustomed to having visions. But we know little about his childhood. His father's voluminous memoirs mention him once, and then only to note his birth and the significance of his name: Emanuel means "God with us."[4] The memoirs, however, do give a clear impression of the Bishop's strong personality, the force of his religious convictions, and the somewhat Baroque imaginative world he inhabited, a world in which the smallest object or occurrence could take on an otherworldly significance, a world in which clothing was strictly controlled for it, too, could signify the religious status of the wearer. Eight years after Jesper Swedberg died in 1735, Swedenborg suffered a religious crisis that prompted him, then in his mid-fifties, to resign from his position as a public official in order to focus exclusively on otherworldly and religious matters. Jesper Swedberg figures prominently in the journal his son kept during and after his crisis, and it may well be that Swedenborg's decision reflects a delayed reaction to his father's death. The earlier death, in 1719, of his stepmother, Sara Bergia, affected his career both more directly and more practically, for she left him an inheritance that enabled him to take the many leaves of absence from his position as Assessor to the Mines that made his scientific pursuits possible.

In 1699, at the age of eleven, Swedenborg entered the university at Uppsala, finishing his studies in 1709 with a dissertation in Latin, a commentary on some maxims by Seneca and Publius Syrus Mimus. Throughout his life, Swedenborg wrote almost exclusively in Latin. He did so in his scientific and visionary works out of a desire to communicate with a European reading public, but his interest in classical literature and poetics was never merely practical, for he composed several long texts in Latin, including an early encomium to the Swedish King Charles XII, *Festivus applausus*, and an unfinished creation epic *De cultu et amore Dei*, which he worked on in the early 1740s, but never finished.[5] In a detailed monograph on the latter work, Inge Jonsson characterizes *De cultu et amore Dei* as a late but worthy example of a genre that had flourished on the continent during the Renaissance. For Jonsson, this work epitomizes Swedenborg's taste for aesthetic and intellectual models of the previous two centuries.

Despite his interest in classical languages and aesthetics, however, Swedenborg did not opt to pursue a career in theology or law, but to study the natural sciences. Did Jesper Swedberg oppose this choice? The records are silent. What we do know is that the Bishop did finance a first study trip abroad, although, young Swedenborg complained in letters home that have been preserved, inadequately. In 1710, he left Sweden for the first of eleven extended sojourns abroad, living in England, where he visited London, as well as Oxford, and attempted to learn as much about the sciences as he could. Returning home to Sweden, he was introduced to Sweden's most brilliant engineer, Christopher Polhem. For two years, Swedenborg was attached to the court of the last Swedish would-be conqueror king, Charles XII, who eventually offered him a position as an adjunct assessor to the mines. In 1716, Swedenborg also published—unusually enough, in Swedish—the first issue of a scientific journal in Sweden, *Daedalus hyperboreus*. In 1723, he assumed responsibilities on the Board of the Mines, a position he would hold, with extended leaves of absence for study abroad, until 1747.

During the next two decades, Swedenborg was an active public official, who sat on the Board of the Mines, supervised mining activities and other engineering projects, participated regularly in the meetings of the Swedish House of Nobles, and pursued his scientific interests on the side, publishing a series of treatises on a wide variety of subjects, including mineralogy, cosmology, physics, and anatomy. These are works of a speculative, rather than empirical, nature, based on his wide reading. Some of Swedenborg's scientific writings were reviewed favorably in scientific journals, but his most ambitious and probably most important treatise, entitled *Principia rerum naturalium*, fell, as the Swedish historian of science Sten Lindroth puts it, "stillborn" into the world of eighteenth-century science.[6] In the 1720s and 1730s, Swedenborg was one of a number of extremely talented scientific pioneers working in Sweden, during a period of extraordinary activity in a relatively impoverished country with little in the way of institutional support to offer its young scientists. He is often compared to his distant relative, Carl von Linné, who, unlike Swedenborg, did attain international recognition as the inventor of a new science of taxonomy, on the basis of years of empirical research. But if Linné's methods differed from those of Swedenborg, the botanist also envisioned a continuity between the visible and invisible aspects of the world in terms that are not unlike Swedenborg's. In a late work entitled *Nemesis divina*, Linné sketched out an invisible moral world that grows out of what he saw as the hierarchical structures of botanical classification.[7]

A comparison between the two men is likely to work to Swedenborg's detriment, but to emphasize the contrast is to overlook the differences in the situations of the two men and in the nature of their works. A professor, Linné managed to become one of Sweden's first professional scientists. A public official whose private means enabled him to pursue his scientific interests during extended leaves of absence, Swedenborg was an amateur in a country where pursuing scientific interests on the side was not easy. From the beginning, Swedenborg worked mainly with texts, the scientific treatises, the records of the experiments and data of other people in other countries. If he had written in a major European vernacular and if he had had a livelier prose style in any language, he might have been a great popularizer or synthesizer. Historians of science have pointed out that Swedenborg's syntheses of the work of others in his scientific treatises are often brilliant and far reaching, but remained at best on the margins of contemporary scientific debate.[8]

In the late 1730s and early 1740s, Swedenborg's scientific interests turned to human physiology and especially to questions of speculative psychology. He began work on two lengthy treatises, *Oeconomia regni animalis* or *The Economy of the Kingdom of the Soul*, and *Regnum animale* or *The Kingdom of the Soul*. Both works approach the question of the relation between mind and body from the perspective, much mocked in the later article on the soul in the French *Encyclopédie*, of the question of the exact location of the soul within the body. Here, as in Linné's *Nemesis divina*, the invisible is construed as a continuation of structures visible to the human eye, except that in the case of Swedenborg's anatomical works, these structures are envisioned as if viewed through a microscope.

In 1743, Swedenborg had more or less completed two volumes of the second study, *Regnum animale,* and he requested and was granted a leave of absence from his position on the Board of Mines in order to publish these volumes and to continue working on the one he planned to follow. He then travelled and, as on previous journeys abroad, he kept a journal, but this one soon turns from a dry if observant record of places and people visited to an account of dreams and visions the traveller experienced alone at night. It seems clear that the journal of 1743–44 records a kind of religious experience that led the writer to change his way of life. It is also, however, and this is a theme to which we shall return in this chapter, a remarkable account of a self-analysis based on the interpretation of dreams, an analysis undertaken by a scientist who was engaged, both theoretically and personally, in deciphering the relations between mind and body. Upon his return to Sweden in 1745, Swedenborg submitted his resignation to the Board of Mines, and began work on a series of works on invisible worlds that parallel our own, treatises no less ambitious than his scientific projects of earlier decades. The first multi-volume work, *Arcana coelestia,* an extended exegesis of Genesis and other books in the Bible, was published between 1749 and 1756. Although Swedenborg kept the price artificially low, it sold miserably. In response to the lack of success of *Arcana coelestia,* Swedenborg composed the far shorter *Heaven and Hell,* which summarizes and popularizes the expository passages of the first work.

Heaven and Hell proved to be Swedenborg's most successful book. The basis for his reinterpretation of the Bible in *Arcana coelestia* was, Swedenborg wrote, his rediscovery of a lost hermeneutic key, which he called the *doctrine of correspondences.* As he explains it, this doctrine is both elaborate and simple. Most basically, the doctrine of correspondences holds that there are three levels of meaning that correspond to three, hierarchically arranged, worlds: the natural, spiritual, and celestial. As in medieval allegorical doctrines, to which Swedenborg's doctrine of correspondences presents striking but imperfect parallels, the act of interpretation is grounded in the belief that language and nature form two, complementary, forms of script, both issuing from God the Author. But within this basic triadic structure, correspondences are nested within correspondences in a dizzying Chinese-box effect that recalls the manner in which Swedenborg, in his physiological treatises, construed the structures of the interior of the human body as a series of nested miniatures of the forms of the visible world.

In *Arcana coelestia,* the doctrine of correspondences served as the basis not only for a reinterpretation of the Bible, but also for the description of invisible worlds that parallel that of everyday experience, but cannot be seen by most people, because knowledge of correspondences, originally possessed by all of humankind during a golden age, has been lost. The mission of Swedenborg's *Arcana coelestia, Heaven and Hell,* as well as subsequent works, was to reintroduce the doctrine of correspondences to Swedenborg's contemporaries, in the hope that the widespread knowledge of correspondences would bring about a new golden age.

Apparently most of Swedenborg's readers—or prospective readers— found the prospect of a multitomed reinterpretation of the Bible along ahistorical lines daunting, if not tedious. *Heaven and Hell,* however, which focused on the visionary passages of the earlier work, omitting almost all the exegeses, and promising readers glimpses into the beyond, exerted an immediate and continuing appeal. Translations into English and French had already appeared by the 1780s.

During the last decade of his life, Swedenborg continued to compose and publish books on visionary and religious subjects, mingling extended exegetical works with briefer popularizing volumes. In the 1760s, he was also the subject of a theological dispute in Sweden: he and two of his followers were charged with heresy by the Swedish Lutheran Church, although they were eventually cleared. Perhaps because of this dispute, in his last works, especially *The True Christian Religion* (1771), Swedenborg emphasized questions of dogma. He died, however, a Lutheran, and it was his followers who, after his death, made him into the founder of what many of them called the New Church.

After his resignation from the Board of Mines, Swedenborg withdrew to his house on Södermalm in Stockholm, where he spent the days writing down his visions of other worlds. He undertook several extended journeys abroad, in order to publish and publicize his works. Legend has it that he lived on little more than coffee and sugar, except when he went out to dine, which, apparently, he did quite frequently. It is difficult to reconcile accounts of Swedenborg in company, where he appeared to be a charming if eccentric old bachelor, with the descriptions of visionary worlds he produced at this time. Some commentators have suggested that he was insane: could any sane person claim to see these visions and expect to be taken seriously? But it is not clear what Swedenborg meant when he said he "saw" these things. His accounts make a certain kind of sense when placed in the contexts of other, similar attempts made in the mid-eighteenth century, to visualize the interior of the human body.[9] Such efforts are not so distant from our own cultural context, for Freud, in his *Interpretation of Dreams,* attempted something similar in passages sketching out an "architecture" of consciousness. The label of mystic seems equally misleading, for if occasional passages in Swedenborg's journal of 1743–44, his so-called *Journal of Dreams,* evoke an experience of a divine Other that seems beyond language and reason, the vast majority of his writing acknowledges its debt to science, reason, and especially language in its construction of orderly, if not always visible, worlds.

Four recent studies have brought Swedenborg's work, especially his doctrine of correspondences, into new perspective. In the field of a linguistically focused intellectual history, a series of monographs by the Swedish intellectual historian, Inge Jonsson, as well as Michel Foucault's *Les mots et les choses*, have refocused attention on the word "correspondences," especially in relation to theories of language in Europe from the Renaissance through the end of the eighteenth century. Interestingly, neither Jonsson nor Foucault account for the fortunes of the word after 1800 or for the apparent interest of nineteenth- and twentieth-century writers in Swedenborgianism. Both suggest that there is an unbridgeable gap between the contexts of "correspondences" and that of Romantic and postromantic poetry and aesthetics, although Jonsson's consideration of Swedenborg's work in relation to the theories of language of seventeenth- and eighteenth-century philosophers raises tantalizing questions concerning the emergence of notions of linguistic structure in late-nineteenth-century French poetics and its debt to the theories of language of the classical age. Neither Jonsson nor Foucault takes into account the popularization of Swedenborgianism or the term "correspondences" in nineteenth-century Europe, for while there does appear to be an abrupt break between the elite science and cultures of the eighteenth and nineteenth centuries, aspects of the scientific culture of the Enlightenment, particularly those such as Swedenborgian and Mesmerism that purported to reconcile science and magic, continued to play a central role in nineteenth-century popular culture.

Significantly, it has been the work of cultural historians, above all Robert Darnton, whose *Mesmerism and the End of the Enlightenment in France* was also published in the 1960s, that has suggested not only how but why doctrines of men such as Swedenborg and Mesmer, both figures marginal to eighteenth-century science, were received and transformed in late-eighteenth- and early-nineteenth-century Europe. For Darnton, Mesmerism, and later Swedenborgianism, serve as explanations for and illustrations of the potential of reason and political participation to transform the world, and both are transformed in the first half of the nineteenth century in conjunction with changing interpretations of the French Revolution. Darnton's *Mesmerism* implies that Swedenborgianism and Mesmerism serve as a kind of popular ideology. In chapter 3, I shall argue that his *Mesmerism* and especially his later work on French print culture imply that the kinds of marginal writers, such as Constant/Lévi, who wrote about Swedenborg in nineteenth-century France, used Swedenborgianism and Mesmerism in order to legitimate their political views. Swedenborgianism

plays an important role in what Jürgen Habermas characterized as "transformations in the public sphere" in his dissertation of 1962.[10]

These four representative studies, then, suggest why it is important to
turn back to the work of Swedenborg, for the writings of this marginalized
figure offer a key perspective on the interrelationships among elite and
popular culture, politics, and theories of language in late-eighteenth- and
early- and mid-nineteenth-century France—and perhaps Europe. In this
context, Inge Jonsson's studies are invaluable in serving as a point of departure for a consideration of the work of Swedenborg that emphasizes its
links to the rationalist tradition and to seventeenth- and eighteenth-century language theory.

Jonsson's emphasis on close textual analysis and on language allowed
him to see beyond the myth of Swedenborg as a preromantic who turned
from this-worldly pursuits to a fascination with the invisible Beyond. Like
most scientists, Swedenborg was preoccupied with what he could not see
throughout his career, but his interests were formed by his lifelong fascination with the work of Descartes and his followers. One of his earliest
works was a treatise on the vortex theory, and Swedenborg's attempts to
work out a solution to the mind-body problem were often couched in language drawn from Cartesians: his use of the terms "correspondences" and
"representations," Jonsson argues, is so close to the usage of Malebranche
in his *De la recherche de la vérité* that it is difficult not to attribute it to
direct influence.[11] In the late 1730s and early 1740s, Swedenborg's attempts to reach a more exact definition of the relation between the two led
him to take a more linguistic approach in his work, and in a series of
studies, notably the unfinished and cryptic *Clavis hieroglyphica*, probably
composed around 1740, he turned to the universal language schemes of
Leibniz and his followers: in an interpretation whose clarity and suggestiveness contrast starkly with the murkiness of Swedenborg's *Clavis*,
Jonsson argues that this fragment represents an attempt to work out a
system of symbols that could be combined, like mathematical symbols, in
order to extend the limits of knowledge, in this instance, knowledge about
the invisible structures of the human body and their relationship to the
soul. For Jonsson, seventeenth-century psychology and language theory
provide the key to the nature of Swedenborg's construction of invisible
worlds in his scientific and his religious writings alike. The Swedish historian argues that unlike later writers who cited him, Swedenborg did not
see science and religion as opposed; he had not undergone what literary
historians sometimes characterize as the "dissociation of sensibility" that
dates back to the mid-seventeenth century in much of Europe, but had
ambitions, like many seventeenth-century Swedish intellectuals who appear as belated Renaissance men, to be a universal scholar.

Inge Jonsson's close readings of Swedenborg's texts and survey of the development of Swedenborg's doctrine of correspondences raise questions concerning Michel Foucault's use of the word "correspondences" in *Les mots et les choses*, first published in 1965. For the French intellectual historian uses the term "correspondences" in a way that coincides with an earlier and much more traditional interpretation of Swedenborg's work and its significance for poets who either cite him or use the word "correspondences" in their work. In *Les mots et les choses*, "correspondences" designates a linguistic model that informs intellectual life in Europe before the seventeenth century. Foucault defines this model in contrast to that of seventeenth- and eighteenth-century science and philosophy, which, he argues, conceived of language as a kind of grid that reproduced the structures of the natural world, whereas intellectuals and artists of earlier centuries saw language and world as infinitely more bound up with each other, as intertwined in a relationship of potentially infinite resemblances or "correspondences," a network that made it all but impossible to construct the kind of taxonomic system that Linné and other eighteenth-century scientists were able to work out on the basis of what Foucault calls an *episteme* or model based on representations.

Although *Les mots et les choses* does not focus on the fortunes of words or their use in ordinary language, its argument implies that Swedenborg's later work is a throwback to earlier notions of language and nature as intimately and chaotically intertwined. Jonsson's studies, however, show that in several key texts, Swedenborg uses both "correspondences" and "representations" in closely related and interconnected ways, and the context that informs this usage is the work of philosophers whose texts are fundamental for Foucault's *episteme* of representation or classical European science: Descartes, Leibniz, and their followers. Foucault's use of the word "correspondences" may well distort our understanding not only of the work of Swedenborg but also of modernist poetry that cites the word as an instance of a particular kind of linguistic and poetic relation.

This brief summary cannot possibly do justice to Jonsson's rich and intricate readings of Swedenborg's texts that point in a variety of directions, many of which cannot be included under the umbrella of Swedenborg's later reception or larger cultural significance. But Jonsson's conclusions, his insistence on the unity of Swedenborg's thought and his attempts to use language as an instrument—the historian compares it to a microscope—to investigate the invisible interior of the human body, also point beyond the range of texts drawn from elite European science and philosophy that he cites.

In a close reading of a journal Swedenborg kept during a journey abroad from 1736 to 1739, Jonsson emphasizes the overwhelming importance of libraries and texts for the development of his scientific work. Biographers who suggest that he frequented anatomical demonstrations, the historian argues, are probably wrong.[12] But if Swedenborg's theories of language drew on a variety of sources, including Leibniz and Descartes, they also reflect a much more mundane aspect of his existence, namely his relation as a scientist and an amateur to the print culture of his time. Printing, Elizabeth Eisenstein has argued in her study of print culture in early modern Europe, transformed both the conditions for the practice and very nature of science in Europe during the centuries following the invention of the press: for the first time, new discoveries could be disseminated widely and uniformly, making it possible for scientists to respond to and build on each other's work more rapidly than ever before. But if printing allowed scientists in relatively underdeveloped countries such as Sweden to communicate with their colleagues in the South, it also brought about an expansion in knowledge that made it almost impossible for distant amateurs such as Swedenborg to keep up. Swedenborg's increasing preoccupation with language, then, suggests not only his fondness for seventeenth-century philosophy and universal language schemes, but also a kind of "language effect" of print culture in which texts—and language itself—begin to take on a life of their own. And printing, the production of still more texts, was the solution to his isolation that Swedenborg envisioned for himself.

In an autobiographical work depicting a hellish period he lived through in Paris in the 1890s, the Swedish writer August Strindberg invoked Swedenborg as a model both for his crisis and for a new kind of writing based on a quest for the absolute. Earlier, however, Strindberg had characterized his precursor, in one of his many phrasings that are pregnant with self-projection, as a late instance of Swedish "Grössenwahn": a fitting translation for this phrase might be "will to power."[13] While there are very great differences between Strindberg's modernist interpretations of Swedenborg and the work of his eighteenth-century model, Strindberg's remarks do point to one striking similarity in their situations: both writers attempted to found a new science or kind of writing in order to break out of an isolation that was not only personal but also cultural. In his study of fin-de-siècle Vienna, Carl Schorske has provided an interpretation of Freud's work that characterizes the Jewish outsider's foundation of a new science as an exemplary modernist move in which the marginalized individual is forced to imagine a new way into the city center and its culture. Schorske's explanations also characterize the situations of Strindberg and many other Scandinavian writers living in exile in the late nineteenth and early twentieth centuries. Or, as Strindberg himself recognized, of Swedenborg or other eighteenth-century figures: one thinks above all of Vico, the title of whose major work, *Scienzia nuova*, might equally well apply to any one of Swedenborg's later texts. Swedenborg may have been quite sincere in denying that he intended to found a Church, but the texts he produced beginning with his journal of 1743–44 take the form of a series of foundational texts designed to transform not only their readers' experience of language, but also the shape of the worlds they described, including the one inhabited by living human beings.

2. Swedenborg's Interpretation of Dreams: The Journal of 1743–44

If many of Swedenborg's later writings present themselves as foundational texts, the most important of these is probably the journal he kept during his trip to England and Holland in 1743–44. For the work, never published during his lifetime, records a series of dreams and visions that eventually led him to resign from the Board of Mines and to devote himself to the description and interpretation of invisible worlds inhabited by angels, spirits, and demons. In its doubleness, however—the little notebook falls into two distinct parts—the diary reflects a structure of experience that can be seen to characterize Swedenborg's work as a whole.

In July 1743, Emanuel Swedenborg set out from Stockholm on a journey that would take him to the Netherlands and to London. He had taken a leave of absence from his position as a state official, Assessor of the Mines, and intended to finish and publish a treatise on speculative psychology called *Regnum animale, The Kingdom of the Spirit*. As he had done on previous journeys abroad, Swedenborg kept a diary, and the first six pages of this manuscript, a somewhat dry record of people met and places seen, do not differ significantly from earlier journals he had kept. The opening account, however, breaks off in mid-sentence, and when the narrative resumes, after a hiatus of several pages, the focus of the account has shifted dramatically. Opening with a list of dreams or visions, the second part of the diary records what the narrator believed he had seen and heard at night, alone in the rooms he inhabited in various Dutch cities and in London. The diary, often called *The Dream Book* or *The Journal of Dreams*, marks a watershed in Swedenborg's career, for after his return, he resigned from his position as a public official on the Board of Mines and turned his attention from natural science to theology and the question of life in other worlds.

What to make of this journal? Its earliest editor, Gustaf Klemming, who published an edition he called *Drömmar* or *Dreams* in 1859, believed it gave evidence both of its author's insanity and of the spuriousness of the doctrines the sectarian followers of Swedenborg preached in mid-nineteenth-century Sweden and the rest of Europe. Swedenborgian interpretations, however, which were quick to follow Klemming's edition, saw the diary as a founding text, but, because of its explicit sexual descriptions, suitable for the eyes of the initiated only. Secular readings have focused on parallels between the diary, which Swedenborg neither published nor apparently intended for publication, and general tendencies in European literature and culture. Swedish intellectual history presents two opposing contextual readings: at the beginning of the century, Martin Lamm argued that the diary recounted the conversion of the author and represented a rejection of science and rationality that situated it among other texts belonging to European preromanticism; more recently, in a series of much more finely tuned interpretations of individual texts, Inge Jonsson has suggested that the diary of 1743–44 finds its place among a number of transitional works Swedenborg composed in the early 1740s, works in which universal language schemes, as well as seventeenth-century psychology and neoclassical aesthetics, play a predominant role. And in the past five years, two very detailed exegeses of the work have appeared: Ross Woofenden has looked at the dreams from a Jungian perspective, and Lars Bergquist has emphasized the parallels between Swedenborg's text and the doctrines of various sects, especially the Herrnhuters. All of these interpretations of the journal, however, present this work as somewhat anomalous in Swedenborg's production, and interesting mainly for the autobiographical information it conveys. Unlike most of Swedenborg's other works, it was written in Swedish and shows an unusual degree of spontaneity. Moreover, its subject matter seems to lie somewhat outside the scope of Swedenborg's carefully constructed Latin treatises which set forth the detailed structures of visible and invisible worlds.

If the diary has figured prominently in the interpretations of Swedenborg scholars, it has yet to receive the attention it deserves among scholars of eighteenth-century culture and psychology. For if, as Swedenborgian scholars and Lamm have suggested, the diary invites a reading as the record of an experience of religious conversion, perhaps mystical union with an ineffable Absolute, it is also a remarkable account of a self-analysis undertaken by an ambitious and talented scientist who had been speculating about the relationship between mind—or soul, as he put it—and body for the past decade and who was anxious to make his reputation abroad. Drawing on a wide variety of intellectual and cultural sources, the diary marks a new stage in its author's speculations concerning the interior of the body and its relation to the mind, for he turned to the recording of his dreams and to attempts to map out the unknown interior in architectural and narrative terms in order to think through problems that had turned out to be insoluble by more conventional means.

Swedenborg's eighteenth- and nineteenth-century readers had in some respects a better understanding than twentieth-century scholars of the relation of his doctrines to the context of eighteenth-century speculative psychology, for, like Constant/Lévi, they often associated his work with that of Mesmer and his followers. As we shall see in chapter 3, this association owes much to the fashion for any kind of occult material in eighteenth-century society, but the prominent emphasis on the human body and on Swedenborg's own physiological speculations in popularizing works such as *Heaven and Hell* suggests a textual basis for the link between the theories of the two men. Swedenborg's journal of 1743–44, I shall argue here, sheds a different light on the nature and the implications of the association.

In an extremely suggestive essay entitled "Sur l'histoire des fluides imaginaires (des esprits animaux à la libido)," Jean Starobinski points to the central importance of the notion of an imaginary fluid in the work of both Mesmer and Freud; drawing on and, in fact, never transcending occult tradition, this notion served as a heuristic model for understanding the relation of consciousness to the world in one tradition in western psychology. Other scholars have described how the practices of Mesmer and his followers in the late eighteenth century, who often had their patients sit in a circle around a *baquet* (a vessel of water), reflect their belief that it was a universal fluid coursing through all of nature that enabled them to influence the minds and bodies of their clients. Scholars have also noted that Mesmer's notion of an occult force was by no means original or unusual in a century still trying to come to grips with Newton's concept of gravity and with the discovery of electricity.[14]

But Swedenborg's journal of 1743–44 goes one step beyond the theoretical underpinnings of Mesmer and other eighteenth-century speculative psychologists, for it suggests the author's partial discovery of the importance of narrative for understanding the processes of consciousness. Evoking moments from Swedenborg's past, as well as his ambition and sexual desires, the text represents an attempt to reground the author's scientific and intellectual work in self-analysis. How did this come about? I submit that the idea was suggested by Swedenborg's understanding of and desire to imitate Descartes, an understanding that reflected the influence of two contradictory models.

If, as Inge Jonsson has shown, much of Swedenborg's intellectual production draws on the work of Descartes and his followers, this text stands in a particularly close relationship to the French philosopher and his texts.

It represents, like Descartes's *Meditations*, a founding text, suggesting that Swedenborg hoped to follow his model's example in beginning anew on the basis of an inner certainty; but the journal also suggests that Swedenborg may well have read and wished to imitate another account of the French philosopher's experience of the absolute, the record of a series of dreams he had on November 10, 1619, which circulated in various textual forms in the eighteenth century. In turning to dreams and perhaps also to the "other" Descartes, Swedenborg placed himself—and his journal—in a tradition of founding texts that take dreams as the point of departure for the establishment of a new science or philosophy, a tradition that includes not only Descartes, but also Freud.

A desire to imitate Descartes, I shall argue here, played a central role in Swedenborg's turn to dreams and their interpretation in his journal of 1743–44. But the desire led in two very different directions, for if it prompted him to note the importance of narrative and language in understanding dreams, the wish to repeat Descartes's experience of mathematical certainty also led Swedenborg to construct a closed system based on what he had understood.

In the pages that follow, I turn first to the shape of the dreams and visions described in the second half of the journal of 1743–44, then to some patterns in the narratives recounted within them, before concluding with a look at one dream passage that represents a remarkable parallel to the extant account of Descartes's dreams in the Baillet biography.

One of the most striking aspects of the journal is its two distinct sections, separated not only by a gap of missing and blank pages, but also distinguished by very different perspectives. And yet there are also clear parallels between the descriptions in the two parts. The accounts of dreams and visions in the second part often evoke little worlds that echo or, better, mirror the landscape and society described in the opening six pages. Linking the two sections—one is tempted to say two worlds—of the journal is a concern with architecture and machinery, and with a force, often portrayed as liquid, that courses through these structures. In its capacity to reflect, permeate, and engulf, water plays a key role in the second part of the diary, a role that may in part derive from the traveler's perceptions of a water-pervaded landscape during the journey described in the first.

The diary has sometimes been compared to Linné's accounts of his travels—to Swedenborg's detriment, for the latter's portrayal of the natural world pales in contrast to the taxonomist's lively and detailed descriptions.[15] Yet the journal of 1743–44 does betray its author's awareness of the beauties of the natural world, as well as those of the city. August 12, 1743, for example, finds the traveller in Hamburg in the company of the brother of the successor to the Swedish throne. Several days later, on his way to Buxtahude, he notices the beautiful countryside:

> The 17th, travelled from Hamburg over the river to Buxtehude, where, for the space of a mile I saw the prettiest country I had seen in Germany; the route lay through a continuous garden of apples, pears, plums, walnuts, chestnut trees, limes and elms. (2)[16]

And the following day, in Bremen, he focuses on the city walls, its bridge and watermills, as well as the town hall, the cathedrals, of which one was called St. Nicholas, and the hospital.

Such landscapes, moreover, crop up again in the second part of the diary. One example, dated the night of October 8–9, 1744, will serve to give a sense of the quality of these inner landscapes, for it combines elements from several entries in the first part of the diary into a complex pattern the dreamer finds resonant with meaning, having to do with his work, its success, and his future:

> [October] 8–9
> This night was the most delightful of all, because I saw the kingdom of innocence. Saw below me the loveliest garden that could be seen. On every tree white roses were set in succession. Went afterwards into a long room. There were beautiful white dishes with milk and bread in them, so appetizing that nothing more appetizing could be imagined. I was in company with a woman whom I do not remember particularly. Then I went back. A pretty little innocent child came to me and told me that the woman had gone away without taking leave and begged me to buy her a book that she might take up; but showed me nothing. Wakened. Besides this it seemed I entertained on my own account a number of people in a house or palace standing by itself, where there were some acquaintances: among them Senator Lagerberg; also, I think, Ehrenpreus and others. It was all at my expense. I realized it cost me much, but my thoughts went to and fro about the expense. Meanwhile I did not care about it for I observed that all was maintained by the Lord, who owned the property or showed it to me. *Was in the kingdom of innocence, and as to my entertaining the other and worldly people without seeing them, does it signify my work, that I should as it were not be with them, although I entertain them therewith; or does it mean something else? The child was innocence itself. I was much moved by it and wished to be in such a kingdom where all is innocence. Lamented that in waking I came away from it. What the woman was that went away without taking leave I am not aware.*

The day after, namely the 9th, I was so clearsighted that I was able to read the finely printed Bible without the least difficulty. (81–82)[17]

Gardens and well-furnished rooms frequented by the best Swedish society are among the spaces most favored by Swedenborg in the second part of his journal. Here, as elsewhere in the text, they serve as settings for little narratives or dramas the writer interprets—to the best of his ability—in allegorical fashion. As in the traditional allegory of Hercules at the cross-roads, which plays a prominent role in Swedish literary tradition, the two female figures, the woman and the little girl, seem to point to choices, and those choices, as is very common in the journal, have to do with books, probably the writer's own, although the sequence does end with the comment that he found it easy to read the Bible.

At times, the inner gardens reflect the current fashion for ruins that provoke a meditation on death, as in a somewhat earlier entry. Interestingly, the sense and tone of the passage turn on the meanings of the Swedish *grafwar*, which can mean either ditches or graves. If the "little bridge" the narrator wants to go over suggests the former, the "abysses on all sides" certainly point to the latter:

> June 15–16. The 16th was a Sunday.
> There was brought to me a representation of my former life, and of how I have since gone where there were abysses on all sides, and of how I turned about. Then I came into a very glorious grove, filled everywhere with the finest fig trees in splendid growth and order. It seemed that there were some withered figs still left on one. The grove was surrounded by graves/ditches; though there was nothing on the side where I was. I wanted to go over a little bridge, which consisted of high earth with grass upon it; but I did not venture it because of the danger. A little way from this I saw a large and very beautiful palace with wings, and I wished to lodge in it because I realized I should then have the prospect of the grove and the graves/ditches. A window a long way down the wing was open. There, I thought, is the room I shall have. It means that on Sunday I shall continue in the spiritual, which is signified by the glorious grove. The palace may be my design for my work, which points to the grove, where I intend to look. (62–63; note that I have modified Wilkinson's translation, which has "ditches" for *grafwar*.)[18]

But even this spooky landscape harbors a palace, its presumably clean neo-classical lines suggesting the dreamer's well-ordered plans for his own work, which is directed toward the living grove, rather than the graves.

The interior landscapes of the second half of the journal do not always point to aristocratic settings of the present: some of the most poignant evoke the rooms of the dreamer's childhood, and they are inhabited by members of his family, his stepmother, siblings, and, above all, his father. The remembered spaces are all marked by some paradox or contradiction that sets them apart from any site in everyday life. In the second-to-last dated entry in the journal, for example, the dreamer describes seeing the interior of his father's house in Uppsala, which seemed, mysteriously, to contain a kind of market fair:

> In the morning in a vision there appeared to me the market called the Disting Fair in my father's house in Upsala in the upstairs parlor, in the entrance and everywhere else in all the upper part. *This signifies the same, showing that it ought to happened with all the more certainty.* (89)[19]

Elsewhere, the dreamer finds himself on a boat, immediately after he has taken a book from his father's library, on a mysterious staircase, or, in the most fantastical entry that concerns Jesper Swedberg, engaging in an orgy with his friend Öhlreich in a room in the doorway of which the father suddenly appears, only to disappear again, having said nothing.

The interiors evoked in the dreams and visions of the journal often appear in a nested arrangement, for there are frequent references to "inner rooms," rooms within rooms, or especially small rooms into which the dreamer penetrates. But the little world described in these accounts also possesses a pronounced vertical dimension; references to stairs and ladders, abysses and hellish chasms abound.[20] There is one reference to a *series mystica*. (Wilkinson 14; Klemming 9)

But the dreamer or seer is not the only moving element of this little world. At times—as in a terrifying vision near the beginning of the second part of the diary—it appears as a giant moving machine that has caught him up in its spokes. (Wilkinson 5; Klemming 4) But more often this is a world in motion whose movements are both made possible and explained by those of water or other fluids. On one occasion, the dreamer sees himself urinate before taking an unfamiliar red-faced woman by the breast. (Wilkinson 56; Klemming 39) This woman is not alone in her associations with a liquid that emerges from the human body; in one particularly suggestive scene, the dreamer asks a woman for something to drink, and she responds by producing from under her clothing a glass filled with a mysterious liquid that resembles either wine or chocolate. (Wilkinson 75; Klemming 52)

Nowhere in the journal is the heuristic function of water clearer than in a complex passage from the entry for the night of April 9–10, which ties water both to the interaction of mind and body and to its relation to God and divine inspiration:

> This night as I was sleeping quite tranquilly, between 3:00 and 4:00 o'clock in the morning, I wakened and lay awake but as in a vision; I could look up and be awake, when I chose, and so I was not otherwise than waking; yet in the spirit there was an inward and sensible gladness shed over the whole body; seemed as if it were shown in a consummate manner how it all issued and ended. It flew up, in a manner, and hid itself in an infinitude, as a center. There was love itself. And it seems as though it extended around therefrom, and then down again; thus, by an incomprehensible circle, from the center, which was love, around, and so thither again.
>
> This love, in a mortal body, whereof I then was full, was like the joy that a chaste man has at the very time when he is in actual love and in the very act with his mate; such extreme pleasantness was suffused over the whole of my body, and this for a long time, lasting all the interval of waking, especially just before I went off to sleep, and after sleep, half an hour or an hour. Now while I was in the spirit, and still awake for I could open my eyes, and be awake, and then again enter the state, I saw and observed that the inward and actual joy came from this source, and that in so far as any one could be therein, in so much cheer has he; and so soon as any one comes into another love that does not concentrate itself thither, so soon he is out of the way; for instance when he came into any love for himself—to any that did not center there—then he was outside of the way. There came a little chill over me and a sort of slight shiver as if it tortured me. From this I found from what my troubles had sometimes arisen, and then I found whence the great anguish comes when the spirit afflicts a man; and that it, at last, ends in everlasting torment and has hell for its portion, when a man unworthily partakes of Christ in the Holy Supper; for it is the Spirit that torments the man for his unworthiness. In the same condition in which I was, I came yet deeper into the spirit, and although I was awake, I could by no means govern myself, but there came a kind of overmastering tendency to throw myself upon my face, to clasp my hands, and to pray as before; to pray for my unworthiness, and with the deepest humility and reverence to pray for grace; that I, as the greatest of sinners, might have the forgiveness of sins. Then also I observed that I was in the same state as the night before last; but could tell nothing further, because I was awake.
>
> At this I wondered; and so it was shown me in the spirit that man in this state is as a man with his feet upwards and his head downwards. And it came before me why Moses had to put off his shoes when he was to go to the holy place, and why Christ washed the apostles' feet, and answered Peter that when the feet are washed all is done. *Afterwards in the spirit I*

found that that which goes out from the very center, which is love, is the
Holy Spirit, which is represented by water; for it is called water or wave.
  In fine, when a man is in the condition of having no love that centers in himself but that centers only in the general or public good, which
represents here on earth in the moral world the love in the spiritual
world, and this not at all for his own sake or society's sake but for Christ's
sake, in whom love is and center is, then is man in the right state. Christ
is the ultimate end, the other ends are mediate ends; they lead direct to
the ultimate end. (28–30; my emphasis)[21]

Nowhere in the journal is the totalizing function of an imagined liquid
more clearly expressed; this entry recalls a passage from the preface to an
earlier physiological treatise, *The Economy of the Kingdom of the Spirit*,
the title of which is often translated as *The Economy of the Animal Kingdom*, for it, too, had portrayed the structures of the body as elements in a
cosmic hierarchy.[22] Yet at least one section suggests that water is also
linked to another network of perceptions and desires: the references to
feet, and to the unsaved individual as upside-down, point to the importance of water as a reflective surface that presents the world as a mirror
image, but also one that may be penetrated.

  Although there is only one direct reference to water in the opening
account of Swedenborg's journey—the town of Leer is surrounded by good
walls and water—recall that much of the journey took place over water:
the writer travels by boat from Sweden to the continent and enters Holland on a kind of barge called a *Treckschuit*. The list that opens the second
part of the journal, however, suggests that the reflective surfaces of the
water that surrounded him played a greater role in his imagination of the
world around him than he had noted, for the laconic but suggestive opening entries begin to make sense if one focuses on the presence and function of the implied or explicit references to water:

1. [Dreamed?] of my youth and the Gustavian family.
2. In Venice, of the beautiful palace.
3. In Sweden, of the white expanse of heaven. [the sky]
4. In Leipsic, of one that lay in boiling water.
5. Of one that tumbled with a chain down into the deep.
6. Of the king that gave away so precious a thing in a peasant's cabin.
7. Of the man servant that wished me to go away on my travels.
8. Of my delights during the nights. (3–4)[23]

If the first entry evokes a memory, probably from the writer's childhood,
the second turns to a city famous for its canals, and the third, strangely, to
the white skies of the heavens in Sweden, perhaps also reflections and

perhaps, if one emphasizes the juxtaposition to Venice, to the reflecting waterways of Stockholm, sometimes called the "Venice of the North." In the fourth entry, the presence of water becomes explicit, although in this case, the perception concerns an individual who is in it, rather than merely looking at it, and in the fifth, the act of penetration beneath the surface is emphasized, for here someone, perhaps the same person as the one in the preceding notation, falls into the deep. Entries 6 and 7 evoke narratives, perhaps memories from the writer's past. And the eighth points forward to the complex entry for April 9–10, which ties the perception of water to the writer's understanding of the relation of his innermost sensations to a totality—although in this instance we hear only of his pleasures at night.

The accounts of dreams and visions in the second part of Swedenborg's journal of 1743–44 are structured as little worlds that mirror that of everyday experience. The relationship of the two is complex, but water, in its functions as a reflective but three-dimensional medium, an iconographic symbol, and a heuristic concept drawn from contemporary science, plays a key role in Swedenborg's construction of the relation between inner and outer experience. In its representation of consciousness in terms of an architectural structure permeated by a force that resembles a fluid, Swedenborg's journal resembles the theories of Mesmer and his followers. But the little worlds evoked in the journal are also sites where little dramas, narratives, are enacted, and in this respect, Swedenborg's text points beyond the doctrines of Mesmer to fantastic literature that tells stories about imaginary worlds and to the work of Freud, who made explicit the central importance of narrative for understanding the workings of consciousness.

But what of the narratives recounted in the journal? Is their sole focus the reconciliation of the dreamer or visionary with God? From a secular perspective, three interrelated subjects stand out here: the first has to do with the narrator's relationship to two male authority figures, his father and Charles XII; another centers around the author's many sexual desires and, occasionally, lack thereof; and the third concerns Swedenborg's intense ambitions, both in general and with respect to the treatise he was writing and publishing at the same time he kept the diary. These subjects coalesce in a kind of narrative Freud was to call the "family romance."

References to Swedenborg's ongoing scientific work—and what, to the author, appears to be its certain success—dot the journal. An early passage, for example, the entry for March 25–26, 1744, interprets a dream or vision focusing on a key as evidence that the dreamer now had the key to anatomy and to the lungs. (Wilkinson 7; Klemming 5) But even after a

series of mystical experiences, the narrator of the journal continues to interpret his dreams and visions as signs pointing to the resolution of problems
in his speculations concerning the human body. At the end of September, he
writes of a dream about a beautiful palace in a garden that "This referred to
that which I have now brought to an end about organic forms in general."
(77)[24] Certainly, the author's ability to see signs even in unlikely places
points to his intense ambition, his desire that the treatise he was writing and
publishing would win him a European reputation. Often this aim takes a
sexual expression; or, at least, sexual and scientific desires overlap in the
representation of half-naked—and, one imagines, statuesque—women, who
beckon to him sexually, but who resemble nothing more than the allegorical
frontispieces found in many scientific texts at this time.

As in Freud's *Interpretation of Dreams*, ambition is a major theme in
the accounts of dreams and visions in Swedenborg's journal of 1743–44.
But the often jarring juxtaposition of experience and interpretation poses
questions concerning the nature and relationship of the worlds described
here. Signs, as well as worlds, appear to proliferate in a seemingly random
fashion. But one passage points to a clear link between the multiplication
of signs and their interpretations and the ambitions of their author.

In this curious passage dated April 15–16, 1744, Swedenborg tells of
receiving a new name, an event that is the occasion for a remarkable transformation and doubling of the name Nicolas, for the new name emerges
out of a neologism the dreamer utters—resembling a Latin comparative, it
suggests something like "more than Nicolas"—and the renaming is linked
not only to a spiritual renewal, but also to the representation of both an
"inner person" and "another self."

> It was said, *Nicolaiter*, and *Nicolaus Nicolai*; whether it can mean my
> new name, I do not know. The most remarkable thing was this, that I
> now represented the inner man and was as another person than myself,
> so that I made salutation to my own thoughts, frightening them; saluted
> my own stores of memory; accused another person; which shows that the
> change has come; that I represent one who is against another; that is to
> say, the inner man, for I have prayed God that I in no wise may be mine
> but that God may be pleased to let me be his. (42–43)[25]

Why the name Nicolas? Swedenborg returns to this event, after the interpretation of two other dreams, to offer an implausible interpretation:

> Nicolaus Nicolai was a philosopher who every year sent bread to Au-
> gustus; meant debts . . ., that I found my duty to be again reconciled to
> the Lord, because I, in spiritual things, am a stinking corpse. (43)[26]

This explanation notwithstanding, it is difficult not to recall the references to churches named St. Nicolas in the opening pages of the travel journal: like the interior landscapes evoked in the second part of the diary, this name suggests a memory or reflection of an experience rather than an otherworldly message. But it also appears to echo more than the sights Swedenborg took in on his way to Holland in 1743.

The doubling of the name here, which is linked to the elevation of the dreamer, recalls the two names Swedenborg had borne during his lifetime, as a result of the ennoblement of his family in 1719, which had transformed the humble Swedberg into Swedenborg. As we shall also see in *Heaven and Hell*, Swedenborg's texts suggest that their author felt pulled between the conflicting values of the worlds of his childhood as the son of an extremely successful clergyman of relatively humble origins and that of the Swedish aristocracy he frequented as an adult. If the conflict was expressed in terms of an emphasis on separate spheres in the later work of popularization, it took a far more literal form in the journal of 1743–44, for the two worlds of Swedberg-Swedenborg and Nicolaus Nicolai are represented in this work in the forms of Jesper Swedberg, Swedenborg's father, and his early patron, King Charles XII.

The ten entries in the diary that refer to Jesper Swedberg nearly all touch on questions of ambition and status. The first, which links the son's clothes to matters of rank and social mobility, as well as rivalry with the father, is probably the most representative:

> Afterwards I saw my father, in a different costume from that he used to wear, nearly of a red color; he called me to him, and took me by the arms, where I had half sleeves with cuffs or ruffles in front. He pulled both the ruffles forwards, and tied them with my strings. My having ruffles signifies that I am not of the priestly order, but I am, and ought to be, a civil servant. Afterwards he asked me how I like the question, that a king has given leave to about 30 persons who were in holy orders to marry, and thus change their estate. I answered that I had thought and written something about such a matter, but it has no relation thereto. Instantly thereupon I found [it in me] to answer, according to my conscience, that no one whatsoever should be permitted to alter the estate to which he has devoted himself. He said that he was of the same opinion. But I said, if the king has resolved, the thing is settled. He said he should deliver in his vote in writing. If there are 50 [votes] the matter will be settled accordingly. I observed it as a remarkable fact that I never called him my father, but my brother; thought afterwards how this was: it seemed to me that my father was dead, and this, that is my father, must thus be my brother. (18)[27]

Two other dreams link the father to questions of clothing, including one in which the dreamer, who finds himself naked in church, is approached by his father: the writer concludes: "This dream perhaps may mean that I am not yet at all clad and prepared as I ought to be."[28] Others recount a conflated memory of the Uppsala market with the family home, and the father's apparent approval of the son's sexuality, perhaps his worldly ambitions. In the entry for July 7–8, the author notes that, in his dream, it had been deliberated whether or not he should be admitted to the society of which his father was a member: "Furthermore, that it was deliberated, whether I should be admitted into the society where my father was."[29]

Jesper Swedberg had died in 1735, and it is clear that on one level the society the author is anxious to enter is not of this world. But both Swedenborg's use of the word *societeten*, "society," and the terms in which he describes his encounters with his father link the questions of clothing and correctness to anxieties concerning his relation to the aristocratic society he frequented. The entry which concludes with the remark about the author's admissibility to his father's society is followed by another, in which he appears in one of the king's chambers, but unsuitably dressed. (Wilkinson 67; Klemming 47) It is one of several such references.[30]

If the entries concerning Jesper Swedberg suggest the author's awareness of the astounding success his family had enjoyed, as well as the anxieties and uncertainties this success provoked, they also point to a desire for a kind of reconciliation with his father, who does not seem to have entirely approved of his son's choice of a secular career. A similar ambivalence runs through the references to the absolute monarch and last Swedish king with imperialist ambitions, Charles XII, whom Swedenborg had served during his youth. These references, however, are far more negative than the entries concerning Jesper Swedberg.

A passage from the first section of the diary suggests that Swedenborg had occasion to remember Charles XII when he visited the house the king had stayed at in Stralsund. (Wilkinson 1; Klemming 1) And one item on the list, which refers to an unnamed king, may mean that the author's initial memories were fond and grateful, for the entry reads: "6. Of the king that gave away so precious a thing in a peasant's cabin."[31] Subsequent entries, however, portray him as bloody, although the final reference to Charles XII concludes with the resolution to continue dedicating his works to this royal patron, as he had done in his youth, because he may have come back to life. (Wilkinson 55; Klemming 38)

In his recent edition of the Latin poem Swedenborg composed in 1714 in honor of Charles XII, Hans Helander has emphasized the ambivalence reflected in this work of conventional praise.[32] Swedenborg, the editor notes, was all too aware of the carnage brought about by Charles's military ambitions, and his absolutism offended the republican sympathies of the still untitled Emanuel Swedberg.

The final reference to Charles XII occurs less than halfway through the journal; subsequent entries refer to other, mostly anonymous kings, who are also mainly participants in warfare. The single wholly positive reference to a monarch in this section of the journal is to a queen, who is presented as superior to her husband, King Fredrick. It was this queen, Ulrika Eleonora, who bestowed the title and new name on the Swedberg/Swedenborg family in 1719.

The two worlds of Swedenborg's diary and, indeed, his later work draw not only on notions of the body as a microcosm and of a universal fluid or substance that courses through all of creation, but also on the author's acute awareness of the relation between names, naming, and social status. In the same way, Swedenborg's insistence on what he will later call "correspondences" between things, perceptions, and names also represents a proliferation of names that repeats and continues an original renaming, which replaced *Swedberg* with its near double, *Swedenborg*.

Jesper Swedberg and Charles XII are not the only earthly father figures to haunt Swedenborg's journal of 1743–44, for a third, textual, model also makes his presence felt. In his studies of Swedenborg's intellectual development, Inge Jonsson has emphasized the importance of Descartes's scientific and philosophical publications for Swedenborg's scientific work. One particularly complex dream recounted in the journal suggests that Descartes and some of his texts continued to play a key role during the crisis that saw Swedenborg turn his attention from the visible world to its invisible counterparts.

Although it does not describe the author's journey in any detail, the second part of the journal does note his presence in various Dutch cities and his move to England in May 1744. The entry which marks his arrival in England, in fact, seems to represent something like a new beginning in the narrative, setting off the English section of the visionary part of the diary from its Dutch counterpart. The dream recounted in the entry for May 4–5 consists of a series of numbered entries, recalling the long undated list at the beginning of the visionary part of the diary. Moreover, the dreamer interprets the dream as pointing to a new beginning in his intellectual work.

> In Harwich, which was on my arrival in England, I slept only some hours; and then there was shown me much that may perhaps concern my work here. It was the 4th–5th of May, according to the English calendar.
> 1. How I lost a bank note, and the person who found it got for it only

nine stivers; and also another who happened upon a similar note, and it
was bought for only nine stivers. And I said in joke that it was sham
piety; maybe it means the condition of people in England, which is part
honest, part dishonest. 2. There were certain who admired my copper
prints, which were well done, and wished to see my rough draft, as if I
was able to conceive them just as they were finished. It may mean that
my work wins approbation, and they believe that I am not the doer of it.
3. There came to hand a little letter, for which I paid nine stivers. When I
opened it there lay within it a great book containing clean blank paper,
and among this a great many lovely drawings: the rest, blank paper. There
sat a woman on the left hand; then she removed to the right and turned
over the leaves, and then drawings or designs came forth. It seemed that
the meaning of the letter was that I should cause a number of such
designs or patterns to be engraved in England. The woman had a rather
broad bust and on both sides down to the lower parts was quite bare; the
skin, shining as if it were polished; and on the thumb a miniature painting. This may perhaps mean that with God's help while in England I shall
be enabled to carry out a number of beautiful designs for my work; and
that afterwards speculation may convert herself *ad priora*, which hitherto
has been *in posterioribus*; as the alteration from the left to the right
seems to suggest. 4. It seemed I was commanded to go with Bergenst-
jierna on a commission for which the money was provided. It seemed to
be all the way to Sicily; and I was well pleased with the commission. But
yet I thought it was needful to take care of scorpions. It may perhaps
mean something that I may afterwards get among the things committed
to me when my work is ready, if haply I am allowed to complete it in
another place; and perhaps in some other cause. (58–59)[33]

Like many other narratives in the visionary part of the diary, this
entry emphasizes the importance of texts, both the author's own and books
he might read. The books, engravings, and writing described in this account, moreover, suggest that the human body might be read like a language: the strangely shiny skin of the woman in the third dream is marked
by the little picture of a ship on her thumb. But here, as elsewhere in the
diary, the half-naked woman suggests not only sexual desire, but also ambition, for she resembles one of those allegorical representations of science
or truth often found on the frontispieces of scientific treatises of the eighteenth century, including Swedenborg's own. Further, the use of an allegorical female figure to represent a choice draws on a literary model that
plays an important role in Swedish literature: that of Hercules at the cross-
roads.[34]

The dream narratives of May 4–5, 1744, thus suggest that Swedenborg drew on an array of models in order to make sense of—and resolve—
a complex of desires in which sexuality and ambition were virtually indis-

tinguishable. The many references to money suggest that avarice, as well as anxiety about being cheated by foreigners, played an important role. And yet, I would argue, there is something else here that cannot be understood without reference to a textual, as well as a personal, model whose presence underlies the project of the diary as a whole, but which is particularly evident in this particular entry. This model is Descartes, whose life and works play a key role in the analysis Swedenborg carried out in his journal of 1743–44. It seems very likely that Swedenborg had in mind the precedent of Descartes's transforming intellectual experience over a century earlier when he chose not only to shut himself up with his manuscripts and his thoughts, but also to shift the focus of his journal to a chronicle of dreams and visions that approached their interpretation from the point of view of divine messages which provide the dreamer with absolute certainty. This likelihood, moreover, seems borne out by the striking parallels between the complicated dream narrative dated May 4, 1744, and accounts of three dreams Descartes experienced around the time he discovered his new philosophy, at least as recounted by his biographer, Adrien Baillet. What seems to be at stake here is Swedenborg's unconscious imitation of a master, his reproduction of a prior text in his dreams, in order to fulfill a wish to equal or replace the French philosopher as the founder of a new philosophy. Significantly, Swedenborg interprets the dreams as indicating a change of direction in the dreamer's approach to knowledge— from a posteriori to a priori—and of marking a new stage in his intellectual career. But in imitating Descartes's dreams, Swedenborg turned to a version of the philosopher's work that emphasized language and poetry over mathematics. He seemed to have hoped to enter a philosopher's heaven through the back door.

Descartes apparently recorded a series of dreams he experienced on the night of November 10, 1619 in a notebook that was among the papers he left in Stockholm after his death, but that was lost sometime during the century that followed. Fortunately, three accounts of the notebook have survived: Hector-Pierre Chanut's inventory of Descartes's papers in Stockholm; the notes Leibniz took based on his reading of the notebook and which were first published in 1859 under the title *Cogitationes Privatae*; and a detailed description of the dreams and the dreamer's interpretation of them in Adrien Baillet's biography of Descartes, first published in 1691. Descartes scholars have sometimes criticized Baillet as a "mere compiler" who was unable to interpret his subject. What may be a limitation in other parts of the biography, however, is a definite advantage in the account of dreams, for Baillet's narrative appears to be a transcription or near transcription of the lost manuscript, and thus brings us as close to Descartes's own record as we are likely to get—unless the original manuscript turns up.[35]

In the first chapter of the second book of his *Vie de Monsieur Descartes*, Baillet recounts three dreams Descartes had during the night of November 10, 1619, at about the same time the philosopher underwent the transforming experience of philosophical illumination and certainty that led to his formulation of a new philosophy. Baillet's account has posed many problems for scholars who base their interpretation of Descartes's philosophy on his published writings. For if the historian's transcription presents at least some dreams as heralds of an absolute truth, in Descartes's published works, they appear as deceptive apparitions that may well be sent by the devil. Although there has been a continuing interest in Baillet's version of Descartes's illumination among Cartesians and Descartes scholars, the general tendency in twentieth-century philosophical interpretations is to portray Baillet's account as marginal and suspect.[36] There have been some notable attempts, however, mostly in the fields of literary criticism and theology, to approach the dreams from an aesthetic or psychoanalytic perspective.[37]

Baillet recounts three dreams. The first and the third emphasize visual impressions, and both have some importance for understanding how Swedenborg construed his dreams—although the third is by far the more important. The second dream consisted of the sound of thunder, followed, after the dreamer woke up, by the impression that the darkened room was full of sparks, as he opened and shut his eyes quickly. This episode is described in such general terms that it would be difficult to prove its relation to any other text. This is fortunately not the case in the retelling of the first and the third dreams.

In the first, the dreamer finds himself walking down a street to escape from some ghosts, unable to walk straight and leaning to the left, because of overpowering gusts of wind and because he felt a weakness in his right side. Entering a school, the dreamer is blown against the church inside its enclosure. He passes an acquaintance without greeting him, but is addressed by another, who tells him that a Monsieur N. has something to give him. The dreamer imagines that the gift is a melon, and is surprised that he is the only individual to be unsteady and bent over; everyone else stands upright. Upon waking, Baillet tells us, Descartes felt a pain and also turned over in bed from his left to his right side. He imagined that this dream might be sent by a demon.

One of Baillet's commentators calls the third dream, quite appropriately, "The Books Dream," for books play a predominant role in this narrative.[38] As the dream begins, the dreamer finds a dictionary open on his table without knowing how it got there and is then surprised to find a second book there, which turns out to be entitled *Corpus Poetarum*. Opening this book, the dreamer reads the verse "Quod vitae sectabor iter?" (What way in life should I follow?), whereupon an unknown man appears out of nowhere to present him with a poem beginning with the words "Est et non" (yes and no). The dreamer responds that he knows it and it comes from the *Idylls* of Ausonius and is, moreover, included in the anthology of poems he has before him on the table. But he is unable to locate it there. The man then asks the dreamer where the book comes from, to which the dreamer responds that he doesn't know, for it seemed to appear out of nowhere as he was leafing through another book that disappeared. At that moment, however, he sees the other book reappear, but when he inspects the dictionary, he finds it less complete than the first version. Then he finds the section in the anthology devoted to the poems of Ausonius, and, although he cannot locate "Est et Non," he tells the man he knows another by the same poet that is much finer: "Quod vitae sectabor iter?" The man begs to see it, and the dreamer leafs unsuccessfully through the anthology, whereupon he comes across several little engravings that lead him to remark that this is not the edition he knows. Suddenly, the man and the books disappear, but the dreamer sleeps on, interpreting the dream in his sleep. The dictionary, he believes, represents the sciences, and the anthology, philosophy and wisdom. The maxims of the poets are wiser than any philosophical writing, because they reflect the working of enthusiasm and the imagination, which work in men's minds "like the sparks of fire in stones." Moreover, the dreamer concludes:

> Voyant que l'application de toutes ces choses réussissoit si bien à son gré, il fut assez hardy pour se persuader, que c'étoit l'Esprit de Vérité qui avoit voulu lui ouvrir les trésors de toutes les sciences par ce songe. (84)

The dreamer goes on to attribute the appearance of the engravings to the visit of an Italian painter the previous day and to interpret the melon as representing the charms of solitude. Upon waking, he considers all three dreams as divine messages urging him to change his way of life.

There is unfortunately no systematic study of the reception of Baillet or other accounts of the dreams that would tell us how and where copies of the text circulated or give us an overview of how it was received. Swedenborg may well have encountered Baillet's account—or perhaps Descartes's own version—in connection with his reading of Malebranche. Malebranche's occasionalism, moreover, his particular solution to the Cartesian mind-body problem that preoccupied Swedenborg at the time he composed the *Journal of Dreams*, may also have suggested that dreams represent proof of the intervention of God that keeps the two together. I have not, however, found evidence—except for textual parallels—that Swedenborg read Baillet or otherwise knew of the dreams of Descartes. This study may well serve as the impetus for a reception scholar to show how the two crossed in a European reading room during one of Swedenborg's many journeys abroad. In any case, I hope that it will attest to the continuing importance of dreams and their interpretation in seventeenth- and eighteenth-century intellectual life, an importance that points to the limits of rationalism, but not its rejection.

In Baillet's account of Descartes's dreams, as in Swedenborg's diary entry for May 4–5, 1744, the third dream is by far the most complex, the most explicit about acknowledging a possible textual origin both of dreams and their interpretation. Swedenborg's third dream is also the one that most closely resembles Descartes's, but before taking a closer look at their common ground, let us review some of the broad similarities and differences between the dream narratives of the two series.

Both accounts focus on questions of intellectual ambition and a choice the dreamer faces. Both raise questions concerning how and when the interpretations arise out of the dreams or dream narratives. Commentators on Baillet's account have expressed puzzlement over the fact that Descartes begins to interpret his third dream while he is asleep, although he continues after he wakes up. Here, as elsewhere in Swedenborg's work, a similar ambiguity reigns: does the act of interpretation form part of the vision or dream, or does it reflect a critical and reflective consideration of what has been experienced? Similarly, neither account comes to terms with the differences among the experiences they relate. In the Baillet account, Descartes makes very little of the contrast between the second dream and the other two. And Swedenborg not only never questions the truth of what he experienced, but also says very little about the nature of his experiences.

Swedenborg's dream narratives seem far rougher, far less composed than the accounts in Baillet. Moreover, unlike Descartes, Swedenborg seems to have been preoccupied with money at the time he recorded his dreams. References to money, both metal and printed, occur in all four dreams. The interpretation of the first, which links an episode in which the author is cheated of the full value of his money to his fears of being duped both by the English in everyday life and by the church in spiritual matters, seems fairly self-evident. The second, as well, refers to the copper engravings the author was having made to illustrate the treatise he wished to publish, and there seems little to question in his association of the admiration of a group of beholders with the future success of his work. Even the third and by far the most complex of the dreams contains a reference to money: the dreamer remembers that he has paid nine stivers for a letter out of which emerge first a book and then a naked woman. The fourth dream, which pales in contrast to the vividness and complexity of the third, takes as its subject a mission Swedenborg is to undertake with a colleague named Bergenstierna and for which he will be paid. A preoccupation with money may be the thread that ties these narratives together; certainly references to it suggest that the first two and the final dream represent expressions of a certain anxiety concerning the dreamer's survival in a foreign country. And the question of cheating also points to issues surrounding what Swedenborg calls *pietasteri*, a word that was probably intended to signify false piety, but the shape of which also suggests pederasty, the "other" sexuality that crops up so often in the visions described in the journal.[39] A similar slippage also characterizes the representation of the body of the half-naked woman who figures prominently in the third dream, for she signifies both an emblem of reason and the awakening and frustration of the dreamer's desires in the overlapping areas of sexuality and ambition.

The "nine stivers" at the beginning of the third dream serve to link this narrative to those surrounding it, but do little to explain it, except to recall a very general association of money and currency with issues related to value, representation, and hence language and textuality. The third dream, however, plunges us into a world that is not only structured like a text, but that also seems to emerge from a text. As in Descartes's third dream, one textual model—a book, a letter, or a poem—displaces another, while also producing human beings who, in turn, hold out or ask for another text.

Both Swedenborg and Descartes link the appearance of engravings which displace an original text to recent experiences in waking life: Descartes remembers the visit of an Italian painter, Swedenborg the illustrations he is having made for the texts he is publishing. Moreover, the woman described in Swedenborg's dream looks very much like an engraving on a frontispiece to an eighteenth-century scientific treatise, perhaps one of Swedenborg's own, in which a partly or wholly clad woman represents truth or wisdom: *scientia* or *veritas*. This woman's link to representation is underscored by what the text calls a miniature painting of a ship on her thumb, and by her act of leafing through the pages of a book. But the rest of her body frustrates any attempt at interpretation, for it is so shiny, the writer tells us, it seems to have been glazed.

Swedenborg's unrevised notations clearly do not represent a conscious imitation of the account of Descartes's dreams. What they do suggest is a dream—and a dream of interpretation—that grows out of a reading of one version of the earlier dream narratives, and that is informed by the emphasis in the text attributed to the earlier philosopher on the importance of language and aesthetic models for the attainment of wisdom. Baillet's Descartes, however, distinguishes between the kind of knowledge or wisdom poetry can provide and that afforded by the sciences. Such a distinction does not come into play in Swedenborg's text, where all texts and visual representations point to the desired success of his scientific work. This difference, however, may have as much to do with the subject of Swedenborg's scientific work as with his lack of what Pascal had called an "esprit de finesse."

References elsewhere in Swedenborg's journal of 1743–44 point to his continuing preoccupation with the nature and function of the interior of the body. The representation of the half-naked shiny woman in the dream in the third dream narrative of May 4, 1744, suggests that the dreamer/ writer was aware that the subject of his inquiry, the interior of the body and its relation to what he called the soul, called for a kind of knowledge in which the distinction Descartes drew in *his* third dream no longer made sense. It is important that the figures that emerge from the texts produced in the dreams of both men differ in gender and appearance: Descartes's is an eminently reasonable man, who asks after another text; Swedenborg's is a tantalizingly naked woman whose prominently decorated thumb and brilliantly shiny skin mock the dreamer's desires to penetrate her by any means, either intellectual or physical. Like Descartes's dreamer in the first dream recounted by Baillet, Swedenborg's woman moves from left to right, a move the dreamer interprets in this passage as pointing to a change in direction in his intellectual life, as Baillet's Descartes had seen his shift from left to right in his first dream and indeed his dreams as a whole as indicating the necessity that he change his way of life.

Although Swedenborg, too, would later decide to change his way of life, largely because of the experiences recorded in this journal of 1743–44, the representation of the textual woman in the third dream of May 4 suggests a dawning discovery of a very different kind. As a whole, the journal invites two divergent readings. Almost certainly, it represents a chronicle of a religious crisis that led the writer to change the focus of his intellectual life. But at the same time, Swedenborg's accounts of his dreams, which are dotted with references both to his speculations about the interior of the human body and to his scientific ambitions, suggest that the journal also chronicles the scientist's attempt to map out those aspects of his own interior he thought he could see, and that what he saw—scene after scene representing various forms of desire, both for worldly success and for other human bodies—told him that the kind of objective proof he was searching for in his scientific work was not possible here.

Both Martin Lamm and Inge Jonsson have noted Swedenborg's increasing interest in language and fiction during the early 1740s. In addition to the journal of 1743–44 and the scientific treatise he set out to publish in these years, Swedenborg also composed a Latin creation epic and a sketch for a hieroglyphic key to the secrets of the human body. The same tendency to turn to narrative in order to explain aspects of the body that could not be seen characterizes the dream narratives of the journal. Like Freud's *Interpretation of Dreams*, Swedenborg's journal juxtaposes two models of human interiority. One, architectural, presents the inside of the human body as a structure: Swedenborg's favorites include rooms, gardens, staircases, and whirling machines. The other, narrative, suggests that the processes that take place there can only be portrayed in the form of stories that reflect the desires of the body and, perhaps, also its spectator. Although Swedenborg does not distinguish among them, there are many kinds of narratives in his journal of 1743–44. Some, such as the dream of the textual woman, seem to represent a response to an earlier textual model. Some suggest that the dreamer had very recently read passages from the Bible, particularly the Book of Revelations. Other passages in the journal unearth memories from the author's childhood and youth, focusing above all on his father and King Charles XII. Still others seem to represent an intense desire for contact or merging with a transcendent Other who appears in the form of a godhead or angel.

As many of Swedenborg's early readers recognized, the texts he produced after 1745 present striking parallels to some of the major doctrines of Mesmer, particularly the Viennese doctor's belief in a universal, fluid-like, force permeating consciousness and the universe. Although several passages in his journal depict fluids that course over and through human bodies, Swedenborg also portrayed the unifying substance in slightly different terms, as light and as language, but its magical powers are much the same, as are its narcissistic implications. Starobinski's essay on imaginary fluids, which emphasizes the importance of this notion both for Mesmerism and for psychoanalysis, can help us situate Swedenborg's journal in the context of one line of development in European psychology that includes both Mesmer and Freud, as well as the Swedish scientist and visionary.

Mesmer's fluid and Swedenborg's understanding of language, an understanding he would come to systematize and call his doctrine of correspondences, serve to map out the invisible regions of human consciousness that fascinated so many eighteenth-century scientists. But if the identification of the structures of the human body with those of the world in Swedenborg's later work differs little from the uncritical totalizing theories of Mesmer, the turn towards memory and narrative in the journal of 1743–44 represents an insight that would not fully surface in European psychology until the work of Freud. The choice confronting Swedenborg at the time he wrote down the dream of May 4 was in reality more complicated than he knew and his oversight may well have been due to his desire to imitate Descartes, not only Descartes the writer and seeker after wisdom, but Descartes the successful founder of a new philosophy. It was partly this desire that led Swedenborg to insist that the at times shattering experiences of otherness and desire that he recorded in his journal represented the absolute Word of God. He was looking for the kind of certainty afforded by mathematical formulas and geometric proofs, rather than an understanding based on the kinds of narratives one spins out of memories, dreams, and desires.

It would be foolish to insist that Swedenborg's failure to develop the insights into the importance of language and narrative was solely due to a mis- or overreading of Descartes. The discovery of free association by Freud and other late nineteenth-century psychologists depended on the presence of at least two people, and Swedenborg was a very solitary man who communicated mainly with texts. And who would have listened? The insights skirted in his journal of 1743–44 would be developed, often in connection with doctrines borrowed from Swedenborg and Mesmer, in gothic and fantastic literary texts written at the end of the eighteenth and in the early nineteenth centuries, but, as Darnton has shown in his study of Mesmerism and popular culture in late eighteenth- and early nineteenth-century France, they were rejected by the most members of the scientific community.[40]

Swedenborg's journal of 1743–44 betrays the importance of both the texts of Descartes and the example of the man himself. In Holland in 1744, Swedenborg found himself attempting to imitate the philosopher's foundational work of the previous century, work based, depending on which account one read, on dreams or on a purely intellectual experience of oneness with God. It was, I have argued here, a desire that permeated his dreams and left traces in the similarity of his dream narratives to those attributed to Descartes and recounted by his biographer, Adrien Baillet. But in his search for the kind of certainty Descartes had described in his published philosophical works, Swedenborg was led to overlook the insights he attained in his own dream narratives, insights concerning the importance of language and narrative for the understanding of the workings of consciousness.

In a series of studies on Freud, the cultural historian Carl Schorske has characterized Freud's *Interpretation of Dreams* as a foundational text that reflects the psychoanalyst's quest both for truth and for power.[41] One might extend his insights back to the texts of both Swedenborg and Descartes, although it makes little sense to characterize earlier thinkers as psychoanalysts *avant la lettre* or, even worse, manqués. By bringing three texts on dreams and their interpretation into alignment, however, we may come to see the importance of a genre of self-examination that turns to dreams in a quest for a new form of knowledge that would bestow not only wisdom but also authority on the dreamer.

3. The Word "Represent" in the Journal of 1743–44

The words "correspond" and "correspondence" do not occur in Swedenborg's journal of 1743–44. Instead, he uses "represent" to denote the relationship between a perception and a meaning he sees as unquestionable.[42] His use of this word, however, draws on several meanings that overlapped in the late seventeenth and early eighteenth centuries. Once, it denotes the political function of acting or standing in for another person—the German *Vertreten* is a reasonable translation for this meaning, as Hanna Pitkin points out.[43] In the following entry for March 24–25, 1744, the author leaves the room because he is inadequately dressed to meet a woman who represents the crown prince:

> 5. Came into a magnificent room and spoke with a lady who was a court attendant; she wished to tell me something; then the queen entered, and went through into another apartment. It seemed to me that it was the same that had represented our successor. I went out, for I was very meanly dressed. (6)[44]

But Swedenborg often uses it in the very general sense of "to symbolize":

> Afterwards in the spirit I found that that which goes out from the very center, which is love, is the Holy Spirit, which is represented by water; for it is called water or wave. (29)[45]

Most often, he uses it in the passive voice, to indicate a communication sent from above in the form of dreams or visions that represent their message in the manner of a play or performance. What is at stake here is the way in which the *whole* dream, performance, or narrative, evokes a meaning, rather than the allegorical relationship among its parts to their conventional counterparts. Thus, towards the end of the diary, the author has a vision of light that reminds him of an earlier experience, but that he interprets as premonitory:

> In the morning when I wakened there came upon me again the same kind of giddiness or swoon that I had six or seven years ago in Amsterdam, when I began the *Economy of the Animal Kingdom*; but much more subtle; so that I appeared to be near death. It came when I saw the light; threw me upon my face; but passed off by degrees; because little periods of sleep came over me. This swoon then was more inward and deep, but soon passed away. *Signifies, as then, that my head is actually swept and cleansed from that which would hinder these thoughts, as also happened on the former occasion, because it gave me penetration, especially with the pen.* This too was now represented to me in that I seemed to write a fine hand. (89–90)[46]

There is little in the diary to suggest that Swedenborg was thinking of Malebranche's use of the term representation—except in the very general sense that he and other seventeenth- and eighteenth-century writers sometimes used the term to indicate the relationship between an object and its perception. What Swedenborg did, however, was to take this commonplace literally and to develop it into a theory of multiple interiorities, so that a correctly perceived object evokes not one, but many, representations in consciousness. One sees the beginning of this process in the journal of 1743–44.

But one passage in particular suggests how this folding inward cannot be divorced from the public world of politics and social roles. For in the entry, already quoted, that describes his receipt of a new, double, name, Swedenborg's use of the word "represent" recalls the first occurrence of the term in the diary, to denote the function of standing in for someone else, of playing their social role:

> It was said, *Nicolaiter*, and *Nicolaus Nicolai*; whether it can mean my new name, I do not know. The most remarkable thing was this, that I now represented the inner man and was as another person than myself, so that I made salutation to my own thoughts, frightening them; saluted my own stores of memory; accused another person; which shows that the change has come; that I represent one who is against another; that is to say, the inner man, for I have prayed God that I in no wise may be mine but that God may be pleased to let me be his. (42–43)[47]

If the context insists that not only the author's clothing and physical appearance, but also his entire social identity, are mere shells that are given life by an inner self, the connotations of *repraesenterade* link the activity of role-playing to the social function of acting for another person; here, in both cases, someone whose prestige exceeds that of his or her representative.

In the later works that use the term "correspondences" to denote the relationships among a series of embedded worlds and meanings, the political and social contexts evoked by "representation" are less apparent. "Correspondences" carries with it no such associations. But like the visions and dreams recounted and interpreted in the journal of 1743–44, the later works still represent—although in sometimes bewildering multiplicity—the structures and activities of a social world they partly deny.

4. *Heaven and Hell*: Utopian Spheres and the Pleasures of Reading

Heaven and Hell (I shall use the short title throughout my discussion) contains an exposition of the doctrine of correspondences that was much quoted in handbooks and popularizations of Swedenborg's work, and yet, as some scholars have complained, there is little to set the doctrine apart, as it is explained in this passage, from medieval theories of allegory or esoteric notions of language. A look back at the contexts of the famous definition of correspondences in this text suggests not only the doctrine's differences from earlier traditions, but also the ideological implications that made it and other theories of a universal language so appealing to social reformers and revolutionaries in France during the century following the Revolution of 1789. Not for nothing did the utopian socialist Charles Fourier invoke a theory of universal analogy that, to Baudelaire and others, recalled Swedenborg's doctrine of correspondences.

Swedenborg's best known work bears as its full title the cumbersome *Heaven and its Wonders and Hell from Things Seen and Heard*, which has the virtue of pointing to one of the major features of the text: its emphasis on sensory experience, especially vision.[48] Yet, despite its prolixity, this title, too, is incomplete, for it fails to recognize that the parallel worlds the text describes belong to three, not two, realms: Heaven, Hell, and an intermediary world inhabited by the spirits of the recently dead.

Of the three realms, Heaven is given by far the fullest treatment, taking up 43 of the 63 chapters of the text as a whole and serving as a model for the other two realms. The section entitled "The World of the Spirits," which follows the section on Heaven, is also second in length, extending over eleven chapters. And Hell comes last in every respect, with eight chapters. It is especially strange that even the long title focuses on only two of the three realms, since the number three recurs incessantly throughout the text. There are not only three distinct realms of visionary experience, but Heaven itself is divided into three parts; there are three kinds of correspondences—celestial, spiritual, and natural—and humankind forgot them over the course of three mythic ages, golden, silver, and copper. But perhaps the omission reflects an uncertainty regarding what one should call the other, intermediary realm. For if Swedenborg's depiction in this work of three realms not immediately visible to the human eye recalls Dante's *Divine Comedy*, the third realm is not Purgatory, even though its inhabitants enjoy the possibility of improving themselves so that they become worthy of Heaven.

Heaven and Hell opens with an affirmation of the importance of the Scriptures, in which each word contains an inner sense that has been forgotten by a degenerate and degenerating humankind. What follows is a series of descriptions that proceed, the text argues, from the kind of re-reading the opening passage argued for. It is a dizzying vision of successive worlds, little spheres closed in upon themselves, that emanate from the sun-like radiance of the Christian God, a radiance that unites them, despite their separateness, into a totality. For the members of the hitherto invisible worlds described in the text, as well as the author and his readers, it is a correct understanding of the relation of language to the divine Origin that allows them to communicate with one another and to know the world around them, for Nature is also a language. And it is a similar understanding that enables the visionary narrator of *Heaven and Hell* to see and write about worlds invisible—or no longer visible—to most naked eyes.

Some sense of the quality of the otherworldly descriptions in *Heaven and Hell* can be gained from the following passage depicting the author's acquaintance with a parallel world inhabited by angels. Here the author portrays himself as an outsider at times free to wander, *flâneur*-like, through land- and cityscapes pregnant with meaning:

> But it is better to present the evidence of experience. Whenever I have talked with angels face to face, I have been with them in their abodes. These abodes are precisely like abodes on the earth which we call houses, but more beautiful. In them there are chambers, parlors, and bedrooms in great number; there are also courts, and there are gardens and flowerbeds and lawns round about. Where they live together their houses are near each other, arranged one next to the other in the form of a city, with avenues, streets, and public squares, exactly like cities on earth. I have been permitted to pass through them, looking about on every side, and sometimes entering the houses. This occurred when my inner sight was opened, and I was fully awake.
>
> 185. I have seen palaces in heaven of such magnificence as cannot be described. Above they glittered as if made of pure gold, and below as if made of precious stones, some more splendid than others. It was the same within. Both words and knowledge are inadequate to describe the decorations that adorned the rooms. On the side looking to the south

there were parks, where, too, every thing shone, in some places the leaves glistening as if made of silver, and fruit as if made of gold; while the flowers in their beds formed rainbows with their colors. Beyond the borders, where the view terminated, were seen other palaces. Such is the architecture of heaven that you would say that art there is in its art; and no wonder, because the art itself is from heaven. The angels said that such things and innumerable others still more perfect are presented before their eyes by the Lord; and yet these things are more pleasing to their minds than to their eyes, because in every one of them they see a correspondence, and through the correspondences what is Divine. (100–101)

The combination of the matter-of-fact with the improbable and strange is typical of the descriptions in *Heaven and Hell*. So, too, the conjunction of virtue and magnificence: the angels inhabit palaces, for, reversing the traditional Christian precept that the meek shall inherit the kingdom of heaven, Swedenborg argues that worldly goods are the just rewards of the deserving. The author, moreover, presents himself as an outside observer, who looks on with the impartial gaze of a scientific expert. These improbable descriptions are merely descriptions of things "seen and heard," as the long title of the text puts it.

But if the passage opens with an invocation of experience, it closes with a qualification of the term that alters its sense markedly, for the knowledge of the author, like that of the angels, seems to be based on an understanding of the divine significance of what they see, an understanding of what the author calls "correspondences." There is an implied comparison here, developed at greater length elsewhere in the text, between the ability of angels and that of even the most visionary of humans to comprehend the meaning of perceptions. If in the minds of angels vision and understanding are fused, the author must work at bringing them together. By learning to read the Bible in a new way, which is attentive to what he calls the "inner meaning of the Word," he—and his readers—can begin to interpret the natural world as a divine language. In so doing, the author and his readers can regain a knowledge that human beings in earlier, less degenerate, times had possessed. Consequently, reacquainting human beings with the knowledge of correspondences might bring about not only the return of an earlier golden age based on the perception of an unchanging divine order underlying the surfaces of appearances, but also the reconciliation of scientific truth and morality.

A passage, often quoted in summaries of Swedenborg's doctrines, describes the loss of the knowledge of correspondences in terms which superimpose the classical myth of the golden age on Christian notions of eschatology. In its evocation of thinking in terms of combinations of words or things, however, it also suggests one of the crucial differences between Swedenborg's doctrine of correspondences and the tradition of neoplatonic allegory, to which it is often compared, namely its debt to eighteenth-century theories of a universal language:

> 115. I have been taught from heaven that the most ancient men on our earth, who were celestial men, thought from correspondences themselves, the natural things of the world before their eyes serving them as means of thinking in this way; and that they could be in fellowship with angels and talk with them because they so thought, and that thus through them heaven was conjoined to the world. For this reason that period was called the Golden Age, of which it is said by ancient writers that the inhabitants of heaven dwelt with men and associated with them as friends with friends. But after this there followed a period when men thought, not from correspondences themselves, but from a knowledge of correspondences, and there was then also a conjunction of heaven with man, but less intimate. This period was called the Silver Age. After this there followed men who had a knowledge of correspondences but did not think from that knowledge, because they were in natural good, and not, like those before them in spiritual good. This period was called the Copper Age. After this man gradually became external, and finally corporeal, and then the knowledge of correspondences was wholly lost, and with it a knowledge of heaven and of the many things pertaining to heaven. It was from correspondence that these ages were named from gold, silver and copper, and for the reason that from correspondence gold signifies celestial good in which were the most ancient people, silver spiritual good in which were the ancient people that followed, and copper natural good in which were the next posterity; while iron, from which the last age takes its name, signifies hard truth apart from good. (63–64)

This passage concludes the two chapters in *Heaven and Hell* which focus on the nature and function of correspondences: chapter 12, "There is a Correspondence of All Things in Heaven with All Things of Man," and chapter 13, "There is a Correspondence of Heaven with All Things of the Earth." These chapters develop the notion that all things have other-worldly equivalents, especially the human body, which "corresponds" to the shape of heaven. (50–51) Recovery of the knowledge of correspondences renders the appearances of everyday life transparent so that the viewer can see through them to their true, moral, significance, a significance which allows the onlooker to situate them within their rightful place in an immutable order that is identified with a nature in harmony with the divine. Each phenomenon, in fact, masks an apparent infinite regress of "correspondences," leading up through a series of spheres, which fall into three broad classifications coinciding with three levels of heaven and leading up to a god whose divine radiance emanates down through creation in much the same way as the sun sheds light.

There is much in the account of correspondences in *Heaven and Hell* that evokes neoplatonic concepts of allegory: the notion of a divine language that emanates from an unknowable godhead; the insistence on levels of meaning and experience; the conception of "man" as a microcosm, or in Swedenborg's terms, a model for the Great Man of the cosmos. Some secular interpreters have, in fact, seen the significance of Swedenborg's later work precisely in its turn towards neoplatonism, which they see as heralding a later, romantic, rejection of the precepts of modern science. But although he incorporates important aspects of the neoplatonic and allegorical traditions into *Heaven and Hell*, there are some important differences in both the context and function of Swedenborgian correspondences.

Elsewhere in the text, the angels are depicted as speaking an ideal language, transparent, musical, and far more suggestive than any human dialect. Their writing, too, is far richer and more evocative than the linear script of human beings. And yet their language is analogous to that of the inhabitants of the earth, and might serve as a model for the development of a universal language capable of bringing about scientific *and* moral progress. That this language would be based on a perfect and unquestionable identity between words and things suggests the importance of the context of contemporary science and language theory for Swedenborg. For Swedenborg's *Heaven and Hell*, which describes a succession of celestial, spiritual, natural, and diabolical orders in terms of both separation and continuity, recalls the structures of eighteenth-century taxonomy, which, like this work, defines its classes against the background of a belief in what Lovejoy called a "great chain of being" emanating down from an unknowable origin.

A cursory reading of Foucault's *Les mots et les choses* might also suggest that Swedenborg's work marks a throwback to an age preceding the formation of modern science. But if one ignores Foucault's use of the term "correspondences", which is possibly based on a misunderstanding of the theory of language underlying not only Swedenborg's work but also that of French writers who cited him after his death, his description of the *episteme* of representation suggests the indebtedness of Swedenborg's doctrine of correspondences to the logic of eighteenth-century science.

Although Foucault does not make this point explicit, the notion of a linguistic grid is already allegorical in its implications, every sign pointing beyond itself to a thing which finds its place in an analogous system. In works by Swedenborg such as *Heaven and Hell*, the allegorical potential already present in the theory of language underlying the taxonomies of the natural world goes wild. Words point not only to things, but also to perceptions and different kinds of spiritual essences. But the resemblances or correspondences make sense only in the context of the systematic mirroring of the different levels of meaning. Thus, in the opening section of *Heaven and Hell*, after Swedenborg insists on the importance of the correspondences evoked by every Word, he goes on to describe a totality of spherical worlds which, monad-like, are separate but which mirror one another. Not for nothing is the resemblance to aspects of the work of Leibniz, whose theory of a universal key or linguistic combinatoria seems to have played an important role in Swedenborg's development of his own theory of language upon which his doctrine of correspondences rests.

As both Lamm and Jonsson have noted, late-seventeenth- and eighteenth-century science and philosophy were crucial for all aspects of Swedenborg's intellectual production, including his writings after 1745. The writer's own references to his own and others' scientific work attest to their continuing importance. For example, this passage in *Heaven and Hell* explicitly incorporates aspects of his scientific work into his visions of invisible, parallel worlds:

> 212. When it comes to the particulars of the form of heaven and how it proceeds and flows, this not even the angels can comprehend. Some conception of it can be gained from the form of all things in the human body, when this is scanned and investigated by an acute and wise man; for it has been shown above, in their respective chapters, that the entire heaven reflects a single man . . . ; and that all things in man correspond to the heavens . . . . How incomprehensible and inexplicable that form is is evident only in a general way from the nervous fibers, by which each part and all parts of the body are woven together. What these fibers are, and how they proceed and flow in the brain, the eye cannot at all perceive; for innumerable fibers are there so interwoven that taken together they appear like a soft continuous mass; and yet it is in accord with these that each thing and all things of the will and understanding flow with the utmost distinctness into acts. How again they interweave themselves in the body is clear from the various plexuses, such as those of the heart, the mesentery, and others; and also from the knots called ganglions, into which many fibers enter from every region and there intermingle, and when variously joined together go forth to their functions, and this again and again; besides like things in every viscus, member, organ, and muscle. Whoever examines these fibers and their many wonders with the eye of wisdom will be utterly bewildered. And yet the things seen with the eye are few, and those not seen are still more wonderful because they belong to an inner realm of nature. It is clearly evident that this form corresponds to the form of heaven, because all the workings of the understand-

ing and the will are within it and are in accordance with it; for it is in accordance with this form that whatever a man wills passes spontaneously into act, and whatever he thinks spreads through the fibers from their beginnings even to their terminations, which is the sources of sensations; and inasmuch as it is the form of thought and will, it is the form of intelligence and wisdom. Such is the form that corresponds to the form of heaven. (113–114)

The passage takes us back to one of Swedenborg's earlier works, in which he explored the hypothesis that invisible fibers formed a network uniting body and soul, or making consciousness possible. It is particularly interesting, because it suggests the one possible motivation for the insistence on vision throughout this text, the likelihood that his speculations were made possible and encouraged by views through a microscope. For Swedenborg, as for many other contemporary scientists, the microscope seems to have suggested that the interior of the body could be imagined as an infinite regress of structures invisible to the naked eye. But Swedenborg, it seemed, not only imagined interiority as such an infinite regress, but also projected the structures of his speculations outwards onto the limits of perception of the cosmos. Thus, what was known, what could be seen of the human body, which had been the focus of his scientific work at the time of the religious crisis that turned him from science to theology and theosophy, became the basis for Swedenborg's own version of the macrocosm, his Great Man. If his macrocosm shares some features with the neoplatonism of the Renaissance and earlier periods, it is important to remember that it is permeated by the fibers and other constructions of eighteenth-century physiology. And if the succession of parallel worlds he describes depends for its coherence on the belief in a continuous "great chain of being," these separate worlds also point more specifically to the monadology of Leibniz and eighteenth-century taxonomy. And finally, if the doctrine of correspondences resembles allegory, it has at least as much in common with the universal language theories of many late-seventeenth- and eighteenth-century thinkers.

Moreover, the worlds of *Heaven and Hell* also bear an uncanny resemblance to the historical setting of Swedenborg's life, as well as his work, a resemblance that might be characterized as ideological. The other worlds of *Heaven and Hell*, it has often been said, look very much like parts of eighteenth-century London, the angelic dwellings described in the passage quoted at the beginning of this discussion evoking the wealthy quarters, depictions of regions of hell in the last part of the work pointing to contemporary slums. In a study of representations of Heaven in western culture, Colleen McDannell and Bernhard Lang have taken this argument a step further, suggesting that Swedenborg's descriptions of life among the angels mark the emergence of a new, anthropocentric vision of Heaven in European cultural history. Swedenborg's visions, they assert, draw not only on contemporary city life, but also on baroque paintings of heaven as a space above the onlooker, inhabited by particularly attractive, but anthropomorphic, beings. I would add that they also reflect a preference for a bourgeois family structure that insisted on the importance of privacy within the home and the right of some members to participate, to communicate, within a public world. Such a bias would partly explain the insistence on separate, but communicating, spheres that runs through *Heaven and Hell*. Like the orders of feudal society, as well as the ideal of the bourgeois family, all regions of the cosmos are organized into spheres that are closed in upon themselves, but can communicate under certain circumstances.

In her study of eighteenth-century taxonomy, Mary Slaughter emphasizes the element of narcissism in the development of notions of species and their interrelatedness at about this time. Eighteenth-century scientists considered the plant and animal worlds in terms that evoked the patterns of kinship in Europe at this time, seeing their relatedness as similar to that of the contemporary bourgeois family. Words such as "species" reflect the connection:

> It is not insignificant that taxonomic concepts and constructs take as their point of departure the most primitive and basic form of order that we have, the order of the family. The word *genus* comes from a word originally related to the family, "what something derives from"; *species* is related to a verb meaning "to see" or "spy out." The genealogical order is something given by the mysterious processes of procreation, of life; it is something confirmed by what we see around us in our first most familiar, familial world. Through the genus we are given our reality, our essence, our nature. Through the external, visible features of mother's eyes and father's chin, (genetic) nature is known and confirmed. The genealogical family is our first (and perhaps our last) intimation of connection, relation and order. (186)

Slaughter might also have added that—as Balzac was to emphasize in his interpretation of Swedenborgianism in *Le livre mystique*—the word *species* is also related to *speculum*, to "mirror." For many eighteenth-century scientists, then, the borderlines separating vision, taxonomy, and self-contemplation tended to be blurred. In much of Swedenborg's late work, however, they tend to disappear.

Some passages of *Heaven and Hell*, however, suggest a subtler relationship to other, roughly contemporary, speculations concerning the nature of interiority and the signs by which it might be read. In a remark that anticipates the work of the physiognomists, Swedenborg compares correspondences to the human face:

> 91. From the human face it can be seen what correspondence is. In a face that has not been taught to dissemble, all the affections of the mind present themselves to view in a natural form, as in their type. This is why the face is called the index of the mind; that is, it is man's spiritual world presented in his natural world. So, too, what pertains to the will is presented in the movements of the body. So whatever effects are produced in the body, whether in the face, in speech, or in bodily movements, are called correspondences. (50–51)

And in yet another passage, the social implications of the focus on the origins of meaning and gesture are made clear. For the visionary is able not only to interpret the signs of the human face, but also to see into minds. Thus, an account of the mind—characterized as a transparent interior—of a righteous individual:

> The interiors of the mind of such have been perceived by me, and were seen as transparent from light of a glistening white, flamy, or blue color, like that of translucent diamonds, rubies, and sapphires; and this in accordance with confirmations in favor of the Divine and Divine truths drawn from science. (210)

Such transparency, it is clear, is inappropriate in a corrupt world in which human beings find it necessary to dissemble, but it remains nevertheless a goal that would make and be made possible by a general regeneration of human society.

As recent studies of changing notions of the afterlife have shown, most versions of heaven, hell, and other worlds inhabited by the dead reflect the practices and values of the societies which shape and transmit them, representing a kind of utopian projection of what an ideal social and moral community would be.[49] The worlds described in Swedenborg's *Heaven and Hell*, one might argue, stand in an even closer relation to the culture and society of mid-eighteenth-century Europe than most other-worldly accounts, for the parallel realms of this text are situated *within* the structures of everyday life and perception. This focus on interiority and an invisible moral and spiritual order underlying the surfaces of everyday experience plays two very different roles in Swedenborg's utopia.

As William Blake was quick to realize, in its insistence that one look inward to find heaven and hell, Swedenborg's work suggests both that the millenium has already arrived—at one point he describes a revolution in the heavens that was to occur in 1757—and that quietistic contemplation, rather than action and conflict, is all that is necessary to bring about a reign of justice and morality on earth.[50] But Swedenborg's focus on interiority also attempts to resolve a series of contradictions in eighteenth-century culture that centered on a conflict between the needs and desires of an upwardly mobile bourgeoisie and the aristocratic values of the social worlds they inhabited. *Heaven and Hell* insists both on the totality of a hierarchical moral and social order and on a separateness of spheres that not only justifies Swedenborg's elaborate classificatory system but also makes possible the continuation of an intimate family life in other worlds. Monogamous marriage characterizes the life of the angels, and although there is no procreation, couples engage in the education of children, the spirits of those who died young. It is useful to juxtapose Swedenborg's representations of heavenly worlds, which reconcile the need for privacy with a desire for universal sincerity, to the social writings of Rousseau, in which the two are in constant contradiction. Rousseau's writings, two commentators note, pit "man" against "citizen," "transparency" against "the obstacle."[51] But one wonders if the kind of reconciliation Swedenborg works out so elaborately in *Heaven and Hell* would be possible outside of the artificial textual worlds he creates.

Work, education, and self-improvement are mainstays of the spirit world and heaven described in *Heaven and Hell*, just as their opposites— laziness, disorder, and ignorance—characterize the underworld. And yet, as McDannell and Lang have argued in their study of heaven, the scenes evoked in Swedenborg's descriptions of other worlds also reflect the values and aesthetic traditions of aristocratic court culture in which the suggestion of an underlying order served to justify an existing social hierarchy. Swedenborg himself, whose family was ennobled in 1719, straddled both worlds, and it is difficult not to see, in his evocation of separate yet connected worlds one can inhabit simultaneously, an attempt to work out a contradiction he experienced on a very personal level in his day-to-day existence. But this aspect of *Heaven and Hell*, as well, finds a striking correlate in eighteenth-century culture. For, like the otherworldly texts Swedenborg began to produce after his religious crisis of the 1740s, European freemasons turned to the invention of elaborate systems of symbolism in order to make it possible for individuals of varying social origins to come together and educate themselves into the participatory practices of a community based on the ideals of self-improvement and work. Although masonic rituals are often presented as very old, sometimes harking back to ancient Egypt, recent scholarship has suggested that many of them were invented in the early eighteenth century, and given the appearance of age in order to lend legitimacy to the practices of the lodges and to provide a language for the description of a process of education and initiation that would enable individuals to work their way up in a moral and social hierarchy that recognized the importance of work and honesty.

Without giving overdue emphasis to the element of cynicism in recent historical accounts of the invention of masonic symbolism, I would like to suggest that Swedenborg's *Heaven and Hell* functions in a similar manner, but in the field of reading, rather than social, practices. As the introduction to this work emphasizes, *Heaven and Hell* wants to teach its readers to learn to see the world and themselves differently *through learning a new set of reading practices*. They must learn to see the "inner sense of the Word." And yet, as we have seen, the nature of this interiority is ambiguous, for the inner sense of the Word contains worlds that look like—and may, in fact, be the same as—the world the reader inhabits. Swedenborg's visionary text invites us to educate ourselves into the understanding of an elaborate symbolism which, like the rituals of freemasonry, affirms the importance both of advancement through education and work and of an aesthetically pleasing hierarchical order that presents clear parallels to the feudal traditions of the European aristocracy. But if the rituals of freemasonry addressed individuals striving to become part of a community, Swedenborg's texts reach out to such individuals at their most solitary: as silent readers free to conjure up visions of parallel worlds inhabited by innumerable angels, demons, and spirits, but not by other human beings.

Swedenborg's *Heaven and Hell* urges the gentlest kind of reform. The regeneration of religion and the world begins with a change in the way individuals view the world and texts, and this is not a change that entails the rejection of established institutions or traditions. There is little in Swedenborg's writings to suggest the potential for rebellion or even the construction of a working-class culture that one finds, for example, in contemporary religious movements, such as the Pietists or the Methodists. In fact, in countries where there was an established Protestant tradition and where religious sectarianism flourished, Swedenborg's doctrines were recognized as a relatively conservative variant of Protestantism.[52] In France, however, which lacked such a tradition, interpretations were less nuanced, and Swedenborgian texts and doctrines tended to carry with them an association with a general Protestant tendency to reject authority and tradition, a tendency that could be viewed either as dangerously subversive or as empowering to the disenfranchised. Despite the fact that Swedenborg never set out to found a sect, it is in the realm of religious

sectarianism that his influence can most clearly be traced, for Swedenborgian churches were founded in many parts of the world and are still
active today.[53]

In the fields of literary and cultural history it is more difficult to
argue that his work exerted any kind of direct influence. The reputation—
and, to some extent, notoriety—of Swedenborg and his doctrines rest
mostly on later writers' interpretations and criticisms of his work.

I have argued that Swedenborg's journal of 1743–44, the so-called
Journal of Dreams, represents a founding text in which the writer, believing that he has received the Word of God, sets out to reground his intellectual enterprise and to embark on a new kind of life. Nowhere in this text,
however, does Swedenborg mention a decision to establish a new religious
community. On the contrary, allusions to Descartes suggest that what he
had in mind was the founding of a new philosophy, similar to the French
philosopher's work over a hundred years earlier.

In this task, Swedenborg failed—at least in terms of the history of
philosophy as it is now told. Mesmer's theories were evaluated and rejected
by the established French medical community at the beginning of the
nineteenth century. The evaluation and rejection of Swedenborg's visionary doctrines by Immanuel Kant marks a similar moment in the cultural
history of Swedenborgianism. One of the earliest purchasers of *Arcana
coelestia*, Kant took Swedenborg to task in his pamphlet, *Träume eines
Geistersehers erläutert durch Träume der Metaphysik* (*Dreams of a Spirit-
Seer, Explained through Dreams of Metaphysics*; 1766), as a raver who
mistook dreams for truth.[54]

Indeed, throughout this chapter, I have argued that Swedenborg's
speculative psychological theories parallel in important respects those of
Mesmer. It is difficult to argue this point in a precise manner, because
Mesmer's theories are notoriously difficult to summarize. Knowledge of his
doctrines seems to have spread by word of mouth rather than through the
publication of theoretical texts.[55] Nevertheless, as Jean Starobinski and
other intellectual historians have pointed out, at the center of Mesmer's
psychology was the notion of a universal substance that united consciousness and the cosmos and also made it possible for the therapist to control
and perhaps cure patients. This imaginary substance, which sometimes
bore a remarkable resemblance to Newton's mysterious gravitational force,
was often conceived in terms of a universal fluid, and, indeed, one finds
such references in the works of both Swedenborg and Mesmer. In Swedenborg's late works, however, the substance most often takes the form of
language.

And it is in the field of speculative theories of language that Swedenborg's doctrines find their place in the middle ground between popular and

elite culture in the eighteenth century. If, as Inge Jonsson has argued, Swedenborg's doctrine of correspondences shows clear traces of the influence of Descartes, Leibniz, and other seventeenth-century philosophers, his inquiry into the origins of language also parallels attempts to come to grips with this problem in mid-eighteenth-century Europe. Swedenborg's theology alone seems to set his work apart from that of many of his contemporaries. True, some eighteenth-century philosophers—notably Condillac—worked out solution to the issue of language origins that shut out the possibility of a divine origin, tracing language back to a single origin in sensation. Others, however, such as Rousseau, were less clear on the subject. If in his unpublished *Essai sur l'origine des langues*, he attributes the birth of language—and music—to human needs for recognition and survival, in a section of *Discours sur l'origine de l'inégalité*, he argues that the origins of language are unknowable, but that he was convinced of the "impossibilité presque démontrée que les langues aient pu naître et s'établir par des moyens purement humains." (*Oeuvres complètes* 3:151)[56] In the works Swedenborg composed during the years immediately preceding and during his religious crisis, the Swede also suggests two possible origins of language, although to a greater extent than Rousseau, he insists on their identity. Language in these texts, as in the *Journal of Dreams* originates in God and in the body.

Rousseau's inclusion of a chapter on language in his *Discours sur l'origine de l'inégalité* suggests the extent to which he saw the question of the origin and nature of language to be bound up with that of the ideal order of society. In this emphasis he was not alone, for other great political theorists—Hobbes and Locke, for example—had also included discussions of language in their political treatises. Although, of course, Swedenborg's purpose in writing texts such as *Heaven and Hell* was not primarily political or theoretical, this text also establishes clear links between its theory of language and an ideal social order. Swedenborg's ideal social order, however, draws on aspects of contemporary bourgeois and aristocratic culture, suggesting that the private spheres of the bourgeois nuclear family might be reconciled—through leaps of the imagination—with the hierarchical traditions of the aristocracy. In this respect, Swedenborg's construction of elaborately detailed, invisible, parallel worlds, as well as of a highly idiosyncratic personal symbolism, parallels the fictions of freemasonry, which also developed highly complex symbolic systems in order to create a set of beliefs and rituals permitting men from various classes to come together and participate in communities that fused aspects of aristocratic and bourgeois cultures.

Like other eighteenth-century theories of language and language origins, Swedenborg's doctrine of correspondences equivocates on the question of the historical origins of language. *Heaven and Hell* does, it is true, sketch out a lost golden age in which language was transparent and human beings could see the divine meanings and origins of words and things. But the sun-like divine origin the text returns to time and again is omnipresent, and, like the parables told by Rousseau to explore how language might have come into being, serves mainly to explore how language functions, rather than how it changes or has changed in human history.

The ambiguities in the theories of language of Swedenborg, Rousseau, and other eighteenth-century writers would come increasingly into focus by the end of the eighteenth century. In Germany, the field of historical linguistics emerged as a scholarly discipline, and its practitioners turned to the study of the evolution of specific words and languages through time. In France, writers who continued to speculate about the origins, nature, and political implications of language in general split into two camps: those, such as the Idéologues, who emphasized the human origins of a universal order underlying nature and consciousness; and those, such as the conservative political theorists, Bonald and Maistre, who argued that the very existence of language not only set humanity apart from nature but also implied the existence of God and a divinely ordained hierarchy in nature and society. In nineteenth-century France, as we shall see, the question was also widely debated outside of elite scientific and philosophical circles.

CHAPTER THREE

Who Has the Word?
Swedenborgianism and Popular Culture in France,
1780–1865

The eclectic blend of politics, esotericism, and pseudoscience one finds in the writings of abbé Constant/Eliphas Lévi was far from unusual among writers in Paris in the 1840s and 1850s. Indeed, one historian of this period, Auguste Viatte, has written of a kind of dizzying proliferation of such personal interpretations at this time, especially among writers of second rank.[1] If some—Hugo, Balzac, and Baudelaire, for example—were able, Viatte suggests, to weld this material into aesthetically suggestive syntheses that deserved to become part of the literary canon, others, such as Constant/Lévi or his contemporaries, Henri Delaage (1825–1882) and Alphonse Cahagnet (1809–1885), were less successful. Although not all of these *mages* of second rank are of proletarian origin, the distinction Viatte suggests is between street occultism, on the one hand, and the tradition of esotericism in elite literature, on the other. Common to both contexts, however, is a concern with politics and political representation, with, in other words, the agendas surroundings the struggles of 1848.

Viatte did not invent the distinction he makes between first- and second-rate interpretations of esoteric and pseudo-scientific doctrines in mid-nineteenth-century Paris. It draws, of course, on traditional literary history, in which Hugo, Balzac, and Baudelaire are recognized as classics. But such distinctions were also being made among the writers themselves at this time. Recall the caustic article on Constant/Lévi often attributed to Baudelaire. The article's disparagement, I have suggested, seems to reflect dismay that a writer of such a background would pretend to literary ambitions; it also points to the author's awareness of the similarities between his life and work and those of his victim. Not so paradoxically, literary (and perhaps would-be-literary) interpretations of esoteric and pseudo-scientific themes, including Swedenborgianism and Mesmerism, often were the sites for an ongoing struggle for literary and political legitimacy, just as these themes were invoked by both sides in the struggles of 1848.

It may be difficult, almost 150 years later, to take the eclectic esotericism of the 1840s and 1850s seriously. Yet there is more at stake here than the superstitious beliefs of uneducated would-be poets or—in the case of Hugo—grieving parents. As Robert Darnton has noted, interpretations of pseudoscientific and occult doctrines in mid-nineteenth-century Paris echo representations in late-eighteenth-century propaganda and popular culture. These echoes, moreover, have much to tell us about attempts to rethink and retool the ideology of the French Revolution in the contexts of ongoing struggles for political representation and participation in nineteenth-century France.

The melding together of disparate doctrines, such as Mesmerism and Swedenborgianism, may well represent, in the words of Darnton's title, "the end of the Enlightenment in France," but it also points to a continuation and transformation of one aspect of Enlightenment culture in the nineteenth century, the extension to the other classes (and the other sex) of the rights to political representation and participation claimed by the educated male bourgeoisie in 1789. For Constant/Lévi and many of his contemporaries, to evoke Swedenborgianism or Mesmerism was also to invoke the context of a revolutionary ideology that promised political participation to the disenfranchised. But if in their eyes, Swedenborgianism's link to theology served to legitimate their writings, not everyone viewed— or views—the connection in such a sanguine fashion. Mid-nineteenth-century popular occultism often appears merely to caricature or parody aspects of the culture of the previous century. Perhaps, as Marx suggested in his *Eighteenth Brumaire*, the repetition involved in these sometimes grotesque nineteenth-century occult syntheses had political, as well as aesthetic, implications, and a certain failure to think beyond the ideology of 1789 led to a series of parodies of the original events.

In his *The Structural Transformation of the Public Sphere*, Jürgen Habermas argues that the French Revolution put an end to the disinterested exchange of opinions among the educated reading public that made possible a rational questioning of the social order. The admission of less educated, unpropertied people into the political process, he suggests in a part of his discussion that has come under attack from a variety of perspectives, made the kind of debate necessary to sustain a democracy impossible. Yet if the terms of Habermas's argument exclude the work of Constant/Lévi and many of his contemporaries, they also make it possible to see both their explicit and implicit claims to authority and participation, and the element of snobbery in the condescending remarks of those whose position in the worlds of politics and literature did not entail the same kind of struggle.

1. Swedenborgian Performances: Alphonse Cahagnet's Séances

If in mid-nineteenth-century Paris, Constant/Lévi was the most prominent and prolific writer to combine—although in somewhat disguised fashion after 1848—socialist and occultist doctrines, the works of his contemporary Alphonse Cahagnet point even more poignantly to some of the problems involved in understanding and evaluating the works of these marginal writers.

Consider, for example, a work Cahagnet published in 1848, whose full title, which might well serve as a summary, is *Magnétisme: Arcanes de la vie future dévoilés, où l'existence, la forme, les occupations de l'âme après sa séparation du corps sont prouvées par plusieurs années d'expérience au moyen de huit somnambules extatiques qui ont eu quatre-vingts perceptions de trente-six personnes de diverses conditions décédées à différentes époques, leur signalement, conversations, renseignements, preuves irrécusables de leur existence au monde spirituel.* In 1854, Cahagnet would publish a digest of Swedenborg's *Heaven and Hell*, based on the first translation into French by Antoine-Joseph Pernety (1716–1801), a translation that misrepresents Swedenborg as a mystic and an admirer of Boehme. The title of Cahagnet's 1848 work, however, clearly suggests one aspect of his interest in Swedenborg: the depiction in *Heaven and Hell* of an intermediary spirit world with the inhabitants of which the visionary individual could communicate. But Cahagnet's interest in this particular translation probably also reflects his distance from more orthodox versions of Swedenborgianism: that of J.-F.-E. Le Boys des Guays, for example, who had made a far more accurate translation of *Heaven and Hell* and was engaged in efforts to establish a Swedenborgian church in France. In Pernety, Cahagnet would have found a predecessor who melded Swedenborgian doctrines with the traditions of freemasonry—even if, probably unknown to Cahagnet or his contemporaries, Pernety's particular brand of freemasonry appears to have been aristocratic and conservative. Despite the existence of Le Boys des Guays's and other translations of *Heaven and Hell*, Cahagnet's version may well have served as a source of information concerning Swedenborgian doctrines for many writers in the 1840s and 1850s. But Cahagnet's own understanding of sources seems to have been quite eccentric: apparently the spirits and demons of *Heaven and Hell* suggested that he bypass texts altogether and that he draw his information directly from the inhabitants of the invisible worlds described there.

In several of the seances described in Cahagnet's *Arcanes de la vie future*, the author conjures up the spirit of Swedenborg in order to interview him—with the help of his medium. Although several individuals claim to have seen him, including a young man called Bruno and a child, it is a young woman by the name of Adèle who, apparently, is able to transmit the messages of the deceased most easily.

A passage from the middle of one of the longest seances conveys the strange mixture of absurdity and authority as the author summons up the spirit in order, in the manner of a doctor or scientist interrogating his subject, to pose questions concerning certain aspects of Swedenborgian dogma that have troubled him:

> 77. J'appelle M. Swedenborg qui vient aussitôt. Je lui ordonne, au nom de Dieu, de se retirer s'il est un esprit faux; il s'avance au contraire, prend la main d'Adèle en lui disant: Ne craignez rien, je suis bien Swedenborg. — Pouvez-vous être remplacé par un mauvais esprit? — Non, tant que vous me désirerez avec l'intention pure de vous instruire, je viendrai; mais si au contraire vous agissez avec mépris et autorité, je ne me présenterais pas, et un autre pourrait venir pour vous tromper. — Pouvez-vous me communiquer de pensée avec moi et me répondre par l'organe de ma lucide? — Non; votre pensée est trop enterrée dans la matière; je pourrais le faire, mais il est mieux de nous servir de Mademoiselle pour éviter les erreurs. (173)

Only magnetism, the spirit assures the author, can permit individuals to communicate with the other world, and he in particular should allow himself to be magnetized behind the ears. (174) The writer then poses a series of questions on a variety of subjects—including madness, free will, talismans, and catoptric mirrors—before going on to ask Swedenborg whether his works contain any errors (yes, a few, the spirit answers) and especially whether he really meant that the heavens are formed like a Great Man (to which the spirit replies no). (174–195)

In *Arcanes de la vie future*, Cahagnet thus presents himself as an expert whose direct knowledge of spirits and other worlds endows him with an authority at least equal to that of priests and professionals. There is, of course, both in the "interviews" of Swedenborg and elsewhere, much that one would never find—at least in the texts Swedenborg left behind. The association of Mesmerism with Swedenborgianism dates from after his death, and Swedenborg himself certainly never used a medium. And yet Cahagnet's dry, expert-like accounts of the seances he conducted and his representation of himself as having direct knowledge of the beyond do recall Swedenborg's claims to absolute certainty and his descriptions of other worlds that draw so strikingly on his work in the natural sciences.

But in their emphasis on the social aspect of visionary experiences, Cahagnet's work harks back, not to Swedenborg's solitary investigations, but to the earliest secular reception of his work, which associated the doctrines of the solitary Swede with the essentially social practices of Mesmerism and freemasonry. That Cahagnet may have been aware of the connection is suggested by his republication of Pernety's translation of *Heaven and Hell*—although he may have done this purely for money. Like Constant/Lévi's books on magic, Cahagnet's writings emphasize the roles of ritual and performance in bringing to life a spirit world otherwise inaccessible to the individual. Whereas Constant/Lévi had sought to ground his beliefs in the objective structures of language itself, however, Cahagnet presented himself as a successor of Mesmer, an expert whose investigations into the beyond were based on knowledge of the human body. Cahagnet was no more successful than Mesmer in gaining the recognition of the French medical establishment, but his many descriptions of his female mediums' ecstatic experiences of apparently irrational phenomena bear a certain resemblance to the performances staged by recognized psychologists such as Charcot, who also employed female subjects to demonstrate the operation of invisible psychological mechanisms.

Charcot's demonstrations at La Salpêtrière attracted a wide variety of spectators. Their theatricality was often noted. One recent critic comments:

> The demonstrations at the famous *leçons du mardi* were immensely successful spectacles, at least for the professional men who, like Freud, crowded into Charcot's clinic to gaze, with some of the master's own scopophilia, at the coached performances of his specimen hysterics. The sexual politics of the situation are dramatically revealed in a well-known lithograph, of which a copy hung in Freud's consulting room, that shows an attractive young female patient leaning back into the arms of Charcot's disciple Babinski, the top of her dress down around her waist, her bodice exposed and shoulders bare, while Charcot, standing stolidly next to her, lectures to his attentive male audience. (Bernheimer, 7)

If there is no mention of nakedness in the references to the female medium in Cahagnet's writings, for both men, the use of female subjects as mediums or case studies served to distance the writer/observer from his observations. Both, moreover, seemed well aware that what they purported to describe could not be made accessible except in the form of a performance, although neither placed much emphasis on his own participation in the performances they described. Juxtaposing the less successful performances of Cahagnet with those of Charcot, however, brings into focus the extent to which recognition of scientific expertise can rest on the ability of an individual to *play the role* of the expert successfully—especially in areas of inquiry, such as psychology or parapsychology, that are disputed by the scientific establishment.

Swedenborg, too, appears as a performer in the rituals Cahagnet enacts in order to demonstrate his own authority, for the spirit who appears in *Arcanes de la vie future* submits to the questioning of the Frenchman and admits to errors in texts that orthodox Swedenborgians view as authoritative. Cahagnet's claim to an authority based on his knowledge of the spirit world may at first suggest a parallel with Protestant thinkers who saw the unmediated experience of God as the source of an individual's right and duty to choose for him- or herself. Indeed, D. G. Charlton has suggested that there was a proliferation of "secular religions" in France in the first half of the nineteenth century that played a role similar to that of Protestant sects in countries with a strong Protestant tradition. (*Secular Religions*) As we shall see, some earlier French Swedenborgians viewed Swedenborgianism in this way, notably Guillaume Oegger, who interpreted a series of ecstatic experiences to mean that he was a new prophet destined to found a Swedenborgian church. But the link between Cahagnet's writings and religion is tenuous, and his representation of Swedenborg as an apparition who readily admits his mistakes to a female medium scarcely capable of understanding what she hears approaches parody.

2. Combien en durera cette société? J.-F.-E. Le Boys des Guays and the French Swedenborgians

Cahagnet's highly personal and flamboyant version of Swedenborg and his doctrines stands in striking contrast to the painstaking work of an isolated group of Swedenborgians who, under the leadership of J.-F.-E. Le Boys des Guays (1794–1864) in Saint-Amand in Cher, labored to present an accurate version of the works and doctrines of the master to the French public. Since the early 1830s, in fact, Le Boys des Guays had been working on a new translation of Swedenborg's major theological and spiritualist works; his version of *Heaven and Hell*, the most accurate French translation to date, came out in 1850, four years before Cahagnet's idiosyncratic *Abrégé des Merveilles du ciel et de l'enfer*. Le Boys des Guays's labors marked the second attempt to translate Swedenborg systematically into French: at the beginning of the century, J. P. Moët, the librarian at the Royal Library at Versailles, had completed a translation of eleven of Swedenborg's works, which were eventually published between 1819 and 1824. (Sjödén, 66–67)[2] In addition, a former priest affiliated with the Swedenborgians at Saint-Amand, a certain Lino de Zaroa, had published a translation of Swedenborg's *Hieroglyphic Key* in 1843. (Sjödén, 109) Le

Boys des Guays and his colleagues also published a Swedenborgian journal, *La nouvelle Jérusalem* from 1838 to 1848. But their proselytizing was largely unsuccessful, and if the small group of faithful was able, in 1878, to set up a Swedenborgian chapel in an apartment at 12, rue Thouin in the Latin quarter, the congregation never seems to have numbered more than about 200 people. (Sjödén, 142)

In his detailed study of French Swedenborgianism, Karl-Erik Sjödén emphasizes the isolation of this group, an isolation that reaches a zenith in the decades of devoted and often fruitless labor of Le Boys des Guays and his circle. Indeed, like other interpretations of Swedenborgian doctrines in mid-nineteenth-century France, that of Le Boys des Guays appears to repeat, even to caricature, earlier versions. In particular, his work raises a question already posed by Henri Grégoire (1750–1831). In his study of religious sects and their compatibility with the aims of the French Revolution, the radical churchman queried:

> Combien en durera cette société? elle n'a plus l'attrait de la nouveauté; elle n'a pour étais que des révélations chimériques adoptées par quelques hommes abondamment pourvus de crédulité; et quoique dans ses sociétés, séparées de l'Eglise catholique, l'absence d'une règle de foi qui éclaire et dirige l'esprit, laisse un libre accès à tous les égaremens, quelques notions de raison universelle qui surnagent au milieu des rêveries les plus répandues, ne promettent à la secte ni beaucoup de prosélytes, ni une longue durée. (5:109)

And yet it was precisely the political context that had drawn Grégoire to Swedenborgianism—only to be dismayed by what he found there—that kept the reputation of Swedenborg alive in the century following the Revolution.

Even an individual as isolated and as scholarly as Le Boys des Guays never seems to have been able entirely to separate Swedenborgianism from politics. If in 1830 he was named subprefect at Saint-Amand, he was dismissed the following year for his political opinions. But his wife's fortune made it unnecessary for him to work, and he was able after his dismissal to turn to what became the all-encompassing study and translation of Swedenborg. In 1837, he began to hold meetings of the faithful, an event he announced publicly. And yet, a document reprinted in Sjödén's study suggests that the local authorities were not convinced that the subject of these meetings was purely religious. A letter dated March 27, 1838, and addressed to the chief of police, complains that an agent had shown up at the meeting held the previous Sunday to verify the number of people assembled and protests, in terms perhaps a little too vehement, the innocence of their purpose. Sjödén also cites passages from unpublished manuscripts that bear witness even more clearly to Le Boys des Guays's ongoing interest in the possible political implications of Swedenborgian doctrines. A manuscript entitled "Concordance de la Nouvelle Eglise avec le système social de Fourier," which also, Sjödén suggests, seems to date from about this time, makes a comparison between Swedenborgian *correspondances* and Fourier's *analogie universelle*, and ties Swedenborgianism to the general context of French socialist theory:

> Ce que Fourier appelle l'*Analogie universelle* n'est autre chose que la *langue des correspondances* dont Swedenborg a donné la grammaire et le dictionnaire perdus. . . Ainsi donc la Nouvelle Dispensation du Seigneur détruit pour jamais les idées fausses et cruelles que le Catholicisme et toutes les Religions passées s'étaient faites de Dieu. La Religion Nouvelle a revêtu un caractère tout opposé, mais l'état social est encore en proie à tous ces fléaux, et demande une transformation radicale. Cette transformation, Fourier l'a offerte au monde, et en a donné les lois mathématiques. Qu'elle l'opère, et l'harmonie sociale ainsi que l'harmonie religieuse se confondront dans une même unité. (Sjödén, 105)

In his famous essay on Victor Hugo first published in 1861, Baudelaire invoked a similar comparison between Fourier and Swedenborg, although with an irony unheard of in Le Boys des Guays's writing: "Fourier est venu un jour, trop pompeusement, nous révéler les mystères de l'*analogie*. . . . D'ailleurs Swedenborg, qui possédait une âme bien plus grande, nous avait déjà enseigné que *le ciel est un très grand homme*; que tout, forme, mouvement, nombre, couleur, parfum, dans le *spirituel* comme dans le *naturel*, est significatif, réciproque, converse, *correspondant*." (2:132–33) The parallel certainly attests to a commonplace association between the works of Swedenborg and Fourier by mid-century and probably points to Baudelaire's ongoing concern with the ideologies of 1848—even in works that appear to have nothing to do with politics.

More significant, perhaps, is the striking similarity between the wording of the last sentence in the quotation from Le Boys des Guays's letter and the opening of the second quatrain in Baudelaire's sonnet "Correspondances," where Le Boys des Guays's somewhat pedestrian "l'harmonie sociale ainsi que l'harmonie religieuse se confondront dans une même unité" seems to become:

> Comme de longs échos qui de loin se confondent
> Dans une ténébreuse et profonde unité,
> Vaste comme la nuit et la clarté,
> Les parfums, les couleurs et les sons se répondent.

Had Baudelaire actually encountered this text or some form of it? Even if one keeps in mind the parallel, however, the second quatrain, which plays off different kinds of sensations rather than social and religious doctrines, is even more ironic than the reference to "pompous Fourier" in the later essay.

There are several references to Fourier in Baudelaire's published works, as well as in his famous letter to Toussenel, and the poet may well have expected his audience to call up a host of ideological *and* mystical associations to his reference to a "profonde unité" that issued from "correspondances." But it would be misleading to identify either Baudelaire's use of the word *correspondances* or his allusions to Swedenborg too closely with any form of socialism, for, as is well known, the poet also invokes the doctrines of the reactionary political theorist, Joseph de Maistre, even more prominently than those of Fourier, in his works. Baudelaire's ironic association of a kind of absolute language that underlies appearances with two opposing political doctrines raises extremely interesting questions concerning the relation of modernist aesthetics both to universal language schemes and to the events and doctrines of 1848, and I shall return to them in the later chapter on Baudelaire. My concern here, however, is the issue of the contradictory political connotations of Swedenborgian doctrines in French culture during the century following the revolution, for Baudelaire did not invent the bizarre triangle: Swedenborg–Fourier–Maistre.

It was a relatively obscure retired army captain by the name of Jean-Jacques Bernard who seems to have been the first to set down in print what may have been a fairly widespread association of Swedenborgianism with the conservative theories of Maistre, for his *Opuscules* were followed by a defense of *Les soirées de Saint-Petersbourg*.[3] Maistre himself had never referred to Swedenborg by name in the dialogues collected in this work, but rather argues against "illuminism" in general, emphasizing that a dangerous Protestant tendency to emphasize individual illumination must give way to a Catholic emphasis on the importance of authority. Central, however, to Maistre's argument was the notion not only of a hierarchy, but also of a hierarchical language that emanated from God and pointed the way to a regeneration of post-revolutionary society through a return to and revival of feudal traditions.

Maistre's conservative emphasis on the divine origin of language, of course, differs markedly from Fourier's representation of a universal order, or harmony or series or analogy, as he sometimes calls it, in his early works, but what is striking about these roughly contemporary accounts of the role of a universal language in thinking about an ideal social order is how well the notion of a language that inhered *in* things lent itself to different political causes. It also played an important role in the work of another group of thinkers, the French Idéologues, who developed it in the direction Fourier took, but with considerably more rigor. If in the 1850s and 1860s, Baudelaire chose to play both sides off against each other, in the 1830s, Balzac, who in 1832 apparently underwent a change of allegiance from liberalism to royalism, was able to exploit both sets of connotations. One might even argue that the ambiguous origins of the notion of a linguistic totality that underlies the construction of his novelistic world accounts in part for its attractiveness to readers of very different political orientations. Be that as it may, most accounts or even citations of Swedenborg and his doctrines were far narrower than those of Balzac and Baudelaire: other writers took sides.

3. Language, Rituals, and Utopias: Eighteenth-Century Interpretations of Swedenborgianism in France

It was not language but freemasonry that supplied the most obvious point of contact between the interests of Maistre and some of the earliest interpreters of Swedenborg in France, for Swedenborgian texts and doctrines were first introduced in that country in the contexts of Mesmerism and freemasonry.

The individual most often cited as the earliest French "Swedenborgian"—his orthodoxy, even his unflagging interest in Swedenborg can be questioned—is Antoine-Joseph Pernety (1716–1801). A defrocked Benedictine monk, Pernety had published two works, *Fables égyptiennes et grecques* and a *Dictionnaire mytho-hermétique* in 1756, had accompanied Bougainville on his voyage to the Falklands, and had served as librarian at the court of Fredrik II of Prussia, before establishing a masonic community at Avignon, which, as Sjödén remarks, "la postérité a trouvé bon d'associer au nom de Swedenborg, bien que rien n'autorise une telle interprétation." (23) It is unclear exactly when Pernety became interested in Swedenborg and his doctrines or even the extent to which he knew and understood his works, but in the 1780s he and several members of the masonic community translated some key texts by Swedenborg. Pernety's translation of *Heaven and Hell*, first published in 1782, is probably the most important, but it is far from accurate, even misleading. As Sjödén comments:

> Mais lorsque Pernety tomba sur un passage qui ne lui convenait pas, il le changea tout simplement. Nous avons déjà constaté qu'il avait introduit

des réponses de son oracle dans sa traduction. Et bien qu'il fût prêtre défroqué, il resta bon catholique. Il se tira d'affaire en rédigeant une célèbre *Note sur l'adoration des saints*, dont le sens était le contraire de celui de l'original. Dans l'introduction, on trouve également des inadvertances: Swedenborg n'avait jamais lu Boehme, comme le prouve une de ses lettres au Dr. Beyer de Göteborg. Pernety l'admirait. Il fait exprimer à Swedenborg sa propre admiration pour Boehme. Swedenborg ne s'était jamais occupé de l'art hermétique. Nous connaissons la passion de Pernety pour cet art. Il la fait partager à Swedenborg. (27)

I cite this passage in full, not only because it presents a useful list of the differences between the views of the two men, but also because it points to one origin of the French understanding—or misunderstanding—of Swedenborg as a mystic in the tradition of Boehme and also, although Sjödén does not make this explicit, Saint-Martin, who, unlike Swedenborg, was one of Boehme's admirers.

Some histories of freemasonry attribute a "Swedenborgian rite" to Pernety's community at Avignon, an attribution contested by Swedenborgians themselves. But if Pernety's faithfulness to Swedenborgian doctrines is extremely questionable, what his interpretation does show is how easily some aspects of Swedenborgianism were assimilated into the culture of freemasonry in the last decades of the eighteenth century. Pernety's early publications, his *Fables égyptiennes et grecques* and his *Dictionnaire mytho-hermétique*, suggest that Pernety, like Swedenborg, was interested in the notion of a natural or hieroglyphic language of things, but that this interest was closely bound up with the kinds of mythological lore that formed the stuff of masonic rites in the eighteenth century.

It is difficult for a nonmason (and a woman) to discuss masonic rituals since, by definition, they are revealed only to initiates. But interpretations and perhaps records of these rituals in novels and the theater suggest that they draw heavily on lore associated with a variety of mythological pasts, but giving pride of place to Egyptian myths and a notion of hieroglyphic writing attributed to Ancient Egypt. The mythological references in the rituals have sometimes led historians to attribute a very ancient origin to the masonic movement. Recent studies from a literary and cultural perspective, however, have suggested that these rituals are themselves a particular kind of fiction that enabled small, restrictive, and somewhat egalitarian communities to define themselves and work out a set of practices that encouraged participation by all members.[4] Although there were many kinds of lodges and there was some segregation on the basis of class, the kinds of rituals the masons invented served to educate members into practices that could become democratic. Certainly, the considerable literature at the end of the eighteenth century on the subject of a masonic conspiracy that led to the French Revolution suggests that their practices were widely perceived as antagonistic to the monarchy.

Pernety seems to have turned to Swedenborg and his doctrines as one source in his construction of a rite that was probably as true to Swedenborg as his earlier works were to Greek or Egyptian tradition. According to one commentator, Pernety also portrayed Swedenborg as a mason.[5] Some of the other known members, however, such as the "Count" Grabianka and Louis-Joseph-Bernard-Philibert de Morveau, also known as Brumore, suggest that the tone of the community was aristocratic, rather than bourgeois, and more oriented towards establishing the power of charismatic individuals than encouraging participation by all members. At this time, freemasonry seems to have been nearly at least as politically and socially protean as Swedenborgianism and the notion of a hieroglyphic language of nature.

It is sometimes difficult to distinguish masonic groups from those based on other kinds of lore. This is especially true of societies devoted to the practices of Mesmer and his followers. Some forms of Mesmerism, notably the cosmological interpretations of Mesmer's rebellious pupil, the marquis de Puységur, could very easily be incorporated into masonic rituals, but such doctrines could equally well become the focus of a rite that in turn drew on the traditions of freemasonry. Certainly the idea of a society of initiates was a potent one at the turn of the eighteenth century, and transcended the kinds of distinctions that individual societies, concerned with establishing the identity of their particular group, were eager to make. Such distinctions, however, seem to have been at the root of a debate carried out in an exchange of letters between two societies at the end of the 1780s, a debate which marks the second point of entry of Swedenborgian doctrines into French culture.

The Strasbourg Société des amis réunis was a group devoted to the doctrines of the marquis de Puységur, who developed a more cosmologically oriented version of Mesmer's theories which he called *animal magnetism*.[6] The Philanthropic and Exegetical Society at Stockholm, on the other hand, believed that their particular combination of masonic, Mesmerist, and, most importantly, Swedenborgian doctrines was superior to the narrower focus of societies such as the one at Strasbourg. In 1787, therefore, the Stockholm society sent a proselytizing letter to the Strasbourg group, a letter that not only was unsuccessful in convincing the animal magnetist society to adopt Swedenborgian doctrines, but was also published in Germany—to widespread ridicule.[7]

Despite the lack of success of the letter, however, it does seem to have evoked some interest in Swedenborgian doctrines in Strasbourg, for a resident of the city, a certain Daillant de la Touche about whom little is known, published an *Abrégé des ouvrages d'Emanuel Swedenborg* in 1788.[8] Like Pernety's translation of *Heaven and Hell*, published six years earlier, the Strasbourg *Abrégé* gave an idiosyncratic interpretation of Swedenborg's doctrines. Daillant de la Touche's version, however, not only emphasized the necessity of reconciling Swedenborgianism with Catholicism but also tied the doctrines of Swedenborg to contemporary debates in social theory, notably the question, widely argued in connection with the reception of Rousseau, whether man and nature were inherently good. In an argument that anticipates the work of Maistre, Daillant de la Touche argues that they are not.

The Strasbourg *Abrégé* might well be titled, like Cahagnet's summary of 1854, *Abrégé des merveilles du ciel et de l'enfer*, for it appears to draw almost exclusively on *Heaven and Hell*, even though other works by Swedenborg are cited. Its focus, however, is what Daillant de la Touche calls "le monde spirituel," which is identified with Heaven. There is one sole chapter on hell, "Des enfers," and the sections, so popular among nineteenth-century spiritualists, on a spirit world in which the recently dead could go on perfecting themselves in preparation for eternal bliss (or degenerating until they were fit for hell), are omitted. The Strasbourg *Abrégé*, which ends with a chapter entitled "De la félicité céleste," transforms *Heaven and Hell* into a theodicy in which the visions of Swedenborg serve to support Catholic dogma. Its version of Swedenborgianism emphasizes the visionary elements of the Swede's work to the almost total exclusion of his theological doctrines. Even Swedenborg's most notorious heterodox belief, his denial of the existence of a trinity, is glossed over in the opening chapter, "De Dieu."

One chapter in the Strasbourg *Abrégé* combines the two principal chapters on correspondences in *Heaven and Hell*, "There is a Correspondence of All Things of Heaven with All Things of Man" and "There is a Correspondence of Heaven with All Things of the Earth," into a single summarizing discussion entitled "De la correspondance du Ciel avec l'homme, et avec tous les objets de la nature." This chapter follows Swedenborg's discussion of four kinds of correspondences—between things and their spiritual equivalents, between the human body and inner spiritual states which it expresses through gesture and facial expressions, between the structures of the body and the cosmos, and between the word and an inner spiritual sense—and describes the gradual loss of knowledge of correspondences in terms of a devolution from a golden to a silver to an iron age. Like Swedenborg's work, the Strasbourg *Abrégé* suggests that the rediscovery of correspondences would bring about a new golden age, a return to a spiritualized natural world. The introduction to the *Abrégé*, however, is more specific than the actual summary itself about the project of reintroducing *correspondances* to the contemporary world in 1788 in Strasbourg and in France.

Very near the beginning of the introduction, the author explains his project in the following terms: "Au torrent de la corruption publique je voudrais opposer la religion et les moeurs; le mal est venu de la terre; c'est dans les cieux qu'il faut chercher le remède." (ii) To what the author sees as a widespread "mépris des lois," he opposes a respect for a Rousseauean "volonté générale," but identifies the general will with "une émanation de la raison suprême." (iv) The doctrines of Swedenborg, he suggests, provide a means for achieving the kind of inner regeneration that alone might be capable of changing society for the better.

Taking issue with the Strasbourg Société des amis de la vérité, Daillant de la Touche argues that Swedenborg's doctrines are compatible not only with Mesmerism, but also with the marvellous in literature. (liii; xxx-xxxii; liv) But for the author of the *Abrégé*, Swedenborg's doctrines seem most attractive for the notion of a gradual and inner regeneration of society they preach. Addressing his patron, a Monsieur N., he writes:

> Joignant de nouvelles objections à celles qui m'ont été déjà faites, vous alleguez, Monsieur, contre la mission de *Swédenborg*, la crainte d'un changement, toujours dangereux quand il a pour objet la religion. —Cette crainte frivole vient de ce que *vous matérialisez la nouvelle Jérusalem*, ce dont il faut bien vous garder. *Swédenborg* n'est point de ces prophètes de malheur qui vous affirment qu'en tel lieu, tel jour, à telle heure, il y aura un tremblement de terre; qui annoncent la peste, la famine, et d'autres fleaux; l'apôtre Suédois ne dit point s'il y aura, ou s'il n'y aura pas sur la terre des révolutions physiques et politiques. Loin de prédire de l'extraordinaire, il dit que les choses iront leur train dans le monde, mais que les esprits seront éclairés par les vérités de la foi pure. . . (xlviii-xlix)

And a little further on:

> Songez, Monsieur, que dans les desseins de ce Dieu infiniment sage tout est gradué et successif. . . (xlix)

Daillant de la Touche's Swedenborgianism is a kind of universal religion—his Swedenborg, a precursor of Balzac's "Bouddha du Nord"— which supports a kind of middle-of-the-road policy of gradual political reform based on the inner regeneration of the individual rather than the rapid transformation or overthrow of social institutions. Such seems also to have been the basis of the appeal of Swedenborgianism to some English radicals in the 1790s, who in the wake of the Terror searched for a doctrine, an ideology, that would emphasize the sanctity of human life at the same time that it called for political change.[9]

It is significant that the two major introductions to Swedenborg's life and works published in the 1780s, Pernety's translation of *Heaven and Hell* and the Strasbourg *Abrégé*, both focused on the visionary aspects of his doctrines, excluding almost all discussion of his theology. Both, moreover, offered highly idiosyncratic interpretations that linked Swedenborgianism to contemporary debates concerning politics and aesthetics in France during the last decades of the eighteenth century. It was a legacy that was to persist well into the nineteenth.

4. Hunger and Hallucinations: The Emigré Perspective

Both Pernety and Daillant de la Touche lived and worked outside of Paris and the mainstream of French culture. At the end of the eighteenth century, a third group of outsiders, aristocratic émigrés who had fled the Terror to London, were instrumental in importing Swedenborgian doctrines into France and French culture. Indeed, another defrocked priest, Bénédict Chastanier, had lived in London since 1774 and was closely associated with the Theosophical Society in that town. (Sjödén, 37) Apparently the most orthodox French Swedenborgian, Chastanier published a *Tableau analytique et raisonné de la doctrine céleste de la Nouvelle Jérusalem* in 1786, several translations of works by Swedenborg, and a Swedenborgian journal, the *Journal Novi-Jérusalémite*, a digest of a Swedish periodical. (Sjödén, 39) Unlike Pernety and his circle at Avignon, with whom he often disagreed vehemently, Chastanier was interested in the theological doctrines of Swedenborg; he was an active supporter of the establishment of a separate Swedenborgian church.

In contrast to Daillant de la Touche's *Abrégé*, which passed over matters of doctrine to focus on the aesthetic, social, and supernatural aspects of Swedenborg's depictions of spirit worlds, Chastanier's *Tableau analytique* focuses on the religious aspects of Swedenborgianism. It is also anything but easy to follow. Published anonymously in London, this work is dedicated to the Archbishop of Paris, but the dedication is only the first of a series of prefaces and prolegomena. This dedication presents Swedenborgianism as a solution to the corruption of the Catholic Church, and is signed only by "les compilateurs." The second, however, called the "Préface de l'auteur français de ce tableau," calls for the establishment of a New Church, taking issue with the point of view that Swedenborg had never advocated separatism. The length and convoluted syntax of the style of this passage, however, suggests that the author's intention was anything but clarity. The distinctness of Swedenborgianism is buried beneath proliferating prefaces and clauses:

> Certains d'entre ses plus zélés partisans, supposent qu'il n'a nulle part entendu que le véritable Chrétien, le vrai membre de la nouvelle Eglise dût jamais faire bande à part, en se séparant d'aucune, et comme rien que ce puisse être de l'Eglise ancienne ou actuelle; ne faisant pas, ce nous semble, assez d'attention à ceci, savoir qu'on ne se sépare point d'une chose qui n'existe pas, et que l'Eglise Chrétienne étant comme l'Ecriture nous le prouve, notamment en l'Apocalypse d'un bout à l'autre, totalement venue à sa fin, toutes ses branches sont également des choses qui n'ont plus d'existence spirituelle; mais il se peut qu'en cette nouvelle dispensation il sera toléré par la Providence qu'elles en ayent une naturelle, pour la même fin, qu'il a été et est encore toléré que la CARCASSE de l'Eglise Judaïque, subsiste encore parmi les hommes, pour servir sans doute de témoignage aux vérités de la nouvelle Eglise. (16)

This preface is followed by an "Avis au public," which is said to be translated from the English by a Mr. ***, and which only appears lead into the body of the text, for the section of the text entitled *Tableau analytique et raisonné des dogmes de la Nouvelle Eglise* opens, in turn, with a series of texts called "Prolégomênes," which already present and justify some of Swedenborg's doctrines. The body of the summary, which does not begin until page 82, begins with a presentation of Swedenborg's beliefs concerning the nature of God, and goes on to discuss redemption and, in the third section, his most controversial doctrine, concerning the Trinity. Here again, the differences of Swedenborg and his followers from more orthodox Christianity are obfuscated by the author's prose. Only at the end of this section of approximately five difficult pages, which not only seem to want to be all things to all people, but also deny the author's desire to meddle with traditional beliefs, do we read:

> Et que par conséquent cette divine Trinité ne consiste point en trois Personnes distinctes l'une de l'autre, mais est unie, comme l'âme, le corps et l'opération en l'homme, en la seule et unique Personne de Jésus Christ notre Seigneur, qui par conséquent est le Dieu du ciel et de la terre, qui seul doit être adoré, comme étant Créateur de toute éternité, Redempteur dans le temps, Régénérateur à perpétuité. (110)

It is difficult to ascertain the purpose of this summary or compilation. If the prefaces suggest the desire to make converts, the presentation of the doctrines does little to clarify Swedenborg's doctrines. The original texts are more accessible.

Chastanier was closely associated with the English Swedenborgian Robert Hindmarsh (1759–1835), whose own summary of Swedenborgian doctrines, *A Compendium of the Chief Doctrines of the True Christian Religion* (1816), was translated into French and published as *Abrégé des principaux points de doctrine de la vraie religion chrétienne d'après les écrits de Swedenborg* in 1820 (it was subsequently republished by Le Boys des Guays in 1862). Hindmarsh's text, which also proceeds point by point through Swedenborg's doctrines, stands in sharp contrast to the obscurity of Chastanier, and probably for this reason, together with Daillant de la Touche's *Abrégé*, was one of the two major popularizing sources for knowledge of Swedenborgianism in the nineteenth century.

Many of the French émigrés who came to London two decades after Chastanier, in the mid-1790s, were less interested—or disinterested. In his autobiographical *Mémoires d'outre-tombe*, for example, Chateaubriand describes with grim humor his contact with a fellow countryman who turned to Swedenborgianism while in the throes of starvation:

> Au lieu d'un schelling par tête, nous ne dépensions plus à dîner qu'un demi-schelling. Le matin, à notre thé, nous retranchâmes la moitié du pain, et nous supprimâmes le beurre. Ces abstinences fatiguaient les nerfs de mon ami. Son esprit battait la campagne; il prêtait l'oreille et l'avait l'air d'écouter quelqu'un; en réponse, il éclatait de rire, ou versait de larmes. Hingant croyait au magnétisme, et s'était troublé la cervelle du galimatias de Swedenborg. (1:416)

While one might argue that Chateaubriand, in turn, suffered from his own brand of hallucinations, he makes a point worth noting: that French interest in Swedenborg often went hand in hand with the kind of marginality both he and his friend experienced while eking out an émigré's precarious existence in London at the turn of the eighteenth century.

5. Eclecticism and *Flânerie*: The Interpretations of Edouard Richer and Guillaume Oegger

Nineteenth-century French Swedenborgians were also, for the most part, an odd lot of outsiders. Some, like Le Boys des Guays and the librarian J.-P Moët, were gentlemen scholars, who developed a burning interest in the doctrines of an eccentric Swede and spent years either inter-preting his doctrines or translating his texts. Among them was a mild-mannered and sickly gentleman from Nantes, Edouard Richer (1792–1834), a writer who, in the 1820s, had edited a literary journal, the *Lycée amoricain*, and published essays on religion, mythology, and romantic lit-erature, and who spent the last decade of his life composing a monumental work in eight volumes, *De la nouvelle Jérusalem*, which attempted to in-tegrate Swedenborgian doctrines into an eclectic system that also em-braced Catholicism, as well as many other mythological and religious tra-ditions.[10]

Richer's *De la nouvelle Jérusalem* represents the culmination of his life's work, an attempt to synthesize earlier work on religious, aesthetic, and social questions, and to present Swedenborg as the herald of a new age and a literary renewal in France. The first part, written second, presents an overview of religious and esoteric tradition; the second focuses on Sweden-borgianism and its relationship to what Richer considered to be essential religious questions. For Richer, Swedenborgianism reconciled science and theology, demonstrating both the possibility of a rational religious order and the necessity of revelation. But Richer was no orthodox Sweden-borgian. Rather, he believed that Swedenborgianism represented a model for the regeneration of Catholicism and French society. Swedenborg was an eclectic visionary whose doctrines resumed and rationalized various re-ligious and esoteric traditions of the past and pointed forward to the fur-ther transformation of these doctrines in nineteenth-century French soci-ety.

Consider the conclusion of the chapter on the doctrine of correspond-ences in *De la nouvelle Jérusalem*. Richer urges the reader to make his or her own dictionary:

> C'est alors à la sagacité du lecteur à voir, selon la place qu'occupent les choses, la signification qu'elles comportent avec elles. Une fois initié, il fait lui-même son propre dictionnaire. (2:402)

For Richer, the doctrine of correspondences is a literary, as well as a reli-gious, concept. His interpretation parallels an early presentation of the doctrine of correspondences, that of the English Swedenborgian Robert Hindmarsh in his introduction to his 1784 edition of Swedenborg's *Clavis hieroglyphica*. This introduction, which has remarkably little to do with the text of this cryptic and unfinished work, suggests that the author chose to publish it because of the suggestiveness of its title. Hindmarsh drew a comparison between correspondences and rhetorical figures that might be read as suggesting that correspondences represented a superior form of rhetoric:

The difference between a mere figure and a correspondence may again appear from the following consideration. A mere figure or simile is the resemblance which one *natural* object or circumstance is supposed to bear to another *natural* object or circumstance; whereas a correspondence is the actual relation subsisting between a *natural* object and a *spiritual* subject, or a *natural* form and a *spiritual* essence; that is between *outer* and *inner*, *lower* and *higher*, *nature* and *spirit*, and not between *nature* and *nature*, or *spirit* and *spirit*. (Preface, 6–8)

Like Hindmarsh, Richer compares the doctrine of correspondences to figures of literary language, concluding that correspondences reflect an original unity of experience, while metaphor and other figures of speech mediate between the fragmentary experience of contemporary humanity and an original unity which cannot be captured in ordinary speech or writing. The doctrine of correspondences thus points the way to the recovery of a universal language that has been lost:

La première langue a donc consisté dans l'usage des objets naturels considérés comme emblèmes des spirituels, afin de rendre appréciables les phénomènes de la vie réelle, de la vie en principe. Nous n'avons pas un terme de moral qui ne soit, pour ainsi dire, une métaphore prise dans l'ordre sensible. Ce sont les états de l'homme physique dans leurs phases diverses et innombrables, qui ont tous fourni les idées dont on s'est servi pour peindre les états de son âme. Il y a une correspondance exacte que l'observateur réfléchi ne peut méconnaître et qui le met sur la trace de la langue primitive. Nous retrouvons le monde moral dans toutes nos expressions familières: la seule différence qu'il y a entre notre langue et celle de nos aieux, c'est que, chez nous, ce monde apparaît comme figure, et que chez eux c'etait une perception. (2:377–78)

Although Richer compares the doctrine of correspondences to the primitive languages described by German philologists, his account of this original language has more in common with eighteenth-century accounts of the origin of language than with historical linguistics. Rousseau's *Essai sur l'origine des langues*, for example, depicted an imagined past in order to explain how language functioned, rather than to trace its historical development.[11] For Richer, imagining the doctrine of correspondences as an original language based on the unselfconscious interaction of virtuous individuals with a spiritualized nature served to demonstrate that language itself was inherently moral:

Une philosophie supérieure nous démontre que ce qui est métaphore dans la bouche de tous les hommes n'a pas toujours été tel, dans la bouche de celui qui, le premier, s'en est servi. Il y a là quelque chose d'antérieur à tous les termes de convention. Des figures si vraies, si naturelles, si bien à la portée de l'esprit de tous les hommes, ne sont point des choses sans réalité. Elles ont procédé, comme tout ce qui est vrai, du seul séjour d'où l'homme puisse recevoir des connaissances. Nous croyons inventer, quand nous ne faisons que répéter ce qui nous est révélé dans l'intérieur de notre esprit. Ce goût des comparaisons est venu d'un souvenir éloigné et confus des relations du monde matériel avec l'univers moral. Les objets, d'abord, n'ont pas été nommés, mais montrés; et le langage emblématique a dû précéder le langage par sons articulés. La langue des objets a été établie avant tous les idiomes de convention, et ce que nous voyons aujourd'hui, dans ceux-ci, de relatif au monde moral, est une traduction de cette première langue. (2:401)

One of the implications of Richer's unorthodox presentation is that the doctrine of correspondences might point the way to a regeneration not only of contemporary society and culture, but also of literary language, the figures of which remind us that "ce goût de comparaisons est venu d'un souvenir éloigné et confus des relations du monde matériel avec l'univers moral."

One recognizes in Richer's work a descendent of the eighteenth-century works, such as Pernety's *Fables égyptiennes et grecques*, that had attempted to fuse mythological and religious traditions to provide a basis for the rituals practiced in masonic and other secret societies. Richer's biographer, Piet, tells us that his subject had been passionately interested in a later book on the subject that had been extremely fashionable at the end of the eighteenth century: Charles-François Dupuis's *Origine de tous les cultes, ou Religion universelle*. But the scope of Richer's project has been reduced to the subjectivity of a single person, a writer who attempts to develop a system that would explain the mysteries of the world in complete isolation—one is constantly reminded of the isolation in which Richer lived—from any kind of social context. But despite Richer's distance from contemporary society, the interpretation of Swedenborg and Swedenborgianism in *De la nouvelle Jérusalem* is remarkably similar to Balzac's in his novels of the early 1830s, which also represent Swedenborgianism as part of an eclectic system made up of aspects of many traditions, but all subsumed under the novelist's particular brand of Catholicism.

In the 1820s, Richer had frequented a kind of Swedenborgian salon held by two other outsiders, the retired army captain, Jean-Jacques Bernard, author of the *Opuscules* to which were appended a defense of *Les soirées de Petersbourg*, and a woman who practiced faith healing, Mme de Saint-Amour. Although little is known concerning what actually went on at the meetings of Bernard and Saint-Amour's little society, their salon seems to have been instrumental in spreading Swedenborgian doctrines—or some form of them—by word of mouth in Paris during this decade. For it was here that one of the most eccentric and interesting French interpreters of Swedenborg, Guillaume Oegger, also encountered his ideas.

One can imagine few starker contrasts than that of the lives and works of the mild-mannered and withdrawn Edouard Richer and the lively and worldly Guillaume Oegger. In contrast to most French Swedenborgians, Oegger (c. 1790–c. 1853)[12] was an insider at the time he encountered the doctrines of Swedenborg and was converted. An extremely talented and successful churchman, the then *abbé* Oegger, by the mid-1820s *grand vicaire* of Notre-Dame and confessor to the queen, had been asked to keep an eye on the activities of Captain Bernard and other spiritualists and magnetists in Paris. Oegger's encounter with Captain Bernard and his circle, however, turned intellectual curiosity and official suspicion into a religious passion. The would-be spy was converted in 1826, and submitted his resignation to the archbishop at the end of the year. He moved to the Faubourg Saint-Germain and then to London, where he underwent a second conversion in which he learned that God had designated him to be a kind of new messiah whose mission was to reacquaint the world with the language of nature to which Swedenborg's doctrine of correspondences provided a key. Captain Bernard died in 1828, less than two years after Oegger's conversion, and his brilliant convert was never fully accepted in orthodox Swedenborgian circles. Le Boys des Guays, for example, found that Oegger's emphasis on a language of *nature* was dangerously irreligious.

Both Oegger and Richer gave a literary turn to French interpretations of Swedenborg's doctrine of correspondences, but while Richer, in his eight—one surmises, little-read—volumes, compared correspondences to figures of speech, Oegger transformed the doctrine so that it accounted for the possible perception of divine meanings not only in dreams and an unadulterated state of nature, but also in the city. Oegger published several interpretations of Swedenborgian doctrines, including *Le vrai Messie, ou l'Ancien et le nouveau Testamens examinés d'après les principes de la langue de la nature* and an *Essai d'un dictionnaire de la langue de la nature, ou Explication de huit cents images hiéroglyphiques*. From the perspective of the development of what one might call an urban literary aesthetic, however, by far his most interesting work is his *Rapports inattendus entre le monde matériel et le monde spirituel, par la découverte de la langue de la nature*, an autobiographical account of his conversion to Swedenborgianism and his call to become a prophet of Swedenborgian correspondences.

Like the *Abrégé* of Daillant de la Touche, this work opens with an invocation of Rousseau:

> Jean-Jacques, que n'ai-je ta plume! Celui peut-être de tous les hommes, qui sympathisa davantage avec ta manière de voir et de sentir, est obligé d'écrire sur des *songes, des visions, des apparitions!* — Après avoir passé pour impie aux yeux des fanatiques, il me faut passer pour fanatique aux yeux des philosophes! — N'importe cependant, le fanatisme religieux. J'ai *trop d'orgueil* pour déguiser aucune de mes pensées, aucun de mes sentimens, devant qui que ce soit, et sous quelque prétexts que ce soit. Et si je ne puis imiter le style de Rousseau, du moins dépend-il de moi d'en imiter la franchise et l'indépendance de caractère. (1)

The narrative then turns to the circumstances that led to the author's conversion to Swedenborgianism. He had already been attending magnetic seances when, in October 1826, he came to spend several nights in the cathedral of Notre-Dame. On one of these occasions, the author began to ruminate about corruption in the Church and his own lack of faith, even going so far as to write down some resolutions on a little strip of paper he concealed in his clothes. On the following two nights, he had what he believed to be otherworldly experiences. The first was a rather remarkable dream, not unlike some of those recounted in Swedenborg's journal of 1743–44. Oegger retells it, however, in an energetic style, punctuated by many underlinings and question marks and quite unlike that of Swedenborg:

> Il est *malade,* il est *malade!* s'écria quelqu'un d'une voix *sifflante.* Aussitôt je voix un être d'un extérieur *misérable* partir de mon lit *comme s'il sortait de moi;* il est entouré de *fumée;* un pan de son *habit, de couleur brune,* est arraché par derrière. — Êtes-vous le *médecin.* lui dis-je? — Oui, oui, répondit-il, d'un *ton qui trahissait un homme plein de fausseté,* c'est moi, êtes-vous prêt? — Puis, il vient sur moi avec une *machine hydraulique,* grossièrement faite avec de l'*écorce de l'arbre;* mais il manquait d'*eau* pour m'*inonder,* et j'en suis quitte pour la peur. La figure de cet être, qui est celle d'un jeune homme d'environ dix-huit ans, s'approche tout près de la mienne; elle est pâle, plutôt triste que gaie, et couverte d'une légère couche de *poussière fine, comme du noir de fumée.* Je distingue tous ses traits plus clairement que si les rayons du midi donnaient dessus, et je m'éveille, me trouvant la tête appuyée sur le coude!
>
> Comme il était grand jour, je réveillai aussitôt mon jeune frère, qui couchait dans un cabinet à côté, en lui criant: Je viens de voir un *ange noir,* un *ange noir!* (4–5)

Like many of the other visions and dreams recounted in *Rapports inat-tendus*, this one bears a clear resemblance to magnetic or spiritualist rit-uals. The hissing voice that chants "il est malade, il est malade!"; the smoke and the trailing garments; above all the pale and ghostly face of the young man—all suggest the conjuring up of apparitions at a seance. But when the author tells the dream to a friend who is a magnetizer, he is told that the dream represents, not a magnetic apparatus or its effects, but a prediction of a future misfortune. (5) And the following night he has an auditory dream in which he hears words that he later interprets as leading him to Swedenborgianism and the doctrine of correspondences:

> *Vous ne comprendrez tout cela que quand vous aurez la TRIPLE LUMI-ERE!* (5)

The author concludes that these were no ordinary dreams, but "de *vérita-bles visions, et des songes* tels qu'en avait eu les anciens." (6) Later, after he had begun to study the doctrine of correspondences, he noticed that all his dreams had become hieroglyphic, "et qu'ils offraient souvent une suite d'emblêmes les plus clairs et les plus significatifs pour celui qui en possède la clef!" (20)

At the end of the year, he submits his resignation to the archbishop, moves to the Faubourg Saint-Honoré, where, except for attending mag-netic seances, he leads a solitary life, and begins to find the world resonant with a meaning intended for him alone. In the Eglise de l'Oratoire, for example, he tells us:

> [j]'avais découvert un prédicateur qui parlait selon mon coeur, et qui dis-ait chaque fois des choses si appropriées à ma position, qu'il semblait, qu'averti incessamment par quelqu'un, il ne prêchait que pour moi. (18)

He also begins to imitate magnetic seances all on his own. One of his first suggests both the kind of performances he had been attending and how the rituals associated with these seances carried over into his understand-ing of Swedenborgianism and the doctrine of correspondences. Like Richer's version of correspondences, these curiously bodiless apparitions point to the relationship between the objects of the world and hidden moral meanings:

> Différentes personnes défuntes m'apparurent alors avec la singulière circonstance de ne montrer que *la tête*, ou une partie plus ou moins grande *du buste*, entres autres mon aïeule maternelle. Je reconnus plus tard que ce devraient être des individus qui avait manqué des *qualités*

morales représentées par les parties éclypsées, mais qui, en même temps, ne voulaient pas se livrer *activement* aux passions opposées. Les *bras* et les *jambes* désignent une *vie active;* le *tronc,* qui renferme le *coeur* et les *entrailles,* les *diverses affections sociales,* etc. Quant à la voix *sifflante* ou *enrouée,* qui a plusieurs fois reparu dans mes songes, je n'en ai pas encore pu déviner au juste la *signification.* L'examen des *causes* qui amènent l'enrouement, pourrait peut-être mettre sur la voie. (19)

The majority of the apparitions he conjures up are feminine, and include his mother (21–22) and a dead sister, who appears in a dream in which he is conducted up a mountain to watch a conflict that he believes is an allegorical representation of the opposition of the Greek and Roman churches and the inevitable triumph of a Swedenborgian new church, a triumph which would occur between 1830 and 1842, but most likely in 1836. (30)

On July 21, 1828, the author left Paris for London, where he stayed at several hotels called *The White Horse.* On the first occasion, he interprets the coincidence of the name with his Swedenborgian interests as fateful. The hand of Providence, it seems, is pointing just at him:

Le hasard, si toutefois hasard il y a, me conduisit à l'auberge du *Cheval blanc,* diligence du *Cheval blanc.* Ce n'est pas que dans ce moment je pensasse plus au *Cheval blanc de l'apocalypse* qu'au *Bucéphale d'Alexandre;* mais on m'y a fait penser depuis. J'allais monter en voiture, lorsque *deux étrangers,* selon toutes les apparences *deux juifs,* arrivent dans un petit char-à-banc, descendent dans la cour en ma présence, me font diverses questions, me demandent si *je suis Allemand, ce que je fais dans le pays;* puis se parlent entre eux, et semblent se dire: *il ne se doute encore de rien;* enfin, au lieu de monter en diligence avec moi, comme je l'avais supposé en les prenant pour des voyageurs comme moi, ils remontent dans leur char et disparaissent.

Nous partons. Pendant près de deux heures on cause de choses indifférentes. De temps à autre je jetais un coup-d'oeil sur une petite Bible que j'avais sur moi. Tout-à-coup *je sens dans ma tête quelque chose de particulier!* Tiens, dis-je, est-ce que la voiture te cause des étourdissemens? Il y a long-temps que cela ne t'est plus arrivé? Quel est ce vertige ou ce délire qui te prend? Tu as bien eu quelquefois des rêves extatiques pendant la nuit; mais jamais tu n'as éprouvé pendant le jour aucune de ces crises, qui ressemblent à l'état d'extase! — Y a-t-il, par hasard, dans la voiture quelque magnétiseur qui te joue ce tour? — Ou bien encore serait-ce un accès de *folie* qui te prendrait? Au milieu de ces soucis, j'entends dans ma tête une voix qui me dit: *Sois tranquille, ne t'inquiète pas; TOUT LE CIEL EST ATTENTIF SUR TOI! Et dans la première auberge où tu t'arrêteras, tu trouveras un FRERE dans le SEIGNEUR!* (38–39)

It is, of course, significant that the two Jews who appear in this scene pose problems related to language and understanding. At the end of the narrative, the author encounters another group of Jewish strangers, but this time they bear a letter with mysterious, half-German, half-Hebrew, letters on it, and it is likely, we are told, that they are students of the cabala. (75–79)

The author travels to Cambridge, where he finds the architecture "too gothic." (41) Upon his return to London, he stops at yet another White Horse Inn. This time the narrative alludes to one of the reasons for his insistence on linguistic coincidences and repetitions: they render familiar a landscape bewildering to a foreigner. He begins to realize that the name is a very popular one for inns in this part of England:

> A Londres nous descendîmes *encore une fois à un hôtel du Cheval blanc*, enseigne vraiment remarquable et dont toute la route était parsemée, en peinture et en sculpture, de toute grandeur et de toute forme. Je le repète, je ne pensais point alors à cette circonstance, mais depuis j'ai acquis la certitude que c'était là une des persécutions que m'avaient ménagées de mauvais esprits; car c'est l'idée du *Cheval blanc* qui, quelques jours après, devint l'idée fixe qui m'égara pendant quelques heures à Londres, tandis que j'étais à la recherche du temple de la *nouvelle Jérusalem*. (42)

Whatever his realization concerning the prevalence of the name *White Horse Inn* in England, however, the author experiences a series of ecstatic revelations at this hotel that lead him to believe that he has been designated by God to be a prophet, the new messiah, of a Swedenborgian new coming. Oegger's account of his experience of the Word resembles only in the most general sense the narrative of Swedenborg's experience of a divine or angelic being at Easter 1744, for the French narrative begins very much like a seance. First, several dead friends of the author appear, then some angels, the Virgin Mary, and a divine voice that chastises the author for his pride, as it affirms his calling.

Interestingly, one of the spirits that appear to the author during the night of magnetic ecstasy is Captain Jean-Jacques Bernard, who had converted Oegger to Swedenborgianism. This is one of the only published accounts of Bernard, and its reference to the author's nervous condition— brought on by his excessive enthusiasm for Swedenborgianism—betrays some ambivalence:

> Je donne enfin la main à mon excellent ami M. B., mort peu de mois auparavant d'une fièvre cérébrale, occasionnée par la trop grande véhémence avec laquelle il avait embrassé *la cause de la nouvelle Jérusalem*.

Nous ne nous parlons pas, mais nous nous serrons long-temps et forte-
ment la main, *en présence de CELUI dont nous nous étions si souvent
entretenus avec attendrissement pendant notre courte connaissance! et
nos coeurs se disent un million de choses!* —
  (M. B. est ce capitaine d'infanterie dont il est parlé plus haut, disci-
ple, et en même temps le plus zélé propagateur de la *nouvelle doctrine,*
qu'il soit possible de rencontrer, et qui a fondé ou encouragé différentes
petites sociétés de *nouveaux chrétiens* à Paris, à Nantes, à Besançon, à
Bayonne, et jusqu'en Espagne, après avoir commencé sa mission dans son
propre régiment, qui compte aujourd'hui plusieurs officiers distingués,
dont les convictions chrétiennes sont aussi franches qu'éclairées. Comme
ç'avaient été également des expériences sur la *magnétisme animal,* qui
l'avaient conduit au *spiritualisme* et de-là à la *nouvelle Jérusalem,* en lui
serrant la main je me rappelai un instant nos *somnambules.* Mais, à mon
grand étonnement, on me représenta ceux-ci comme des *somnambules*
ou *extatiques naturels,* par opposition aux somnambules ou extatiques
spirituels; et persuadé, qu'*ils avaient besoin d'être mis sous la protection
d'un ordre d'êtres plus élevés,* je les recommandai aux soins d'une Mme
X., *qu'il est inutile de faire connaître,* puis je me tins dans le silence.)
(47–48)

Rapports inattendus is followed by an appendix on dreams and their
interpretation. Dreams, the author argues, are the means by which we can
come to understand the language of nature. We should be careful, however, to use a Christian key, for those associated with Egyptian, Greek, and
Roman lore, which somnambulists often draw on, are dangerously misleading. There are three kinds of dreams, associated with three degrees of
spiritual progression: dreams included in the first category represent the
babbling of one's inner self, "l'homme intérieur," before the individual has
become conscious of the spiritual world; in the second are dreams that
suggest incomplete knowledge of the spiritual world; and those of the third
reveal a complete understanding of the language of nature.
  While Oegger's understanding of dreams and their interpretation is
clearly prepsychoanalytic in its emphasis on their prophetic significance,
on some points he does anticipate Freud's discussion of the role of puns.
One remarkable dream narrative, for example, turns on the interpretation
of an apparently nonsensical phrase:

C'est ainsi qu'une autre fois, après m'être beaucoup occupé de *l'immortalité,* je me réveillai le matin, en prononçant ces paroles étonnantes:
C'est moi qui ai doré la tombe du papillon! —On sait que nombre de
chrysalides sont ornées de taches *dorées,* d'où vient même le mot grec de
corset doré. Le *cercueil,* ou plutôt le *cadavre,* est donc la vraie *chrysalide*

de l'homme, d'où il sort *Ange,* comme la *chenille* sort *papillon* de la sienne. (93)

Other dream narratives concern serpents, spiders, and the tomb of Casimir Périer, who was still alive at the time of the experiences recounted in *Rapports inattendus.* Even the author recognizes this dream as a form of wish fulfillment:

> Le 8 juillet, 1828, j'ai rêvé que M. *Casimir Périer avait une tombe au Père Lachaise; que Benjamin Constant était gouverneur des enfans d'Orléans, et même du duc de Bordeaux;* que M. C., publiciste religieux, m'avait permis *d'ôter la poussière de dessus les reliquaires dont toutes ses fenêtres étaient garnies;* que le même M. C. *voulait imprimer un manuscrit qui n'était entre ses mains que depuis une quinzaine de jours.* Qu'enfin la plupart de ces événements devaient s'accomplir vers le temps que le *tonnerre tomberait sur un hôtel situé près de la place Vendôme.*
> 1. La *tombe de Casimir Périer* peut signifier *sa mort naturelle,* aussi bien que la *mort du système politique* dont il était le *type.* La première s'est réalisée cette année (1832) et l'autre ne tardera probablement pas à la suivre. Par-là le tableau a commencé à se remplir. 2. *Benjamin Constant* était ici le *type* du *principe constitutionnel,* et probablement aussi du principe du *protestantisme.* Le *principe constitutionnel* est bien déjà devenu celui de la *famille d'Orléans,* qui peut-être dans peu sentira également la nécessité d'admettre *de fait* une *liberté de conscience, aussi illimitée,* qu'elle l'a été déclarée de *droit.* (115–16)

The manuscript in the dusty hall, the author believes, was a Deist text. He cannot—or will not—explain the building in the Place Vendôme on which thunder must fall.

The Périer dream represents one of two passages in *Rapports inattendus* which allude to the author's political interests. The other occurred in the midst of the ecstatic visions of the White Horse Inn:

> —On me donna aussi à entendre que j'avais eu tort, dans certaine rencontre, de dire *que je ne rentrerais en France que quand nous y aurions un roi* COMME JE L'ENTENDAIS, *c'est-à dire un roi* libéral. (70)

Such an event, which, of course, had already taken place by the time *Rapports inattendus* was published, depends on the will of God, the author learns.

Rapports inattendus thus ties Swedenborgianism—at least officially—to the fortunes of liberalism in France. One is reminded of another, almost contemporaneous, representation of the city as a hieroglyphic landscape and an allegory of desire, Balzac's *La peau de chagrin*, which contains a single reference to Swedenborg (10:87) and was first published in 1831, while its author was still an avowed liberal. If Balzac's representation of contemporary Paris is more aesthetically successful and certainly more developed than Oegger's depiction of London in 1828, *Rapports inattendus* ties the representation of the city as a conglomeration of hieroglyphic meanings more explicitly than any more self-consciously literary text in nineteenth-century France to the transformations of Swedenborgianism in the contexts of animal magnetism and spiritualism in the 1820s and 1830s.

From a late-twentieth-century perspective, then, Oegger's interpretation of Swedenborgianism has more in common with what is most interesting in French literature than that of his contemporary Edouard Richer. Yet it was Richer who explicitly addressed the issue of the relation of Swedenborg and his doctrine of correspondences to French literary tradition and Richer, the provincial writer and editor of a literary journal, whose interpretation would have probably been recognized by readers in the 1830s as the more literary of the two. But despite their many differences of temperament, style, and focus, the writings of Oegger and Richer on Swedenborgianism have much in common. Both represent Swedenborg as an eclectic visionary, whose doctrine of correspondences points to the universal significance of apparently diverse mythological and religious traditions. This is a significance inherent in language itself that can be brought to light by the initiated reader who is able—with the help of a mythological key, the doctrine of correspondences—to see beyond the most obvious "meaning" of words, the mere objects they appear to designate. For Oegger, as for Richer and for Swedenborg, the meanings, the "correspondences," that words point to are only apparently historical; the origins that all three men attribute to the doctrine of correspondences are as mythological as the origins Rousseau was concerned with in his essay on language, for the doctrine of correspondences points to an element in language that has been obscured by the corruption of language, as well as contemporary society, but that can be recovered at any moment. As for many other writers who evoked the image of a lost golden age of perfection, for Swedenborg and his interpreters the myth pointed to a future utopian order, but one that was very near. If Swedenborg had written of a revolution in the heavens in 1757, his French followers saw the event as much closer to hand. Successive interpretations of Swedenborgianism tie the doctrines of the master very closely to the French Revolution and its aftermath.

Oegger and Richer, then, invented a Swedenborg to appeal to French culture in the late 1820s and 1830s. Their visionary's eclecticism was suited to a reading public accustomed to versions of Victor Cousin's philosophical method, but it also drew on widespread interest in animal magnetism and spiritualism. Richer's Swedenborgianism was, moreover, compatible with Catholicism and had a distinct contribution to make to the renewal of literary language in France. Oegger's version, like its author, was less pliant, and Oegger seems to have been the sole French Swedenborgian to move from the position of an insider to that of an outsider. Perhaps for that reason, his discovery of serendipitous correspondences, *Rapports inattendus*, in the city points forward to many interpretations, in avant-garde literature and art of the following century, of the city as text.

In their representation of Swedenborg as an eclectic visionary, Oegger and Richer draw on earlier interpretations, such as that of Pernety, which had seen him as one element in a wide variety of mythological traditions that fed the invention of new forms of social ritual in the mid- and late-eighteenth century, including the rites of the freemasons and other secret societies. Both Oegger and Richer, however, do take care to distinguish—if they do not always do so accurately—the doctrines of Swedenborg from other traditions. Later writers were not always so careful. Toward the end of the narrative part of Oegger's *Rapports inattendus*, the author encounters three Jews, who hand him texts or make signs that seem to have a hieroglyphic significance. He attributes the meaningfulness of the signs to the Jewish tradition of the cabala:

> Je sais seulement, comme je le ferai voir plus bas, qu'un grand nombre d'Israélites connaissent la *crise extatique* et que quelques élémens de *la langue de la nature*, et que ce n'était pas la première fois que ces *sortes d'initiés de la cabbale* s'étaient mêlés à mes songes et même à mes aventures de la veille. (76)

But if for Oegger, Swedenborg and the doctrine of correspondences suggested how Jewish traditions might be reconciled with those of Christianity, for some later writers, notably Constant/Lévi, the two traditions seem to have melted into each other. It was left to scholars and academics, nonparticipants in the culture of religious sectarianism, animal magnetism, and spiritualism of mid-nineteenth-century France, to revive distinctions that had been lost in popular culture.

6. Beyond the Myth? Mid-Nineteenth-Century Accounts

Le Boys des Guays, laboring in relative isolation in Saint-Amand, Cher, to produce accurate translations of Swedenborg's texts and to proselytize for the New Church, was not alone in seeking to revive a more accurate assessment of Swedenborg. Two scholarly accounts reflect attempts to come to terms with an interest in a cult that looked as puzzling in the 1850s as it had to Henri Grégoire in the first decades of the century.

In 1857, Edouard Chambefort presented a thesis on Swedenborgianism to the Faculty of Protestant Theology at the University of Strasbourg. His *Essai sur Swedenborg et ses idées eschatologiques* gives a brief overview of the history of Swedenborgianism in France and evaluates Swedenborg's doctrines from the point of view of Protestant theology. Chambefort criticizes the realism and materialism of Swedenborg's representation of the afterlife, but sees these as the result of mental illness brought on by long years of meditation in isolation.

And in 1863, the religious scholar, Jacques Matter (1791–1864), the author of the influential *Histoire critique du gnosticisme*, published a scholarly study of Swedenborg in which he pointed to the parallels between Swedenborg's doctrines and seventeenth-century French religious thought. For the religious scholar, however, who had published a study of Saint-Martin the year before, Swedenborg and his works also raised questions concerning the legacy of the Enlightenment. In his introduction, he writes:

> Swedenborg, c'est le surnaturel en face de la critique du dix-huitième siècle. Or le surnaturel n'est pas seulement la question la plus haute et la plus agitée pour nous, enfants du dix-huitième siècle plus que nous ne pensons, mais encore a toujours été et sera toujours la plus grosse question de l'intelligence, la question auprès de laquelle pâlissent toutes les autres. (iii)

But he also aims to put to rest certain myths concerning Swedenborg, the *fable* surrounding his life and work:

> D'après ce genre d'histoire que le grand juge du dernier siècle appelait la fable convenue, Swedenborg est un *rêveur*, un *visionnaire*, un *esprit faible* ou *malade*, un *halluciné* dupe de ses illusions. Voilà le portrait et le jugement reçues, la fable convenue. Or la fable convenue a des raisons d'être, sans doute, mais ce n'est pas l'histoire. (vi)

The most accurate French account of Swedenborg to date, Matter's book was, Sjödén tells us, pillaged by at least one preacher at the Swedenborgian chapel on the rue Thouin in Paris. (144)

Writing under the pseudonym Alexandre Erdan, a certain Alexandre André Jacob (1826–78) published a compendious overview of religious and utopian sects—he sees the two as identical—that could not be less academic. Although his views of Swedenborg could scarcely be more contemptuous, ironically enough, Erdan believed, like many of Swedenborg's followers, that social change would have to begin with language; he also published a work entitled *Les révolutionnaires de l'A–B–C*. Erdan's *La France mistique* [sic] reflects the views and orthography of an eccentric who was interested in the rationalization and reformation of spelling, as well as society. It cites Swedenborg as the first of a long line of founders of sects responsible for the derailing of the Enlightenment and the Revolution in France.

Erdan's *La France mistique* takes us from Swedenborg, Fourier, and Mesmer, through a host of lesser-known nineteenth-century prophets and occultists, to the religion of humanity of Auguste Comte. The work opens with a dedication to Voltaire (i), and a plea for religious toleration and the separation of Church and State. For Erdan, the Restoration and the reinstatement of the Catholic Church marked a step backwards in the history of France:

> Ma conviction profonde et inébranlable est qu'il n'y avait pas lieu, au commencement de ce siècle, de réparer l'édifice religieuz qu'avait détruit la révolution française. Ni l'intérêt politique dans son acsepsion la plus étendue, ni même l'intérêt gouvernemental de la haute personalité qui était alors au pouvoir, n'exigeaient une pareille restauration. Le parti le plus sage, come le plus juste, était alors, ainsi qu'il serait aujourdui ainsi qu'il sera éternelement, d'organiser la liberté des sectes, et de rendre l'administration nationale complètement et absolument étrangère à ces sortes de choses. (1–2)

Erdan writes that the Catholic revival, in both its aesthetic and politically conservative forms, represented a return to the worst aspects of medieval culture. But if the proponents of Catholicism in the nineteenth century tended to play down the demoniacal aspects of theology, Erdan takes it upon himself to remedy this oversight in his survey of religious, esoteric, and pseudoscientific thinkers and sects.

Swedenborg is the first cult leader Erdan takes up. The chapter, "Les Swedenborgiens," appears at the beginning of Book I of *La France mistique*, which is entitled "Eudémons et Cacodémons." Erdan admits that his knowledge of Swedenborg's life and works is extremely limited—he cites the Strasbourg *Abrégé* and a work by Emile Broussais as sources—but this does not prevent him from adopting an extremely critical view of the man and his doctrines. Erdan's criticisms begin with the man himself:

> Non! il n'y a pas là de somnambule. Il y a un home qui a sucé dans la maison paternèle la croyance aux aparitions d'esprits. Il y a un home qui

a toujours vécu célibataire, et chez lequel la nature est en désordre. Il y a
un home qui ne mange prèsque pas, et qui au dire de ses biografes, boit
du café cinq à siz fois par jour. Il y a un savant qui a toujours eu un
remarquable esprit d'analise, mais qui a presque toujours manqué de
droiture dans le jugement quand il a fallu sintétiser. Il y a un esprit
fatigué de ses études multipliées et profondes. Il y a une nature prédis-
posée au délire. Il y a un fou: voilà ce qu'il y a. (32–33)

Erdan's analysis of Swedenborg's representation of love is equally simplis-
tic, although one does wish he had taken on the subject of angelic sexuality:

> Une autre idée de Swedenborg, c'est que l'amour consiste essensiele-
> ment en ceci: L'home est le bien; la femme est le vrai (Oh! oh! oh!) et
> alors, quoi de plus simple? L'amour, c'est l'union du bien et du vrai; ce
> que l'home aime dans la femme, c'est le vrai, et ce que la femme aime
> dans l'home, c'est le bien. (37)

Erdan criticizes the style and quantity of Swedenborg's works, their lack of
originality, and prosaic nature. Like Blake, he prefers Dante: "Je donerais
toutes les visions célestes et infernales de Swedenborg pour vingt vers de
Dante . . ." (23) Like Grégoire, he finds the practices of contemporary
Swedenborgians absurd; unlike Grégoire, however, he sees them as typical
of French sectarianism at this time:

> . . . [j]e dois le dire sincèrement, ce que je conais de la secte sweden-
> borgiène à Paris est si faible, si profondément illogique, que je ne puis me
> décider à entrer dans le détail de ce qu'a produit parmi nous la Nouvèle
> Jérusalem. Le seul moyen de tenir ce chapitre à un certain hauteur, c'est
> d'étudier Swedenborg lui-même. Cet étude, je l'espère, aura quelque util-
> ité; ele arachera son voile à une idole qui n'est respectable que parce
> qu'ele est cachée, et, de plus, ele jetera un jour lumineuz sur les origines
> de cet immense mouvement spiritualist dont les deuz mondes vienent
> d'être témoins. (20)

The hallucinations of a solitude-crazed Swede, in other words, not
only point to the origins, but also suggest the nature and implications, of
contemporary sectarian beliefs. Erdan's ironic and often ill-informed consideration of various sects, including Swedenborgianism, serves to distance
himself and the reader from the esoteric and utopian themes surrounding
the popular cause in 1848.

The poet, Gérard Labrunie or Gérard de Nerval, as he called himself, also surveyed the context of late-eighteenth- and early-nineteenth-

century esotericism in a collection of essays written between 1839 and 1850 and known as *Les Illuminés, ou les précurseurs du socialisme*. As the title indicates, the poet was interested in the connections between esotericism and politics: there are fragments of a second collection on nineteenth-century writers on esoteric and social themes. But Nerval also emphasized the aesthetic aspects of these doctrines, as well as their relation to abnormal psychological states. His poetry draws on a wide variety of esoteric traditions, as freemasons and their interpreters had done the century before. Indeed, both the eclecticism of *Les Illuminés* and its frequent references to freemasonry and other secret societies suggest that Nerval's work draws either on masonic rites or on the kinds of all-embracing mythologies, such as those of Pernety, Dupuis, or even Richer, invented to explain or construct them.

It is ironic that Paul Valéry, in his review of Martin Lamm's book on Swedenborg, cites Nerval as one of the "sources" for his knowledge of the Swede, because the references to Swedenborg in *Les Illuminés*, which contains essays on many other esoteric and pseudoscientific figures of the time, are few and oblique at best.

Two occur in the context of an essay on Cazotte (1847). The poet mentions that the practices of the masonic lodge at Lyons owed more to the doctrines of one of the founders of French illuminism, Martinez de Pasqually, than to Swedenborg. The second links Swedenborg and the doctrine of correspondences to turn-of-the-century millenarianism:

> Rien dans la masse d'écrits qu'on a conservés de cette époque de la vie de Cazotte n'indique un affaiblissement quelconque dans ses facultés intellectuelles. Ses révélations, toujours empreintes de ses opinions monarchiques, tendent à présenter dans tout ce qui se passe alors des rapports avec les vagues prédictions de l'Apocalypse. C'est ce que l'école de Swedenborg appelle la science des correspondances. (2:1164)

This apparently slight reference is all there is in *Les Illuminés* to tie the doctrine of correspondences to the poetics of Nerval's work.

The essay on Cagliostro (1850) refers to the French Swedenborgian Pernety and his work on hermeticism and again to Swedenborgianism as part of the masonic movement. Both occur in the section of the essay entitled "Du mysticisme révolutionnaire."

Of the Swedenborgians, Nerval writes:

> Ensuite les *convulsionnaires* et certaines sectes du jansénisme; vers 1770, les *martinistes*, les *swedenborgiens*, et enfin les illuminés, dont la doctrine, fondée d'abord en Allemagne par Weisshaupt, se répandit bientôt en France où elle se fondit dans l'institution maçonnique. (2:1175)

The "illuminés" Nerval writes of here were a German radical secret society often believed to be part of a revolutionary conspiracy.

Finally, several references to Swedenborgianism occur in Nerval's extremely ironic discussion of the Polish theosopher Towiansky. These are by far the most specific references to Swedenborgianism in *Les Illuminés* and they do not indicate that Nerval had much respect or reverence for Swedenborg or his doctrines. As for Erdan, the apparent absurdity of Swedenborg's doctrines pointed up the absurdity of more recent writers' work. On the subject of Swedenborg and Towiansky, Nerval writes:

> Ceux-là qui sont des philosophes, car il y en a aussi de tous états, arrivent dans leur dispute à un moment si ardu et si embrouillé, leurs discours s'imprègnent tellement de sophismes et de paradoxes grossiers, que le jour spirituel qui les éclaire s'affaiblit, et que l'erreur descend matériellement en colonnes sombres dans le palais céleste où ils sont rassemblés. Alors un ange d'un ciel supérieur descend vers eux, rétablit les questions sous leur vrai jour et dissipe ainsi l'obscurité. (2:1224)

And further, regarding Towiansky's argumentation:

> N'est-ce pas là une discussion à obscurcir le ciel lui-même, comme dans la fameuse dispute des anges philosophes de Swedenborg? (2:1224)

Nerval's brief and ironic references to Swedenborg and Swedenborgianism in *Les Illuminés* suggest that for this writer these doctrines played a very small role in the larger context of eighteenth-century esotericism. Whereas for Erdan, however, esoteric elements in contemporary political theory pointed up the absurdity of these doctrines, for Nerval they transposed the vision of would-be social reformers into the inner world of dreams and madness. His most telling reference to Swedenborg links the doctrine of correspondences to predictions of the end of the world. Nerval looks back with nostalgia at the millenarian doctrines of the late eighteenth century; in his own work, however, the notion of the end of history points to the limits of consciousness and the end of meaning.

If Nerval's remarks concerning Swedenborg in *Les Illuminés* are brief and disparaging, at least one of his prose works, the novella *Sylvie* suggests a general sense in which the poet's temporal understanding of the doctrine of correspondences contributed to a poetics that emphasized the presence of the past within the present.

In *Sylvie* (1850), the hero undertakes a journey from Paris into the countryside, leaving behind the world of the theater and the city for nature and the rituals of the peasants. His trip takes him from the worlds of artifice into nature, from the present into the past, and his journey through time and space teaches him not only that the past survives into the present, but also that the present is, in many respects, no more than a repetition of the past. A passage near the beginning of the text links this discovery to the experience of disillusionment he and his generation underwent in the years following the Revolution of 1830:

> Nous vivions alors dans une époque étrange, comme celles qui d'ordinaire succèdent aux révolutions ou aux abaissements des grands règnes. Ce n'était plus la galanterie héroïque comme sous la Fronde, le vice élégant et paré comme sous la Régence, le scepticisme et les folles orgies du Directoire; c'était un mélange d'activité, d'hésitation et de paresse, d'utopies brillantes, d'aspirations philosophiques ou religieuses, d'enthousiasmes vagues, mêlés de certains instincts de renaissance; d'ennui des discordes passées, d'espoirs incertains,—quelque chose comme l'époque de Pérégrinus et d'Apulée. (1:266)

The strange brilliance of the years following 1830 appears to be repeated in those following 1848. The apparent correspondence between present and past is underscored by the narrator's encounter with a young peasant woman who resembles a lost love of his youth and the dead woman herself. In the context of esotericism and pseudoscience at the time *Sylvie* was published, communication with the dead was often associated with Swedenborgianism. One need not look for a relationship of influence, however, to see that the concept of language associated with Swedenborg's doctrine of correspondences has in Nerval's work taken on the connotation of a "correspondence" between past and present and of the attempt to recover, through writing, an experience of wholeness which is unattainable, except in the writer's dreams.

7. Swedenborgianism and Popular Culture

In *Mesmerism and the End of the Enlightenment in France*, Robert Darnton characterized Swedenborgianism and other forms of religious sectarianism in late-eighteenth- and nineteenth-century France as a "source of the irrational" for postrevolutionary thinkers eager to "develop a nonorthodox system that would account for irrationality and the existence of evil." (127) While this view certainly accords with the views of writers such as Alexandre Erdan, who were eager to distance themselves and their readers from popular political movements, and of Joseph de Maistre, whose emphasis on evil served to bolster his authoritarian views, it does not match the transformations of Swedenborgian doctrines in France during these years.

French writers, we have seen, turned to aspects of Swedenborgian doctrines because they helped them make sense of political and cultural issues: they supplemented and explained existing masonic rites; they provided a key, some writers believed, for the interpretation of the dreams and visions they experienced in connection with the seances of Mesmerists and animal magnetists; they pointed the way to a reconciliation of Catholicism and other religious and mythological traditions; and they suggested that individual conviction was a source of authority for anyone, including the marginal and excluded. French Swedenborgians most often had good reasons for turning to these doctrines. Those who characterized their choice as irrational—at least in the nineteenth century—usually disagreed with them on other matters, such as politics or aesthetics.

If this chapter has taken issue with Darton's contention that Swedenborgianism was a source of irrationalism in nineteenth-century French culture, however, it has thus far left unquestioned his assumption that Swedenborgianism belongs to popular culture. My chronicle of transformations of Swedenborgianism in France between 1780 and 1865, in fact, follows his account of Mesmerism closely. But what does the term "popular culture" mean? And can one fit all French interpreters of Swedenborgianism under its umbrella?

Certainly, Matter and Erdan (not to mention Baudelaire!) would resist this classification, although their disdain for writers they considered beneath them points to one common definition of popular culture, a definition that aligns "popular culture" with "mass culture," the culture of the faceless crowd: it comes from the "people," but is a term used only by individuals who do not see themselves as part of this group. Except for Constant/Lévi and Cahagnet, however, none of the individuals I have discussed belong to the people in the sense that they come from families of artisans, workers, or peasants. Is popular culture then defined by its rejection by members of the scientific and cultural elite? This seems to be one of the definitions that informs Darnton's discussion of Mesmerism, which certainly was disdained by the scientific community in nineteenth-century France and it also characterizes one aspect of the reception of Swedenborgianism in late-eighteenth- and nineteenth-century France: that most of the individuals who were drawn to it were in some sense outsiders who turned to a cult not officially recognized in a Catholic country. But Darnton includes far more literary texts in his discussion than I have in this chapter. Is popular culture, is popular Swedenborgianism, then, set off from the literary canon? If so, how and why?

Recent disputes about the nature of the canon and its classics, the debates concerning the existence and nature of multicultural courses on university campuses, for example, have emphasized the extent to which definitions of culture and its distinctions are negotiated and subject to change. It would be misleading, I think, to insist on a rigid distinction between "literary" and "nonliterary" interpretations of Swedenborgianism in nineteenth-century France. One of the reasons I have included Nerval in this chapter is that his work, which ranges from journalism to highly esoteric poetry, suggests how difficult it is to characterize a writer as belonging wholly to either context. I have separated off my discussion of Balzac and Baudelaire, then, not only because they use Swedenborgian doctrines in particularly rich ways but also because in their works Swedenborg's doctrine of correspondences is closely bound up with new concepts of literary structure and effect, with the very ways of distinguishing literature from other uses of language. But the kinds of distinctions that Balzac and Baudelaire are beginning to incorporate into their writing are also bound up with new definitions of popular culture in France after 1840.

Not for nothing do we notice a clear stand-off in the 1840s and 1850s between writers such as Constant/Lévi and Cahagnet, on the one hand, and Baudelaire, Erdan, and Matter, on the other. There is more at stake than a battle for literary turf in the belittlement of Constant/Lévi in the article attributed to Baudelaire, for the article suggests that the kind of distinctions the author wished to make were up for grabs and that what mattered was the very act of distinction itself. In his study, *Distinction*, the French sociologist, Pierre Bourdieu, has argued that modern culture relies on a conflation of aesthetic and class distinctions, and, indeed, that aesthetic complexity often serves the interests of class distinctions. If Bourdieu draws his evidence from surveys of cultural preferences in the 1960s and 1970s, however, his conclusions are also highly suggestive for our understanding of French culture at the beginning of the Second Empire—probably because in a society in which all kinds of social distinction were increasingly called into question, aesthetic and cultural distinctions came to the fore.

The splintering off we have seen of interpretations of Swedenborgianism into points of view related to class and professional identity points to a larger transformation in concepts of popular and elite culture in mid-nineteenth-century France. Historians of early modern Europe, such as Peter Burke, write of a kind of cultural bilingualism among the social elite: aristocrats, he argues, knew, loved, and participated in the rituals and festivities of the other orders in society. The literary theorist, Bakhtin, makes a similar point about literature in the age of Rabelais: that the texts of a learned writer such as the French doctor were likely to capture and represent points of view related to very different kinds of social standing; that some early modern texts are multivoiced or polyphonic.[13] It may well be that the apparent openness and tolerance of the points of view of those of different social ranks in the art and culture of early modern Europe reflect a certain security in a world in which everyone's place was well defined. What does seem certain is that by the first half of the nineteenth century, tolerance of the rites and rituals of social others diminishes, especially when the others belong to the still disenfranchised ranks of artisans, workers, and peasants.

Erdan's contempt for the sectarian and utopian cults he discusses is perhaps exemplary in this regard, for in both style and spelling he places himself and his text outside of the bounds of elite writing and literature in mid-nineteenth-century France. He/I/we are not the ones we most resemble. The writers I discuss in the second part of this study, Balzac and Baudelaire, are as anxious as Erdan to distinguish themselves and their work from writers of the people and their causes, and yet their texts point beyond the sympathies of their writers. If Balzac and Baudelaire both evoke little aesthetic worlds that mirror, but are separate from, the larger world of experience, their texts also embrace, albeit in distorted form, the points of view of social and aesthetic others, including practitioners of doctrines such as Swedenborgianism and Mesmerism which, as we have seen, in mid-nineteenth-century Paris were often identified with the cause of the working or popular classes.

PART II

Fictions of Wholeness:
Swedenborgianism and the French Canon

CHAPTER FOUR

The Underside of History: Swedenborgianism and La comédie humaine

During the early 1830s, Balzac composed a series of novels with fantastic themes that he eventually came to group together in a section of *La comédie humaine* called *Les études philosophiques*. Sometimes denigrated by critics who would like to see Balzac as a serious novelist preoccupied with contemporary society, rather than what they regard as superstition, this section of *La comédie humaine* includes two works, *Louis Lambert* and *Séraphîta*, which refer extensively to Swedenborg and Swedenborgianism. Both written—and rewritten—between 1832 and 1835, these novels certainly do present a contrast to the narratives depicting both the city and the country in by far the largest section of *La comédie humaine, Les études de moeurs. Louis Lambert* recounts the life of a genius who fails to make his way in society and pays little attention to the details of contemporary life; *Séraphîta* takes place in an elaborately constructed landscape, the frigid and snowy fjords of an imaginary Norway, but its protagonist, an androgyn who also dies by the end of the novel, is as solitary as Louis Lambert. Both novels, moreover, bear the clear imprint of Germanic philosophy and aesthetics: if Louis Lambert has an early encounter with Mme de Staël, the popularizer of German culture in France, *Séraphîta* takes an admirer on a tour that includes the viewing of a mysterious green flower that looks very much like a transposition of a prominent emblem of German Romanticism, Novalis's *blaue Blume*.

While much recent work on Balzac has focused on the role of fantastic themes in the *construction* of contemporary society in his novels, few critics have attempted to situate *Louis Lambert* and *Séraphîta* in the context of the novel cycle or to consider the relation of his references to Swedenborgianism to the popularization of Swedenborgianism in France. They have focused mainly on the hybrid *Etudes philosophiques*, such as *La peau de chagrin* or *L'histoire des treize*, which relate visionary and fantastic themes explicitly to the representation of contemporary society, especially the city. But *Louis Lambert* and *Séraphîta* are important for our understanding of *La comédie humaine* both because they represent an extended meditation on and an attempt to systematize some of the visionary themes sketched out elsewhere and also because they suggest, even at this early date, the indebtedness of Balzac's fiction to popular culture, an indebtedness that becomes increasingly apparent in his novels of the 1840s.

Other than *Louis Lambert* and *Séraphîta*, there are relatively few references to Swedenborg in *La comédie humaine*, but they do occur in one of the earliest works to be included, *La peau de chagrin* (1831), as well as two of the latest, *Le cousin Pons* (1847) and *L'envers de l'histoire contemporaine* (1848). These references point to the continuing importance of Swedenborgianism for Balzac's construction of a novel system that became ever more ambitious and ever more idiosyncratic and personal.

Balzac's system, of course, cannot be identified with Swedenborg or Swedenborgianism alone. This is true even for *Louis Lambert* and *Séraphîta*. Many of his novels, including some of the greatest in *Les études de moeurs*, such as *Illusions perdues*, emphasize the importance of visionary themes without mentioning Swedenborg. But I shall argue here that references to Swedenborg, his doctrines, and French interpretations of them in *La comédie humaine* provide a red thread through the novelist's attempts to work out the nature and importance of contemporary theories of the afterworld and of language for his fictional world.

1. Swedenborgianism and Representation in *La comédie humaine*

The title of one of the last works by Balzac to be published during his lifetime, *L'envers de l'histoire contemporaine*, refers back to a passage in *Séraphîta*:

> Il est en nous-mêmes de longues luttes dont le terms se trouve peut-être une de nos actions et qui font comme un envers à l'humanité. Cet envers est à Dieu, l'endroit est aux hommes. Plus d'une fois Séraphîta s'était plu à prouver à Wilfrid qu'elle connaissait cet envers si varié qui compose une seconde vie à la plupart des hommes. (11:797)

In *Séraphîta*, the notion of a hidden underside to human existence provides moral justification for the acceptance of the limitation of desire and a restricted role in society. The one reference to Swedenborg in *L'envers de l'histoire contemporaine* also relates his doctrines to an ethic of suffering and renunciation:

Dieu réserve-t-il ces dernières, ces cruelles épreuves à celles de ses
créatures qui doivent s'asseoir près de lui le lendemain de leur mort? dit
le bonhomme Alain, sans savoir qu'il exprimait naïvement toute la doctrine de Swedenborg sur les anges. (8:318)

But in *L'envers de l'histoire contemporaine*, the inner world of *Séraphîta*
has been transformed into a vision of the underside of Parisian society, a
world associated with the darkest and oldest parts of Paris, with poverty,
crime, and disease, and with mysterious forces which apparently transform
individuals into crowds.

References to Swedenborg or Swedenborgianism occur in eight narrative works in *La comédie humaine*, as well as the Avant-propos, the
programmatic introduction to the whole written in 1842. In the *Etudes
philosophiques*, Swedenborgian doctrines serve as a model for the representation of unconscious processes; the later works in *Les études de
moeurs* shift focus to the unconscious or marginal aspects of the history of
society as a whole, and from individual consciousness to the body and to
the social world, which is depicted in terms of an organism corresponding
to the human body. There are no references to Swedenborg in the third
section of the cycle described in the Avant-propos, *Les études physiologiques*, but it is important to remember the importance Balzac accorded to
the body and its desires, both around 1830 and later. *Les études philosophiques* seem to have grown out of his reaction to the events of the Revolution of 1830, a reaction that took the form of a conviction that individualism and desire were dangerous and needed to be restrained; visionary
themes, however, play a vital role throughout his work in allowing him to
imagine and depict desire and its consequences.

Swedenborgianism in *La comédie humaine* is linked both to the affirmation of the continuity between all forms of life, visible and invisible,
natural and social, and to a belief in the separateness of spheres, a separateness which is expressed not only in the depiction of class differences,
but also in statements concerning the incomprehensibility of God and the
necessary conflict between individual consciousness and desire, and the
social order. In *Les études philosophiques*, Swedenborgianism represents
one pole of an opposition first described in *La peau de chagrin*, the conflict between *Volonté* and *Savoir*. The counterpart to Swedenborgian *Savoir* is Mesmerist *Volonté*. The oppositions evoked in the context of references to Swedenborgianism have been renamed in our century: Curtius,
for example, suggests that the central conflict in Balzac's work is between
magic and mysticism; Philippe Bertault argues that Balzac's religiosity is
marked by a penchant towards both mysticism and a belief in rationalist
science and the mediating structures of Catholic tradition.[1]

The Avant-propos opens with an analogy between the structures of society and the animal world. According to the Avant-propos, both natural and social species have evolved from an original and unknowable unity. The role of the doctrines of Swedenborg and Mesmer, as well as other pseudoscientific and esoteric thinkers, is to extend the taxonomic structures of natural history beyond the limits of perception, thus making possible the depiction and classification of most forms of human consciousness and, therefore, man, *homo duplex* himself. The doctrines of Swedenborg and Mesmer are, however, incapable of comprehending either the totality of creation or the mentality of the genius. Within the deterministic structures described by the allegorical correspondence between consciousness and the natural world, the genius is free. Here Balzac's interpretation of Swedenborgianism serves as a model for the representation of the freedom of the individual:

> Ceux qui veulent apercevoir chez moi l'intention de considérer l'homme comme une créature finie se trompent donc étrangement. *Séraphîta*, la doctrine en action du Bouddha chrétien, me semble une réponse suffisante à cette accusation assez légèrement avancée d'ailleurs. (1:16)

In a letter to Eve Hanska, Balzac pointed to a major idiosyncracy in his interpretation of Swedenborgianism: "Le Swedenborgisme," he wrote, "qui n'est qu'une répétition dans le sens chrétien d'anciennes idées, est ma religion, *avec l'augmentation que j'y fais de l'incompréhensibilité de Dieu*." (1:510; my emphasis) For Swedenborg, God, as well as the spiritual world, was inaccessible to those of inferior intelligence, but He was not unknowable. Balzac's modification of Swedenborgianism transformed Swedenborg into a mystic and brought his beliefs into line with the precepts of biological transformism, which postulated an unrecoverable unity as the origin of the natural world, as well as the doctrines of conservative political philosophers, such as Bonald and Maistre, who had argued that the social world devolved from God, who made His presence felt only through the mediating forms of tradition.[2] The invisible taxonomies suggested by the doctrines of Swedenborg and other esoteric thinkers enable the writer to map out the presence, beneath the surfaces of contemporary French society, of a hidden hierarchical order based on the structures of natural history, theology, and feudal tradition. The representation of this hidden order is a central aspect of the aesthetics of the novel and its utopian possibilities: "L'histoire n'a pas pour loi, comme le roman," Balzac writes in the Avant-propos, "de tendre vers le beau idéal. L'histoire est ou devrait être ce qu'elle fut; tandis que *le roman doit être le monde meilleur*, a dit Mme Necker, un des esprits les plus distingués du dernier siècle." (1:15)

Balzac's interpretation of Swedenborgianism not only diverges from the doctrines of Swedenborg in this important respect, but also appears to have been based on a limited knowledge of Swedenborg's works. In *Les études philosophiques*, Swedenborgianism is linked principally to the concept of an immutable hierarchical order informing nature, consciousness, and society, and to the visionary individual, often described as an angel, who is able to see beyond appearances and to get in touch with a spiritual reality inaccessible to most human beings and beyond the limits of language. In *Les études de moeurs*, the interiority of the visionary individual comes to be associated with the hidden places and interiors of the city, and the unknowable God with the mysterious resonance of objects in the city, a resonance which suggests a lost experience of unity and wholeness.

Critics who have taken up the issue of the relationship of Balzac's work to Swedenborgian doctrines have usually done so from the point of view of sources or the contribution Swedenborgianism may have made to the literary system the novelist worked out in the years 1830–1835.[3] Although there has been some speculation concerning what Balzac may have read by or about Swedenborg, there is little evidence concerning this question outside the novels themselves. Balzac's mother was interested in illuminism, but we know little concerning her beliefs.[4] *Séraphîta* lists seven works by Swedenborg, and we know that Balzac sent an order to his bookbinder for the binding of eight unspecified volumes by Swedenborg.[5] It is possible only to suggest parallels among Balzac's works and those by Swedenborg and his interpreters. The genetic studies of Philippe Bertault, Maurice Bardèche, and Bernard Guyon have attempted to place Swedenborgianism in the larger context of Balzac's interest in natural history, political theory, and intellectual and social history during this period; they have emphasized the systematic nature of Balzac's interpretation and its close association with the the theories of contemporary natural history, especially the work of Geoffroy Saint-Hilaire. What these studies fail to take into account, however, is the marginal nature of Swedenborgianism in France at this time and the changing function of these doctrines in works of *La comédie humaine* written after 1840.

The histories of the intellectual development of characters such as Balthazar Claës in *La recherche de l'Absolu*, Louis Lambert, and Denis Minoret in *Ursule Mirouët* suggest that Balzac was quite familiar with the historical development of esoteric and pseudoscientific doctrines and that he saw their role as ideological in nature: they pointed the way beyond the materialism of the Enlightenment to a new synthetic philosophy capable of undoing the work of the Revolution of 1789. The utopian associations of esoteric and pseudoscientific doctrines are closely allied with their representational function in *La comédie humaine*: the hierarchical taxonomic system Balzac describes in the Avant-propos applies less to the way things are than the way he believes they should be. Mesmerist and Swedenborgian doctrines suggest the presence beneath the surfaces of nature and society of a hidden hierarchical order often in conflict with the status quo. But perhaps the most important connection between the work of Balzac and esoteric doctrines is the concept of the hieroglyph. In Swedenborg's work, the concept of a natural language had been closely related to the development of his doctrine of correspondences, a key for the "natural" exegesis of the Scriptures and also a system for the allegorical representation of the relationship among nature, consciousness, and an invisible spiritual world. In *La comédie humaine*, a passage near the beginning of *Louis Lambert* focuses on the recent history of the concept of the hieroglyph and its implications for the development of the protagonist who, as a child, manifested an extraordinary love of reading—in both nature and books. (11:591–92) And throughout *La comédie humaine*, language is characterized as possessing a mysterious power—"l'occulte puissance des noms," Balzac calls it in *Ursule Mirouët*. (3:372) The etymologies of words and names in *La comédie humaine* often suggest natural characteristics of the people or things they refer to, and the identities of names in genealogies point to a concept of history as an ever-repeating process, its cycles limited by the structures inherent in nature, consciousness, and language. In the works of the 1840s, especially, the concept of the hieroglyph is closely related to the novelist's representation of the city in terms of an organism which preserves the myths and life forms of different epochs in its strata. Finally, Swedenborgian doctrines form an important part of the novelist's attempt to endow the disparate objects of city life with a sense of a sacred wholeness, or what Walter Benjamin has called an *aura*.[6]

It is extremely doubtful that Swedenborg can be named as the sole or even the major source for any of these themes in *La comédie humaine*. Balzac's interpretation of Swedenborgian doctrines and the hieroglyph shows, however, that he understood the context of eighteenth- and nineteenth-century esotericism and pseudoscience well. Although he may have read very little of Swedenborg's work, in *La comédie humaine*, Balzac transmitted a literary myth of Swedenborg which was, perhaps in spite of itself, relatively faithful to the original.

2. Balzac's "Swedenborgianism" and Its Contexts

In his essay "The Concept of Romanticism in Literary History," René Wellek writes: "A study of Balzac's religious views reveals that he declared himself a Swedenborgian many times." (174)[7] Wellek speaks for many critics who have taken the expositions of Swedenborgian doctrines in

Louis Lambert and *Séraphîta*—where in both cases they are presented by
a skeptical and ironic narrator—as evidence of the author's religious beliefs. Outside *La comédie humaine*, the few references to Swedenborg or
Swedenborgianism are scarcely less ironic. In his letter to Charles Nodier
of October 1832 and in five letters to Madame Hanska written between
1836 and 1841, Balzac emphasizes the secular context of his interest in
Swedenborgianism. The doctrines of Swedenborgianism mediate between
science and aesthetics, and provide a model for the mapping out of human
consciousness. Furthermore, Swedenborgianism enters into the language
of gallantry with which Balzac attempted to woo an aristocratic foreigner
who lived hundreds of miles from Paris.

In his letter to Nodier, Balzac criticizes Nodier's article, "De la palingénésie humaine et de la résurrection," for its failure to recognize the
limits of science. Balzac suggests that Nodier's speculations, like those of
"mystics" such as Swedenborg, Saint-Martin, and Madame Guyon, are
fictions useful for what they reveal about the operations of human consciousness, but which in themselves have no truth value. Balzac describes
Swedenborg's works as "ces oeuvres mystiques où les abîmes de l'infini
semblent organisés, et où bien des intelligences trop faibles, trop fortes
peut-être, aiment à se perdre comme un voyageur dans les souterrains de
Rome"; his characterization makes it seem probable that he had read very
little of Swedenborg's work, but the architectural comparison will recur
in later works of *La comédie humaine* in connection with references to
Swedenborgianism and other esoteric and pseudoscientific doctrines. Balzac furthermore suggests that Nodier's concept of a superman, his "être
compréhensif," can be traced back to Swedenborg's concept of the angel.
(582) For Balzac, Nodier's principal mistake was that he attempted to describe the totality of the world in conceptual language, rather than in the
language of literature, which alone is capable of evoking a unity that
eludes the discourses of both analytical science and metaphysics.

In contrast, all of the references to Swedenborg in the letters to Madame Hanska reflect Balzac's desire to please his aristocratic correspondent by referring to a "mystical" doctrine which interested her, rather than
a burning personal interest in the doctrines themselves or the issues they
raise.

The earliest reference occurs in a letter dated the end of June 1836, in
the context of a commentary on *Séraphîta*, which he had dedicated to
Madame Hanska. Here Balzac emphasizes the heterodoxy of Swedenborgianism and places Swedenborg in the context of other religious thinkers
such as Saint Theresa, Fénelon, Boehme, and Saint-Martin.

The letter of May 31, 1837 contains what at first glance appears to be
Balzac's most unequivocal statement of his belief in Swedenborgianism:

"Le Swedenborgisme qui n'est qu'une répétition dans le sens chrétien d'anciennes idées, est ma religion, avec l'augmentation que j'y fais de l'incompréhensibilité de Dieu." (1:510)

The statement takes issue with one of the central tenets of Swedenborg's work and doctrines—the comprehensibility of the Absolute. An examination of the immediate context of the statement suggests further limitations. Balzac's declaration appears to have been made in response to Madame Hanska's query concerning his religious beliefs and it appears that she made the future of their relationship rest on this issue. The situation echoes the dialogue between Faust and Gretchen in the scene in Martha's garden in which Gretchen asks whether Faust believes in God and he evades the issue with a vague declaration of pantheistic beliefs. Whether or not Madame Hanska and Balzac were conscious of the parallel—given the extent to which the language of "Germanic mysticism" colored their dialogue, it is difficult to believe they were not—Balzac apparently felt it necessary to give a more specific reply to his correspondent and one which, at least superficially, denied the pantheistic tendencies of Goethe and the German Romantics.[8]

"Votre lettre me fait beaucoup de mal," Balzac writes:

> Croyez-moi, il y a dans les idées religieuses une certaine mesure au delà de laquelle tout est vicieux. Vous savez quelles sont mes religions, je ne suis point orthodoxe et ne crois pas à l'Eglise romaine; je trouve que s'il y a quelque plan digne de Dieu, ce sont les transformations humaines faisant marcher l'être vers des zones inconnues, c'est la loi des créations qui nous sont inférieures, ce doit être la loi des créations supérieures. Le Swedenborgisme qui n'est qu'une répétition dans le sens chrétien d'anciennes idées, est ma religion, avec l'augmentation que j'y fais de l'incompréhensibilité de Dieu. (1:510)

The declaration of Swedenborgian belief with the contradictory denial of pantheism is all but overshadowed by the reference to biological transformism. Yet perhaps what we are looking at in this apparent attempt to placate Madame Hanska is one of the origins of the strange marriage between Swedenborgianism and natural history later elaborated in the Avant-propos to *La comédie humaine* and elsewhere.

The letter of November 7, 1837 refers to Swedenborg in the context of the ability of Romantic music (here, above all, the work of Beethoven) to evoke a synaesthetic effect:

> J'aurais voulu être plutôt Beethoven que Rossini et que Mozart. Il y a dans cet homme une puissance divine. Dans son *finale*, il semble qu'un

enchanteur vous enlève dans un monde merveilleux, au milieu des plus beaux palais qui réunissent les merveilles de tous les arts et là, à son commandement, des portes, semblables à celle du Baptistère, tournent sur leurs gonds et vous laissent apercevoir des beautés d'un genre inconnu, les fées de la fantaisie, ce sont des créatures qui voltigent avec les beautés de la femme et les ailes diaprées de l'ange, et vous êtes inondé de l'air supérieur, de cet air qui selon Swedenborg, change et répand des parfums, qui a la couleur et le sentiment et qui afflue et qui vous beautifie. (1:554)

And the letter of June 4, 1839 links Swedenborg to a certain kind of language which appears incomprehensible:

Je ne sais pas si des phrases ne vous paraîtront pas du Swedenborg, mais comme elles tiennent à mon histoire, je vous les expliquerai quelque jour. (1:647)

The reference to sentences which "paraîtront . . . du Swedenborg" reduces to a cliché the potential role of the apparently incomprehensible and irrational language of mystics which Balzac explores more seriously in *Séraphîta* and other works.

The final reference to Swedenborg suggests how allusions both to Swedenborg and to women as angels in *La comédie humaine* are informed by a discourse which identifies women with the sublime and uses this identification to justify their claustration in marriage and the family:

Décidément l'envoi du v[otre] profil, chère adorée, est une coquetterie, car on croirait voir une jeune fille; mais j'y vois q[ue]lq[ue] chose de plus saint, de plus sacré qui m'émeut aux larmes, c'est une preuve de cette gracieuse affection qui semble renaître par une nouvelle offrande, et mon coeur vous a répondu de toutes ses fibres, par tous ses sentiments. J'ai reconnu l'âme de mon choix, la créature élue, tout ce qu'il y a de beau et de bon pour moi, comme dit Swedenborg, l'élégance de la maison, et ce que j'ai pris la liberté d'appeler *le beau moi* de l'homme. Plus j'ai connu l'espoir d'une existence sans nuage, d'une entente de toutes les heures et d'un attachement également senti. (2:160)

References to Swedenborg in the correspondence with Madame Hanska reveal little concerning the details of Balzac's knowledge of Swedenborgianism. What they do suggest, however, are the sexual (and sexist) connotations of a discourse which purports to provide a key to the true nature of both the "other" world and the "other" sex.

3. Desire and Tradition: The Other Worlds of *Les études philosophiques*

Le livre mystique

Most of the references to Swedenborg or Swedenborgianism in *La comédie humaine* occur in two novels, *Louis Lambert* and *Séraphîta*, published together in 1835 as the second and third works of a trilogy entitled *Le livre mystique*. In these two novels, Balzac attempts to develop a system which would draw together and explain his use, in earlier works, of different kinds of esoteric and pseudoscientific themes to represent individual consciousness and its relationship to the world.

From the "Avertissement du *Gars*" to *Louis Lambert*

The preface to the first version of *Les Chouans* entitled *Le Gars*, the "Avertissement du *Gars*," probably written in 1828,[9] recounts the biography of the pseudonymous author Victor Morillon, who in some respects appears to be the prototype for Louis Lambert. *Les Chouans*, which went through several titles as well as revisions, is the first novel Balzac signed with his own name and later chose to include in *La comédie humaine*. None of the versions of *Les Chouans* contains any reference to Swedenborg, and the narrative itself, which focuses melodramatically on a fictional episode of love and betrayal in the Chouan uprising in 1799, can scarcely be characterized as visionary or fantastic. Nevertheless, the remarkable parallels between the "Avertissement du *Gars*" and *Louis Lambert* suggest that Balzac's interest in Swedenborgianism grew out of his preoccupation with a Leibnizean model of the mind as a little mirror capable of reflecting and expressing the universe in its totality.

Born in 1788 to a tanner and his wife, Victor Morillon showed an early passion for reading. Educated by an Oratorian in hiding during the Revolution, he often escaped into the countryside with his books. He was orphaned at an early age, and left to his own devices. As a young man, he was found by a teacher at the Collège de Vendôme, who was impressed by his extensive knowledge of modern literature and ancient—especially Oriental—languages. The teacher was able to procure him a position at the Collège, where he (like Balzac) wrote his first novel under the influence of Walter Scott. The brief account of the life of Victor Morillon revolves around the paradox that an isolated consciousness could perceive and express an entire world. In a central passage of the Avertissement, Balzac uses the Leibnizean metaphor of the *miroir concentrique* to describe the relationship of Victor Morillon's consciousness to the world:

> L'homme qui n'a d'imagination que ce qu'il en faut pour faire le soir
> ou le matin, en se couchant ou s'éveillant, cette rêverie délicieuse nommé

un château en Espagne, doit concevoir cette suave et mensongère existence plus brillante mille fois qu'une vie réelle et importune. Ces lignes
contiennent toute l'histoire de M. Victor Morillon. Les gens excentriques,
cherchant toujours à sortir d'un logis vide et querellant l'existence de ce
qu'elle ne leur fournit pas assez d'événements, ne trouveront dans cette
biographie de l'auteur ni faits, ni aventures. Il a eu cinq, sept, quinze,
vingt-cinq ans, trente-neuf ans et pas une pierre jetée dans l'eau n'a trou-
blé la surface de cette vie pleine, limpide et profonde, semblable à un lac
tranquille et inconnu où viennent se réfléchir des milliers d'images, et où
s'élèvent aussi les vagues dans la tempête. Cette âme était enfin, selon la
magnifique expression de Leibniz, *un miroir concentrique de l'univers*.
(8:1675)

The metaphor of the *miroir concentrique* suggests that representation
originates in a mysterious correspondence between the expressive powers
of consciousness and the world which enables a solitary consciousness to
capture the entirety of the world, rather than merely imitating a model—
as in neoclassical aesthetics—or reproducing a "squelette chronologique."
(8:1680) Language and aesthetic models, however, mediate between the
artist's vision and his expression of this vision in a work of art. Thus,
Victor Morillon's childhood reading and interest in Oriental languages
serve as important influences on the development of his imagination. And
an important passage affirms the importance of aesthetic models for stim-
ulating an artist's imagination. Attacking French critics who make an artificial distinction between imitation and inspiration, the narrator writes: "Je
ne sache pas qu'en Allemagne les critiques aient arrêté M. de Goethe, en
lui opposant qu'il ne serait que le Singe de Shakespeare." (8:1678) Further,
it is the novels of Scott that teach young Morillon about the world. Despite
its acknowledgement of the heuristic importance of language and aesthetic
models, however, the Avertissement tends to emphasize the spontaneity of
the artist's perception and representation of the world around him. It is
Morillon's childhood closeness to nature, rather than his early reading,
which stands at the origin of his later creative work. One passage in particular, emphasizes the organic nature of his development and relationship to
the world:

Orphelin de bonne heure, M. Victor Morillon végétait, pour ceux qui
vivent exclusivement de ce qu'ils digèrent, dans un état voisin de l'indi-
gence. N'importunant personne du spectacle de sa misère, il *poussait*
comme une plante, s'abandonnant à une contemplation perpetuelle possédé d'une haine curieuse pour les réalités et les corps, ignorant sa propre
existence physique; vivant, pour ainsi dire, par les seules forces de ces
sens intérieurs qui constituent, selon lui, un double être en l'homme,
mais épuisé par cette intuition profonde des choses. (8:1672)

In contrast, the opening pages of *Louis Lambert* dwell on the nature of the child's reading and interest in language, sketching out a theory of an original hieroglyphic language.

A far longer work, *Louis Lambert* emphasizes the role of time in perception and in the protagonist's development, which is depicted as occurring in stages. The concept of the mirroring consciousness, here called *Spécialité*, is temporalized; *Spécialité* grasps not only the total structure of the world, but also things in their original and future form. *Louis Lambert*, however, does not reject the notion of an immutable order underlying appearances in favor of a concept of historical development which would emphasize organic development and infinite possibilities of differentiation. The novel draws a distinction between human perception and the real order of things which has much in common with—and probably derives from—Kant's distinction between noumental and phenomenal worlds.

Seven editions of *Louis Lambert* were published during Balzac's lifetime: the *Notice biographique sur Louis Lambert*, published in the *Nouveaux contes philosophiques* in 1832 by Gosselin; the substantially expanded *Histoire intellectuelle de Louis Lambert*, published separately by Gosselin in 1833; the version included in the collection of *Études philosophiques* published by Werdet in 1836, but probably prepared between 1833 and 1835; the version published in the first edition of *Le livre mystique* in 1835; a corrected version included in the second edition of *Le livre mystique* in 1836; an edition titled *Louis Lambert*, published by Charpentier in 1842; and, finally, the Furne edition of 1846.[10] The text underwent substantial changes, mostly in the form of additions, between 1832 and 1835. Concerning Swedenborgianism, the most important of these additions are the summary of the *Traité de la Volonté* first included in the 1833 edition, and the fourth letter from Louis Lambert to his uncle and the series of philosophical fragments which make their appearance in the fourth edition. The text of 1835 is far more complex than the original *Notice biographique sur Louis Lambert*. In the 1835 edition, references to Swedenborgianism occur at three crucial moments in the narrative: during his childhood, he reads Swedenborg, whose works correspond to his innate visionary qualities; at the Collège de Vendôme, his passionate interest and belief in Swedenborgianism precede his construction of a philosophical system which unites theology and science; in the letter to his uncle, Louis Lambert writes that Swedenborgianism represents a universal religion capable of reconciling political and sectarian differences and of rejuvenating contemporary society. In all three cases, Swedenborgianism serves as a model or key explaining Louis Lambert's intellectual development, and representing moments in this process.

The narrator of *Louis Lambert* tells us that his friend's life falls into three stages: his childhood, school days, and adult life at Paris and Villenoix. (11:644) References to Swedenborg and Swedenborgianism occur at the beginning of each of these three stages, foreshadowing and providing a context for the understanding of Louis Lambert's intellectual development in the years that follow.

The first direct reference to Swedenborg or Swedenborgianism occurs near the beginning of the novel, when the child's future benefactor, Madame de Staël, comes upon him in a field while he is reading a copy of *Heaven and Hell*. Louis Lambert's interest in Swedenborg, however, forms part of his general passion for reading and language. Here the description of the child's early reading and concept of language parallels the Swedenborgian doctrine of correspondences as an interpretative key for the rediscovery of the original, inner, sense of the word. Louis Lambert's favorite reading was the Bible. The narrator poses the following series of rhetorical questions:

> Cette enfantine imagination comprit-elle déjà la mystérieuse profondeur des Ecritures, pouvait-elle suivre l'Esprit-Saint dans son vol à travers les mondes, s'éprit-elle seulement des romanesques attraits qui abondent en ces poèmes orientaux; ou, dans sa première innocence, cette âme sympathisa-t-elle avec le sublime religieux que des mains divines ont épanché dans ce livre? (11:589)

More important are the narrator's reflections on the child's early experience of language and meaning. These reflections lead from the interpretation of the Scriptures to the concept of an original, hieroglyphic language, to the question of the origins of language in sensation:

> La plupart des mots ne sont-ils pas teints de l'idée qu'ils représentent extérieurement? A quel génie sont-ils dus! S'il faut une grande intelligence pour créer un mot, quel âge a donc la parole humaine? L'assemblage des lettres, leurs formes, la figure qu'elles donnent à un mot, dessinent exactement, suivant le caractère de chaque peuple, des êtres inconnus dont le souvenir est en nous. Qui nous expliquera philosophiquement la transition de la sensation à la pensée, de la pensée au verbe, du verbe à son expression hiéroglyphique, des hiéroglyphes à l'alphabet, de l'alphabet à l'éloquence écrite, dont la beauté réside dans une suite d'images classées par les rhéteurs, et qui sont comme les hiéroglyphes de la pensée? L'antique peinture des idées humaines configurées par les formes zoologiques n'aurait-elle pas déterminé les premiers signes'dont s'est servi l'Orient pour écrire ses langages? Puis n'aurait-elle pas traditionnellement laissé quelques vestiges dans nos langues modernes, qui toutes se sont partagé des débris du verbe primitif des nations, verbe

majestueux et solennel, dont la majesté, dont la solenneté décroissent à
mesure que vieillissent les sociétés; dont les retentissements si sonores
dans la Bible hébraique si beaux encore dans la Grèce, s'affaiblissent à
travers les progrès de nos civilisations successives? (11:591–592)

This passage sketches the history of the concept of the origin of language
from eighteenth-century sensualism, with its preoccupation with the origins of language in sensation, through the work of conservative political
philosophers, such as Bonald and Maistre, who saw the conventions of
contemporary society, including language, as degenerate forms of an original, divinely inspired, system. The historicization of an eighteenth-century
philosophical and scientific concept we see here is typical of Balzac's treatment of scientific and pseudoscientific concepts. Thumbnail sketches of
the history of a concept or doctrine, such as the one in the passage above,
often serve to allegorize recent developments in French history and to
show how a concept gradually took on ideological connotations during the
decades following the Revolution of 1789. As we shall see, other such passages include the early history of Balthazar Claës's life and scientific interests in *La recherche de l'Absolu*, and the history of animal magnetism and
Swedenborgianism in *Ursule Miroüet*. In these works, Swedenborgianism
and Mesmerism mediate between the mechanistic and analytical science of
the Enlightenment—a science associated with a dangerous individualism
which isolates the individual and threatens to fragment society as a
whole—and organic concepts of society. In *Louis Lambert*, the narrator's
meditation on the origins of language and the nature of an original language also spans this development. The narrator's point of view, however,
has much in common with eighteenth-century rationalism; his dilemma is
that, while he recognizes destructive and sterile tendencies in the thought
and science of the previous century, he is unable to invent or believe in a
new synthesis.

  While at the Collège de Vendôme, the narrator tells us, he and Louis
Lambert were known as "*le Poète-et-Pythagore.*" (11:606, 676) Literature
represents the narrator's principal strategy for understanding and inter-
preting the experiences of his friend. He writes his friend's biography at
least in part to come to a clearer understanding of his life. Even at the
beginning of the novel, however, the narrator interprets his friend's accounts of a visionary world based on Swedenborg's *Heaven and Hell* as a
literary phenomenon, referring to Louis Lambert's attempts to convince
him as "ses récits empreints de ce merveilleux qui font dévorer avec tant
de délices, aux enfants comme aux hommes, les contes où le vrai affecte
les formes les plus absurdes." (11:616)

  Like Balzac in his letter to Nodier, the narrator speculates on the psychological significance of the visionary narratives contained in the works of Swedenborg and other religious and theosophical writers, suggesting that they represent the mythic beliefs of an earlier stage of history:

> Louis tâchait alors, en m'expliquant Swedenborg, de me faire partager ses croyances relatives aux anges. Dans ses raisonnements les plus faux se rencontraient encore des observations étonnantes sur la puissance de l'homme, et qui imprimaient à sa parole ces teintes de vérité sans lesquelles rien n'est possible dans aucun art. La fin romanesque de laquelle il dotait la destinée humaine était de nature à caresser le penchant qui porte les imaginations vierges à s'abandonner aux croyances. N'est-ce pas durant leur jeunesse que les peuples enfantent leurs dogmes, leurs idoles? Et les êtres surnaturels devant lesquels ils tremblent ne sont-ils pas la personnification de leurs sentiments, de leurs besoins aggrandis? (11:616)

The narrator calls the passage which follows this psychological explanation of Louis Lambert's beliefs a "Précis" of his friend's Swedenborgian beliefs. As the summary presents it, Louis Lambert's "Swedenborgianism" consists in his belief in a hierarchy of angelic spheres inhabited by spirits of the dead who find their place in this visionary order according to their merits. Here the concept of an angelic order serves as the justification of social hierarchies and the privileges of genius:

> Quand leur separation arrive sous cette forme que nous appelons la Mort, l'ange, assez puissant pour se dégager de son enveloppe, demeure et commence sa vraie vie. Les individualités infinies qui différencient les hommes ne peuvent s'expliquer que par cette double existence; elles la font comprendre et la démontrent. En effet, la distance qui se trouve entre un homme dont l'intelligence inerte le condamne à une apparente stupidité, et celui que l'exercice de sa vue intérieure a doué d'une force quelconque, doit nous faire supposer qu'il peut exister entre les gens de génie et d'autres êtres la même distance qui sépare les Aveugles des Voyants. (11:617)

According to the narrator, Swedenborg's greatest contribution to Louis Lambert's thought lay in his attempts to map out the order of the invisible world:

> La doctrine de Swedenborg serait donc l'ouvrage d'un esprit lucide qui aurait enregistré les innombrables phénomènes par lesquels les anges se révèlent au milieu des hommes. (11:617)

For the narrator, however, the language of Swedenborg, like that of Boehme and Madame Guyon, is poetic and illogical, giving rise to "des fantaisies aussi multiformes que peuvent l'être les rêves produits par l'opium" (11:618) Like Balzac in the preface to *Le livre mystique*, the narrator admits that he has found it necessary to "translate" the doctrines of Swedenborg and his friend into more logical form. (11:505–506, 617) Both emphasize the role of language in mediating an experience of the Absolute which cannot be expressed directly in words.

The next reference to Swedenborg occurs in the context of Louis Lambert's experience of déjà vu during a school expedition to the castle of Rochambeau, an experience which awakens him to the realization of the physiological origins of interiority, and causes him to reject Swedenborgianism for the moment. Louis Lambert compares the experience of déjà vu to that of sleep and dreams, which, he believes, attest to the existence of faculties in consciousness which generate experience:

> Si, pendant la nuit, les yeux fermés, j'ai vu en moi-même des objets colorés, si j'ai entendu des bruits dans le plus absolu silence, et sans les conditions exigées pour que le son se forme, si dans la plus parfaite immobilité j'ai franchi des espaces, nous aurions des facultés internes, indépendantes des lois physiques extérieures. La nature matérielle serait pénétrable par l'esprit. (11:622)

Again, the narrator's explanation of Louis Lambert's interest in visionary phenomena recalls Nodier, whose essay, "De quelques phénomènes du sommeil," Balzac had mentioned in his letter of 1832. ("Lettre à Nodier," 563) Louis Lambert's realization of the role of consciousness in generating experience causes him to doubt the reality of Swedenborg's visions:

> Mais, reprit-il après une pause et en laissant échapper un geste de doute, peut-être n'existe-t-il pas en nous deux natures? Peut-être sommes-nous tout simplement doués de qualités intimes et perfectibles dont l'exercice, dont les développements produisent en nous des phénomènes d'activité, de pénétration, de vision encore inobservés. Dans notre amour du merveilleux, passion engendrée par notre orgueil, nous aurons transformé ces effets en créations poétiques, parce que nous ne les comprenions pas. Il est si commode de déifier l'incompréhensible! Ah! j'avoue que je pleurerai la perte de mes illusions. J'avais besoin de croire à une double nature et aux anges de Swedenborg! Cette nouvelle science les tuerait-elle donc? Oui, l'examen de nos propriétés inconnues implique une science en apparence matérialiste, car l'ESPRIT emploie, divise, anime la substance; mais il ne la détruit pas. (11:622)

The experience at Rochambeau prompts Louis Lambert to begin work on a treaty on the origins of experience in consciousness and the unity of the spiritual and material worlds, his *Traité de la Volonté*, which was confiscated and destroyed by a teacher at Vendôme. While Swedenborg served as the point of departure for Louis Lambert's concept of *homo duplex* and the importance of the "inner man," the work of Mesmer, Gall, and Lavater guided the construction of his unitary system. What links the system of the *Traité* and Louis Lambert's interpretation of Swedenborgianism is the concept of a series which emanates from a first cause. The *Traité* posits the existence of two series: one emanating from thought, *Pensée*, and the other from the will, *Volonté*:

> Ainsi, la Volonté, la Pensée étaient les deux moyens générateurs; la Volition, l'Idée étaient les deux produits. La Volition lui semblait être l'idée arrivée de son état abstrait à un état concret, de sa génération fluide à une expression quasi solide, si toutefois ces mots peuvent formuler des aperçus si difficiles à distinguer. Selon lui, la Pensée et les Idées sont le mouvement et les actes de notre organisme intérieur comme les Volitions et la Volonté constituent ceux de la vie extérieure. (11:626)

The two series are mutually antagonistic, but linked by a relationship of causality between the inner being, which Louis Lambert calls the *être actionnel*, and the outer, the *être réactionnel*:

> L'être *actionnel* ou intérieur, mot qui lui servait à nommer le *species* inconnu, le mystérieux ensemble de fibrilles auxquel sont dues les différentes puissances incomplètement observées de la Pensée, de la Volonté; enfin cet être innommé voyant, agissant, mettant tout à fin, accomplissant tout avant aucune démonstration corporelle, doit, pour se conformer à sa nature, n'être soumis à aucune des conditions physiques par lesquelles l'être réactionnel ou *extérieur*, l'homme visible est arrêté dans ses manifestations. (11:628)

The use of the term *species* here to designate a species or *espèce* points forward to the use of the Latin term in the fragments at the conclusion of the novel, where it occurs in the context of the etymology of Balzac's term, *Spécialité*:

> (Spécialité, *species*, vue, spéculer, voir tout, et d'un seul coup; *speculum*, miroir ou moyen d'apprécier une chose en la voyant tout entière.) (11:688)

In both cases, the text plays on the double meaning of the Latin *species*, which means both sight and species, as well as form, visionary experience, idea, and apparition.[11] Curiously, however, Balzac does not invoke the economic resonances of the word, although both earlier and later narratives emphasize this dimension of supernatural themes.[12] But in *Louis Lambert*, the summary of the *Traité* brings to light the importance of the connection between vision and visionary experience in the novel and the taxonomic structures of natural history, a connection which is less apparent in the fragments at the end of the novel.

References to Swedenborg occur twice within the narrator's summary of the *Traité de la Volonté*. The first instance dates from the manuscript version of the novel, but is included in successive editions; it cites an incident in which the location of receipts necessary for the resolution of a court case in favor of the Lambert family is revealed to the clairvoyant great-grandfather of Louis Lambert by his dead wife, and represents a reworking of one of the anecdotes circulated about Swedenborg's ability to communicate with the dead. For Louis Lambert, the incident in his childhood serves as evidence of the "post-existence de l'être intérieur," (11:635) and hence of a view of man as double—*homo duplex*—and of Louis Lambert's version of Swedenborgianism:

> Cette aventure arrivée sous le toit paternel, aux yeux de Louis, alors âgé de neuf ans, contribua beaucoup à le faire croire aux visions miraculeuses de Swedenborg, qui donna pendant sa vie plusieurs preuves de la puissance de vision acquise à son *être intérieur*. En avançant en âge et à mesure que son intelligence se développait, Lambert devait être conduit à chercher dans les lois de la nature humaine les causes du miracle qui dès l'enfance avait attiré son attention. (11:636)

The passage again emphasizes the heuristic role of Louis Lambert's Swedenborgian beliefs.

The second reference to Swedenborg is skeptical, and represents an addition to the second edition of 1833:

> Certains hommes ayant entrevu quelques phénomènes du jeu naturel de *l'être actionnel* furent, comme Swedenborg, emportés au-delà du monde vrai par une âme ardente, amoureuse de poésie, ivre du principe divin. Tous se plurent donc, dans leur ignorance des causes, dans leur admiration du fait, à diviniser cet appareil intime, à bâtir un mystique univers. De là les anges! délicieuses illusions auxquelles ne voulait pas renoncer Lambert, qui les caressait encore au moment où le glaive de son Analyse en tranchait les éblouissantes ailes. (11:628)

This skeptical remark, however, represents the narrator's point of view, rather than that of Louis Lambert, who persists in his beliefs, even though analysis "en tranchait les éblouissantes ailes."

During Louis Lambert's childhood and adolescence, Swedenborgianism plays a role both in his naive perception of nature and language and in
his first reflective attempts to construct a system which would reconcile
his spiritualist and scientific interests. References to Swedenborg also occur in what the narrator calls the third stage of his existence:

> La troisième phase dut m'échapper. Elle commençait lorsque je fus
> séparé de Louis, qui ne sortit du collège qu'à l'âge de dix-huit ans, vers le
> milieu de l'année 1815. (11:644)

It is significant that the beginning of this third phase of Louis Lambert's
life coincides with the Restoration in France. In this phase, Louis Lambert
goes to Paris, where, penniless, he encounters French society and enrolls
in a course of study at the university. In a series of letters to his uncle, he
reflects on his experiences in the world. The letters reveal an increasing
level of abstraction. The first letter focuses on the role of money and hy-
pocrisy in Parisian society; the second on the conflict between society and
nature; and the third and fourth on the possibility of a new social science
capable of regenerating contemporary society and on the relationship of
this science of society to the natural sciences—especially natural history—and theology. The references to Swedenborg occur in the fourth
letter to Louis Lambert's uncle, in connection with the role of theological
systems in the construction of a model for an ideal society. Significantly,
these references appear again in the context of an opposition between science and materialism, on the one hand, and spiritualism and theology, on
the other. The exposition of a theoretical social science based on a theological system Balzac identifies with Swedenborgianism suggests a very
different conclusion to the novel—or at least to the social problems the
novel suggests—from that represented by Louis Lambert's withdrawal into
apparent madness and death.

Here, Louis Lambert represents Swedenborgianism as a universal religion which reconciles and rationalizes the doctrines of East and West.
Despite his obscurity, Swedenborg points the way to a new concept of
society:

> Enfin Swedenborg reprend au Magisme, au Brahmaïsme, au Bouddhisme
> et au Mysticisme chrétien ce que ces quatre grandes religions ont de
> commun, de réel, de divin, et rend à leur doctrine une raison pour ainsi
> dire mathématique. Pour qui se jette dans ces fleuves religieux dont tous
> les fondateurs ne sont pas connus, il est prouvé que Zoroastre, Moïse,
> Bouddha, Confucius, Jésus-Christ, Swedenborg ont eu les mêmes prin-
> cipes, et se sont proposé la même fin. Mais le dernier de tous, Sweden-

borg, sera peut-être le Bouddha du Nord. Quelque obscurs et diffus que soient ses livres, il s'y trouve les éléments d'une conception sociale grandiose. (11: 656)

Despite his recognition of the possible role of Swedenborgianism in the reintegration of society, however, Louis Lambert's Swedenborgianism propels him, not into a life of action and social engagement, but into solitude and isolation. He reasons:

Chaque homme peut savoir s'il lui est réservé d'entrer dans une autre vie, et si ce monde a un sens. Cette expérience, je vais la tenter. Cette tentative peut sauver le monde, aussi bien que la croix de Jèrusalem et le sabre de la Mecque. L'une et l'autre sont fils du désert. Des trente-trois années de Jésus, il n'en est que neuf de connues; sa vie silencieuse a préparé sa vie glorieuse. A moi aussi, il me faut le désert. (11:657)

Louis Lambert thus suggests that the fourth stage of his life will represent a rejection of Swedenborgianism and the science of society which might be based on its tenets for a more radical attempt to reform human consciousness itself. It is significant that the narrator fails to take into account this fourth stage, insisting upon a triadic division of his friend's life.

There are no further direct references to Swedenborg or to Swedenborgianism after the fourth letter to Louis Lambert's uncle. His occasional utterances during the period immediately following the onset of his madness suggest that he has chosen to close himself off in an interior world which resembles the parallel worlds described by Swedenborg. Louis Lambert's uncle tells the narrator that his nephew is in the habit of saying: "*Cet homme n'est pas de mon ciel,* là où les autres disaient: Nous ne mangerons pas un minot de sel ensemble." (11:677) When the narrator finally confronts his friend, Louis Lambert does not respond to him, but merely says: "*Les anges sont blancs!*" (11:682) And both Louis Lambert and his fiancée are themselves described by the narrator as angels.

Important parallels to Swedenborgianism also occur in the series of philosophical fragments which, beginning with the third edition, were appended to the end of the novel. The narrator distinguishes between two series of fragments: the first, he says, appears to represent the ruins of a unitary system Louis Lambert was unable to construct in its entirety; the second, which he is unable to make sense of, consists of a series of mathematical and numerological speculations concerning the structure and meaning of the world. Both series present parallels to Swedenborgian doctrines discussed earlier in the text, but stand in degrees of increasing abstraction, both to Swedenborgianism and to the world itself. The second series appears to represent an attempt to explore the limits of language and representation and to construct a pure system of signs based on mathematics.

The narrator presents the fragments as the ruins of Louis Lambert's mature philosophical system. As such, the fragments or "pensées," as he calls them, have much in common with the genre of the philosophical fragment developed by German Romantics such as Friedrich Schlegel and Novalis, in whose works the concept of the fragment was based on a belief in the impossibility of a system, at the same time that it suggested an ineffable totality. But, of course, in calling Louis Lambert's meditations *pensées*, Balzac also harked back to the French tradition of the philosophical fragment, notably Pascal's *Pensées*.

The fragments at the end of *Louis Lambert* are arranged in two series. The narrator invites us to decipher their relationship:

> Mais entre ces deux fragments, il est un correlation évidente aux yeux des personnes, assez rares d'ailleurs, qui se plaisent à plonger dans ces sortes de gouffres intellectuels. (11:689)

It is the narrator, of course, who has arranged the fragments and given them "des formes en rapport avec notre entendement." (11:689) Thus the fragments are twice mediated, first by the memory of Louis Lambert's wife, and then by the efforts of the narrator to translate what he has heard into what he considers to be comprehensible terms. The systematic connotations of the fragments may therefore be the result of the interference of Pauline or of the narrator. The complex narrative structure here emphasizes the paradoxical nature of the fragments and calls into question the ability of language to communicate a form of knowledge which does not carry with it notions of a system and a centered ego.

The relationship between the two series recalls the parallel between metaphysical speculation and scientific analysis set forth in the letter to Nodier. The twenty-two fragments of the first series take us from the origins of life and thought in a "substance éthérée," which is called variously electricity, heat, light, or magnetic fluid, to different levels of consciousness, to an experience of the Absolute based on the understanding of the Word and—this is the most interesting and original aspects of this series—through the experience of the Absolute, the retranslation and re-spiritualizing of the world into language:

XXI

Aussi, peut-être un jour le sens inverse de l'ET VERBUM CARO FACTUM EST sera-t-il le résumé d'un nouvel évangile qui dira: ET LA CHAIR SE FERA LE VERBE, ELLE DEVIENDRA LA PAROLE DE DIEU. (11:689)

The second series, consisting of fifteen fragments, begins with the origins of the world in the Word, the source of movement and numbers which, in their conflict with the inertia of matter, give rise to the differentiated forms of life; through knowledge of numbers of mathematics, the individual has the possibility of regaining knowledge of the Word, and thus of reintegration with the Absolute. The movement of both series is circular, but the first takes as the point of departure for its spiral movement the smallest conceivable element of the material world, and the second, the origins of consciousness in the "spiritual" world. A passage from the eighth fragment in the first series makes explicit the analytical bias of the first group, as well as its correspondence to the second:

> On décomposera l'homme en entier, l'on trouvera peut-être les éléments de la Pensée et de la Volonté, mais on rencontrera toujours, sans pouvoir le résoudre, cet X contre lequel je me suis autrefois heurté. Cet X est la PAROLE, dont la communication brûle et dévore ceux qui ne sont pas préparés à la recevoir. Elle engendre incessamment la SUBSTANCE. (11:686)

The juxtaposition of the "analytical" and "speculative" series, and their ironic presentation through a skeptical and uncomprehending narrator suggest the impossibility of systems at the present time, but continue to project the possibility of a system into the future.

The most important parallel to Swedenborgian doctrines occurs in the first series and has to do with the distinction between three levels of consciousness, based on the Swedenborgian distinction between the "natural," "spiritual," and "divine" worlds:

> XX
>
> Il existe trois mondes: le NATUREL, le SPIRITUEL, le DIVIN. L'Humanité transite dans le Monde Naturel, qui n'est fixe ni dans son essence ni dans ses facultés. Le Monde Spirituel est fixe dans son essence et mobile dans ses facultés. Le Monde Divin est fixe dans ses facultés et dans son essence. Il existe donc nécessairement un culte matériel, un culte spirituel, un culte divin; trois formes qui s'expriment par l'Action, par la Parole, par la Prière, autrement dit, le Fait, l'Entendement et l'Amour. L'Instinctif veut des faits, l'Abstractif s'occupe des idées; le Spécialiste voit la fin, il aspire à Dieu qu'il pressent ou contemple. (11:688–89)

In *Séraphîta*, Pastor Becker explicitly identifies these three levels with the doctrines of Swedenborg. (11:778) In both *Séraphîta* and *Louis Lambert*, they correspond to levels of consciousness which parallel Swedenborg's distinction between the *animus, mens,* and *anima.* These corresponding levels of consciousness, called instinct, abstraction, and *Spécialité* in *Louis*

Lambert, are also temporalized. They can best be understood in the context of Balzac's explorations of questions of perception and representation in works written up until this time, rather than by reference to Swedenborgianism. The relationship among instinct, abstraction, and *Spécialité* is developed in four fragments near the conclusion of the first series:

XIII

Le monde des Idées se divise en trois sphère: elle de l'Instinct, celle des Abstractions, celle de la Spécialité.

XIV

La plus grande partie de l'humanité visible, la partie la plus faible, habite la sphère de l'Instinctivité. Les Instinctifs naissent, travaillent et meurent sans s'élever au second degré de l'intelligence humaine, l'Abstraction.

XV

A l'Abstraction commence la Société. Si l'Abstraction comparée à l'Instinct est une puissance presque divine, elle est une faiblesse inouïe, comparée au don de Spécialité qui peut seul expliquer Dieu. L'Abstraction comprend toute une nature en germe plus virtuellement que la graine ne contient le système d'une plante et ses produits. De l'Abstraction naissent les lois, les arts, les intérêts, les idées sociales. Elle est la gloire et le fléau du monde: la gloire, elle a créé les sociétés; le fléau, elle dispense l'homme d'entrer dans la Spécialité, qui est un des chemins de l'Infini. L'homme juge tout par ses abstractions, le bien, le mal, la vertu, le crime. Ses formules de droit sont ses balances, sa justice est aveugle: celle de Dieu voit, tout est là. Il se trouve nécessairement des êtres intermédiaires qui séparent le Règne des Instinctifs du Règne des Abstractifs, et chez lesquels l'Instinctivité se mêle à l'Abstractivité dans des proportions infinies. Les uns ont plus d'Instinctivité que d'Abstractivité, et *vice versa*, que les autres. Puis, il est des êtres chez lesquels les deux actions se neutralisent en agissant par des forces égales.

XVI

La Spécialité consiste à voir les choses du monde matériel aussi bien que celles du monde spirituel dans leurs ramifications originelles et conséquentielles. Les plus beaux génies humains sont ceux qui sont partis des ténèbres de l'Abstraction pour arriver aux lumières de la Spécialité. (Spécialité, *species*, vue, spéculer, voir tout, et d'un seul coup; *speculum*, miroir ou moyen d'apprécier une chose en la voyant tout entière.) Jésus était Spécialiste, il voyait le fait dans ses racines et dans ses productions, dans le passé qui l'avait engendré, dans le présent où il se manifestait, dans l'avenir où il se développait; sa vue pénétrait l'entendement d'autrui. La perfection de la vue intérieure enfante le don de Spécialité. La Spé-

cialité emporte l'intuition. L'intuition est une des facultés de L'HOMME IN-
TERIEUR dont le Spécialisme est un attribut. Elle agit par une impercept-
ible sensation ignorée de celui qui lui obéit: Napoléon s'en allant
instinctivement de sa place avant qu'un boulet n'y arrive. (11:687–88)

The formulation of the evolution of *Abstraction* and its role in the consti-
tution of society parallels the justification, in the preface to *Les études de
moeurs* of 1835 signed by Félix Davin, of the ordering of the parts of *Les
études de moeurs* according to degrees of abstraction from nature.[13]

The concept of *Spécialité*, however, has roots as far back as the "Avertissement du *Gars*," which, we recall, used the Leibnizean metaphor of a
concentric mirror in order to describe the origins of the work of art in the
consciousness of the artist. In the Avertissement, the metaphor of the mirror served to illustrate and justify a concept of representation opposed to
the neoclassical concept of imitation; the mysterious correspondence between the artist's consciousness and the world justified a concept of the
novel as reflecting the structure of the social world in its entirety. The
mirror metaphor recurs in the citation of the preface to *La peau de chagrin*, and in the preface to the *Romans et contes philosophiques* signed by
Philarète Chasles, (10:1193), but here the belief in the spontaneous nature
of artistic creation has given way to a consideration of the work as the
result of a twofold process consisting of observation and expression: the
artist combines elements of remembered experience in order to construct
an aesthetic world. By the 1835 version of *Louis Lambert*, the mirror metaphor is linked to the problem of the perception of unity in time and to
the creation of a typology which would represent the universal in the particular. This typology, in turn, serves as a fixed frame of reference which
limits the development of consciousness and society. Thus the conclusion
of *Louis Lambert* points forward to the discussion in the Avant-propos of
the role of ideal scientific types in the construction of a novel system.

The relationship of the conclusion of *Louis Lambert* to the concept of
a system, however, is ambiguous. For if, on the one hand, the fragments
suggest the conditions for the construction of both a conceptual and a
novelistic totality, on the other, it is this idea which leads to Louis Lambert's madness and death.

The history of Louis Lambert's Swedenborgianism follows the reception and secularization of Swedenborgianism in France from the publication of the first translations and *Abrégés* of his work in the 1780s to
Richer's *De la Nouvelle Jérusalem* of 1834–1835. The section of the novel
depicting Louis Lambert's childhood associates Swedenborgianism both
with the rejection of reason and a return to a more naive view of the world
and with the discovery of the historical dimension of language; in his

meeting with Madame de Staël, the works of the theosopher and the context of late eighteenth-century German philosophy and aesthetics converge; his years at Vendôme see the attempt to reconcile science and theology and the fusion of Swedenborgianism and Mesmerism which was common during the early decades of the nineteenth century; finally, during the Restoration, Louis Lambert comes to interpret Swedenborg as an eclectic theosopher whose doctrines are capable of resolving political and sectarian differences. This position parallels Edouard Richer's interpretation of Swedenborg in *De la nouvelle Jérusalem*. In significant respects, the account of Louis Lambert's intellectual development even suggests the development of Richer himself, who evolved from an early interest in the origin of religion to a gradual recognition of the role of theology in explaining the apparently irrational aspects of human existence and in maintaining the social order.[14] It is important, however, that Balzac chooses to represent his protagonist's development from the point of view of an eminently reasonable and very limited narrator, who sees his friend's interests as impressively ambitious, but misleading and even dangerous.

Thus Louis Lambert's successive attitudes towards Swedenborgianism not only illustrate his movement from spiritualism to materialism to an attempted synthesis of the two positions and eventual madness, but also offer a history of French Swedenborgianism that suggests how spiritualist doctrines represent various political, as well as intellectual, strategies over a period of about forty years. If Louis Lambert's development allegorizes recent French cultural history, his fate suggests the dangers of all intellectual and ideological systems—when not mediated by a dialogue with other people or by the precedents of tradition and authority.

Séraphîta

Like *Louis Lambert*, *Séraphîta* contains several expository passages of considerable length which serve as a frame of reference for the interpretation of the narrative. The novel is set in Norway, in May 1800, at the end of a long and severe winter. There are five principal characters: the hermaphrodite Séraphîta-Séraphîtüs, who appears as a man to women and as a woman to men; a couple, Minna and Wilfrid, both of whom are in love with Séraphîta-Séraphîtüs at the beginning of the novel; and two older men, the rationalist pastor, Becker, who is interested in, but skeptical of, visionary phenomena, and the servant of Séraphîta-Séraphîtüs, David, who is uneducated and who, unlike Becker, believes naively in the truth of Séraphîta-Séraphîtüs' visions. Thus the five characters (six, if one takes into account the doubleness of Séraphîta-Séraphîtüs), establish a series of oppositions between masculine and feminine, reason and faith, and understanding and love. Séraphîta-Séraphîtüs represents a unity which is invisible to human eyes and incomprehensible to human reason, but which is nevertheless the source of the phenomenal world. In the course of the novel, the hermaphrodite sickens and dies, the long winter comes to an end, and Minna and Wilfrid discover their love for each other. The death of Séraphîta, the impending marriage of Minna and Wilfrid, and the coming of spring are all linked to a renunciation of transcendental aims and a return to the human world, which is characterized by mediations and duality. "Tout principe extrême porte en soi l'apparence d'une négation et les symptômes de la mort," the narrator tells us at the beginning of the novel. "La vie n'est-elle pas le combat de deux forces? Là rien ne trahissait la vie. Une seule puissance, la force improductive de la glace régnait sans contradiction. (11:735) A similar sterility characterizes Séraphîta-Séraphîtüs, who tells Minna: "Mon coeur ne palpite plus; je ne vis que par moi et pour moi." (11:746)

The novel comprises seven chapters: 1. Séraphîtüs; 2. Séraphîta; 3. Séraphîta-Séraphîtüs; 4. Les Nuées du Sanctuaire; 5. Les Adieux; 6. Le Chemin pour aller au Ciel; and 7. L'Assomption. The ordering and number of the chapters recall Fragments XIV and XV of the second series in *Louis Lambert*:

XIV

TROIS et SEPT sont les deux plus grands nombres spirituels.

XV

TROIS est la formule des Mondes créés. Il est le signe spirituel de la création comme il est le signe matériel de la circonférence. En effet, Dieu n'a procédé que par des lignes circulaires. La ligne droite est l'attribut de l'infini; aussi l'homme qui pressent l'infini la reproduit-il dans ses oeuvres. DEUX est le nombre de la génération. TROIS est le nombre de l'existence, qui comprend la génération et le produit. Ajoutez le Quaternaire, vous avez le SEPT, qui est la formule du ciel. Dieu est au-dessus, il est l'Unité. (11:691)

The first three chapters, "Séraphîtüs," "Séraphîta," and "Séraphîta-Séraphîtüs," give us the points of view of Minna, Wilfrid, and Becker on Séraphîta-Séraphîtüs and the Absolute. Pastor Becker's perspective is based on his reading of Swedenborg and Jean Wier, and in chapter 3 he expounds a version of Swedenborgianism which serves as the basis for the interpretation of the second part of the novel, the "Quaternaire." Chapter 3 also contains the suggestion of a fourth point of view, that of David, the servant of Séraphîta-Séraphîtüs, who arrives in a hysterical state at the end of Becker's Swedenborgian discourse, and announces his mistress-master's visions and illness.

Chapter 4 describes the four characters in terms which emphasize their identification with different points of view, which, taken together, represent a totality:

> L'humanité dans tous ses modes et attendant la lumière on ne pouvait être mieux représentée que par cette jeune fille, par cet homme et par ces deux vieillards, dont l'un était assez savant pour douter, dont l'autre était assez ignorant pour croire. (11:805)

The difference between the points of view of the first three characters is emphasized in chapter 3 after the return of David to Séraphîta-Séraphîtüs' manor:

> David était rentré. Ils revinrent en silence; aucun d'eux ne comprenait les effets de cette vision de la même manière: M. Becker doutait, Minna adorait, Wilfrid désirait. (11:792)

Chapter 4 suggests why David's point of view is not included in this passage: it emphasizes the difference between faith and other approaches to knowledge. David's perceptions of Séraphîta-Séraphîtüs can only be presented in the visionary language of the mystics. In *Séraphîta*, Swedenborg figures as the last of a tradition of mystics and visionaries whose works elaborate experiences in other worlds in a language which is opposed to human logic and which exercises a dangerous influence on human perception. Becker warns Wilfrid of the dangers of reading Swedenborg: "En le lisant, il faut ou perdre le sens, ou devenir un Voyant." (11:775) He compares the visionary writings of Swedenborg to the works of Dante, Klopstock, Milton, and Tasso, (11:760) thus emphasizing the parallel between the discourses of mysticism and literature.

Chapter 4, which opens the second series of chapters, the "Quaternaire," is in many respects the mirror image of Chapter 3. Here, Séraphîta-Séraphîtüs expounds her/his system, a system which grows out of Becker's skeptical exposition of Swedenborgianism in much the same way that Louis Lambert's "systems" derived from his Swedenborgian beliefs. In both novels, Swedenborgianism appears as an inadequate representation of the transcendental world, but one which is nonetheless extremely useful because it mediates between human perception and logic and the Absolute, thus providing a model for the language of literature, which purports to do the same. The relationship between Becker's version of Swedenborgianism in chapter 3 and Séraphîta-Séraphîtüs' transcendental system in chapter 4 forms the crux of the argument concerning the role of Swedenborgianism in this novel. The two major expository passages form a frame of reference for the interpretation of other, less direct, references to Swedenborgianism and to the visionary in general, in the work as a whole. Here, as in *Louis Lambert*, Swedenborgianism points, above all, to questions of perception and representation. This is already clear in the opening pages of the novel, the exposition which establishes both the setting and the central themes of the novel. The narrator describes the majesty of the landscape, but focuses above all on the technical achievement of the cutting of a canal from Stromfiord to Sweden, an accomplishment he attributes to Swedenborg. It is crucial to note the stress on the practical and technical potential of the visionary consciousness at the beginning of the novel: it points towards the conclusion, in which Minna and Wilfrid are persuaded to renounce their dreams for a practical and productive existence centered around the family:

> Le Village de Jarvis aurait peut-être pu communiquer avec la Norvège intérieure et la Suède par la Sieg; mais pour être mis en rapport avec la civilisation, le Stromfiord voulait un homme de génie. Ce génie parut en effet: ce fut un poète, un Suédois religieux qui mourut en admirant et respectant les beautés de ce pays, comme un des plus magnifiques ouvrages du Créateur.
>
> Maintenant, les hommes que l'étude a doués de cette vue intérieure dont les véloces perceptions amènent tour à tour dans l'âme, comme sur une toile, les paysages les plus contrastants du globe, peuvent facilement embrasser l'ensemble du Stromfiord. (11:732)

The visions described in chapters 3 and 7 also allude to Swedenborg and his works. These visions, however, have more to do with Balzac's attempts to demonstrate the poetic force of literary language than with Swedenborg's orderly expositions of parallel worlds. Possible models for these visions include the writers Becker mentions: Dante, Klopstock, Milton, and Tasso.

Like the "system" of Séraphîta-Séraphîtüs, Becker's exposition of Swedenborgianism falls into two parts: the first anecdotal and biographical, recounting aspects of the life and works of Swedenborg and focusing on the unity of his scientific and theosophical work, a unity which has already been announced at the beginning of the novel (see 11:732); the second, centering on aspects of his doctrines which have a heuristic value in explaining the nature and limits of perception and the role of language in determining human experience. The cornerstone of his interpretation of Swedenborgianism, as well as the "system" of Séraphîta-Séraphîtüs, is the concept of what Balzac calls "la Parole," the Divine Word which mediates between consciousness and nature and between the spiritual and material worlds.

Balzac's account of Swedenborg's life and works in the first part of Becker's exposition appears to draw from a variety of sources. The beginning probably follows Sandels's *Eloge*, which had been translated and published in Pernety's 1782 translation of *Heaven and Hell*. But Balzac omits much of Sandels's account of Swedenborg's early life and works, emphasizing only the unity of his scientific and theosophical interests and the precocious nature of many of his scientific discoveries. The discussion of the parallels between the doctrines of Swedenborg and Mesmer may draw exclusively on the "Remarques de M. de Thomé," which Balzac mentions here and which was sometimes bound together with the *Abrégé* of Swedenborgian doctrines published by Bénédict Chastanier in 1786. It should, however, be noted that the parallels are also discussed in the introduction to the Strasbourg *Abrégé* of 1788 and were commonplace in literature on the subject of both Mesmerism and animal magnetism in general in the first part of the nineteenth century in France.[15]

The biographical part of Becker's exposition concludes with a series of criticisms of Swedenborg's visions, the details of which Becker often finds ridiculous. These attest to Becker's skeptical point of view and serve to distance the reader from the exposition of Swedenborg's doctrines which follows. Furthermore, Becker prefaces his remarks with the admission that, since he speaks from memory, his version may differ from that of Swedenborg, and that he will only discuss those mysteries which relate to the death of Séraphîta-Séraphîtüs. (10:776)

The second part of the exposition opens with a reference to Swedenborg and mathematics:

> Après avoir mathématiquement établi que l'homme vit éternellement en des sphères, soit inférieures, soit supérieures, Swedenborg appelle Esprits Angéliques les êtres qui, dans ce monde, sont préparés pour le ciel, où ils deviennent Anges. (11:776)

Inge Jonsson has pointed to the importance of mathematics in Swedenborg's language treatise, *Clavis hieroglyphica*, but mathematics play relatively little part in Swedenborg's later discussions of symbolism, exegesis, and the nature of visionary or moral worlds. Balzac's emphasis on mathematics and the parallel he develops between language and mathematics, both in *Louis Lambert* and in *Séraphîta*, draws on the novelist's earlier speculations concerning the nature of language and its relationship to consciousness: the "Dissertation sur l'homme," for example, which focuses on the origins of language in sensation and the formation of concepts through a kind of secondary process or reflection, which he calls "secondes idées";[16] the critique of the language and various social theories in *La peau de chagrin*, and the discussion of the relationship between the logics of scientific analysis and metaphysical speculation in the letter to Nodier of 1832 are also important in this context. In *Louis Lambert* and *Séraphîta*, however, the analogy between language and mathematics suggests a concept of language as a purely logical, rather than representational, medium and points forward to non-representational concepts of language in French poetry of the second half of the century.

The opening of the second part of Becker's exposition thus emphasizes the role of mathematics, language, and logic in our perception of the "visionary" world of the angels. Séraphîta-Séraphîtüs will criticize the inadequacy of human mathematics and logic in the exposition of her/his system in chapter 4, suggesting at the same time the inadequacy of Swedenborg's visions as a medium for knowledge of a transcendental world. Becker, however, proceeds to develop the concept of the angel, or interior being, who undergoes a series of inner metamorphoses which take her/him into higher spheres. These transformations are characterized by a passage through three kinds of love: love of self, which characterizes the human genius; love of the world, which produces prophets; and, finally, love of heaven, the love of angels. (11:777) Angels undergo two successive metamorphoses: the first, through three stages of love; the second, through three stages of wisdom. Love and wisdom represent the feminine and masculine principles, as well as two corresponding, but opposite, approaches to knowledge and the Absolute:

> L'Esprit d'Amour a conquis la force, résultat de toutes les passions terrestres vaincues, il aime aveuglément Dieu; mais l'Esprit de Sagesse a l'intelligence et sait pourquoi il aime. Les ailes de l'un sont déployées et l'emportent vers Dieu, les ailes de l'autre sont repliées par la terreur que lui donnee la Science: il connaît Dieu. L'un désire incessamment voir Dieu et s'élance vers lui, l'autre y touche et tremble. L'union qui se fait d'un Esprit d'Amour et d'un Esprit de Sagesse met la créature à l'état divin pendant lequel son âme est FEMME, et son corps est HOMME, dernière expression humaine où l'Esprit l'emporte sur la Forme, ou la forme se débat encore contre l'Esprit divin; car la forme, la chair, ignore, se révolte, et veut rester grossière. (11:778)

In this passage, Swedenborg's distinction between the masculine *Mens* and the feminine *Anima*, which, for him, represent different, but not successive, levels of intelligence, becomes the basis for a doctrine of metamorphosis and the transformation of opposites which, like the hermaphrodite, Séraphîta-Séraphîtüs, has far more in common with the gnostic tradition than with the work of Swedenborg.[17]

Becker also describes three states of regeneration or nonregeneration:

> Ainsi le NATUREL, état dans lequel sont les êtres non régénérés; le SPIRI-
> TUEL, état dans lequel sont les Esprits Angéliques; et le DIVIN, état dans
> lequel demeure l'Ange avant de briser son enveloppe, sont les trois degrés
> de l'*exister* par lesquels l'homme parvient au ciel. (11:778)

Balzac's formulation of the three states here corresponds to the description
of the three spheres of the world of ideas in Fragments XIII–XIV of the
first series in *Louis Lambert*, where they are called Instinct, Abstraction,
and *Spécialité*. (11:686–687) In *Séraphîta*, as well, the three levels correspond to different modes of experience, but here Balzac is mainly preoccupied with the role of language in mediating between the natural and
spiritual worlds. The distinction between the natural, spiritual, and the
divine is followed by an exposition of the meaning of *correspondances* and
of *la Parole*.

The exposition of the doctrine of correspondences begins with a distinction between two kinds of knowledge:

> Pour les hommes, dit-il [Swedenborg], le Naturel passe dans le Spirituel,
> ils considèrent le monde sous ses formes visibles et le perçoivent dans
> une réalité propre à leur sens. Mais pour l'Esprit Angélique, le Spirituel
> passe dans le Naturel, il considère le monde dans son esprit intime, et
> non dans sa forme. Ainsi, nos sciences humaines ne sont que l'analyse des
> formes. (11:778)

The doctrine of correspondences, as Balzac's narrator elaborates it here,
represents a means for overcoming the limits of contemporary science
through the exegesis of an inner sense hidden in language and phenomena. According to this presentation, the concept of correspondences is primarily allegorical; it points to the relationship between natural objects and
spiritual equivalents or types. The discussion of the nature of an original
language at the beginning of *Louis Lambert* (11:591–592) focused on the
relationship of language to the developing consciousness of the individual.
Here the emphasis is more external. By locating the source of meaning in
language and phenomema themselves, Balzac displaces the origin of meaning from individual consciousness to the structures of society and also—
this becomes clearer later, especially in the Avant-propos—the natural
sciences.

Balzac's interpretation in *Séraphîta* of the inner sense of language
revealed by correspondences remains close to classical concepts of representation. Correspondences reveal the thought which precedes the word:

> L'Esprit Angélique va bien au-delà, son savoir est la pensée dont la science
> humaine n'est que la parole; il puise la connaissance des choses dans le
> Verbe, en apprenant LES CORRESPONDANCES par lesquelles les mondes con-
> cordent avec les cieux. (11:778)

Correspondences mediate between the divine and spiritual worlds, as well
as between the spiritual and natural worlds; they translate the living word,
the *Parole* of God, into writing:

> LA PAROLE de Dieu fut entièrement écrite par pures Correspondances, elle
> couvre un sens interne ou spirituel qui, sans la science des Correspond-
> ances, ne peut être compris. (11:779)

In its primary sense, then, the doctrine of correspondences, as it is set
forth in *Séraphîta*, is linked to a neoclassical concept of the correspondence between words and things, which is extended to comprise a secondary
relationship between phenomena and their spiritual equivalents. Balzac's
interpretation agrees with the presentation in popularizations of Swedenborgianism of the doctrine of correspondences as allegory and as an original language hidden in natural phenomena. In its association with mathematics, however, Balzac's version of the doctrine of correspondences
parallels his earlier discussions of the role of the imagination and memory
in the composition of the work of art. The inner being, the "Esprit," is
entirely free of the constraints which determine the situation of the outer
being in time and space. The parallel between the description of the Esprit's perception of numbers and the discussion of the artist's "seconde
vue" in the preface to *La peau de chagrin* is striking. In that work, Balzac
writes:

> Outre ces deux conditions essentielles au talent [the ability to ob-
> serve and to express], il se passe chez les poètes ou chez les écrivains
> réellement philosophes, un phénomène moral, inexplicable, inouï, dont la
> science peut difficilement rendre compte. C'est une sorte de seconde vue
> qui leur permet de deviner la vérité dans toutes les situations possibles;
> ou, mieux encore, je ne sais quelle puissance qui les transporte là où ils
> doivent, où ils veulent être. Ils inventent le vrai, par analogie, ou voient
> l'objet à décrire, soit que l'objet vienne à eux, soit qu'ils aillent eux-
> mêmes vers l'objet. (10:52)

In *Séraphîta*:

> Il existe deux perceptions: l'une interne, l'autre externe; l'Homme est tout
> externe, l'Esprit Angélique est tout interne. L'Esprit va au fond des

Nombres, il en possède la totalité, connaît leurs signifiances. Il dispose du mouvement et s'associe à tout par l'ubiquité: *Un ange*, selon le Prophète suédois, *est* présent à un autre quand il le désire (*Sap. Ang. De Div. Am.*); car il a le don de se séparer de son corps, et voit les cieux comme les prophètes les ont vus, et comme Swedenborg les voyait lui-même. (11:781)

In the preface to *La peau de chagrin*, the two faculties, observation and expression, are seen as complementary; in *Louis Lambert* and *Séraphîta*, the inner and outer "man" are seen as opposed. Balzac, however, envisages two possible resolutions to the conflict between inner and outer selves: on the one hand, the dissolution of meaning and communication suggested by Louis Lambert's decline into madness; on the other, a rejection of subjectivity and submission to the traditional structures of the Church and State, evoked by the death of the heroine and the marriage of Wilfrid and Minna in *Séraphîta*.

The conclusion of Becker's exposition of Swedenborgianism takes up the subject of heavenly marriage, a subject Swedenborg had discussed at length and in great detail in his treatise on love and marriage among the angels, *The Delights of Wisdom pertaining to Conjugial Love, after which Follow the Pleasures of Insanity Pertaining to Scortatory Love*, a work which has often disappointed those who have been led by its title to expect a libertinist tract. According to Becker, the division of the individual into male and female components becomes the basis for a social union based on sentiment and choice. In heavenly marriage:

L'homme a donné l'ENTENDEMENT, la femme a donné la VOLONTE: ils deviennent un seule être, UNE SEULE CHAIR ici-bas. (11:782)

Becker's exposition of heavenly marriage, however, has little in common with Swedenborg's work, which catalogues various aspects of heavenly marriage; it is rather a visionary elaboration of the cliché that "marriages are made in heaven," and its implications are the sublimation of sexuality and the subjection of women in bourgeois marriage. What is remarkable about this novel, however, is the extent to which it suggests that the hermaphrodite is more interesting than either of the two differentiated sexes. In this context, Pastor Becker's reply to Wilfrid's declaration of his desire for Séraphîta is extremely ironic:

—D'accord, cher pasteur; mais pour moi Séraphîta doit être une femme divine à posséder.

—Elle est toute intelligence," répondit dubitativement M. Becker. (11:832)

The third chapter ends with David's announcement of Séraphîta-Séraphîtüs' illness, which he interprets as an attack by demons, and which, whatever its causes, announces her/his death. The fourth chapter unites Minna, Wilfrid, Becker, and David at the bedside of the dying hermaphrodite, who expounds her/his knowledge of the Absolute as if possessed by another voice or intelligence. The exposition of a system which follows consists of two parts: the first, apparently given by Séraphîtüs, concerns the limits of human understanding and the duality of man and nature; the second, apparently given by Séraphîta, focuses on faith and its relationship to reason.

The first part of Séraphîta-Séraphîtüs' exposition opens with an invocation of the power of *la Parole*:

> La parole est le bien de tous, reprit gravement l'être mystérieux. Malheur à qui garderait le silence au milieu du désert en croyant n'être entendu de personne: tout parle et tout écoute ici-bas. La parole meut des mondes. (11:807)

The speaker then moves on to the subject of the inability of human reason to prove the validity of a monistic system: Séraphîtüs' formulation of the paradox recalls Kant's famous antinomies in the *Critique of Pure Reason*. It also points back to Balzac's discussion of the relationship between scientific analysis and speculation in the letter to Nodier. Séraphîtüs emphasizes that both materialist and spiritualist systems are true, according to human reason, because human beings are themselves double, consisting of material and spiritual components:

> Les générations spiritualistes n'ont pas fait moins de vains efforts pour nier la Matière que n'en ont tenté les générations matérialistes pour nier l'Esprit. Pourquoi ces débats? L'homme n'offrait-il pas à l'un et à l'autre système des preuves irrécusable? ne se rencontre-t-il pas en lui des choses matérielles et des choses spirituelles? (11:807)

The remainder of Séraphîtüs' argument attempts to prove that the spiritual is prior to Matter, and that God exists outside of the universe. This represents a reversal of Balzac's earlier position in the letter to Nodier, in which he emphasized the superiority of analysis and the role of experience in verifying theory. Finally, a series of paradoxes illustrates the incomprehensibility of God.

In contrast to the first, critical, part of Séraphîta-Séraphîtüs' discussion, the second sets forth the principles of a system based on faith. It opens with the affirmation of the difference between knowledge based on faith and reason, a subject which leads into a discussion of language, representation, and logic:

> La pensée, faisceau des rapports que vous apercevez entre les choses, est une langue intellectuelle qui s'apprend, n'est-ce pas? La Croyance, faisceau des vérités célestes, est également une langue, mais aussi supérieure à la pensée que la pensée est supérieure à l'instinct. Cette langue s'apprend. Le Croyant répond par un seul cri, par un seul geste; la Foi lui met aux mains une épée flamboyante avec laquelle il tranche, il éclaire tout. Le Voyant ne redescend pas du ciel, il le contemple et se tait. (11:815–16)

This passage depicts faith both as a supplement to the language of thought and as a return to an earlier, original, language of gestures and cries. The parallels to Rousseau's and Herder's discussions of the origin of language are striking and, at least in the case of Rousseau, probably intentional. Where Balzac differs from his predecessors, however, is in his characterization of the return to an original language as marking a break in the normal circuits of communication, leading to silence and perhaps to madness.

Séraphîta's subsequent attempts to prove the existence of God center on the concepts of origin and the series:

> En vous la matière aboutit à l'intelligence; et vous pensez que l'intelligence humaine aboutirait aux ténèbres, au doute, au néant? Si Dieu vous semble incompréhensible, inexplicable, avouez du moins que vous voyez, en toute chose purement physique, un conséquent et sublime ouvrier. Pourquoi sa logique s'arrêterait-elle à l'homme, sa création la plus achevée? (11:816)

For Séraphîta, the key to the problem of the logical proof of God's existence lies in mathematics, in our perceptions of numbers as both the origin of thought and the key to the absolute structure of the universe. The logic of numbers parallels the higher concept of God: both are characterized by paradox and by the nonapplicability of the categories of time and space:

> En un moment, je vais vous prouver que vous croyez fermement à des choses qui agissent et ne sont pas des êtres, qui engendrent la pensée et ne sont pas des esprits, à des abstractions vivantes que l'entendement ne saisit sous aucune forme, qui ne sont nulle part, mais que vous trouvez

> partout; qui sont sans nom possible, et que vous avez nommées; qui, semblables au Dieu de chair que vous vous figurez, périssent sous l'inexplicable, l'incompréhensible et l'absurde. Et je vous demanderai comment, adoptant ces choses, vous réservez vos doutes pour Dieu. Vous croyez au Nombre, base sur laquelle vous asseyez l'édifice des sciences que vous appelez exactes. (11:817–18)

Séraphîta proceeds to suggest that all human knowledge is based on antinomies—from the opposition between quality and quantity to the conflict between reason and experience in the apparent discrepancy between the laws of geometry and the movement of the spheres. Between the two, says Séraphîta, lies an abyss which can only be bridged by faith:

> Entre ces deux lignes est un abîme, comme entre le fini et l'infini, comme entre la matière et l'esprit, comme entre l'homme et l'idée, entre le mouvement et l'objet mu, entre la créature et Dieu. Demandez à l'amour divin ses ailes, et vous franchirez cet abîme! Au-delà commence la Révélation du Verbe. (11:822)

Furthermore, if the "languages" of mathematics and geometry are incapable of representing more than the surfaces of things, the sciences such as chemistry which claim to investigate the interior of things are unable to come to terms with the most essential aspect of inwardness—life itself:

> Vous n'obtenez que des substances mortes d'où vous avez chassé la force inconnue qui s'oppose à tout ce qui se décompose ici-bas, et dont l'attraction, la vibration, la cohésion et la polarité ne sont que des phénomènes. La vie est la pensée des corps; ils ne sont, eux, qu'un moyen de la fixer, de la contenir dans sa route; si les corps étaient des êtres vivants par eux-mêmes, ils seraient *cause* et ne mourraient pas. (11:823)

Mathematical science is incapable of explaining relationships among things: "Où enseignez-vous," asks Séraphîta, "l'étude des rapports qui lient les choses entre elles? Nulle part. Vous n'avez donc rien d'absolu." (11:824) Only the "occult sciences" are capable of generating synthetic knowledge:

> Vos thèmes les plus certains reposent sur l'analyse des Formes matérielles dont l'Esprit est sans cesse négligé par vous. Il est une science élevée que certains hommes entrevoient trop tard, sans oser l'avouer. Ces hommes ont compris la nécessité de considérer les corps, non seulement dans leurs propriétés mathématiques, mais encore dans leur ensemble, dans leurs affinités occultes. (11:824)

This is the most explicit statement thus far in Balzac's work on the role of the "occult sciences" in mediating between scientific analysis and metaphysical speculation, between consciousness and the material world. In the final stage of her argument, Séraphîta elaborates upon the social and political connotations of an age of faith. Religious tradition not only unites what would otherwise be a chaotic collection of autonomous individuals, but also keeps civilization alive in an age which lacks great men—the allusion to Napoleon is clear in this passage:

> Si la science matérielle devait être le but des efforts humains, avouez-le, les sociétés, ces grands foyers où les hommes se sont rassemblés, seraient-ils toujours providentiellement dispersés? Si la civilisation était le but de l'Espèce, l'intelligence périrait-elle? resterait-elle purement individuelle? La grandeur de toutes les nations qui furent grandes était basée sur des exceptions: l'exception cessée, morte fut la puissance. (11:826)

The visions recounted in *Séraphîta*—the old servant David's report of Séraphîta's experiences, Séraphîta's own version, and finally, the experience of Wilfrid and Minna of Séraphîta-Séraphîtüs' apotheosis—bear only a superficial resemblance to Swedenborg's visions. In their emphasis on movement and conflict, the visions recounted in *Séraphîta* have more in common with the works of William Blake than with those of Swedenborg: we find in *Séraphîta* none of the concern with exegesis and the taxonomy of the spirit world which often characterizes the visionary works of Swedenborg. The key to the difference lies in Balzac's attempts—both here and elsewhere—to formulate a concept of poetic language which, like the "occult sciences," would mediate between consciousness and nature. For Balzac, Swedenborg's visions represented a model for the development of such a language.

The oblique relationship of the doctrines of Swedenborg to the "system" both expounded in and represented by the novel *Séraphîta* is nowhere demonstrated more clearly than in the central figure, the androgynous Séraphîta-Séraphîtüs. Unlike Balzac, Swedenborg emphasized the sexual differentiation of angels.[18] The androgyn Séraphîta-Séraphîtüs, however, represents the combination of contradictory qualities in a single being, reflecting both a general tendency to give a dialectical interpretation to Swedenborgian doctrines in the nineteenth century and also the romantic fascination with the hermaphrodite as a contradictory being whose nature reflects a pure and undifferentiated wholeness and, at the same time, the appearance of doubleness.

What does link Balzac's Séraphîta-Séraphîtüs and Swedenborg's angels, however, is a common concern with the invisible aspects of sexuality, which both writers attempt to represent in terms of an analogy to the taxonomic systems of natural history. In *Séraphîta*, however, the most obvious link between the representation of sexuality and sexual differentiation and the taxonomic systems of the previous century is natural history—especially Linné's sexual system. The connection is most obvious in the passage in the first chapter, "Séraphîtüs," in which the mysterious green flower represents the bisexuality and sterility of Séraphîta-Séraphîtüs:

> Çà et là, sur ce tapis, s'élèvaient des étoiles blanches, bordées d'un filet d'or du sein desquelles sortaient des anthères pourprées, sans pistil. Une odeur qui tenait à la fois de celle des roses et des calices de l'oranger, mais fugitive et sauvage, achevait de donner je ne sais quoi de céleste à cette fleur mystérieuse que Séraphîtüs contemplait avec mélancolie, comme si la senteur lui en eût exprimé de plaintives idées que, lui seul! il comprenait. Mais à Minna, ce phénomène inouï parut être un caprice par lequel la nature s'était plu à douer quelques pierreries de la fraîcheur, de la mollesse et du parfum des plantes.
>
> "Pourquoi serait-elle unique? Elle ne se reproduira donc plus? dit la jeune fille à Séraphîtüs qui rougit et changea brusquement de conversation. (11:739)

At first glance, the flower appears to have much in common with the *blaue Blume*, the blue flower of Novalis' *Heinrich von Ofterdingen*, which became for the German Romantics a symbol for the possibilities of infinite development and differentiation, a symbol akin to the suggestiveness inherent in the concept of a fragment. The metaphor of the green flower in *Séraphîta*, however, operates quite differently, pointing to an allegorical correspondence between different levels of experience in a phenomenal and noumenal world which are both seen to be closed and unchanging.

Les proscrits and the Préface au *Livre mystique*

In addition to *Louis Lambert* and *Séraphîta*, *Le livre mystique* also includes the novella, *Les proscrits*, first published in 1831, and a preface written at the end of November 1835.

Les proscrits, which tells a story about Dante in Paris, relates the doctrines of Swedenborg both to medieval allegory and to the representation of the city, providing a historical and social context for the exploration of psychological questions in the two novels. The novella focuses on an encounter—probably entirely fictious—between Dante and a French theologian, abbé Sigier, and draws a line of descent from medieval scholasticism through the work of Boehme, Madame Guyon, Swedenborg, and other "mystics":

La Théologie se divisait en deux Facultés, celle de THEOLOGIE proprement dite, et celle de DECRET. La Faculté de Théologie avait trois sections: la Scolastique, la Canonique et la Mystique. Il serait fastidieux d'expliquer les attributions de ces diverses parties de la sciencee, puisqu'une seule, la Mystique, est le sujet de cet étude. La THEOLOGIE MYSTIQUE embrassait l'ensemble des *révélations divines* et l'explication des *mystères*. Cette branche de l'ancienne théologie est secrètement restée en honneur parmi nous. Jacob Boehm, Swedenborg, Martinez Pasqualis, Saint-Martin, Molinos, Mmes Guyon, Bourignon et Krudener, la grande secte des Extatiques, celle des Illuminés, ont à diverses époques, dignement conservé les doctrines de cette science, dont le but a quelque chose d'effrayant et de gigantesque. Aujourd'hui, comme au temps du docteur Sigier, il s'agit de donner à l'homme des ailes pour pénétrer dans le sanctuaire où Dieu se cache à nos regards. (11:538)

Here, as in *Louis Lambert* and *Séraphîta*, theology is presented as a model for literature. Per Nykrog has suggested that the three principal characters, Godefroid, Dante, and abbé Sigier, represent three approaches to knowledge: emotion, poetry, and metaphysics. The language of literature mediates between feeling and concepts.[19]

The preface to *Le livre mystique* addresses the question of the relationship of mysticism to the representation of contemporary society. The trilogy, Balzac tells us, is "destiné à offrir l'expression nette de la pensée religieuse jetée comme une âme en ce long ouvrage." (1:501) The "soul" is personified in the form of the characters Louis Lambert and Séraphîta, who are represented, Balzac claims, "selon les lois de Swedenborg sévèrement appliquées." (1:505) Swedenborg's work is particularly relevant here because it represents a kind of universal mysticism which allows for the importance of science, but also recognizes the limits of human knowledge and the importance of faith, and because Swedenborg's concept of the angel provides a model for the representation of the genius or "être parfait." Here, as in *Séraphîta*, Balzac's description of the language of Swedenborg's work suggests that he had read very little, if any, of it:

Si vous pouvez imaginer les milliers de propositions naissant dans Swedenborg les unes dans les autres, comme des flots; si vous pouvez vous figurer les landes sans fin que présentent tous ces auteurs; si vous voulez comparer l'esprit essayant de faire rentrer dans les bornes de la logique cette mer de phrases furieuses, à l'oeil essayant de percevoir une lumière dans les ténèbres, vous apprécierez les travaux de l'auteur, la peine qu'il a prise pour donner un corps à cette doctrine et la mettre à la portée de l'étourderie française qui veut deviner ce qu'elle ne sait pas, et savoir ce qu'elle ne peut pas deviner. Mais, de bonne heure, il avait pressenti là comme une nouvelle Divine Comédie. Hélas! le rythme voulait toute une vie et sa vie a exigé d'autres travaux; le sceptre du rythme lui a donc échappé. La poésie sans la mesure est peut-être une impuissance? peut-être n'a-t-il fait qu'indiquer le sujet à quelque grand poète, humble prosateur qu'il est! Peut-être le Mysticisme y gagnera-t-il en se trouvant dans la langue si positive de notre pays, obligé de courir droit, comme un wagon sur le rail de son chemin de fer. (11:506)

The representation of the language of Swedenborg as a landscape, however, not only recalls the symbolic Nordic landscape of *Séraphîta*, but also has important implications for Balzac's interpretation of Swedenborgianism and the concept of the hieroglyph in the novels of the 1840s, in which the language of the text will be seen to correspond, in depth and substance, to the structures of nature and of the city.

   Louis Lambert and *Séraphîta* mark the limits—both temporal and thematic—of Balzac's exploration of esoteric and pseudoscientific doctrines as models for the representation of individual consciousness and its relationship to the world. These novels refer to the social and historical situation of their protagonists only indirectly; the social and political implications of the representation of invisible worlds in *Le livre mystique* are expressed more clearly in two *Etudes philosophiques* which emphasize esoteric and pseudoscientific doctrines, but which were not included in *Le livre mystique*: *La peau de chagrin* (1831), and *La recherche de l'Absolu* (1834).

La peau de chagrin

   Published the year following the July Revolution, *La peau de chagrin* allegorizes recent French history in the character Raphaël de Valentin, who, bankrupt and on the verge of suicide, barters his life for a talisman which will allow him to satisfy all his desires immediately, thereby depleting himself dangerously quickly of his limited supply of vital forces.[20] Raphaël is offered a choice between *Volonté* and *Savoir*: in choosing the first, he opts for a personal disaster which Balzac sets against the situation in France in 1830–1831. *La peau de chagrin* refers to esoteric and pseudoscientific doctrines in order to suggest the existence of an occult world of invisible forces which point to the necessary limitation of individual desires.

   The one reference to Swedenborg in *La peau de chagrin* occurs in the famous scene between Raphaël de Valentin and the mysterious old man who inhabits the third floor of the antiquary shop he enters while contemplating suicide. The old man urges him not to accept the talisman, which, he says, represents *Pouvoir* and *Vouloir*, but instead to devote himself to *Savoir*, and his admonition reveals the extent to which Raphaël's choice carries with it associations with sexual desires, revolutionary ideologies, and also the circulation of money:

> Ceci, dit-il d'une voix éclatante en montrant la peau de chagrin, est le *pouvoir* et le *vouloir* réunis. Là sont vos idées sociales, vos désirs excessifs, vos intempérances, vos joies qui tuent, vos douleurs qui font trop vivre . . . (10:87)

The talisman itself bears an inscription in strange Oriental characters which are so deeply etched in the skin that they appear to have been been produced by the animal itself. The novel translates the characters for the reader, although Raphaël is unable to read them:

> SI TU ME POSSEDES, TU POSSEDERAS TOUT. MAIS TA VIE M'APPARTIENDRA. DIEU L'A VOULU AINSI. DESIRE, ET TES DESIRS SERONT ACCOMPLIS. MAIS REGLE TES SOUHAITS SUR TA VIE. ELLE EST LA. A CHAQUE VOLOIR JE DECROITRAI COMME TES JOURS. ME VEUX-TU? PRENDS. DIEU T'EXAUCERA. SOIT! (10:84; I have not attempted to reproduce the triangular shape of the inscription in the novel.)

Raphaël's refusal of the old man's warning appears as a failure to recognize the meanings inherent in language or hidden in the objects around him in the antiquary shop. *Savoir*, he suggests, does not pay:

> — J'avais résolu ma vie par l'étude et par la pensée; mais elles ne m'ont même pas nourri, répliqua l'inconnu. Je ne veux être la dupe ni d'une prédication digne de Swedenborg, ni de votre amulette orientale, ni des charitables efforts que vous faites, monsieur, pour me retenir dans un monde où mon existence est désormais impossible. (10:87)

In the course of the novel, the shrinking skin and the depletion of Raphaël's vital forces reveal the truth of the old man's predictions, the hidden meaning of the inscription on the skin, and the validity of the "prédication digne de Swedenborg." Raphaël, like the reader of novels, must be taught to interpret the objects which surround him in the city as signs of an underlying moral system, rather than commodities which beckon to one's desires.

La recherche de l'Absolu

The one direct reference to Swedenborg in *La recherche de l'Absolu* occurs in the context of the description of Balthazar Claës's physiognomy near the beginning of the novel. The narrator attempts to interpret the appearance of Balthazar according to the point of view of Gall, Lavater, and a priest:

> Son large front offrait d'ailleurs les protuberances dans lesquelles Gall a placé les mondes poétiques. (10:671)

> Lavater aurait voulu certainement étudier cette tête pleine de patience, de loyauté flamande, de moralité candide, où tout était large et grand, où la passion semblait calme parce qu'elle était forte. (10:672)

> A un prêtre, il eût paru plein.de la parole de Dieu, un artiste l'eût salué comme un grand maître, un enthousiaste l'eût pris pour un Voyant de l'Eglise swedenborgienne. (10:673)

The summary of the life of Balthazar Claës at the beginning of the novel allegorizes the relationship between the development of science and nature philosophy, on the one hand, and French history, on the other. Balthazar, who was born in 1761, traveled to Paris in 1783, in time to acquaint himself both with scientific and pseudoscientific circles and with court life before the Revolution, which put an end to his hopes of worldly or scientific success. Already, his early abandonment of his scientific pursuits for the facile eroticism of the salon suggests an opposition between science and instinct. What sets Balthazar apart from the mainstream of late-eighteenth-century science and philosophy, however, is his fascination with those sciences and pseudosciences, such as chemistry and Mesmerism, which focus on the invisible aspects of phenomena. It is probably this fascination which leads him to marry the extraordinarily ugly, but noble-minded, Mlle de Temninck upon his return to Douai. In 1805, the death of Mme Claës's brother leaves the family with a sizeable inheritance. The visit of a Polish refugee, Adam de Wierzchownia, in 1809, revives Balthazar's interest in chemistry, and by 1815, the year of Napoleon's defeat, the family is nearly ruined. Madame Claës dies shortly thereafter, and her daughter, Marguerite, is able to extract a promise from her father to give up his experiments, but by 1830, he has nearly ruined them again. Marguerite, however, is able to solve the family's problems in a manner that is fundamentally opposed to her father's strategy, for rather than attempting to invent a new technique, she seeks an alliance with an aristocratic family, marrying a young noble with the Swedenborgian name, Emmanuel. Returning from her honeymoon in Spain that year, however, Marguerite finds the house stripped of every valuable belonging: "L'idée de l'Absolu avait passé partout comme un incendie." (10:829)

Marguerite's marriage and Balthazar's scientific mania are presented as two alternatives for the solution of the tensions in French society in 1830: on the one hand, a peaceful reconciliation of the interests of a very docile bourgeoisie and a piously rigid aristocracy, represented by the marriage of the self-effacing Marguerite and her noble suitor, Emmanuel; on the other hand, revolution, whose destructive effects are captured in Balzac's use of hyperbole to describe the consequences of Balthazar's obsession. "L'idée de l'Absolu avait passé partout comme un incendie": these words suggest that the novelist viewed the July Revolution in similar terms—as the extreme expression of an individualistic mania which bordered on the insane. Two years later, Balthazar dies. His dying word—"Eureka!"—suggests that he found the Absolute in death, and perhaps ultimately, that this is what the idea of the Absolute—or Revolution—leads to.

La recherche de l'Absolu draws a distinction between two kinds of systems: one, scientific, analytical, mechanistic, and hostile to human life; the other consisting of forms of tradition which mediate between human interests and a natural world viewed in hierarchical terms. The relationship between the nature-philosophical doctrines which fascinate Balthazar Claës and the forms of tradition which oppose the destructive advances of modern science (and also political change) is complex. Both mediate between consciousness and the material world. In themselves, however, the doctrines of Gall, Lavater, and, especially, Mesmer are incomplete. They focus on the relationship of the individual will to the material world, and their fragmentary approach entails all of what Balzac believes to be the evil consequences of individualism. Only in connection with theological or theosophical doctrines, such as Swedenborgianism, which complete their theories concerning the nature of the invisible world and transform them from mere sciences into cosmologies, do nature-philosophical doctrines such as phrenology, physiognomy, and animal magnetism become appropriate models for the ordering of society. Here, as in *Les proscrits*, Swedenborgianism is assimilated to the concept of a theological system much like that of traditional Catholicism.

Like *Louis Lambert* and *Séraphîta*, *La peau de chagrin* and *La recherche de l'Absolu* dramatize the inadequacy of individual consciousness either to comprehend the totality of the world or to control his or her own destiny. Both Raphaël de Valentin and Balthazar Claës suffer from an excess of *Vouloir* over *Savoir*, but whereas Raphaël is in love with appearances, Balthazar is obsessed with interiority: the two loves of his life are chemistry and a noble but hunchbacked wife.

Against the inability of the protagonists to comprehend or control their worlds, the novels set a world of objects, both natural and aesthetic or artificial, which speak to the reader like a language. The meaningfulness of the settings of the novel derives from a concept of a natural taxonomy or hieroglyphic language inherent in nature itself, but also manifest in the forms of art and tradition.

The opening of *La recherche de l'Absolu* suggests that architecture forms the basis for the novelist's activity, which consists, like that of the archaeologist, in the reconstruction of the life of an epoch in which the subjects of history, the creators of the buildings and artifacts he or she examines, are curiously absent:

> Les événements de la vie humaine, soit publique, soit privée, sont si intimement liés à l'architecture, que la plupart des observateurs peuvent reconstruire les nations ou les individus dans toute la vérité de leurs habitudes d'après les restes de leurs monuments publics ou par l'examen de leurs reliques domestiques. L'archéologie est à la nature sociale ce que l'anatomie comparée est à la nature organisée. Une mosaïque révèle toute une société, comme un squelette d'ichthyosaure sous-entend toute une création. De part et d'autre, tout se déduit, tout s'enchaîne. (10:657–58)

In both *La peau de chagrin* and *La recherche de l'Absolu*, however, it is above all the collection—of works of art and bric à brac—that suggests the task of representing life in contemporary French society. Here, as elsewhere in Balzac's work, from the "Avertissement du *Gars*" to *Le cousin Pons*, the highest aesthetic value is accorded to Dutch and Flemish masterpieces because they appear to combine the reproduction of appearances with the evocation of interiority. Yet this interiority turns out, like human life itself, to be governed by an economy which resembles the circulation of money. Raphaël de Valentin, for example, climbs up to the third and highest level of the antiquary shop, the level which contains the most "spiritual" works of art, only to encounter an old man who looks like Gerrit Dou's *Le peseur d'or*. (10:78) The jumbled collections of resonant artifacts from all periods suggest the task of the writer and his or her reader: the reconstruction of a unity in a world which consists of alien but suggestive ruins.

The Fragments: *Les deux amis, Les martyrs ignorés*, and *Aventures administratives d'une idée heureuse*

References to Swedenborg also occur in three fragments written in the 1830s.

The earliest reference to Swedenborg in a fictional work by Balzac occurs in the first version of the unfinished work, *Les deux amis*, written in 1830. The reference occurs in the context of a confrontation between the two friends and a woman whom they both desire and to whom one of them has just proposed:

> Quelles actions de grâces nous devons rendre à la nature pour
> n'avoir départi qu'à quelques malheureux cette seconde vue, dont la pré-
> voyance et la prudence sont deux pales rayons! . . . Si Swedenborg avait
> été là, Claire serait peut-être tombée morte. (12:683)

The association of Swedenborg with the gift of second sight points forward
to the discussion of *Spécialité*, a higher state of consciousness, in *Louis
Lambert* and *Séraphîta*, but the frivolous context of the allusion scarcely
suggests serious interest in his doctrines. The reference, moreover, evokes
no resonances with other aspects of the plot or thematic structure of the
novella.

The 1845 *Catalogue* of works to be included in *La comédie humaine*
lists, among other projected works, two narratives which, in their unfinished form, contain references and allusions to Swedenborgianism. *Les
martyrs ignorés* was to form part of a larger work, *Le Phédon d'aujourd'hui*, which was to stand at the beginning of *Les études philosophiques*. *Aventures administratives d'une idée heureuse*, renamed in the
Catalogue La vie et les aventures d'une idée, was to come near the end of
this section of *La comédie humaine*; it was to be the last work to precede
the final trilogy, *Les proscrits*, *Louis Lambert*, and *Séraphîta*. The position
of these two titles in the *Catalogue* suggested that Balzac saw the works—
in their projected form—to be of central importance to the development
of *Les études philosophiques*. In the form in which we have them, however, the two fragments do not live up to our—and probably Balzac's—
expectations.

Aventures administratives d'une idée heureuse, probably written in
1833, allegorizes the history of one man's idea for the building of a canal.
The opening of the narrative, the "Fantasque Avant-propos," takes the form
of a conversation in a salon. Here an allusion to Swedenborg occurs in the
context of a Prussian scientist's mockery of Louis Lambert's system:

> Mais, madame, répondit en souriant le Prussien, est-ce un système?
> Je n'oserais ni le nier ni l'affirmer. De l'autre côté du Rhin, plusieurs
> hommes se sont élevés dans les régions éthérées et se sont cassé la tête
> contre les étoiles. Des écrivains en *org*, en *ohm*, en *oehm*, ont trouvé, dit-
> on, dans ces mêmes étoiles, de sublimes pensées que comprennent quel-
> ques gens presque fous, selon nos informes opinions vulgaires. (12:769)

The Prussian goes on to recount a story which also mocks the notion,
central to Louis Lambert's system, of the material nature of thought. The
story concerns a German abroad who complained to the authorities that
his thoughts had been stolen. The Prussian comments:

A Paris, personne ne se serait étonné de ces vols; on y prend sans façon
les idées des gens qui ont des idées, seulement on ne les met pas en bocal,
on les met en journal, en livre, en entreprises. (12:769)

The significance of the Prussian's ironic comments on the nature of genius
and its role in society lies, first of all, in his association of genius and the
sublime with technical achievement (recall, for example, that in the opening chapter of *Séraphîta*, the narrator emphasizes Swedenborg's role in
the construction of a canal from Stromfiord to Sweden; 12:732); and, second, in his parody of themes and situations associated with the *genre fantastique* in order to represent a problem in social relations, rather than
epistemology.

   Les martyrs ignorés appeared in the edition of *Les études philosophiques* published by Werdet in 1837; it bore the subtitle *Fragment du
Phédon d'aujourd'hui*. *Les martyrs ignorés* takes the form of a philosophical conversation in the tradition of Maistre's *Les soirées de Saint-Petersbourg*. There are seven participants: the young doctor, Physidor, interested in phrenology and insanity; Doctor Phantasma, whose name is
related to his passion for animal magnetism; the Lithuanian, Grodninsky,
mathematician, chemist, and inventor; the dreamy and foolish German,
Tschoern; the poor and tubucular Raphaël, whom Balzac called Raphaël de
Valentin twice in the manuscript; the Byronic Irishman, Théophile Or-
mond; and the bookseller. In the one completed conversation, here called
the eighth, Phantasma, the bookseller, Théophile, Tschoern, and Physidor
recount stories of moral crimes, instances in which the actions of one
individual were responsible for the demoralizing of another, to the extent
that the victims died or went insane. Various explanations for the apparent powers of suggestion to bring about changes in a person's physical, as
well as mental, health are explored. The reference to Swedenborgianism
occurs in the context of the last speaker's discussion of the occult sciences
as models for more recent attempts to create systems which would account for the apparent unity of spirit and matter. Here Swedenborgianism
is identified with the tradition of magic. Physidor describes thinkers such
as Becher, Stahl, Paracelsus, and Agrippa as magic thinkers:

> Dans les infiniment petits, ils voulaient surprendre les secrets de la Vie
> universelle dont ils apercevaient le jeu. La réunion de ces sciences con-
> stitue le Magisme, ne le confondez pas avec la magie. Le Magisme est la
> haute science qui cherche à découvrir le sens intime des choses, et qui
> recherche par quels fils déliés les effets naturels s'y rattachent. (12:743)

To which Grodninsky replies:

Vous arriverez quelque jour, en France, aux concordances de Swedenborg.
(12:743)

Grodninsky's reply suggests that Swedenborg's theories are the natural
complement, rather than an alternative, to the doctrines of animal magnetism and phrenology, as well as "magisme." His comparison is similar to
Louis Lambert's words concerning the relationship between Swedenborg
and magical traditions, which Madeleine Ambrière-Fargeaud cites in her
notes to the second Pléiade edition:

> Swedenborg reprend au Magisme, au Brahamaïsme, au Bouddhisme et au
> Mysticisme chrétien ce que ces quatre grandes religions ont de commun,
> de réel, de divin, et rend à leur doctrine une raison pour ainsi dire mathé-
> matique. (11:656)

As we have seen, references to Swedenborg or Swedenborgianism in
Balzac's novels of the early 1830s are embedded in a rich intertextual context that includes the work of Leibniz, other German philosophers and
aestheticians, Mesmer, his followers and wayward disciples, and various
visionary writers, such as Dante, Milton, and Tasso.

Although the novelist says nothing of his sources, his knowledge of
and interest in Swedenborgian doctrines in the early 1830s seem to go
hand in hand with his concern with the political issues at stake in the
revolution of 1830. The earliest reference to Swedenborg in a novel published in *La comédie humaine* occurs in *La peau de chagrin*, written in
that year and presenting an argument for the containment of individual
desires. At the time of that novel's composition and publication, Balzac's
declared political allegiances were liberal. *Louis Lambert* and *Séraphîta*,
however, were written the year of his notorious "conversion" to royalism,
and reflect the influence of conservative political theory, for they interpret
Swedenborgianism as a doctrine that emphasizes the importance of authority and tradition and that represents language as emanating from an
unknowable origin, but becoming increasingly corrupt in an age that has
severed its ties with the past. At the same time, however, Balzac also saw
Swedenborg as a kind of eclectic theosopher, as his contemporary Edouard
Richer also had. Did Balzac know Richer or Oegger? Was he familiar with
Jean-Jacques Bernard's defense of Maistre's political theory? His novels say
nothing on this subject, but the thumbnail sketches of the lives of principal characters do suggest that he was very familiar with the history and
political and cultural implications of the development of Swedenborgianism, Mesmerism, and other occult traditions in France in the late eighteenth and early nineteenth centuries.

Despite the rarity of explicit references to Swedenborg and Sweden-borgianism outside *Louis Lambert* and *Séraphîta*, there is plenty of evidence in other Balzacian narratives to suggest that Swedenborgianism, especially in its interpretations in various French milieux, played an important role in the evolution of the novelist's concept of a fictional system that would capture the totality of contemporary society. This seems nowhere clearer than in three novels Balzac published in the 1840s.

4. Through A Glass Darkly: Swedenborgianism in *Les études de moeurs*

The Avant-propos of 1842

In 1842, Balzac composed a preface to the novel cycle he had come to call *La comédie humaine*. This essay or Avant-propos represents his most programmatic statement on the nature and structure of his novel cycle, looking back and consolidating many remarks made elsewhere during the late 1820s and 1830s.

The essay opens with an invocation of the mystical notion of emanation, dear to conservative political theorists such as Bonald and Maistre, as well as some French interpreters of Swedenborgianism. But it ties this notion both to dreams and to the taxonomies of natural history, which, Balzac argues, form the basis for the discernment of an immutable hierarchal order in human society. History and the novel should, like the taxonomic systems of natural history, aim to capture the totality of the species, but this is somewhat more difficult in human affairs because human beings are double, *homo duplex*. How then to capture the totality of the human world? Balzac argues that such an interpretation must take a threefold form:

> Ainsi l'oeuvre à faire devait avoir une triple forme: les hommes, les femmes et les choses, c'est-à-dire les personnes et la représentation matérielle qu'ils donnent de leur pensée; enfin l'homme et la vie. (1:9)

One sees here a justification for the division of *La comédie humaine* into three sections: *Les études de moeurs*, *Les études philosophiques*, and *Les études physiologiques*. But the emphasis on the importance of different points of view for the representation of human society also forms part of a more general argument concerning what history and the novel can and should do. Historians, Balzac complains in a passage that recalls the reference to the "squelette chronologique" of bad history in the "Avertissement du *Gars*," have often treated events too superficially, forgetting the importance of customs and culture, of *moeurs*. Here the novel has an important role to play in illustrating how different kinds of narrative can bring to life a variegated portrait of human society.

In the Avant-propos, as in many of Balzac's earlier prefaces and statements on the novel, including the "Avertissement du *Gars*," Walter Scott is invoked as an important but flawed model. Scott's historical novels had suggested the idea of a novel cycle about *contemporary* French society, but, Balzac argues, the Protestant perspective of the Scottish novelist had blinded him to the mysteries of love and womanhood—as perceived through one set of Catholic lenses. Moreover, the novelist asserts, "Le Catholicisme et la Royauté sont deux principes jumeaux." (1:13) The Avant-propos presents *La comédie humaine* as a novel cycle that illustrates the validity of these two principles—although, from the point of view of many later commentators, the greatness of Balzac's novel cycle stems from how unsuccessful it was in this attempt.

There are two references to Swedenborg or Swedenborgianism in the preface. The second reference is the simpler of the two, tying Swedenborg and *Louis Lambert* to the Catholic and conservative political vision of the preface as a whole:

> L'unique religion possible est le Christianisme (voir la lettre écrite de Paris dans *Louis Lambert*, où le jeune philosophe mystique explique, à propos de la doctrine de Swedenborg, comment il n'y a jamais eu qu'une même religion depuis l'origine du monde). Le Christianisme a crée les peuples modernes, il les conservera. De là sans doute la nécessité du principe monarchique. Le Catholicisme et le Royauté sont deux principes jumeaux. (1:13)

The first links Swedenborg to the kind of mystical theories that demonstrate the continuity among the structures of natural history, religion, and human psychology:

> En relisant les oeuvres si extraordinaires des écrivains mystiques qui se sont occupés des sciences dans leurs relations avec l'infini, tels que Swedenborg, Saint-Martin, etc., et les écrits des plus beaux génies en histoire naturelle, tels que Leibniz, Buffon, Charles Bonnet, etc., on trouve dans les monades de Leibniz, dans les molécules organiques de Buffon, dans la force végétatrice de Needham, dans l'*emboîtement* des parties similaires de Charles Bonnet, assez hardi pour écrire en 1760: *L'animal végète comme la plante*; on trouve, dis-je, les rudiments de la belle loi du *soi pour soi* sur laquelle repose l'*unité de composition*." (I, 7–8)

Although it does not name it explicitly, this passage implies the presence and importance of a hidden language informing visible and invisible worlds and mapping out an ideal order that the attentive individual might discern. In his third letter from Paris, Louis Lambert had written of a new social science capable of comprehending modern society. This passage pulls together many of the disparate elements in that work and other early novels in *La comédie humaine* to show how they fit together as part of such a system.

It is a system that one is tempted to call "ideological"—in two senses. First, it points to a system of beliefs that few of Balzac's readers agree with. But second, and more importantly, it also recalls the work of the Idéologues, who emphasized the role of a universal language of nature in the reformation of human society. If Balzac never discussed his work in relation to that of the Idéologues, it may be because in France in the first part of the nineteenth century, their work was associated with the fortunes of liberalism, a position Balzac renounced after 1832. But the work of the Idéologues also aimed to undermine the very structures of authority and hierarchy Balzac so painstakingly constructed in the Avant-propos. Despite obvious differences in religious and political loyalties, the structures mapped out in Balzac's preface resemble works by Idéologues such as Destutt de Tracy in that both attempt to describe an unchanging scientific grid underlying all of experience. And for both, the belief in an unchanging order underlying appearances serves as a point of departure for criticizing the organization of contemporary society. But it is precisely this notion of a timeless, universal, and psychological order that Balzac's novels of the 1840s call into question.

A consolidating work, the Avant-propos has more to do with Balzac's work of the previous decade than with the novels he composed in the decade preceding his death in 1850. It emphasizes the continuing importance of *Le livre mystique* and the other *Etudes philosophiques* within the context of *La comédie humaine* as a whole, arguing that both visionary or occult doctrines and the taxonomies of natural history are necessary for the representation of *homo duplex* in society. Far more consistently than the novels written in the early 1830s, however, the Avant-propos assimilates these doctrines to a conservative political vision emphasizing the importance of Catholic orthodoxy and feudal tradition for the creation of good literature and the maintenance of order in society. But Balzac's novels rarely seem to demonstrate what the Avant-propos lays down. Narratives of the 1840s also reconsider the mystical and occult themes of *Les études philosophiques*, but with very different implications.

Ursule Mirouët

Published in 1842, *Ursule Mirouët* also relates the doctrines of Swedenborgianism and Mesmerism to the representation of a hierarchical series which informs nature, society, and human consciousness. In contrast to the Avant-propos, however, *Ursule Mirouët* presents this "natural" order as out of kilter with the structures of contemporary society; its existence is evoked through language, especially what Balzac calls the "occulte puissance des noms," (3:772) and the electrifying apparitions of the heroine's uncle, which safeguard her inheritance and see to it that she marries her aristocratic neighbor, rather than her bourgeois cousin. The early novels of *La comédie humaine* collected in the section entitled *Les études philosophiques* had been concerned with the conflict between *Volonté* and *Savoir* in individual consciousness and had tended to represent the doctrines of Swedenborgianism and Mesmerism as two terms of an opposition. *Ursule Mirouët* presents us with a version of Mesmerism which has incorporated elements of Swedenborgianism to form a system which could mediate, like the hierarchical totality evoked in the Avant-propos, between science, theology, and the feudal traditions of the aristocracy; but the marriage of Ursule to her neighbor Savinien, rather than to her cousin Désiré, suggests the victory of *Savoir* over *Volonté*, rather than the fusion of the two.

The plot of *Ursule Mirouët* conforms to the conventions of melodrama. A young and innocent orphan, Ursule Mirouët, is almost cheated of her inheritance by a group of greedy relatives, but in the nick of time, both her virtue and her money are saved and she is able to marry her true love, the equally virtuous but penniless aristocrat, Savinien de Portenduère. Here the melodramatic twists of the plot bring into play the interests of a hierarchical class society. A greedy but enterprising and energetic provincial bourgeoisie competes with an impoverished and exhausted aristocracy for the dowry of a young girl whose questionable origins (her father was illegitimate) and docility make her an appropriate mediator between the money of the bourgeoisie and the traditions of the aristocracy. The novel plays off the degraded world of the Nemours bourgeoisie against an ideal hierarchical social order which, it suggests, can be seen in the highly stratified society of Paris. Once the greedy relatives have renounced their claim to the inheritance, Ursule and her husband leave Nemours for Paris, in a move which the novel describes in terms of transcendence. At the end of the novel, the young couple appears to both the narrator and his readers as a kind of apparition: we catch a brief glimpse of a couple which *may* be the Portenduères in a luxuriously equipped carriage. While the novel attempts to give precedence to the hierarchical structures suggested by Ursule's movement from the degraded world of the Nemours bourgeoisie to the upper reaches of Parisian society, it is unable to evoke them directly. *Ursule Mirouët* uses the language of Mesmerism and Swedenborgianism in order to suggest the existence of a hidden hierarchical order which validates and to some extent safeguards the interests of an aristocracy whose position in contemporary society is based on tradition alone.

The seances and apparitions in *Ursule Mirouët* point to a hidden order of things in which Ursule's desire, money, and an aristocratic name are identical. Mesmerism mediates between the thematic oppositions established by the text: between nature and morality, interiority and society, money and a good name—the possibilities seem endless. In terms of the plot, these revelations bring about both the recovery of her inheritance and her marriage to Savinien de Portenduère. However, the suggestion of a hidden order of things which stands in opposition to the surfaces of post-Revolutionary French society also calls into question the system of representation which this novel, like the Avant-propos, insists on.

There are two movements in the novel: one essentially metaphoric, associated with the ascendence of Ursule and Savinien to a superior sphere of French society in Paris; the other, a lateral movement in which language and money proliferate metonymically, without regard for origins. On the one hand, the "occulte puissance" of the language of the novel evokes the resonances of tradition; on the other, the attempt to imitate a tradition which is no longer alive results in a kind of parody in which words take on a life of their own. The narrator's summary of the history of the main families of the Nemours bourgeoisie in terms of a parody of aristocratic genealogies, for example, is obviously intended to suggest the universality of the preoccupation with names and origins in French society; what it points to, however, is the absurdity of an obsession with an anachronism:

> Sous Louis IX époque à laquelle le Tiers Etat a fini par faire de ses surnoms de véritables noms dont quelques-uns se mêlèrent à ceux de la Féodalité, la bourgeoisie de Nemours se composait de Minoret, de Massin, de Levrault et de Cremière. Sous Louis XIII, ces quatre familles produisaient déjà des Massin-Cremière, des Levrault-Massin, des Massin-Minoret, des Minoret-Minoret, des Cremière-Levrault, des Levrault-Minoret-Massin, des Massin-Levrault, des Minoret-Massin, des Massin-Massin, des Cremière-Massin, tout cela bariolé de junior, de fils aîné, de Cremière-François, de Levrault-Jacques, de Jean-Minoret, à rendre fou le père Anselme, si le Peuple avait jamais besoin de généalogiste. (3:782)

In similar fashion, the conclusion of the novel, in which a brief glimpse of an isolated aristocratic couple is played off against a panorama of the Nemours bourgeoisie, suggests problems in the attempt of the language of the novel to revive the traditions of the past and to bring about a reconciliation between bourgeois money and aristocratic names and traditions. We are never sure of the identity of the couple; the young blond woman, aristocratic and unattainable, could be anyone whom the reader—or, more significantly, the narrator or Balzac—happened to see and desire on one of his walks through Paris. The passage, with its fetishization of the details of the carriage and the woman's person, both evokes and warns against desire.

> Quand en voyant passer aux Champs Elysées une de ces charmantes petites voitures basses appelées *escargots*, doublée de soie gris de lin ornée d'agréments bleus, vous y admirerez une jolie femme blonde, la figure enveloppée comme d'un feuillage par des milliers de boucles, montrant des yeux semblables à des pervenches lumineuses et pleins d'amour, légèrement appuyée sur un beau jeune homme; si vous étiez mordu par un désir envieux, pensez que ce beau couple, aimé de Dieu, a d'avance payé sa quote-part aux malheurs de la vie. Ces deux amants mariés seront vraisemblablement le vicomte de Portenduère et sa femme. Il n'y a pas deux ménages semblables dans Paris. (3:987)

Here, one suspects, is the real origin of the text, an initial moment of desire which is then sublimated into the narrative of the poor blond orphan, a narrative which recounts a quest for origins which may be seen either in atemporal religious or metaphysical terms or as a golden age of the past.

The movement to repress or negate desire is repeated in the names of the principal characters, which possess what Balzac refers to in an early part of the novel as the "occulte puissance des noms." (3:772) There are two principal contenders for Ursule's fortune and hand, the aristocratic Savinien and her bourgeois cousin, Désiré Minoret-Levrault. Their names echo the opposition, given its most famous expression in *La peau de chagrin*, between *Volonté* and *Savoir*, recalling the fate of Raphaël de Valentin, who was killed by his addiction to desire. The young Désiré, too, dies, but in a manner which is much more violent and almost completely unmotivated by the narrative. At the end of the novel, he is simply run over by a carriage, losing his legs and later his life. The death and castration of Désiré-desire seems to have been the price the narrator was willing to pay for the marriage of Ursule and Savinien and for the maintenance of a hierarchical model of representation.

The conclusion of *Ursule Mirouët*, which takes us from Nemours to Paris and back again to Nemours, establishes the continuity of the hierarchical structures which the novel, like the Avant-propos, characterizes as informing nature, society, and human consciousness. The reference here to the momentary impression of the *flâneur*, his glimpse of the wealthy pair in their carriage, suggests that the function of narrative is to integrate the fragmentary experiences of the city-dweller into a "natural" totality embracing both nature and society, and through the "occulte puissance des noms" to convince him—or perhaps her—of the necessity of renouncing desires which threaten the structures of authority and tradition.

The analogy suggested here, between esoteric and occult doctrines, on the one hand, and language, on the other, serves to point up the function of language in the novel. *Ursule Mirouët* presents us with a synthesis of the doctrines of Swedenborgianism and Mesmerism, a synthesis which embraces both individual psychology and cosmology; Swedenborgian Mesmerism is a unitary doctrine which reconciles, rather than opposes, the structures of science, theology, and feudal tradition. The energy previously ascribed to the individual is now located in things themselves in the form of "original" meanings which have been obscured by time, but which can be discerned in the form of traces of past traditions inscribed in the world in the way that past meanings are preserved in the etymologies of words. The presence of "original" or "natural" meanings is suggested, above all, by the names of characters in the novel. Minoret-Levrault's name prophesies his size at the conclusion of the novel (3:772); his wife's name, Zélie, reflects her zeal (3:804); the name Désiré points to his father's possible impotence and the ambiguity of his own sexual preferences (3:773), as well as his desire for money and his cousin; Ursule, the narrator tells us, means wild or "sauvage" (3:848), but it is tempting to read in the English sense of "wild" as a wild card or joker here, an interpretation perhaps justified by Ursule's lack of a legitimate origin and uncanny ability to move between different strata of society—although perhaps a more motivated association would be with Saint Ursula, who died a martyr to her virginity; the name of the corrupt clerk, Goupil, is, we are told, a corruption of the Latin *vulpes*, or fox (3:870), an epithet which suits him admirably. Balzac's name play here echoes, as it often does, the work of Sterne. "En pensant que cette espèce d'eléphant sans trompe et sans intelligence se nomme *Minoret-Levrault*," says the narrator, "ne doit-on pas reconnaître l'occulte puissance des noms, qui tantôt raillent et tantôt prédisent les caractères?" (3:772) Minoret-Levrault's withering away at the end of the narrative suggests that Balzac's novel will, in other respects, attempt to demonstrate the "occulte puissance," not only of names, but of language in general. As the narrator explains it, an understanding of language—and names in particular—leads not only to the revival of the past, but also to the understanding that the present is nothing but the repetition of the past:

> En quelque pays que vous alliez, changez les noms, vous retrouverez le
> fait, mais sans la poésie que la féodalité lui avait imprimée et que Walter
> Scott a reproduite avec tant de talent. (3:783)

This passage points both to the arbitrariness of the sign and to the literary
or linguistic strategy for overcoming it. In the novel, the concept of a
hidden order of things, an original language, compensates for the deficien-
cies of human language. The suggestion of an original "occult" language
hidden in nature and society is doubled in the narrative by an invitation to
interpret the names of the central characters both in terms of a moral
meaning and in terms of their origin. We are invited, in other words, to
interpret the names of the characters metaphorically, a process which
serves both to give the narrative an illusion of depth and to locate the
characters in terms of the invisible hierarchy suggested by the "occulte
puissance" of language, by the doctrines of Swedenborgianism and Mesmerism, and by the emphasis on feudal origins.

The most obvious example of reduplication in the novel is Ursule Mirouët herself, who bears the name of Denis Minoret's wife, who had died of
terror during the Terror. Ursule, who is born during the siege of Paris in
1814, represents a second chance, both for her uncle and, the narrative
suggests, for French society as a whole. Her survival of 1830 and subsequent marriage to Savinien de Portenduère suggest an alternative to revolution in the nineteenth century. If, for Balzac, in real life the identity of
historical circumstances is masked by shifts in human language and
names, his narrative insists on the identity of names in order to suggest
correspondences between historical events which are not at first apparent.

Like many of Balzac's novels, *Ursule Mirouët* is set in the years immediately surrounding 1830. The novel is less concerned, however, with the
causes and effects of the revolution, than with imagining an alternative to
revolution: the repression of bourgeois desire and the marriage of money
and aristocratic names. The alternative is proposed as a model for the
resolution of tensions inherent in French society in 1840. Thus Balzac re-
writes the Revolution of 1830 in order that it may be reread in 1840 in
terms of a revolution which never was and which, therefore, cannot be
repeated.

Le cousin Pons

First published in 1847, *Le cousin Pons* links Swedenborgianism,
Mesmerism, and other occult beliefs to the invention of new forms of mechanical reproduction, especially the daguerreotype, and to the beliefs and
practices of "new" characters in *La comédie humaine*: Parisian petit bourgeois, workers, and artisans. Recounting the story of an old man, an *artiste*

manqué turned collector who is robbed of his art collection and murdered by his concierge and her confederates, the novel calls into question the validity of the supernatural doctrines that *Les études philosophiques* and the Avant-propos of 1842 had insisted were a necessary—and natural— part of the representation of society.

The two collections in *Le cousin Pons* (1847) recall those of *La peau de chagrin* and *La recherche de l'Absolu*. Both the old bourgeois Pons's private collection and that of Rémonencq, the peasant who comes to Paris to make good, sets up shop, and poisons Pons in order to steal his trea- sures, contain works from different periods, although Pons's collection, like the aesthetic objects kept on the third tier of the antiquary shop in *La peau de chagrin* or the collection of the Claës family in *La recherche de l'Absolu*, gives pride of place to Dutch and Flemish painting. The two col- lections in *Le cousin Pons* are above all linked by the circulation of these paintings from one to the other, but the movement of the spiritual works of art from Pons's private collection to the window of Rémonencq's shop on the boulevards points to one of the most important differences between *Les études de moeurs* of the 1840s and *Les études philosophiques* of the early 1830s. This difference has to do with the shift in focus from the individual's relationship to nature to his or her place in the city. The ob- jects in Rémonencq's shop window not only represent a haphazard collec- tion from different periods and contexts; they have been removed from any kind of sacred place, where they might receive the veneration of a few connoisseurs, to be exposed to the glance of every passerby on the boule- vards. They have, to use Walter Benjamin's expression, lost their "aura." Like the collections in earlier novels, those of *Le cousin Pons* suggest an organic unity which has been lost in the city and must be reconstituted by the individual viewer. Like the earlier novels and like the Avant-propos to *La comédie humaine*, *Le cousin Pons* sets the fragmentary and jumbled experience of the city against a concept of the world as a hierarchical totality, a totality which is described in terms of occult and pseudoscien- tific doctrines which mediate between the structures of natural science and what are projected as invisible worlds of morality and consciousness. In *Le cousin Pons*, the evocation of this totality has come to rest almost exclusively in language itself. The language of the novelist is perceived as possessing the depth and substance of the buildings and streets he de- scribes; it functions like a machine in order to spin out a narrative which draws the most momentary and fleeting of the *flâneur*'s impressions into a drama which encompasses the entirety of society.

Like *Louis Lambert*, *Séraphîta*, and *Ursule Mirouët*, *Le cousin Pons* contains an expository passage on the history and function of an occult science. In *Pons*, however, this passage focuses on the survival of occult beliefs among the popular classes in the city, and the description of a visit to a fortuneteller takes us back in time, as well as down into the city, where both the language and the beliefs of the inhabitants reflect the elite culture of earlier epochs. The inhabitants of poorer districts of the city are described in terms of the inert matter out of which the city is constructed: Balzac compares the closed mind of a visionary proletarian to a "diamant brut [qui] garde l'éclat de ses facettes." (7:488) The journey down into quarters of the city most often "forgotten" by the bourgeoisie takes us into regions where consciousness and its objects merge. The occult beliefs of the past merge with the most advanced technological developments of the 1840s: the "monde spectral" evoked by the fortuneteller is identified with the image caught by the daguerreotype. The apparatus of both fortuneteller and daguerreotype, moreover, are described in terms of a linguistic metaphor: both demand that we read an isolated event or image in terms of its representation of the whole; both operate, in other words, according to the principle represented by the rhetorical figure of synecdoche.

Swedenborg's Great Man, together with Rabelais's microcosm, is cited as one of the antecedents for this kind of reading of the city:

> Quand aux moyens employés pour arriver aux *visions*, c'est là le merveilleux le plus explicable, dès que la main du consultant dispose les objets à l'aide desquels on lui fait représenter les hasards de sa vie. En effet, tout s'enchaîne dans le monde réel. Tout mouvement y correspond à une cause, toute cause se rattache à l'ensemble; et, conséquemment, l'ensemble se représente dans le moindre mouvement. Rabelais, le plus grand esprit de l'humanité moderne, cet homme qui résuma Pythagore, Hippocrate, Aristophane et Dante, a dit, il y a maintenant trois siècles: L'homme est un microcosme. Trois siècles après, Swedenborg, le grand prophète suédois, disait que la terre était un homme. Le prophète et le précurseur de l'incrédulité se rencontraient ainsi dans la plus grande des formules. Tout est fatal dans la vie humaine, comme dans la vie de notre planète. (7:587)

The metaphor of the correspondence between the individual body and the world has two related functions in the novel: it allows the novelist to represent French society, and particularly parts of the city, as a diseased organism, and it provides a justification for the spinning of a narrative out of an isolated perception in the street.

The metaphor of the city as a diseased organism informs one of the most striking and unusual passages in *Le cousin Pons*, the description of the Passage Bordin and its inhabitants:

Schmucke suivit comme un mouton Topinard, qui le conduisit dans une de ces affreuses localités qu'on pourrait appeler les cancers de Paris. La chose se nomme cité Bordin. C'est un passage étroit, bordé de maisons bâties comme on bâtit par spéculation, qui débouche rue de Bondy, dans cette partie de la rue ombombrée par l'immense bâtiment du théâtre de la Porte-Saint-Martin, une des verrues de Paris. Ce passage, dont la voie est creusée en contrebas de la chaussée de la rue, s'enfonce par une pente vers la rue des Mathurins-du-Temple. La cité finit par une rue intérieure qui la barre en figurant la forme d'un T. Ces deux ruelles, ainsi disposées, contiennent une trentaine de maisons à six et sept étages, dont les cours intérieures, dont tous les appartements contiennent des magasins, des industries, des fabriques en tout genre. C'est le faubourg Saint-Antoine en miniature. On y fait des meubles, on y cisèle les cuivres, on y coud des costumes pour les théâtres, on y travaille le verre, on y peint les porce- laines, on y fabrique enfin toutes les fantaisies et les variétés de l'article- Paris. Sale et productif comme le commerce, ce passage, toujours plein d'allants et de venants, de charrettes, de haquets, est d'un aspect repous- sant, et la population qui y grouille est en harmonie avec les choses et les lieux. C'est le peuple des fabriques, peuple intelligent dans les travaux manuels, mais dont l'intelligence s'y absorbe. (7:750–51)

Like Rémonencq's shop, the Passage Bordin represents an ironic double of the bourgeois interior, the lodgings of Pons and Schmucke or the apart- ment of the Camusot family. The passage represents a city in miniature and, at the same time, a space removed from the boulevards. It swarms with an alien life which the narrator can capture only with comparisons to disease or insect life. Like Rémonencq's shop, the passage and the alien life which fills it appear to represent a future in which the individualism of Pons, with his small room filled with works of art reflecting a humanism of the past, will be meaningless.

The analogies between the body and the city and the part and the whole also make possible the narrator's interpretation at the beginning of the novel of the isolated and alien figure of an old man dressed in the style of the Empire, who appears on the boulevards every afternoon. Only grad- ually does this anachronistic figure assume an identity, to draw us into a drama which comes to encompass all of French society. The language of the narrator reproduces—and replaces—the totality of the visible and in- visible worlds he believes is represented by the occult sciences and the daguerreotype. "Quant aux moyens employés pour arriver aux *visions*," the narrator declares in his digression on the subject of the occult sciences, "c'est là le merveilleux le plus explicable, dès que la main du consultant dispose les objets à l'aide desquels on lui fait représenter les hasards de sa vie." (7:587) His analysis of the fortuneteller's technique characterizes the role of language in the novel; working on the basis of an analogy between the part and the whole, the language of the novel functions like a machine which, in the manner of a film projector, transforms the momentary impression of the *flâneur* on the boulevards into a "moving" narrative. This is not a chance comparison, for *Le cousin Pons* contains several striking references to new forms of technology, such as the daguerreotype and the railway, as well as classes of people not represented in Balzac's novels of the 1830s.

In his essays on Baudelaire, Walter Benjamin suggested that the form of Baudelaire's poetry mimicked the architecture of the Paris streets and the movements of the crowd within them.[21] In *Le cousin Pons*, we find an explicit justification for the correspondence between the structures of language and the City. The analogies Balzac works with here—city/body, writing-archaeology/geology—lead to a conception of language as a substance which, like bodies and artifacts, conceals mysteries within its interior.

By the 1840s, however, Balzac had come to identify these mysteries with a specific historical past: the feudal order that had been disrupted by the Revolution of 1789. One passage illustrates how far he had come from the airy discussion of *correspondances* in *Séraphîta*:

> L'avilissement des mots est une de ces bizarreries des moeurs qui, pour être expliquée, voudrait des volumes. Ecrivez à un avoué en le qualifiant d'*homme de loi*, vous l'aurez offensé tout autant que vous offenseriez un négociant en gros de denrées coloniales à qui vous adresseriez ainsi votre lettre: "Monsieur un tel, épicier." Un assez grand nombre de gens du monde qui devraient savoir, puisque c'est là toute leur science, ces délicatesses du savoir-vivre, ignorent encore que la qualification d'*homme de lettres* est la plus cruelle injure qu'on puisse faire à un auteur. Le mot monsieur est le plus grand exemple de la vie et de la mort des mots. Monsieur veut dire monseigneur. Ce titre, si considérable autrefois, réservé maintenant aux rois par la transformation de sieur en sire, se donne à tout le monde; et néanmoins *messire*, qui n'est pas autre chose que le double du mot monsieur et son équivalent, soulève des articles dans les feuilles républicaines, quand, par hasard, il se trouve mis dans un billet d'enterrement. . . . Mais à Paris, chaque profession a ses Oméga, des individus qui mettent le métier de plain-pied avec la pratique des rues, avec le peuple. Aussi l'*homme de loi*, le petit agent d'affaires existe-t-il encore dans certains quartiers. comme on trouve encore à la Halle le prêteur à la petite semaine qui est à la haute banque ce que M. Fraisier était à la compagnie des avoués. (7:630–31)

The discussion of the doctrine of correspondences in *Heaven and Hell* had also emphasized the importance of recovering meanings that had been lost in the corrupt social and religious cultures of the present, but the past Swedenborg refers to is a distant, mythological, golden age. For Balzac in the 1840s, in contrast, pre-Revolutionary France represents a golden age of stable meanings and a social order in which the machinations of people such as Cousin Pons's upstart enemies would be controlled, if not prevented.

Yet, paradoxically, this past lives on in the present in the popular culture the novel depicts so ambivalently. The fortuneteller keeps the Mesmerist and Swedenborgian traditions of popular culture alive. Whether or not she also transmits their political connotations the narrative does not say. Calling for a return to a stable past, the novel demonstrates the impossibility of such a goal, pointing, instead, to the splintering of languages, cultures, and classes within the world it describes. In *Le cousin Pons*, the hidden hieroglyphic language identified with nature has been transferred to the city, where it no longer bears any relationship to nature or truth. In the novels of the early 1830s, the depiction of an underlying immutable order bore striking resemblances to the concept of language of the Idéologues, who suggested that its decipherment might point the way to a more rational ordering of the social world. In *Le cousin Pons*, on the other hand, the hieroglyphic language of the city had come to resemble the later association of ideology with error, with perceptions that take mechanical reproductions too literally, and with beliefs that distort in order to further class interests. It has lost all connection to nature and to truth. The end of the novel shows that the predictions of the fortuneteller simply do not come true.

> Mme Rémenoncq, frappée de la prédiction de Mme Fontaine, ne veut pas se retirer à la campagne, elle reste dans son magnifique magasin du boulevard de la Madeleine, encore une fois veuve. En effet, l'Auvergnat, après s'être fait donner par contrat de mariage les biens au dernier vivant, avait mis à portée de sa femme un petit verre de vitriol, comptant sur une erreur, et sa femme, dans une intention excellente, ayant mis ailleurs le petit verre, Rémenoncq l'avala. Cette fin, digne de ce scélérat, prouve en faveur de la Providence que les peintres de moeurs sont accusés d'oublier, peut-être à cause des dénouements de drames qui en abusent.
> Excusez les fautes du copiste! (7:765)

No ending, it seems at first glance, could be more easily viewed as watertight. Here, as in the digression on the occult, the supernatural is cited as proving the truth and the morality of the novelist's tale. Yet the conclusion stands in direct contradiction to the fortune predicted for Mme Rémonencq when she was still Mme Cibot:

Plus tard vous vous repentirez dans les angoisses de la mort, car vous mourrez assassinée par deux forçats évadés, un petit à cheveux rouges et un vieux tout chauve, à cause de la fortune qu'on vous supposera dans le village où vous vous retirerez avec votre second mari. (7:591)

Moreover, the arbitrary punishment of Rémonencq and not his wife offers little in the way of argument for the existence of any kind of Providence. We are, it seems, asked to take very seriously the narrator's apology: "Excusez les fautes du copiste!"

The representation of the occult in *Le cousin Pons* is far closer to one current use of the term "ideology" than to "science." If "ideology" is one of the slipperier words in our political vocabulary, in present-day usage it often serves little more than a deprecatory function, pointing to what one considers the misguided beliefs of others, almost never one's own.[22] But references to the invention of the daguerreotype that link it to the occult recall the famous remarks on the camera obscura in Marx and Engels's *The German Ideology*, written earlier in the 1840s:

Men are the producers of their conceptions, ideas, etc., that is, real, active men, as they are conditioned by a definite development of their productive forces and of the intercourse corresponding to these, up to its 'furthest forms. Consciousness [das Bewusstsein] can never be anything else than conscious being [das bewusste Sein], and the being of men is their actual life-process. If in all ideology men and their relations appear upside-down as in a *camera obscura*, this phenomenon arises just as much from their historical life-process as the inversion of objects on the retina does from their physical life-process. (42)

These remarks occur in the context of a series of polemical and journalistic essays on the group of philosophers known as the Young Hegelians, which generally emphasize the wrong-headedness of their work and German thought in general. If the term "ideology" is never given a precise definition in *The German Ideology*, what seems clear enough in the remarks on the camera obscura is that the analogy between natural and mechanical representation serves to emphasize the insufficiency of any kind of simple reproduction of images. Merely to reproduce the surface of the world is to repeat and reinforce the status quo; the viewer misunderstands his or her position in the world as a subject who is engaged, consciously or not, in the processes reflected, with deceptive objectivity, on the receptive surfaces of the camera obscura or the retina.

The references to Daguerre and his invention in *Le cousin Pons* also focus on the relationship between vision and understanding. Here, as in the work of Marx and Engels, the mechanical device fails to register what one might expect. And in *Le cousin Pons*, even the daguerreotype reproduces a ghost world.

The first reference holds up recent occult doctrines and the daguerreotype as two inventions with far-reaching implications for the reorganization of social life:

> En ne regardant que le côté possible de la divination, croire que les événements antérieurs de la vie d'un homme, que les secrets connus de lui seul peuvent être immédiatement représentés par des cartes qu'il mêle, qu'il coupe et que le diseur d'horoscope divise en paquets d'après des lois mystérieuses, c'est l'absurde; mais c'est l'absurde qui condamnait la vapeur, qui condamne encore la navigation aérienne, qui condamnait les inventions de la poudre et de l'imprimerie, celle des lunettes, de la gravure, et la dernière découverte, la daguerréotypie. Si quelqu'un fût venu dire à Napoléon qu'un édifice et qu'un homme sont incessamment et à toute heure représentés par une image dans l'atmosphère, que tous les objets existants y ont un spectre saisissable, perceptible, il aurait logé cet homme à Charenton, comme Richelieu logea Salomon de Caus à Bicêtre, lorsque le martyr normand lui apporta l'immense conquête de la navigation à vapeur. Et c'est là cependant ce que Daguerre a prouvé par sa découverte. (7:585)

The second reference resembles earlier discussions in *La comédie humaine* of an invisible hierarchical order which made possible both the taxonomies of natural history and the representation of French society in the novel. It also takes the daguerreotype as a point of departure for a consideration of how one should interpret representations:

> Le monde moral est taillé pour ainsi dire sur le patron du monde naturel; les mêmes effets s'y doivent retrouver avec les différences propres à leurs divers milieux. Ainsi, de même que les corps se projettent réellement dans l'atmosphère en y laissant subsister ce spectre saisi par le daguerréotype qui l'arrête au passage, de même les idées, créations réelles et agissantes, s'impriment dans ce qu'il faut nommer l'atmosphère du monde spirituel, y produisent des effets, y vivent *spectralement* (car il est nécessaire de forger des mots pour exprimer des phénomènes innomés), et dès lors certaines créatures douées de facultés rares peuvent parfaitement apercevoir ces formes ou ces traces d'idées. (7:587)

The daguerreotype, like the novel, registers the surfaces of a world that only appears to be solid, present, meaningful. What it really indicates is an absence, a kind of fragmentary spectral trace of the past which needs to be integrated into a larger narrative. A wise reader, Balzac's narrator suggests, will take the fragmentary impression on the daguerreotype as an evocation of an invisible totality. It will lead to a realization that "tout s'enchaîne dans le monde réel."

Le cousin Pons thus looks back at earlier works in *La comédie humaine* in a manner which resembles the criticism of the Young Hegelians in *The German Ideology*. Both works point to the role of theology in masking class interests and in misrepresenting society. Both caution us to examine representations carefully and to see them as historically determined. In *Le cousin Pons*, Balzac criticizes the perspectives of his novels of the 1830s. He teaches us to read his earlier work as a kind of "French ideology."

L'envers de l'histoire contemporaine

L'envers de l'histoire contemporaine, published in 1848, but begun in 1841, also presents a plea for a return to linguistic origins, in this instance the guild traditions of pre-Revolutionary Europe. This narrative, which focuses on the activities of a clandestine Catholic society, argues that this is the only living kind of association because it is the only kind that keeps alive a certain kind of thinking about social bodies and corporatism:

> L'association, une des plus grandes forces sociales et qui a fait l'Europe du Moyen Age, repose sur des sentiments qui, depuis 1792, n'existent plus en France, où l'Individu a triomphé de l'Etat. L'association exige d'abord une nature de dévouement qui n'y est pas comprise, puis une foi candide contraire à l'esprit de la nation, enfin, une discipline contre laquelle tout regimbe, et que la Religion catholique peut seule obtenir. (8:328)

Moreover, the narrator argues, the death of association derives from the alienation of individuals from *le Corps collectif*:

> L'amour de soi s'est substitué à l'amour du Corps collectif. Les corporations et les Hanses du Moyen Age, auxquelles on reviendra, sont impossibles encore; aussi les seules SOCIETES qui subsistent sont-elles des institutions religieuses auxquelles on fait la plus rude guerre en ce moment, car la tendance naturelle des malades est de s'attaquer aux remèdes et souvent aux médecins. (8:328)

References in *Le cousin Pons* that link the occult to the daguerreotype present an analogy to Marx and Engels's famous passage comparing ideology to the reversal of the image in the camera obscura. The context of the remarks on associations and corporatism in *L'envers de l'histoire contemporaine* suggest yet another link to the work of the communist theorists, for the Catholic clandestine society described in Balzac's novel sets itself against and is an ironic double of Communist workers' associations.[23] Thus the concept of linguistic origins enables Balzac's narrator to argue that contemporary workers' associations are not genuine: for if autonomous workers' organizations detached words such as *corps* from their origins, Balzac's text insists that the prerevolutionary meaning of a word is its only true meaning. The recourse to origins in Balzac's narrative functions to convince the reader that what he or she sees is not really there.

Yet in its linguistically focused discussions of corporatism and workers' associations, *L'envers de l'histoire contemporaine* draws once more on a contemporary interpretation of the culture of the late Enlightenment, of which Swedenborgianism formed an important part. Recent studies such as William H. Sewell's *Work and Revolution in France* have emphasized the importance of terminology and rituals associated with prerevolutionary guild traditions for the formation of a language of class consciousness in Paris in the 1840s. Significantly, the words *corps* and *corporation* played a key role in this process, coming increasingly to designate solidarity among workers as a class, rather than as members of smaller organizations with more restricted interests. Sewell points out, moreover, that autonomous workers' organizations were outlawed under the July Monarchy; only organizations sponsored by the Church were legal and could operate openly. Balzac's invention of a clandestine *Catholic* association thus attempts to substitute a conservative for a radical organization, a move that forms part of a more general argument that history could be rewritten if we would only change the words we use to describe it. Here the word *corps* also plays a central role, for the novel describes a displacement of social malaise not only from illegal to legitimate societies, but also from groups of any kind to a suffering human body. *L'envers de l'histoire contemporaine* comes full circle to the earliest *Etudes philosophiques*, which developed as an alternative to the representation of bodily desires so openly portrayed in *Les études physiologiques*.

A single direct reference to Swedenborg occurs at the end of the first "episode" of this short novel in two parts. The first, "Madame de la Chanterie," recounts the background and history of the clandestine Catholic community in central Paris. The leader of this community, based on an alliance between the Church and the great banks, is a Breton aristocrat, who had been arrested and imprisoned, perhaps unjustly, for participation in the Chouan revolt. It is not until the conclusion of the section named after her that we learn of Madame de Chanterie's background. An older member of the community, a Monsieur Alain, tells her story to the young initiate, Godefroid, through whose eyes we see the community and its leader. Alain concludes his narrative with a reference to Swedenborg which links the apparently angelic nature of Madame de la Chanterie to a social theodicy:

> Par certains jour[s] je me demande quel est le sens d'une pareille existence? . . . Dieu réserve-t-il ces dernières, ces cruelles épreuves à celles de ses créatures qui doivent s'asseoir près de lui le lendemain de leur mort? dit le bonhomme Alain, sans savoir qu'il exprimait naïvement toute la doctrine de Swedenborg sur les anges. (8:318)

Balzac's interpretation of Swedenborgianism here runs directly counter to Swedenborg's optimism, his belief that not only the meek and the poor, but especially the rich, the reasonable, and the prosperous, were the natural inheritors of the Kingdom of Heaven. The misinterpretation is a logical development of Balzac's earlier depiction of Swedenborgianism as the counterweight to Mesmerism. From the beginning, the principle of *Savoir*, associated with Swedenborgianism and mysticism in general, had been linked to an ethic of renunciation; here it has become the justification for suffering and self-abnegation in the interests of the regeneration of society as a whole.

The conclusion of the second part of the novel contains a reference to Madame de la Chanterie's "angelism," which echoes the ending of the first part and the reference to Swedenborg there. In this part, entitled "L'Initié," the young novice, Godefroid, is charged with the mission of infiltrating the household of a judge who lost his position after 1830. The judge lives in very great poverty with his invalid daughter, Vanda, and grandson, Népomucène, in a rooming house kept by a Madame Vauthier, whose name recalls the witch-like Madame Vauquer of *Le père Goriot*. Vanda fell ill in 1829. Since then, she has inhabited a room decorated with objets d'art and bric à brac from the past—although her father and son often do not have enough to eat. Vanda's illness mystifies conventional doctors. She has been extraordinarily receptive to the techniques of magnetizers and somnambulists—even manifesting a high degree of clairvoyance—but they, too, are unable to cure her. All they can do is diagnose her condition as a neurosis. The local doctor refers the Baron de Bourlac to a Polish refugee, a doctor by the name of Halpersohn who is both a communist and a Jew, but the Baron lacks money and Halpersohn is unwilling to treat Vanda without payment. Godefroid is able to supply money from the community, which is very wealthy, and Vanda is removed from her room for treatment in isolation. Eventually she is returned in a state of health to her family. Her return coincides with the revelation of the source of the money to the Baron de Bourlac, who realizes that he has been saved by a woman whom he sent to prison—he now believes unjustly—during the Chouannerie, and whose daughter he condemned to death. The baron, prostrate with remorse, comes to beg her forgiveness, which she grants him:

> Il tomba sur ses genoux, baisa le parquet, fondit en larmes, et d'une voix déchirante, il cria:
> "Au nom de Jésus, mort sur la croix, pardonnez! pardonnez! car ma fille a souffert mille morts!"
> Le vieillard s'affaissa, si bien que les spectateurs émus le crurent mort. En ce moment, Mme de la Chanterie apparut comme un spectre à la porte de sa chambre, sur laquelle elle s'appuyait défaillante.
> "Par Louis XVI et Marie-Antoinette, que je vois sur leur échafaud, par madame Elisabeth, par ma fille, par la vôtre, par Jésus, je vous pardonne. . ."
> En entendant ce dernier mot, l'ancien procureur leva les yeux et dit:
> "Les anges se vengent ainsi." (8:412–13)

His words may be given a conventional, Christian interpretation. At this moment, it appears that Madame de La Chanterie has chosen forgiveness over vengeance. Even if this is the case, however, it is also apparent that she is killing him with kindness. And furthermore, it is possible that she may have had a hand in causing Vanda's illness and her father's misfortune. She may indeed have taken vengeance.

"Madame de La Chanterie," the passage reads, "apparut comme un spectre à la porte de sa chambre." The words are ambiguous, evoking both an image of a woman in a state of shock, perhaps close to death, and of a creature belonging to another world. The other world, however, is not the realm of spiritual transcendence and light evoked in *Séraphîta*, but rather the sinister world of ghouls, the unconsecrated dead—*revenants*, Balzac calls them in *Ursule Mirouët*, in a passage which links the circulation of *revenants* to that of *revenus*. (3:976) Far from being an angel, Madame de La Chanterie is, like the arch-criminal Vautrin, a creature of the underworld. And like Vautrin, who, at the end of *Splendeurs et misères des courtisanes*, becomes chief of police, Madame de La Chanterie appears to represent the alliance of the reactionary and repressive powers in contemporary society with the underworld of crime and shady financial deals. (The ambiguity of this character is reflected in her name, which suggests both music [*le chant*]—and blackmail [*le chantage*]—as well as *une chanterelle*—a decoy.)

Her apparition at the end of the novel and her pronunciation of words of forgiveness which evoke past allegiances and grudges represent the return of the repressed—the return to the community of Godefroid, whose initiation consisted for the most part of his learning to repress and sublimate his desire for Madame d La Chanterie, and the resurfacing of "forgotten" identities. Much of the novel is concerned with establishing the identities and origins of its characters and their relation to the past of Madame de La Chanterie. Only at the conclusion of the novel do all recognize both themselves and their role in this woman's fate. The unearthing of the past brings guilt and also, perhaps, death. The charity of Madame de La Chanterie's order, which distributes money to the destitute in order to keep them happy with their lot, is lethal.

The Baron de Bourlac's recognition of his guilt is probably the illness which Halpersohn, the communist-Jewish doctor, predicted would strike another if Vanda were cured. It is clear that here, as elsewhere, Balzac is working with an analogy between individual neurosis—or even psychosis—and contradictions in society as a whole. Vanda's illness, which strikes first at her reproductive organs, killing her second child, is evidently an indictment of contemporary society: its means of production have been strangled, it exists in a state of paralysis, its head is dissociated from its body, and, like Vanda, who lives in a single room decorated with the luxury of the past century in the midst of poverty, it has lost touch, both with the present and with the living conditions of the majority of its citizens. In an earlier novel, Vanda would probably have been cured—or at least correctly diagnosed—by Bianchon. Here it is a Polish Jew and a communist who is able to cure her, and we learn little of his methods. Halpersohn may be the instrument of Madame de La Chanterie. In that case, like the representatives of other ideologies in *La comédie humaine*, he may be seen to subsist only through the control and manipulation of a Church which has entered into a sinister alliance with capitalism in order to perpetuate the traditions of the past.

L'envers de l'histoire contemporaine concludes the *Scènes de la vie parisienne*, and, according to the Catalogue of 1845, was intended to do so. (1:cxxiv) Like many of Balzac's late works, its relationship to earlier parts of *La comédie humaine* is complex. It refers especially to the early utopian novel, *Le médecin de campagne*, to *L'histoire des Treize*, which recounts episodes from the lives of members of another secret association, to *Les Chouans*, and to *Le livre mystique*. Its references to these texts are, however, dark and ironic. The sinister nature of Madame de La Chanterie contrasts with the melancholy honesty of Bénassis in *Le médecin de campagne*, and the mediocrity of Godefroid and other members of Madame de La Chanterie's order with the heroism of the *Treize*. The documents which recount Madame de La Chanterie's condemnation evoke in Godefroid's mind a project for a novel similar to Balzac's *Les Chouans*—a project which, we surmise, he will never carry through. The vision of a spiritualized nature depicted in *Séraphîta* has been transformed into a revelation of the dark powers which control contemporary society and the existence of the individual in the city. It is possible to see the Godefroid of *L'envers de l'histoire contemporaine* as the counterpart of the naive young lover by the same name in *Les proscrits*. This Godefroid, however, is stupid, rather than naive. Unable to manage his inheritance or find a job on his own, he joins an association which gives him a sense of power which can only be dangerous in the hands of one so weak minded.

In earlier works in *La comédie humaine*, religion and what Balzac calls mysticism are linked, on the one hand, to the ability of tradition to overcome individualism, which Balzac so often characterized as the greatest problem in contemporary society, and, on the other, to a kind of vision which enables the individual to see into the nature of things, to penetrate beyond appearances. In *L'envers de l'histoire contemporaine*, the characters do not *see*, and the loss of self in a larger group is seen as potentially threatening to the social order. The fusion of the individual with the whole evokes the tremendous political potential of groups of individuals from what Balzac called "les classes inférieures."

At the beginning of the 1840s, in the Avant-propos to *La comédie humaine*, Balzac drew up a hierarchical model for the representation of contemporary French society, a model in which Swedenborgianism, together with other esoteric and pseudoscientific doctrines, served as a means for the representation both of the totalitarian nature of this model and of its invisiblity—and partial inaccessibility—to individual consciousness. Novels of the forties often refer to the hierarchical model described in the Avant-propos, but the narratives themselves suggest the inappropriateness of the model for the representation of contemporary society. The structures of contemporary life do not completely correspond to those described in the Avant-propos, and the esoteric and pseudoscientific doctrines cited there as proof of the universality of Balzac's hierarchical models turn out, in the novels themselves, to suggest their anachronistic or even chimerical nature. In the later novels, the concept of a totality is preserved in the language alone, the instrument by which the novelist constructs, or attempts to construct, a unified and coherent picture of contemporary society.

Balzac's understanding of Swedenborgian doctrines appears to have been very general, and it was marked by a fundamental divergence from the original. His most extended interpretations of Swedenborgianism occur in the two novels of *Le livre mystique, Louis Lambert* and *Séraphîta*. Here, Swedenborgianism is associated with the concept of an angelic order which continues the taxonomic structures of natural history into the invisible world; Swedenborg's angels are depicted as fictional models which are useful for our understanding of the invisible and which explain the existence of outstanding individuals and their conflict with society. In *Le livre mystique*, as in *La peau de chagrin*, Swedenborgianism represents *Savoir*, a wisdom which entails a detachment from the things of this world and the desires they provoke. *Savoir* is set against *Volonté* or *Pouvoir*, which is, in *Les études philosophiques*, associated with the doctrines of Mesmer and his followers. In order to portray Swedenborgianism as the counterpart to Mesmerism, Balzac was led to interpret the doctrines of Swedenborg as a form of mysticism, insisting, unlike Swedenborg, on the incomprehensibility of God.

References to Swedenborg and Swedenborgianism in Balzac's novels of the 1840s refer back to the novelist's presentation of Swedenborgianism in *Les études philosophiques*, especially *Le livre mystique*, rather than to the works of Swedenborg themselves. Balzac's interpretation insists on the necessity for the renunciation of individual desires in the interests of society as a whole, the submission of *Volonté* to *Savoir*. But in *Les études de moeurs* the incomprehensible God of *Les études philosophiques* makes His presence felt only in the form of a mysterious aura or resonance inherent in things themselves, which the reader is invited to interpret in terms of a language referring back to a lost unity or wholeness. Balzac's association of Swedenborgianism with the concept of the hieroglyph, particularly in connection with the representation of the city, proved to be of greatest importance for the later literary reception of Swedenborgianism in France.

Balzac refers to Swedenborg as only one of many antecedents for the concept of a hieroglyphic language which informs the representation of French society in *La comédie humaine*; he ascribes far more importance, for example, to the novelist Sterne. Above all, however, Balzac saw the hieroglyph, like the doctrines of occultism, pseudoscience, and esotericism in general, in historical terms. The passage in *Louis Lambert* describing the evolution of theories of language origins in the late eighteenth and early nineteenth centuries parallels the expositions of the development of pseudoscientific and esoteric doctrines, including Swedenborgianism, in novels such as *La recherche de l'Absolu*, *Ursule Mirouët*, and *Le cousin Pons*, as well as *Le livre mystique*. In these works, pseudoscientific and esoteric doctrines are presented as models for a synthetic philosophical system, an ideology for a society which would have returned to the hierarchical order upset by the Revolution of 1789. From the beginning, Balzac expresses an awareness of the marginality of these doctrines, nowhere more clearly, however, than in the last novel to be published during his lifetime, *Le cousin Pons*, where occult beliefs are ascribed to the popular classes, whose ideology and way of life hark back to an earlier period than those of the scientific elite and upper classes.

The doctrines expounded in the *Le livre mystique* and developed in the later novels thus have more to do with French Swedenborgianism and the context of esoteric and pseudoscientific thought during the late eighteenth and early nineteenth centuries than with the work of Swedenborg himself. One can, however, point to at least one important parallel between the work of Balzac and Swedenborg: the relationship between the concept of the hieroglyph, the representation of the city, and the generation of textual worlds which are seen to correspond in toto to the structures of the city and nature, but which are founded in a movement into language, a "discovery" of the interiority of language itself.

Like Swedenborg, Balzac was led to ontologize language in his late work, in part as the result of his desire to represent the city in human terms, to imagine himself as part of the interiors of the buildings which lined the streets of the city. For both writers, taxonomy served as a means for the representation of the writer's simultaneous involvement in and detachment from the world around him. The late works of Balzac, like those of Swedenborg, reveal an increasing preoccupation with the coherence of the little worlds generated by a linguistic system, worlds which are intended to "correspond" allegorically to the world outside the text, but which leave behind them signs, traces, of their increasing distance from natural or theological origins.

CHAPTER FIVE

Baudelaire's Correspondances:
Language, Censorship, and Mourning

We now come full circle to the work of Baudelaire, whose sonnet "Correspondances" bears as its title the resonant word that served as the point of departure for this study. It is with some puzzlement, then, that we find that our goal, perhaps the vanishing point of our journey, is a delicate sonnet of fourteen lines that makes no doctrinal statement whatsoever:

Correspondances

La Nature est un temple où de vivants piliers
Laissent parfois sortir de confuses paroles;
L'homme y passe à travers des forêts de symboles
Qui l'observent avec des regards familiers.

Comme de longs échos qui de loin se confondent
Dans une ténébreuse et profonde unité,
Vaste comme la nuit et comme la clarté,
Les parfums, les couleurs et les sons se répondent.

Il est des parfums frais comme des chairs d'enfants,
Doux comme les hautbois, verts comme les prairies,
—Et d'autres, corrompus, riches et triomphants,

Ayant l'expansion des choses infinies,
Comme l'ambre, le musc, le benjoin et l'encens,
Qui chantent les transports de l'esprit et des sens.

Confronted with the resonant vagueness of this poem, one wonders how and why historians and critics of poetry searched for doctrinal origins, for the sonnet certainly seems to undercut any possible references to theology:

as generations of critics have pointed out, if the opening quatrain suggests "vertical correspondences" between the world-as-temple and a great beyond, the remaining lines evoke this-worldly, "horizontal correspondences" among sense impressions. And the relation between the two kinds of *correspondances* may be construed in several ways: as aspects of a desirable experience of unity; as rhetorical figures; as parallel, but different kinds of experience; or as fundamentally opposed, so that the sensuous relationships suggested in the second part of the poem undermine the transcendental *correspondances* of the first. However one chooses to interpret the poem, it is clear that it makes no theological or doctrinal statement. A search for the origins of the allegory only suggested in the sonnet's opening lines would tell us little about the way the poem works as a whole.

And yet it is precisely this indeterminacy that invites a comparison of the poem's language to that of mysticism: both Baudelaire's sonnet and the language of mystics strain at the limits of language and representation, suggesting experiences which lie outside them. Perhaps, as many twentieth-century critics have suggested, a view of language that is akin to mysticism is a determining characteristic of modern poetry. A surprising number of critics have situated Baudelaire's "Correspondances" at a pivotal point in a line of development in European poetry that runs from Romanticism, often German Romanticism, to Surrealism. Many cite Swedenborg as a source, albeit one source among many, for an unstated theory of language that underlies his innovative poetics—although, as we have seen, it is difficult to see much of Swedenborg's work as mystical. Others write more generally of the continuity between the esoteric references in the poet's work and esoteric tradition. Few ask what it meant for Baudelaire to use the term *correspondances* in mid-century Paris.[1]

Baudelaire's sonnet, moreover, looks more enigmatic in isolation than it does against the background of the other poems in *Les fleurs du mal* and his prose. "Correspondances" finds its place in the collection as the fourth poem in the first grouping, whose title, "Spleen et Idéal," invites the reader to focus on the opposition between a disappointing this-worldly experience and ideals which are perhaps unattainable. It is also the fifth poem in a cycle that emphasizes the representation of contemporary Paris. In this context, it is impossible to read the first quatrain as referring unambiguously to nature. And *Les fleurs du mal*, in turn, finds its place in the context of Baudelaire's prose, which, in quantity if not quality, dwarfs the poet's output of verse. In the case of Baudelaire, it seems all the more important to consider the prose and verse as part of a single *oeuvre*, since the poet, one of the inventors of the prose poem in France, called into question conventional distinctions between the two.

In *Les fleurs du mal*, the title of Baudelaire's sonnet, "Correspondances," stands alone. If, as the heading of the first group of poems, "Spleen et idéal," suggests, the notion of a transcendent reality plays an important role in the thematic structure of the collection, there are no further occurrences of the word *correspondances* and no references to Swedenborg. In Baudelaire's prose, however, one finds references to Swedenborg and Swedenborgianism in eight works and to *correspondances* in seven more. Although these are brief—especially in contrast to Balzac's discursive use of Swedenborg in his *Livre mystique*—they provide an invaluable guide to the function and connotations of the word *correspondances* in Baudelaire's work.

If the focus of many critics and historians who have attempted to tie Baudelaire's sonnet and his use of the word *correspondances* to the language of modern poetry is too narrow, the questions they pose lead in the right direction. Baudelaire's references to Swedenborg and *correspondances* form a red thread through the thinking of a poet whose poetry was an inspiration to later writers. These references, moreover, emphasize the continuing importance of the language of representation in the work of Baudelaire and also, perhaps, later French poets.

They point, moreover, to the central role of what we now see as popular culture in the evolution of Baudelaire's aesthetics and thinking about language. As we have seen, by the 1840s, *correspondances* evoked not only the work of an obscure visionary writer whose theories had come to resemble those of Mesmer and Fourier, but also the revolutionary culture of the 1790s, a culture that was particularly alive in the nineteenth century for those, such as Constant/Lévi, who questioned the emancipatory limits of the Revolution of 1789. To overlook this context and to attempt to jump directly from Baudelaire's sonnet or his references to *correspondances* in his prose to the work of Swedenborg or other exponents of mysticism or esotericism is to overlook not only how this poet developed, but also how modernist poetry and literature came to define itself within and against a context of what we now view as popular culture in mid-nineteenth-century Paris. Critics have tended to portray Constant/Lévi and *his* poem, "Les correspondances," as examples of a belated and second-rate Romanticism which Baudelaire overturned in his own, more adroit, informed, and cosmopolitan work. But this view is very incomplete: what comes into focus when one looks at the careers of the two men is that in the years following 1848 both apparently turned away from politics and towards a view of language as both absolute and curiously powerful. But if Constant/Lévi took care to distinguish his post-1848 work from his political engagement of the 1840s, Baudelaire makes a more complicated gesture of refusal. His texts of the 1850s and 1860s proclaim the differences of poetry and aesthetics not only from politics, but also from other kinds of writing and

language. Distinction becomes an end in itself, and the references to theological and esoteric tradition that masked Constant/Lévi's continuing interest in politics come in the work of Baudelaire after 1850 to play the role of
a hallmark of aesthetic apartness.

But, as the sociologist Pierre Bourdieu has emphasized in his study,
Distinction, the act of distinguishing cannot be understood apart from the
complex web of social meanings in which it is embedded.[2] In the years
following 1848, many French artists and writers eschewed political involvement. As the art historian, T. J. Clark, has emphasized in his studies
of French artists in the 1840s and 1850s, Baudelaire was in the company of
Courbet, Daumier, and many others at this time. But as Clark has also
argued, art that proclaims its apartness is not—despite the intentions of
its author—apolitical.[3] The apparent objectivity of Courbet's painting in
the 1850s makes sense when viewed in the context of the artist's ambivalence concerning the events of 1848 and 1851. Similarly, the move to
objectify language in the work of Baudelaire (and also Constant/Lévi) can
only be understood against the backgrounds of 1848 and the Fourierist
invocation of a universal analogy which, we have seen, bears a resemblance
to the Idéologues' notion of a universal language of nature that could serve
as a point of departure for the establishment of a more rational social
order. As late as 1861, in a famous essay on Victor Hugo, Baudelaire compares *correspondances* to Fourier's universal analogy, concluding, however, that both serve as inadequate models for the language of the true
poet. But elsewhere in Baudelaire's work, the political implications of the
notion of a language of nature that is universal and that aims at capturing
the totality of the social and natural worlds are never far from the surface.

1. A Volume of Swedenborg under His Arm:
Baudelaire and Swedenborgianism

How and when did Baudelaire encounter the doctrines of Swedenborg? Apart from a letter to the Fourierist, Alphonse Toussenel, which
mentions the word *correspondances*, there are no references or allusions
to Swedenborg or Swedenborgianism in his letters. Did Baudelaire read
Swedenborg? If so, which works? Or did the poet merely absorb what was
in the air at the time from interpretations such as those of Constant/Lévi
or contemporary Fourierists?

Two passages from the memoirs of Baudelaire's contemporary, the
writer Champfleury, suggest that the poet's interest in Swedenborg was
neither deep nor very serious, at least around 1850. Rather, he seems to

have affected an interest in Swedenborgianism as part of his presentation of himself as a poet and a dandy:

> Baudelaire est allé ennuyer Bellegarigue pour écrire dans le *Moniteur de l'épicerie*. Dans le temps il tracassait Veuillot pour écrire à *L'Univers*, Baudelaire aurait été fort enchanté de dire partout qu'il rédigeait le journal des épiciers, histoire de se singulariser et de se faire remarquer. C'est dans le même but qu'il se promène tantôt avec des livres de Swedenborg sous le bras, tantôt avec de gros livres d'algèbre; son prétendu livre *Conversations de Ch. Baudelaire avec les Anges* est encore un moyen de donner à causer aux farceurs. Mais il n'en écrit pas une ligne de plus et perd son temps à se *maniérer* de la sorte. (2:1239)

Moreover, Swedenborg is only one among an imposing gallery of enthusiasms Baudelaire displayed at the time. Champfleury recounts:

> Un jour, Baudelaire se montrait avec un volume de Swedenborg sous le bras... Dans nos promenades au Louvre, il me donnait le Bronzino, un maître maniéré, comme le grand peintre de toutes les écoles. Un autre jour, le Polonais Wronski faisait oublier Swedenborg... Une autre fois, Van Eyck et les peintres primitifs remplaçaient ce coquin de Bronzino. [Champfleury, *Souvenirs*, p. 134, quoted in Lemonnier, iii.]

That Baudelaire knew Constant/Lévi and was familiar with some of his work is suggested not only by the article in *Les mystères galants de Paris* attributed to him, but also by their collaboration on the same journals in the late 1840s. Baudelaire's association of Swedenborgianism with Mesmerism, Fourierism, and, eventually, the cabala, suggests that he had read or heard of Constant/Lévi's summaries of esoteric tradition, but Baudelaire's contempt for the defrocked priest, probably based as much on social origins as aesthetic pretentions, would scarcely have permitted him to acknowledge Constant/Lévi and his work as sources or models.

Balzac was a very different matter. As Graham Robb has shown in his comprehensive thesis, the contact between the two men and their works was pervasive and many-sided, far surpassing their chance meetings. Baudelaire's view of Balzac was by no means entirely positive: he seems to have regarded the older writer as a kind of literary father figure, whose work inspired the younger man, but who also stood in his way. References to Balzac are scattered throughout Baudelaire's prose, including one in the early preface to the translation of Poe's "Mesmeric Revelation" that attributes the notion of totality that informs *La comédie humaine* to the influence of the doctrines of Swedenborg, but his most suggestive remarks are included in an essay on Théophile Gautier first published in 1857:

Si Balzac a fait de ce genre roturier une chose admirable, toujours curieuse et souvent sublime, c'est parce qu'il y a jeté tout son être. J'ai
mainte fois été étonné que la grande gloire de Balzac fût de passer pour
un observateur; il m'avait toujours semblé que son principal mérite était
d'être visionnaire, et visionnaire passionné. Tous ses personnages sont
doués de l'ardeur vitale dont il était animé lui-même. Toutes ses fictions
sont aussi profondément colorées que les rêves. Depuis le sommet de
l'aristocratie jusqu'aux bas-fonds de la plèbe, tous les acteurs de sa *Comédie* sont plus âpres à la vie, plus actifs et rusés dans la lutte, plus patients
dans le malheur, plus goulus dans la jouissance, plus angéliques dans le
dévouement, que la comédie du vrai monde ne nous les montre. Bref,
chacun, chez Balzac, même les portières, a du génie. Toutes les âmes sont
des armes chargées de volonté jusqu'à la gueule. C'est bien Balzac lui-
même. Et comme tous les êtres du monde extérieur s'offraient à l'oeil de
son esprit avec un relief puissant et une grimace saisissante, il a fait se
convulser ses figures; il a noirci leurs ombres et illuminé leurs lumières.
Son goût prodigieux du détail, qui tient à une ambition immodérée de
tout voir, de tout faire voir, de tout deviner, de tout faire deviner, l'obli-
geait d'ailleurs à marquer avec plus de force les lignes principales, pour
sauver la perspective de l'ensemble. (2:120)

Significantly, however, it is the nonrepresentational aspects of Balzac's visionary style that interest the poet most, especially the dream-like qualities
of his narratives and their tendency to exaggerate, which brings them close
to caricature. It is possible, in turn, to view the notion of totality that
underlies both Baudelaire's poetry and his art criticism as a caricature of
Balzac's novel system: what's left in the work of the poet is an abstraction,
the idea of a system that recedes as one attempts to look more closely at it,
the details having vanished. And the same might be said of Baudelaire's
very sketchy interpretations of Swedenborgianism.

Balzac's work finds its place as one of a number of *narrative* models
Baudelaire acknowledges as important sources for his own aesthetics.
Others include the works of Gautier, Hugo, and, especially, Poe. That all
three of these men also wrote poetry attests to the increasing vagueness of
distinctions between poetry and prose in mid-century Paris, distinctions
which Baudelaire's *Petits poèmes en prose* further undermined. But the
poet's characterization of Balzac's style seems, like his choice of narratives
by Poe, to have suggested that characteristics of fantastic narrative, especially its use of irony to undermine belief in the totality it suggested,
played an especially important role in his imaginative transformation of
their aesthetics.

The best evidence we have of Baudelaire's knowledge and interpretation of Swedenborgianism and the doctrine of correspondences consists of

the references to them in his works. Like Champfleury's remarks, these references suggest that the French poet took the phenomenon of Sweden-borgianism with less than entire seriousness, but not as the joke the title of the never-written *Conversations de Ch. Baudelaire avec les anges* suggests. Even Champfleury's somewhat contemptuous remark that Baudelaire traded off volumes of Swedenborg and algebra suggests that the poet understood the link between language and mathematics that informed the work of not only Swedenborg, but also the French Idéologues, Fourier, and Balzac.

Baudelaire's references to Swedenborg and to *correspondances* do not entirely overlap. Allusions to Swedenborg occur in a variety of texts published between 1847 and 1865, while the word *correspondances* crops up in a narrower range of prose works published between 1855 and 1861. That there is a gap between the two groups suggests that the poet gave an interpretation to the term that diverges from its use both in Swedenborg's published works and in French interpretations of his doctrines. In order to gauge the differences, I turn first to the works in which Baudelaire refers to Swedenborg, before taking up the question of the metamorphoses of *correspondances* in his prose and, finally, his poetry.

2. Fictional Polarities and the Aesthete's Dilemma: Baudelaire's References to Swedenborg

La Fanfarlo

Baudelaire's earliest known reference to Swedenborg occurs in the novella, *La Fanfarlo*, which was published in 1847, but which may have been written several years earlier.[4] This narrative, which seems to caricature the plot of many novels by Balzac, focuses on the experiences of a jaded young dandy with two women: a married woman (one presumes *une femme de trente ans*) and her husband's mistress, a dancer and a prostitute. The protagonist, Samuel Cramer, resembles the young men in Balzac's novels who cannot cope with the intricacies of Parisian society, such as Lucien de Rubempré and, especially, Godefroid of *L'envers de l'histoire contemporaine*. Like Godefroid, Samuel Cramer ends by throwing in his lot with a collective ideology, although he chooses one on the left, rather than the right. This remarkable work, which has not received the attention it deserves, focuses on the dilemma of the aesthete, unable to integrate his intellectual interests with his need to act.

In *La Fanfarlo*, Swedenborgianism represents one pole of the hero's interests, a theological system evidently beyond his comprehension; the other is represented by the works of Crébillon fils. The account of Baudelaire's hero's unsuccessful attempts to interpret the signs of nature or society correctly, however, already links Swedenborgianism to the question of the relationship of the world of the city, particularly the language of commodities, to nature and to art.

Before leaving his lodgings for a walk which will bring him into contact with the woman who will initiate his encounter with the dancer called La Fanfarlo, Samuel Cramer snuffs out two candles, "dont l'une palpitait encore sur un volume de Swedenborg, et l'autre s'éteignait sur un de ces livres honteux dont la lecture n'est profitable qu'aux esprits possédés d'un goût immodéré de la vérité." (1:555) Swedenborgianism and eroticism figure as one of the oppositions which characterize the life and personality of Cramer. As the introduction to the novella makes clear, Samuel Cramer is a dandy and a Romantic. The summary of his character consists of an ironic compilation of Romantic clichés: he is subject to the contradictions and ambiguities of the generation described, mocked, and diagnosed at greater length by Musset in his *Confessions d'un enfant du siècle* and Gautier in *Mademoiselle de Maupin*. Samuel Cramer suffers from a dualism in his character explained, in part, by his Northern father and Southern mother; this dualism is expressed, above all, in a certain sexual ambiguity: "Il raffolait d'un ami comme d'une femme, aimait une femme comme un camarade." (1:555) Like many Romantics, he is obsessed with the idea of originality, but so susceptible to the sensations of the moment that he is unable either to produce an original work or to finish anything he has started. Samuel Cramer, according to the narrator, is typical of an entire generation of dandies and *flâneurs*:

> Dans le monde actuel, ce genre de caractère est plus fréquent qu'on ne le pense; les rues, les promenades publiques, les estaminets, et tous les asiles de la flânerie fourmillent d'êtres de cette espèce. Ils s'identifient si bien avec le nouveau modèle, qu'ils ne sont pas éloignés de croire qu'ils l'ont inventé.—Les voilà aujourd'hui déchiffrant péniblement les pages mystiques de Plotin ou de Porphyre; demain ils admireront comme Crébillon le fils a bien exprimé le côté volage et français de leur caractère. (1:554)

Mysticism and esotericism, this passage suggests, represent the limits of the kinds of experiences offered to Cramer in contemporary society.

In the course of the encounter described in *La Fanfarlo*, Samuel Cramer will attempt to leave behind the fragmentary and ambivalent experience of the dandy and *flâneur*, preoccupied with creating a persona for himself out of the sensations of the moment, for the salvation his generation saw in contemporary socialism and utopian movements. Baudelaire's narrator depicts Samuel Cramer's "conversion" with lacerating irony:

Pauvre chantre des Orfraies! Pauvre Manuela de Monteverde! Il est tombé bien bas. — J'ai appris récemment qu'il fondait un journal socialiste et voulait se mettre à la politique. — Intelligence malhonnête! — comme dit cet honnête M. Nisard. (1: 580)

Baudelaire himself had edited a socialist journal, *Le salut public*, which appeared briefly in 1848. His irony is no less vituperative in that it applies to his own experience, which is depicted as typical of an entire generation which fell prey to its own clichés: "Ils s'identifient si bien avec le nouveau modèle, qu'ils ne sont pas éloignés de croire qu'ils l'ont inventé." (1:554)

In *La Fanfarlo*, Swedenborgianism and utopianism, theology and politics, represent alternatives in the public life of the individual, just as Swedenborg or Plotinus and the kind of eroticism represented by the works of Crébillon fils point to poles in his private life. Swedenborgianism is coupled with a contemporary taste for eroticism and sensualism, designating one extreme—the theological—of the experience of a generation concerned above all with the relationship between sensation, sensualism, and meaning. Socialism and political engagement appear as one means to overcome the contradictions of a life based solely on aesthetic principles. The alternative to immersion in the undialectical models of contemporary social theory, which appears in Baudelaire's later writings as a preoccupation with the relationship between sensation and the absolute, is missing in *La Fanfarlo*, although it is perhaps suggested by the unsatisfactoriness of the ambivalent and fragmentary experience of the dandy and the blind commitment of his political contemporary.

In the dancer La Fanfarlo, Samuel Cramer meets his match. He is the master of the Romantic cliché; she is the mistress of the suggestive gestures of dance and mime. He seduces her with a language which is as artificial as it is asexual; his lack of response appears to egg her on:

A défaut du coeur, Samuel avait l'intelligence noble, et, au lieu d'ingratitude, la jouissance avait engendré chez lui ce contentement savoureux, cette rêverie sensuelle, qui vaut peut-être mieux que l'amour comme l'entend le vulgaire. Du reste, la Fanfarlo avait fait de son mieux et dépensé ses plus habiles caresses, s'étant accoutumée à ce langage mystique, bariolé d'impuretés et de crudités énormes. — Cela avait pour elle du moins l'attrait de la nouveauté. (1:578)

The combination of the languages of spiritualism and eroticism which recalls the two candles set on the volumes of Swedenborg and "un de ces livres honteux dont la lecture n'est profitable qu'aux esprits possédés d'un goût immodéré de la vérité," excludes sexual fulfillment. At one point,

Cramer demands that La Fanfarlo make herself up and play the part of Colombine—at three o'clock in the morning. (1:577) The gap between language and experience is, however, perhaps clearest in the description of the denouement of the relationship between the two, which refers back to Samuel Cramer's forgotten promise to Madame de Cosmelly to seduce La Fanfarlo away from M. de Cosmelly, a promise he had made in the hopes of seducing a woman he had believed to be innocent and naive. In a reversal he has difficulty understanding, Samuel Cramer finds himself in the arms of a woman he had completely identified with the artifice of her profession, confronted with the duplicity of a woman he had believed to be natural:

> Samuel, vautré sur de la dentelle, et appuyé sur une des plus fraîches et des plus belles épaules qu'on pût voir, sentit vaguement qu'il était joué, et eut quelque peine à rassembler dans sa mémoire les éléments de l'intrigue dont il avait amené le dénouement; mais il se dit tranquillement: Nos passions sont-elles bien sincères? qui peut savoir sûrement ce qu'il veut et connaître au juste le baromètre de son coeur? (1:579)

Neither Samuel nor La Fanfarlo are able to come to terms with the contradictions inherent in their situation. The conclusion of the novella sees La Fanfarlo the mother of twins, and Samuel Cramer an adherent of the socialist cause.

In *La Fanfarlo*, Swedenborgianism is associated with one pole, a spiritualism made up of clichés from many theological and visionary traditions, of the dandy or aesthete's experience; Swedenborgianism forms part of "ce langage mystique, bariolé d'impuretés et de crudités énormes" (1:578), which Samuel Cramer substitutes for the sexual act. In the course of the novella, we see the contradictory and fragmentary language of aestheticism subsumed in two new stances, the fall back into nature and the espousal of visionary political theories, both of which are characterized as inadequate by the narrator.

The Essays on Poe:

"Présentation de *Révélation magnétique*" (1848)
"Edgar Allan Poe: sa vie et ses ouvrages" (1852)
"Notes nouvelles sur Edgar Poe" (1857)

If the ending of *La Fanfarlo* portrays the hero's turn to politics despite the inadequacies of doctrines such as Swedenborg's, Baudelaire's earliest work on Edgar Allan Poe, his translation of and preface to "Mesmeric Revelation," also links visionary systems to the politics of 1848, for the French poet first read Poe in a translation published in the Fourierist journal, *La démocratie pacifique*, and he published his first translation in *La liberté de penser*, July 15, 1848. But Baudelaire's interpretation of Poe differs radically from that of his Fourierist source, who presented the American writer as a drunkard who, under the influence of alchohol, showed "à quels singuliers arguments sont réduits les derniers partisans du dogme de la *perversité native*." (cited by Pichois in Baudelaire, *Oeuvres complètes*, 2:1200) For Baudelaire, in contrast, Poe was a solitary genius who, unlike Samuel Cramer, was able to see through the clichés of the marketplace. Baudelaire's Poe shares with Samuel Cramer an interest in Swedenborg, but in this case it is a Swedenborg linked to the conservative doctrines of Joseph de Maistre, rather than the collectivist beliefs of Fourier and his followers.

At first glance, "Mesmeric Revelation" seems a strange choice for a first translation into French. "Le conte de Poe—si c'est un conte—est d'intérêt bien moindre que la présentation de Baudelaire," notes Pichois in his commentary on Baudelaire's preface (*Oeuvres complètes*, 2:1205). Yet, from the point of view of Baudelaire's evolving interest in visionary systems and aesthetics, it makes perfect sense and suggests that his knowledge of this context exceeded what the brevity of his comments might lead one to believe.

In translating "Mesmeric" as *magnétique*, Baudelaire made explicit a distinction Poe's narrative only implies, a distinction between two traditions among the followers of Mesmer: those who emphasized the therapeutic aspects of his theories and those who saw them in more cosmological terms, often marrying them with aspects of Swedenborgianism and other doctrines of the supernatural. In Poe's tale, the first-person narrative of an animal magnetist frames an account of a dialogue between the practitioner and his patient, who has come to him for treatment of a "confirmed phthisis." (88) Once under the magnetist's influence, however, the sufferer begins to talk of a world beyond the senses which is organized in the form of a hierarchy that emanates from God. His account reads like a pastiche of Swedenborg—or Balzac:

> V. (*après une longue pause, et en marmottant*). Je le vois, —je le vois, —mais c'est une chose très difficile à dire. (*Autre pause également longue.*) Il n'est pas esprit, car il existe. Il n'est non plus matière, *comme vous l'entendez*. Mais il y a des *gradations* de matière dont l'homme n'a aucune connaissance, la plus dense entraînant la plus subtile, la plus subtile pénétrant la plus dense. L'atmosphère, par exemple, met en mouvement le principe électrique, pendant que le principe électrique pénètre l'atmosphère. Ces *gradations* de matière augmentent en raréfaction et en subtilité jusqu'à ce que nous arrivions à une matière *imparticulée*, — sans molécules —indivisible, —*une*; et ici la loi d'impulsion et de péné-

tration est modifiée. La matière suprème ou *imparticulée* non seulement pénètre les êtres, mais met tous les êtres en mouvement, —et ainsi elle *est* tous les êtres en un, qui est elle-même. Cette matière est Dieu. Ce que les hommes cherchent à personnifier dans le mot *pensée*, c'est la matière en mouvement. (Lemonnier, 232–33)

V. [*After a long pause, and mutteringly.*] I see—but it is a thing difficult to tell. [*Another long pause.*] He is not spirit, for he exists. Nor is he matter, *as you understand it*. But there are *gradations* of matter of which man knows nothing; the grosser impelling the finer, the finer pervading the grosser. The atmosphere, for example, impels the electric principle, while the electric principle permeates the atmosphere. These gradations of matter increase in rarity or fineness, until we arrive at a matter *unparticled*—without particles—indivisible—*one*; and here the law of impulsion and permeation is modified. The ultimate or unparticled matter not only permeates all things, but impels all things; and thus *is* all things within itself. This matter is God. What men attempt to embody in the word "thought," is this matter in motion. (90–91)

The interview continues along these lines in what is, until its end, an extremely static narrative. But it is, I suspect, the ending that drew Baudelaire to this tale, for it calls into question not only the perceptions of the limited man of science (or pseudoscience) and his sickly patient, but also the nature of the cosmological theories he recites. The patient literally wakes up dead, and in the final sentence of the tale, the narrator asks:

Le somnambule, pendant la dernière partie de son discours, m'avait-il donc parlé du fond de la région des ombres? (240)

Had the sleep-walker, indeed, during the latter portion of his discourse, been addressing me from out the region of the shadows? (95)

In several of his novels published during the 1840s, as we have seen, Balzac also discussed animal magnetism and related visionary doctrines, only to undermine belief in their validity. They may well have taught Baudelaire the necessity of imagining a totality, while resisting belief in any specific body of doctrines that claimed to represent it. Certainly, both in the preface to his translation of this tale and elsewhere, Baudelaire pays tribute to the French novelist and his visionary representation of contemporary French society. What he seems to have taken from Poe, however, was the technique of undermining belief in any system with a concise, ironic point that was particularly effective when it came at the end of a text.

Baudelaire's "Présentation" depicts both animal magnetism and the work of Poe as emblematic of a kind of systematic writing which attempts to reconcile science and theology. Giving way to a kind of intertextual excess, the poet compares Poe to Diderot, Laclos, Hoffmann, Goethe, Jean-Paul, and Maturin. (2:245) For Baudelaire, however, the significance of the "systems" of these writers lies, not in the specific doctrines attached to their works, but in what they reveal concerning the psychology of the artist and the process of artistic creation. They represent an attempt to recapture the harmonious world of childhood; these writers' works are a reflection, not of the objective structure of the world, but of themselves:

> Tous ces gens, avec une volonté et une bonne foi infatigable, décalquent la nature, la pure nature. — Laquelle? — La leur. Aussi sont-ils générale-ment bien plus étonnants et originaux que les simples imaginatifs qui sont tout à fait indoués d'esprit philosophique, et qui entassent et align-ent les événements sans les classer, et sans en expliquer le sens mysté-rieux. J'ai dit qu'ils étaient étonnants. Je dis plus: c'est ce qu'ils visent généralement à l'étonnant. Dans les oeuvres de plusieurs d'entre eux, on voit la préoccupation d'un perpétuel surnaturalisme. Cela tient, comme je l'ai dit, à cet esprit primitif de *chercherie*, qu'on me pardonne le barbar-isme, à cet esprit inquisitorial, esprit de juge d'instruction, qui a peut-être ses racines dans les plus lointaines impressions de l'enfance. (2:248)

The single reference to Swedenborg in this essay occurs in the context of a comparison of Balzac and Poe:

> On connaît Séraphîtus, Louis Lambert, et une foule de passages d'autres livres, où Balzac, ce grand esprit dévoré du légitime orgueil encyclopé-dique, a essayé de fondre en un système unitaire et définitif différentes idées tirées de Swedenborg, Mesmer, Marat, Goethe et Geoffroy Saint-Hilaire. L'idée de l'unité a aussi poursuivi Edgar Poe, et il n'a point dé-pensé moins d'efforts que Balzac dans ce rêve caressé. (2:248)

Lest the reader be lulled into thinking the systems of writers such as Swedenborg, Balzac, or Poe innocuous, Baudelaire slips a reference to Marat into yet another list of sources, this time for Balzac's "légitime or-gueil encyclopédique." Yet, if the overall tone of this preface is skeptical, its references to the energy and ambition of system builders and imitators point to the writer's admiration of them, although he presents himself clearly as a nonparticipant. A later reference to "Mesmeric Revelation" is far more negative.

In "Notes nouvelles sur Edgar Poe" (1857), Baudelaire writes of Poe's "Mesmeric Revelation" and presumably his translation of it:

> Les Swédenborgiens se félicitent de sa *Révélation magnétique*, semblables à ces naïfs Illuminés qui jadis surveillaient dans l'auteur du *Diable*

amoureux un révélateur de leurs mystères; ils le remercient pour les grandes vérités qu'il vient de proclamer,—car ils ont découvert (ô véri-ficateurs de ce qui ne peut être vérifié!) que tout ce qu'il a énoncé est absolument vrai;—bien que d'abord, avouent ces braves gens, ils aient eu le soupçon que ce pouvait bien être une simple fiction. Poe répond que, pour son compte, il n'en a jamais douté. (2:322)

Already in "Edgar Allan Poe: sa vie et ses ouvrages," first published in 1852, Baudelaire refers to Swedenborg in the context of the marginal and powerless situation of the artist, misunderstood by a public interested only in money:

Mais il paraît que Poe était fort difficile sur le choix de son auditoire. Que ses auditeurs fussent capables de comprendre ses abstractions ténues, ou d'admirer les glorieuses conceptions qui coupaient incessamment de leurs lueurs le ciel sombre de son cerveau, il ne s'en inquiétaiet guère. Il s'asseyait dans une taverne, à côté d'un sordide polisson, et lui dévelop-pait gravement les grandes lignes de son terrible livre *Eureka*, avec un sang-froid implacable, comme s'il eût dicté à un secrétaire, ou disputé avec Kepler, Bacon ou Swedenborg. (2:270)

And yet, in this relatively early essay, Poe appears as the model of an artist, a poet, who through sheer willpower and force of understanding is able to understand the world in the comprehensive terms of a great philosopher or visionary. He is the polar opposite of a Samuel Cramer, Godefroid, or Lucien de Rubempré.

Baudelaire's "Notes nouvelles sur Edgar Poe" of 1857 contains the earliest references in his prose to "correspondences." This essay, which modifies Baudelaire's earlier interpretation of "Mesmeric Revelation," takes up again the depiction of the artist as a soul in exile, here explicitly in connection with a concept of allegorical *correspondances* between the ob-jects of a degraded and alienating world and those of a transcendent be-yond:

C'est cet admirable, cet immortel instinct du Beau qui nous fait con-sidérer la terre et ses spectacles comme un aperçu, comme une corre-spondance du Ciel. La soif insatiable de tout ce qui est au delà, et que révèle la vie, est la preuve la plus vivante de notre immortalité. C'est à la fois par la poésie et à *travers* la musique que l'on entrevoit les splendeurs situées derrière le tombeau; et quand un poème exquis amène les larmes au bord des yeux, ces larmes ne sont pas la preuve d'un excès de jouis-sance, elles sont bien plutôt le témoignage d'une mélancolie irritée, d'une postulation des nerfs, d'une nature exilée dans l'imparfait et qui voudrait s'emparer immédiatement, sur cette terre même, d'un paradis révélé. (2:334)

Clearly, however, the emphasis has shifted in this essay from inadequate or unknowable philosophical situations to the aesthetic intuitions associated with the poet's "instinct du Beau."

"Notes nouvelles sur Edgar Poe" represents Baudelaire's most extensive comments on Poe's aesthetics; its emphasis on form and function resembles the American writer's "Philosophy of Composition." One notes here the increased importance accorded to language in the evocation of ideal beauty and also the analogy between language and music, which was to become increasingly prominent in Baudelaire's aesthetics. And yet *correspondances* also stand for the kind of negative analogy that the totalizing systems of Swedenborg and some philosophers had represented in earlier essays.

> L'Imagination n'est pas la fantaisie; elle n'est pas non plus la sensibilité, bien qu'il soit difficile de concevoir un homme imaginatif qui ne serait pas sensible. L'Imagination est une faculté quasi divine qui perçoit tout d'abord, en dehors des méthodes philosophiques, les rapports intimes et secrets des choses, les correspondances et les analogies. Les honneurs et les fonctions qu'il confère à cette faculté lui donnent une valeur telle (du moins quand on a bien compris la pensée de l'auteur), qu'un savant sans imagination n'apparaît plus que comme un faux savant, ou tout au moins comme un savant incomplet. (2:329)

Correspondances cannot be identified with theological allegory, not only because they are evoked as products of the poet's imagination and sense of beauty, but also because the relationship between the real world and the experience produced by the work of art grows out of an opposition between consciousness and its surroundings: "et quand un poème amène les larmes au bord des yeux, ces larmes ne sont pas la preuve d'un excès de jouissance, elles sont bien plutôt le témoignage d'une mélancolie irritée, d'une postulation des nerfs, d'une nature exilée dans l'imparfait et qui voudrait s'emparer immédiatement sur cette terre même, d'un paradis révélé."

The *imagination* of otherworldly *correspondances*, then, is the basis for the survival and integrity of the artist, as well as the creation of aesthetic objects and the depiction of analogies among the arts. The development of the concept of *correspondances* here parallels the movement of the sonnet "Correspondances," which begins by evoking a hieroglyphic language of nature and moves on to suggest the equivalence of different sense impressions.

"Le poème du hachisch"

Like *La Fanfarlo* and the essays on Poe, the essays by Baudelaire collected in *Les paradis artificiels* are about what poetry is *not*. If the earlier works distinguished it from philosophical, theological, or political systems, these texts focus on its similarities to—but fundamental differences from—the experience of taking opium.

Two references to Swedenborgianism occur in the fourth section of "Le poème du hachisch," first published in 1860, in the context of a discussion of the drugged subject's tendency to read anthropomorphic meanings into objects and to consider him- or herself, narcissistically, as the equal of God. The first passage links Swedenborgianism to a concept of a natural language which yet indoctrinates:

> La sinuosité des lignes est un langage définitivement clair où vous lisez l'agitation et le désir des âmes. Cependant se développe cet état mystérieux et temporaire de l'esprit, où la profondeur de la vie, hérissée de ses problèmes multiples, se révèle tout entière dans le spectacle, si naturel et si trivial qu'il soit, qu'on a sous les yeux,—où le premier objet devient objet parlant. Fourier et Swedenborg, l'un avec ses *analogies*, l'autre avec ses *correspondances*, se sont incarnés dans le végétal et l'animal qui tombent sous votre regard, et au lieu d'enseigner par la voix, ils vous endoctrinent par la forme et par la couleur. L'intelligence de l'allégorie prend en vous des proportions à vous-mêmes inconnues; nous noterons en passant que l'allégorie, ce genre si *spirituel*, que les peintres maladroits nous ont accoutumés à mépriser, mais qui est vraiment l'une des formes primitives et les plus naturelles de la poésie, reprend la domination légitime dans l'intelligence illuminée par l'ivresse. (1:430)

But the second reference undermines the affirmation of the connection of Swedenborgianism with a moral vision of things, for, alluding to Swedenborg's characterization of "man" as a "natural devil," it ties Swedenborgianism to the drugged individual's diabolical belief in his equality with God.

> Avais-je tort de dire que le hachisch apparaissait, à un esprit vraiment philosophique, comme un parfait instrument satanique? Le remords, singulier ingrédient du plaisir, est bientôt noyé dans la délicieuse contemplation du remords, dans une espèce d'analyse voluptueuse; et cette analyse est si rapide que l'homme, ce diable naturel, pour parler comme les Swedenborgiens, ne s'aperçoit pas combien elle est involontaire, et combien, de seconde en seconde, il se rapproche de la perfection diabolique. Il *admire* son remords et il se glorifie, pendant qu'il est en train de perdre sa liberté. (1:434)

The satanic interpretation of Swedenborgianism here recalls the section of *Les fleurs du mal* entitled "Révolte," in which the rebellion of Satan suggests the events of 1848. The context here, however, is very different. The satanism of the drug addict is characterized by inertia and unawareness; he is essentially a solitary being, perceiving anthropomorphic significances in animal and vegetable matter, rather than in other human beings.

"Le poème du hachisch" was published in the collection *Les paradis artificiels*, which also included the early "Du vin et du hachisch, comparés comme moyens de multiplication de l'individualité."[5] In the earlier work, wine is described as an intoxicant which renders the individual sociable and productive, hachisch as one which isolates and exhausts. The artificial paradise of the drugged subject is opposed to the sociable intoxication of the working classes and, by association, to the notion of revolution. "A quoi bon, en effet," Baudelaire writes, "travailler, labourer, écrire, fabriquer, quoi que ça soit, quand on peut emporter le paradis d'un seul coup? Enfin le vin est pour le peuple qui travaille et qui mérite d'en boire." (1:397) One suspects in these words, which appear near the end of "Du vin et du hachisch," an ironic concession to conventional morality, but the last words of the piece imply that the solidarity produced by wine is indeed superior to the solitude produced by hachisch and also, probably, by art and poetry: "Le vin est utile, il produit des résultats fructifiants. Le hachisch est inutile et dangereux." (1:397)

"Le poème du hachisch" establishes an analogy between drugs and poetry: both turn the former revolutionary into a solitary daydreamer.[6]

Réflexions sur quelques-uns de mes contemporains: "Victor Hugo"

Baudelaire's essay on Victor Hugo was published in the *Revue fantaisiste* in 1861, the year following the publication of the first edition of *Les paradis artificiels*.[7] In this work, which contains Baudelaire's most famous references to Swedenborg and Fourier, he focuses above all on the link between Hugo's moral vision of the world and his belief in the anthropomorphic significance of his perceptions. Baudelaire's remarks on the relationship of Hugo's poetry to the doctrines of Swedenborg and Fourier recall his earlier comparison, in *Les paradis artificiels*, of the work of these two writers to the lethargic megalomania of the drug addict. Here, as well, the doctrines of the two earlier writers are linked to a moral vision of the world, a vision Hugo shares and even intensifies in his work, but about which Baudelaire voices considerable ambivalence. On this subject, it is helpful to recall the more openly critical remarks at the end of "Notes nouvelles sur Edgar Poe," in which Baudelaire took the older poet to task for his fondness for "l'enseignement":

> Nous connaissons cette loyale escrime. Les reproches que les mauvais critiques font aux bons poètes sont les mêmes dans tous les pays. En lisant cet article, il me semblait lire la traduction d'un de ces nombreux réquisitoires dressés par les critiques parisiens contre ceux de nos poètes qui sont le plus amoureux de perfection. Nos préférés sont faciles à deviner, et toute âme éprise de poésie pure me comprendra quand je dirai que, parmi notre race antipoétique, Victor Hugo serait moins admiré s'il était parfait, et qu'il n'a pu se faire pardonner tout son génie lyrique qu'en introduisant de force et brutalement dans sa poésie ce qu'Edgar Poe considérait comme l'hérésie moderne capitale, — *l'enseignement*. (2:336–37)

In the 1861 essay on Hugo, the references to Swedenborg and Fourier occur in the context of a discussion of the structure and function of poetic language in the second part of the text. Baudelaire opens with a discussion of the resources of a hieroglyphic language of nature:

> La nature qui pose devant nous, de quelque côté que nous nous tournions, et qui nous enveloppe comme un mystère, se présente sous plusieurs états simultanés dont chacun, selon qu'il est plus intelligible, plus sensible pour nous, se réflète plus vivement dans nos coeurs: forme, attitude et mouvement, lumière et couleur, son et harmonie. (2:132)

Victor Hugo's poetry, a reflection of his temperament, emphasizes the musical, sculptural, and painterly resources of language, and it is the interplay of these three aspects of language which evokes what Baudelaire calls either "le mystère de la vie" (2: 131) or "la morale des choses." (2:132) Hugo is at his most subtle when he is able to evoke "sensations morales," which are transmitted to us

> par l'être visible, par la nature inanimée, ou dite inanimée; non seulement, la figure d'un être extérieur à l'homme, végétal ou minéral, mais aussi sa physionomie, son regard, sa tristesse, sa douceur, sa joie éclatante, sa haine répulsive, son enchantement ou son horreur; enfin, en d'autres termes, tout ce qu'il y a d'humaine dans n'importe quoi, et aussi tout ce qu'il y a de divin, de sacré ou de diabolique. (2:132)

The evocation of "sensations morales," then, derives from the poet's ability to see anthropomorphic significance in his perceptions. This process is linked to what Baudelaire calls, in the fourth part of the essay, "la conjecture poétique," or the ability of the poet to play with and even extend the language of contemporary science. (2:138–139) The poetic practice of Hugo, like the attitude of the drug addict, involves the acceptance and repetition of existing structures.

It is in this context that we can perhaps best understand the significance of Baudelaire's references to Fourier and Swedenborg in the second part of the essay:

> Ceux qui ne sont pas poètes ne comprennent pas ces choses. Fourier est venu un jour, trop pompeusement, nous révéler les mystères de l'*analogie*. Je ne nie pas la valeur de quelques-unes de ses minutieuses découvertes, bien que je croie que son cerveau était trop épris d'exactitude matérielle pour ne pas commettre d'erreurs et pour atteindre d'emblée la certitude morale de l'intuition. Il aurait pu tout aussi précieusement nous révéler tous les excellents poètes dans lesquels l'humanité lisante fait son éducation aussi bien que dans la contemplation de la nature. D'ailleurs Swedenborg, qui possédait une âme bien plus grande, nous avait déjà enseigné que *le ciel est un très grand homme*; que tout, forme, mouvement, nombre, couleur, parfum, dans le *spirituel* comme dans le *naturel*, est significatif, réciproque, converse, *correspondant*. Lavater, limitant au visage de l'homme la démonstration de l'universelle vérité, nous avait traduit le sens spirituel du contour, de la forme, de la dimension. (2:132–133)

Fourier's analogies are far less suggestive, according to Baudelaire, than Swedenborg's correspondences. The description of the suggestiveness of Swedenborg's work—"tout, forme, mouvement, nombre, couleur, parfum . . . est significatif, réciproque, converse, *correspondant*"—recalls the comparison, at the beginning of the second part of the essay, of Hugo's poetic lexicon to the infinite possibilities of a language of nature. Baudelaire associates Swedenborgianism with a concept of a natural language that is far richer in associative possiblities than existing human languages. The kind of "meaning" evoked by *correspondances*—the poet must use a series of adjectives to suggest the complex relationships brought into play by this language—stands in opposition to the limited anthropomorphic significance evoked by poetry such as that of Hugo. To be sure, Swedenborgianism is, in its turn, anthropomorphic: "D'ailleurs Swedenborg, qui possédait une âme bien plus grande, nous avait déjà enseigné que *le ciel est un très grand homme*." Swedenborgianism, like the work of Fourier and Hugo, merely points the way to the poet's creation of a language superior to those already existing in either nature or society.

"Peintures murales d'Eugène Delacroix à Saint-Sulpice"

Baudelaire's reference to Swedenborgianism in his review of Delacroix's murals in Saint-Sulpice also emphasizes the distance between the allegorical interpretations of Swedenborgianism and the cabala, on the one hand, and his aesthetics, on the other. His remarks occur in the context of his evaluation of the first of three murals (covering the left- and right-hand walls of the chapel and its ceiling). The painting on the left depicts Jacob wrestling with the angel. Baudelaire cites the Biblical version of the narrative (Genesis 32: 23–32), and goes on to comment:

> De cette bizarre légende, que beaucoup de gens interprètent allégo-riquement, et que ceux de la Kaballe et de la Nouvelle Jérusalem tradui-sent sans doute dans des sens différents, Delacroix, s'attachant au sens matériel, comme il devait faire, a tiré tout le parti qu'un peintre de son tempérament en pouvait tirer. (2:730)

It is the natural, rather than the spiritual, aspect of the narrative that interests Delacroix. Baudelaire's interpretation of the painting focuses, in turn, on the concrete detail of the scene:

> L'homme naturel et l'homme surnaturel luttent chacun selon sa nature, Jacob incliné en avant comme un bélier et bandant toute sa musculature, l'ange se prêtant complaisamment au combat, calme, doux, comme un être qui peut vaincre sans effort des muscles et ne permettant pas à la colère d'altérer la forme divine de ses membres. (2:730)

Swedenborg had interpreted Genesis 32 in his *Arcana coelestia* 4232–4317. He summarizes his analysis, which extends over eighty pages in the American Swedenborg Society edition, in these terms:

> 4232. The subject here treated of in the internal sense is the inversion of state in the natural, in order that the good may be in the first place, and truth in the second. The implantation of truth in good is treated of (verses 1 to 23) and the wrestlings of the temptations which are then to be sustained (verses 24 to 32). At the same time the Jewish nation is also treated of, because although that nation could receive nothing of the church, it nevertheless represented the things of the church. (*Arcana coelestia* 6:6)

For Baudelaire, the core of the narrative was its reflection of the Romantic cliché of the duality of man. For Swedenborg, on the other hand, the conflict between Jacob and the angel represented the reconciliation be-tween goodness and truth and between the will and consciousness, rather than their opposition. His exegesis moved from the details of the scene to moral abstractions. Baudelaire, in contrast, translates the language of reli-gious tradition into sensation. The poet gives us two versions of each nar-rative: the first is a repetition of the Biblical version; the second is his transposition of Delacroix's paintings into language. He explicitly opposes his view of the scene to interpretations proposed—or likely to be proposed—by Swedenborgians and believers in the cabala, but what he is objecting to here is not the notion of allegory per se, but rather the divorce between language and its "sens matériel." Baudelaire's retelling of the story and the painting in the words of Genesis 32 and in his own terms also allegorizes the painting; but his opposition of the "spiritual" and the "material" sense undermines the coherence of the narrative framework in order to bring the onlooker closer to the *sensuous detail* of the work.

Swedenborgianism is mentioned here for the first and only time in Baudelaire's work in connection with the mystical concept of language associated with the cabala. As we have seen, the cabala probably influenced Swedenborg only indirectly, through the work of Leibniz and through his study of hermeneutics.[8] At the time Baudelaire was writing, however, interest in the cabala was widespread in aesthetic circles in France. The poet may well have encountered Adolphe Franck's *La kabbale ou la philosophie des Hébreux*, first published in 1843, or the interpretations of his old acquaintance, Constant/Lévi. For Baudelaire, as for his contemporaries, the cabala appears to have been important because of its focus on language and its apparent ability both to resume and reconcile divergent cultural traditions, but here, like Swedenborgianism, to which it is explicitly compared, it plays a purely heuristic role, providing an interpretive model that enables the spectator and critic to understand how Delacroix's painting functions as a whole.

"Les bons chiens"

The prose poem "Les bons chiens," first published in *L'indépendance belge* in June 1865, plays with the relationship between natural history, morality, and the world of the city. Swedenborgianism figures here, as it had in the work of Balzac, as a doctrine which extends the taxonomies of natural history beyond the limits of perception. Baudelaire's reference to Swedenborgianism is, however, heavily ironic; it occurs in connection with the question of the existence of a heaven for well-behaved dogs:

> Et que de fois j'ai pensé qu'il y avait peut-être quelque part (qui sait, après tout?), pour récompenser tant de courage, tant de patience et de labeur, un paradis spécial pour les bons chiens, les pauvres chiens, les chiens crottés et désolés. Swedenborg affirme bien qu'il y en a un pour les Turcs et un pour les Hollandais. (1:362)

Claude Pichois suggests that the immediate reference of this prose poem is to the lines jotted down near the beginning of *Pauvre Belgique II*: "Les chiens seuls sont vivants; ils sont les nègres de la Belgique." (Baudelaire, *Oeuvres complètes* 2:823) "Les bons chiens" also recalls the earlier prose poem, "Le chien et le flacon" (1862), in which the fondness of dogs for excrement stands for the execrable taste of the poet's public. Moreover, the earlier poem contains a variation of the word *correspondances* in a context that suggests that it, too, mocks the contexts of Swedenborgianism and, indeed, any kind of aestheticized spiritualism, for the narrator characterizes the tail-wagging of dogs as: "le signe correspondant du rire et du sourire." (1:284)[9]

The dogs in "Les bons chiens" obviously represent their owners in Brussels who, in turn, represent the worst of the mid-century European bourgeoisie. At one point, Baudelaire links his evocation of these creatures explicitly to Belgium:

> Connaissez-vous la paresseuse Belgique, et avez-vous admiré comme moi tous ces chiens vigoureux attelés à la charette du boucher, de la laitière ou du boulanger, et qui témoignent par leurs aboiements triomphants, du plaisir orgueilleux qu'ils éprouvent à rivaliser avec les chevaux? (1:361–362)

The reference to "la paresseuse Belgique," of course, is ironic; what characterizes Belgian dogs (and their owners) here is their senseless activity, their imitation of bourgeois habits:

> Où vont ces chiens, dites-vous, hommes peu attentifs? Ils vont à leurs affaires.
> Rendez-vous d'affaires, rendez-vous d'amour. A travers la brume, à travers la neige, à travers la crotte, sous la canicule mordante, sous la pluie ruisselante, ils vont, ils viennent, ils trottent, ils passent sous les voitures, excités par les puces, la passion, le besoin ou le devoir. Comme nous, ils se sont levés de bon matin, et ils cherchent leur vie ou courent à leurs plaisirs. (1:361)

The subject of the poem strains the limits of the classificatory language of natural history, as well as that of literary tradition. "Les bons chiens" opens with a reference to the poet's admiration for Buffon and his inability to reconcile his theme with Buffon's work. Instead, he realizes that this is a subject for Sterne, whom he calls "sentimental farceur, farceur incomparable." (1:360) The poem then goes on to invoke the appropriate muse: "Arrière la muse académique! . . .J'invoque la muse familière, la citadine, la vivante, pour qu'elle m'aide à chanter les bons chiens . . ." (1:360) The Swedenborgian concept of different spheres of heaven appears here both as a caricature of the classificatory systems of natural history and physiognomy, and as a mocking reference to the self-satisfied aesthetic and moral beliefs of Baudelaire's bourgeois audience.

3. Toward a Universal Language of Art? Baudelaire's *Correspondances*

From *La Fanfarlo*, published in 1847, but perhaps written earlier, to "Les bons chiens," published in 1865, Baudelaire's brief references to Swedenborgianism focus on the importance of fictions of totality in making sense of the world. These fictions may be allied with the interests of the political right or left, with the followers of Maistre or Fourier, and they are most often beyond the grasp or even the intuition of individuals. Certainly Samuel Cramer of *La Fanfarlo* might have had more success in directing his life if he had better understood the relationship between the ideas of Crébillon fils and Swedenborg, whose books he kept next to each other in his room. But even Baudelaire's hero, Poe, is unable to act on what appears, in "Mesmeric Revelation," as well as the French poet's interpretations of his work, to be a sound and aesthetically suggestive understanding of the systems of Swedenborg and Mesmer. *La Fanfarlo* and the essays on Poe tie Swedenborgianism to two very different political orientations, represented by the utopian politics of 1848 and the doctrines of Joseph de Maistre. "Le poème du hachisch," however, compares Swedenborgianism to the essentially apolitical and isolating experience of taking drugs. In the essay on Hugo of 1861, it stands for a moral vision of the world that is akin but inferior to really good poetry. In the late essay on Delacroix's murals at Saint-Sulpice and the prose poem, "Les bons chiens," Swedenborgianism had come to resemble a caricature of a philosophical, theological, or aesthetic system, but one which, despite its *dépouillement*, still played an important role in understanding the world or a work of art as a totality. But those two late works point to a polarity in Baudelaire's interpretation of Swedenborgianism that is important for our understanding of his interpretation and reworking of what he understood as the doctrine of correspondences.

"Les bons chiens" invokes Swedenborg in connection with a caricature of the taxonomic systems that made it possible, in the eighteenth century, to begin to classify within the natural world and, in the nineteenth, to imagine classes of human beings. If it represents a particularly dark and bitter interpretation of the theme of totality, "Les bons chiens" nevertheless emphasizes the role of such systems, however preposterous, in enabling the individual to imagine him- or herself as part of a social world, a community, or a crowd. The prose poem thus marks the end of one line of development in Baudelaire's very sketchy interpretation of Swedenborgianism, one which, beginning with *La Fanfarlo*, emphasized the social and political importance of these doctrines as one kind of system that took the poet out of himself.

"Peintures murales," on the other hand, emphasizes the isolation of the artist and the autonomy of the work of art, which stands independently of any moral system or political platform. It is this view that we find most clearly expressed in the works which, beginning with "Notes nouvelles sur Edgar Poe" of 1857, use the term *correspondances* in connection with a notion of the work of art as a closed system that generates a certain effect. The view of the work of art as a little world, of course, echoes the affirmation of the importance of systems for understanding the world outside, but Baudelaire consistently emphasizes their difference. The work of art is *like* the world, but fundamentally distinct. Like Swedenborg's doctrine of correspondences, its language, its structures, evoke the invisible, but in the case of aesthetic artifacts, the invisible has little to do with the classificatory systems of natural history. Like the language of mysticism, good poetry and good art point beyond the known structures of representation.

And yet, if Baudelaire's meditations on *correspondances* suggest that, like Constant/Lévi, his turn towards language went hand in hand with a retreat from political issues and overt political statements, they also betray their essential connection to contemporary politics and society. Baudelaire's references to *correspondances* most often emphasize the distinctness of art and aesthetic experience, an experience as solitary as that of the drug taker, but they are best understood as a movement of withdrawal from something. The little aesthetic worlds marked out by Baudelaire's *correspondances* stand in an implied opposition to the discursive works of Constant/Lévi and other writers of working-class or artisan origins in mid-nineteenth-century Paris. Similarly, the use of the term to evoke an experience of unity that grows out of the most private kinds of sensations, those such as smell or touch that are closest to the body, serves, as Walter Benjamin has suggested, to insulate the poet from the experience of the city crowds.[10]

In his commentary to "Correspondances," Claude Pichois notes seven references to the term in Baudelaire's prose: in *Exposition universelle—1855—Beaux-Arts*, the letter to Toussenel of January 21, 1856, "Le Poème du hachisch," the preface to Poe's *Nouvelles Histoires extraordinaires* (repeated in "Notes nouvelles sur Edgar Poe" and the essay on Gautier of 1859), the prose "Invitation au voyage," the *Salon de 1859*, and the essay on Hugo of 1861.[11] Analogies among the arts, the artistic process (which is described in terms of a linguistic model), and utopianism frame Baudelaire's use of the term in all seven references.

As we have seen, the texts which explicitly link *correspondances* to

Swedenborg—"Notes nouvelles sur Edgar Poe," "Le Poème du hachisch," and the essay on Hugo—all represent Swedenborg's doctrine of correspondences as a model, but an inadequate model, for poetry: its moral and political connotations sound a false note in what the poet sees as the essentially solitary and solipsistic pleasures of art. In the texts that refer to *correspondances* alone, the word is used in a more positive sense, denoting an essential aspect of the isolating experience the poet opposes to politics and morality. Yet its use here is also paradoxical, for in his essays on painting and music, *correspondances* comes to stand not only for the relationship among the various components of little aesthetic systems, but also for the way in which the apparently sealed-off worlds of art communicate.

Although he removes it from its Swedenborgian context, Baudelaire's use of the word *correspondances* in these texts harks back to eighteenth-century aesthetics and language theory. His insistence on an analogy between the arts recalls the unitary aesthetics of eighteenth-century writers such as Charles Batteux, who represented "les beaux arts sous un même principe." But his emphasis on the role of feeling and sensation in the creation of a good work of art, which may echo eighteenth-century accounts of the origins of language, especially Rousseau's, undercuts the prescriptive element in neoclassical aesthetics. The authority of the poet and the artist is grounded not in his or her ability to imitate worthy models, but in intuitions of a language hidden in things.

In the *Exposition universelle* (1855), for example, the term *correspondances* occurs in connection with the rejection of prescriptive aesthetics:

> L'insensé doctrinaire du Beau déraisonnerait, sans doute; enfermé dans l'aveuglante forteresse de son système, il blasphémerait la vie et la nature, et son fanatisme grec, italien ou parisien, lui persuaderait de défendre à ce peuple insolent de jouir, de rêver ou de penser par d'autres procédés que les siens propres;—science barbouillée d'encre, goût bâtard, plus barbare que les barbares, qui a oublié la couleur du ciel, la forme du végétal, le mouvement et l'odeur de l'animalité, et dont les doigts crispés, paralysés par la plume, ne peuvent plus courir avec agilité sur l'immense clavier des *correspondances*! (2:557)

In contrast to the precepts of prescriptive aesthetics, living works of art are founded on a secret sympathy between the imagination of the artist and his world, a sympathy which evokes similar resonances in the consciousness of his audience. This sympathy allows the work of art to become the instrument for the creation of "new worlds of ideas" rather than the representation of systems already formulated. The generative capacity of the work of art is closely allied to its tendency to distance the reader from his or her everyday experience:

> Si, au lieu d'un pédagogue, je prends un homme du monde, un intelligent, et si je le transporte dans une contrée lointaine, je suis sûr que, si les étonnements du débarquement sont grands, si l'accoutumance est plus ou moins longue, plus ou moins laborieuse, la sympathie sera tôt ou tard si vive, si pénétrante, qu'elle créera en lui un monde nouveau d'idées, monde qui fera partie intégrante de lui-même, et qui l'accompagnera, sous la forme de souvenirs, jusqu'à la mort. (2:576)

Baudelaire's *Exposition universlle* (1855) is devoted to a discussion of paintings by Ingres and Delacroix and a comparison of their work. The reference to "l'immense clavier des *correspondances*" recalls earlier discussions of Delacroix's method of composition, which Baudelaire compares to the poet's use of words in a dictionary and the pianist's manipulation of notes on a keyboard. In the *Salon de 1846*, for example, he writes:

> Pour E. Delacroix, la nature est un vaste dictionnaire dont il roule et consulte les feuillets avec un oeil sûr et profond; et cette peinture, qui procède surtout du souvenir, parle surtout au souvenir. L'effet produit sur l'âme du spectateur est analogue aux moyens de l'artiste. (2:433)

What is at stake in the 1846 essay, however, is the embellishment of the surfaces of everyday life:

> La vie parisienne est féconde en sujets poétiques et merveilleux. Le merveilleux nous enveloppe et nous abreuve comme l'atmosphère; mais nous ne le voyons pas. (2:496)

Baudelaire's letter of 1856 to the Fourierist, Alphonse Toussenel, emphasizes the importance to poetry of the individual's ability to intuit analogies and correspondences that are not immediately visible. Here the poet takes care to distinguish this ability from any ideological tradition; it has its roots in the individual consciousness, and every good poet must discover it for him- or herself. Baudelaire compares Toussenel's attempt to create a Fourierist natural history to the work of the poet, which, he implies, is superior to politics or social theory. Like the poet, Toussenel uses language to mediate between the structures of natural science and his imagination. Baudelaire's emphasis on the scientific nature of the imagination and of the language of poetry points forward to his discussion of Hugo's use of language in the essay of 1861:

Ce qui est positif, c'est que vous êtes poète. Il y a bien longtemps que je dis que le poète est *souverainement intelligent*, qu'il est *l'intelligence* par excellence, — et que l'imagination est la plus scientifique des facultés, parce que seule elle comprend l'analogie universelle, ou ce qu'une religion mystique appelle la *correspondance*.

A further reference to *correspondances* occurs in a passage from his "Notes nouvelles sur Edgar Poe" of 1857, in the context of a discussion of Poe's "Poetic Principle" and its implications for a unity of the aesthetic object based, not on unity of conception, but on unity of impression—on the totality of effect: "je ne veux pas parler de l'unité dans la conception, mais de l'unité dans l'impression, de la totalité de l'effet . . . " (2:332) *Correspondances* again point to the production of effects based on an instinctive, rather than a rational or even conscious, concept of beauty:

C'est cet admirable, cet immortel instinct du Beau qui nous fait considérer la terre et ses spectacles comme un aperçu, comme une correspondance du Ciel. (2:334)

The one prose poem to mention *correspondances* in isolation, the prose version of "Invitation au voyage" (*Le Spleen de Paris* XVIII) links *correspondances* and analogy to desire generated by aesthetic objects, a desire which leads to a kind of lassitude reminiscent of a drugged state— "Chaque homme porte en lui sa dose d'opium naturel" (1:303)—which leads to immobility and, here again, death. The central paradox of the prose "Invitation au voyage" is that the "trip" suggested by the work of art is a desire for immobility:

Qu'ils cherchent, qu'ils cherchent encore, qu'ils reculent sans cesse les limites de leur bonheur, ces alchimistes de l'horticulture! Qu'ils proposent des prix de soixante et de cent mille florins pour qui résoudra leurs ambitieux problèmes! Moi, j'ai trouvé ma *tulipe noire* et mon *dahlia bleu*!

Fleur incomparable, tulipe retrouvée, allégorique dahlia, c'est là, n'est-ce pas, dans ce beau pays si calme et si rêveur, qu'il faudrait aller vivre et fleurir? Ne serais-tu pas encadrée dans ton analogie et ne pourrais-tu pas te mirer, pour parler comme des mystiques, dans ta propre *correspondance*? (1:303)

The aesthetic dream of the trip to Cocagne contrasts with the philistine's belief in "jouissance positive":

Des rêves! toujours des rêves! et plus l'âme est ambitieuse et délicate, plus les rêves l'éloignent du possible. Chaque homme porte en lui sa dose d'opium naturel, incessamment sécrétée et renouvelée, et, de la naissance à la mort, combien comptons-nous d'heures remplies par la jouissance positive, par l'action réussie et décidée? Vivrons-nous jamais, passerons-nous jamais dans ce tableau qu'a peint mon esprit, ce tableau qui te ressemble? (1:303)

The effect of the intoxicating language of *correspondances* is to transform the seer into an object.

As Barbara Johnson has pointed out, in the prose "Invitation au voyage" Baudelaire has translated the sublime poetic vision of the version in *Les fleurs du mal* into its commercial equivalent.[12] The prose version points to the ambiguous relationship of the languages of art and poetry to that of advertising. The negative *correspondances* of the prose "Invitation" mediate between the two.

The *Salon de 1859* also reveals a consciousness of the commercial possibilities of the languages of art and poetry. Here, Delacroix's dictionary has become an "immense magasin d'observations" (2:622):

Tout l'univers visible n'est qu'un magasin d'images et de signes auxquels l'imagination donnera une place et une valeur relative; c'est une espèce de pâture que l'imagination doit digérer et transformer. (2:627)

The language of analogy not only decomposes and recreates the world for the artist, it also creates the very profitable "sensation du neuf." (2:621)

Finally, the first two quatrains of the sonnet "Correspondances" are cited in Baudelaire's "Richard Wagner et *Tannhaüser* à Paris," first published in the *Revue européenne* of April 1861, in the context of a discussion of the relationship between different kinds of sensation and art forms:

Le lecteur sait quel but nous poursuivons: démontrer que la véritable musique suggère des idées analogues dans des cerveaux différents. D'ailleurs, il ne serait pas ridicule ici de raisonner *a priori*, sans analyse et sans comparaisons; car ce qui serait vraiment surprenant, c'est que le son *ne pût pas* suggérer la couleur, que les couleurs *ne pussent pas* donner l'idée d'une mélodie, et que le son et la couleur fussent impropres à traduire des idées; les choses s'étant toujours exprimées par une analogie réciproque, depuis le jour où Dieu a proféré le monde comme une complexe et indivisible totalité.

La nature est un temple où de vivants piliers
Laissent parfois sortir de confuses paroles;
L'homme y passe à travers des forêts de symboles
Qui l'observent avec des regards familiers.

Comme de longs échos qui de loin se confondent
Dans une ténébreuse et profonde unité,
Vaste comme la nuit et comme la clarté,
Les parfums, les couleurs et les sons se répondent.

(2:784)

Here, paradoxically enough, the resonant opening of the sonnet is evoked as a kind of proof for the existence of a God-created totality that guarantees communication among the otherwise closed worlds of art. Significantly, the poet's language recalls Leibniz's monadology: "les choses s'étant toujours exprimées par une analogie réciproque, depuis le jour où Dieu a proféré le monde comme une complexe et indivisible totalité." This was not an unusual allusion in mid-nineteenth-century French literature. Recall the importance of Leibniz for Balzac's early "Avertissement du *Gars*," which depicts the consciousness of the artist as a "miroir concentrique de l'univers." But Baudelaire is far less concerned than Balzac with the surface detail of things than with their hidden structure, which resembles a universal language akin to mathematics, although we can only intuit it in the kind of dream-like receptive state the sonnet "Correspondances" evokes.

In his prose, Baudelaire most often uses the word *correspondances* in connection with an argument for the structural analogies among the arts that draws on eighteenth-century aesthetics, as well as language theory. If *correspondances* point to a universal language that originates in the sensations and emotions of individuals, the emphasis here on the unity of the arts recalls arguments of the previous century, such as Batteux's *Les beaux arts réduits à un même principe*. And Baudelaire's reworking of the aesthetics and language theory of the previous century also points forward to the invention and spread of semiotic theories during the century which followed his death.

But there is more at stake here than the spread of a structural principle. Indeed, looking back at the work of Baudelaire, at the tendency to abstraction and closure in the poet's texts, one is reminded of what he shut out and what we often forget. For the poet defined his work against the contexts of the modern city and many of its cultures. *His correspondances* have to do, he emphasizes, with music, harmony, and an aesthetic balance that has little to do with the unpredictability and frequent ugliness of the social world; they may look like Fourier's analogies, but, he argues, they are really quite different. Yet naming them together also stresses their kinship, and points, as well, to the importance of the *other correspondances*, those of Constant/Lévi and the other marginal authors who invoked visionary and esoteric doctrines as the basis for their authority to speak out on matters of social and political concern.

The sonnet "Correspondances" may look at first glance like a poem about nature, but on further examination, particularly in relation to its place in *Les fleurs du mal*, it turns out to lend itself equally well to a reading as a poem about the city. The "vivants piliers" can be read either as trees, or as architectural pillars, or as moving figures in a city crowd. The poem thus functions as a kind of Gestalt switch. Like the famous drawing of the duck/rabbit, it can be seen as a poem about either nature or the city, depending on the reader's point of view. The oscillation between meanings, moreover, serves to emphasize the interdependence of the two and also, perhaps, to point toward some kind of utopian synthesis of them.[13]

Certainly, the last point is a central aspect of Walter Benjamin's interpretation of Baudelaire and mid-nineteenth-century Paris. For Benjamin, Baudelaire's *correspondances* evoke a state of blissful enjoyment one often associates with the world of childhood, but the term can only be understood in the context of the evocation of the fragmentary and jarring experience of the city crowds elsewhere in Baudelaire's works, such as the sonnet "A une passante." In a broader context, however, the German critic suggests that the word finds its place in the culture of commodities of mid-nineteenth-century Paris, in which artifacts reminded the onlooker of the unnaturalness and inhumanity of the city. At best, in the works of artists such as Baudelaire, they are transformed into dialectical images—or one might also say, dialectical texts—that point beyond themselves to a very different, better, way of life, but one, Benjamin emphasizes, that can never be named. There is no originary state of unity and bliss, but texts such as "Correspondances" are, nonetheless, works of mourning. But by forcing the reader to imagine what is not there, or what is there only very fleetingly, they point to what has been lost, not only in the past, but also in the present.

Throughout his prose, Baudelaire defines art and poetry negatively: they cannot be identified with the moral or political systems of philosophers, visionaries, second-rate poets, or social theorists; nor have they much in common with the lethargic ecstacy of the opium eater. This is also true of his use of the word *correspondances*, although he sometimes, in "Le Poème du hachisch" and the essay on Hugo, for example, takes care to distinguish Swedenborg's doctrine of correspondences from the language of good poetry. For if *correspondances* serves as a negative analogy of what good poetry and art should do, the distance between Baudelaire's use of the word and that of Swedenborg points as clearly as the city poems in *Les fleurs du mal* to what has been lost in the poet's careful construction of little aesthetic worlds sealed off from the politics and poverty of the city crowds.

Consider the discussion of the doctrine of correspondences in Swedenborg's *Heaven and Hell*, which, if Baudelaire did, in fact, walk the streets of Paris with a volume by Swedenborg under his arm, was very likely to have been the one he had chosen. In *Heaven and Hell*, correspondences link not only parts of the human body, but also whole communities, which are able to communicate with one another through the transparent languages of things, gestures, and facial expressions, as well as words. Even in Swedenborg, the rediscovery of correspondences serves a utopian social function, pointing the way to a restoration of a just social order based on transparency and virtue. This was the one point in Swedenborg's work that most of his later interpreters, including Constant/Lévi, got right about his work—however little else they knew of it.

What is missing in Baudelaire's invocation of *correspondances* is the world—and other people. His sonnet by that name restricts the meaning of the term to the kinds of impressions characteristic of a dream or dreamlike state and intimate bodily sensations. For the poet, the problem of communication turns on how apparently different works of art speak to individual members of their audiences. And yet, like the "forêts de symboles" in the sonnet, the word also carries with it the memory of other meanings and contexts.

Baudelaire's withdrawal into language and the aesthetic worlds generated by art, music, and poetry marks both his distance from and similarity to popular esoteric thinkers and writers of the 1850s. Baudelaire's aesthetic system was far more coherent and informed than that of Constant/Lévi, yet the works of both men represent a retreat from social questions into invisible worlds generated by language. The poet's attempt to lose himself in the impersonal structures of art parallels an experience of the crowd as a threat to the Parisian bourgeois's sense of his or her individuality. Yet the writer's language is also that of the crowd. Through the words of the text, *it* speaks.

Conclusion

I began this study with a quotation from Paul Valéry's essay on Swedenborg, which opened somewhat quizzically with a reference to the Swedish thinker's "beau nom." Despite its resonance, the Swedish writer's name, like his life, jarred with certain myths that had grown up around it in French culture. What to make of the resonant dissonance? The French poet gave no answer.

I have taken my cue from Valéry, however, in focusing not only on the fortunes of this and another resonant *nom*, "correspondences" or *correspondances*, but also on the cultural contexts that informed their transformations in France during the century following Swedenborg's death in 1772. I found that these contexts often were, as Valéry suggested in his nostalgic evocation of late-eighteenth-century French culture, millenarian and oriented towards the decipherment of dreams, but that, far from emphasizing the past and the end of the world as it was known, the dreams and visions many French writers and movements evoke in connection with the name of Swedenborg and the word *correspondances* betray clear links to practical projects for the transformation of society. As we have seen, even Nerval, whom Valéry named as a source for his knowledge of French Swedenborgianism, was aware of this aspect of the tradition.

For Valéry, the apparent paradox of the presence of Swedenborgian doctrines in nineteenth-century French literature was partly explained by the reawakening of interest in eighteenth-century culture in the final decades of the nineteenth. Without stating so explicitly, his essay suggests that this turning back represents a millenarian temper among late-nineteenth-century French writers, as well, a sense (one that Valéry seemed to share) that the world as they knew it was inevitably coming to an end. But the fashion for eighteenth-century models in late-nineteenth-century France had many facets, of which millenarian pessimism was only one.

Another is certainly linguistic. In his collection of essays, *From Locke to Saussure*, Hans Aarsleff has emphasized the parallels between eighteenth-century language theory and the concept of structure underlying

249

the work of Ferdinand de Saussure and other linguists at the turn of the last century, parallels he in part attributes to the reawakening of interest in many aspects of eighteenth-century culture at that time. Aarsleff's essays focus on the work of philosophers and linguists, attempting to explain how notions of linguistic structure persisted and were transformed even during those decades of the nineteenth century when the dominant linguistic paradigm was historical. My emphasis here has been somewhat different. In tracing the reception of Swedenborg in different kinds of French texts from the early and mid nineteenth century, I have aimed to show that the contexts of literature, popular culture, and religious sectarianism also played an important role in the transmission and transformation of concepts of structure that were to re-emerge in the last years of the nineteenth century as what was to become part of one officially recognized branch of linguistic inquiry. Studies in popular culture, such as Robert Darnton's *Mesmerism and the End of the Enlightenment in France*, called my attention both to the persistence of eighteenth-century models in early-nineteenth-century French culture and to the role of political dreams, goals, and programs in their reception and transformation during the century following the Revolution of 1789.

My study, then, has emphasized the parallels and continuities between the work of Swedenborg, including his doctrine of correspondences, and its reception in France. Thus, I take issue with the thesis of Michel Foucault, who used the term "correspondences" to denote a concept of language that stands in opposition to what he calls the model or *episteme* of representation, a kind of linguistic grid that made it possible to develop taxonomic systems in the eighteenth century. The dizzying proliferation of grid-like parallel worlds in Swedenborg's later texts, I have argued, points to the common ground of the two models. Significantly enough, in texts such as *Correspondences and Representations* or *Heaven and Hell*, the Swedish writer uses the words "correspondences" and "representations" in interchangeable or overlapping senses. And in the next century, as we have seen, the references to Swedenborg or "correspondences" in the work of Balzac and Baudelaire are intimately bound up with the representation of contemporary French society, especially the city, in terms of a totality.

In his very early "Avertissement du *Gars*" (1828), Balzac wrote of the difficulty of producing a portrait of an age or a society that was more than a "squelette chronologique." He cited Leibniz as a model for the apparently paradoxical reflection of the totality of the world through the single consciousness of an isolated individual. For Balzac, the model of a Leibnizean totality was an alternative to what he saw as the mere arrangement of events in sequence, allowing the novelist to represent events in many different kinds of relationships. But in *La comédie humaine*, the notion of a totality is implicit and underlies the representation of French society as it evolved during the fifty years following the French Revolution; it fleshes out, but does not displace, the chronological skeleton. As I traced the fortunes of Swedenborgianism and the word "correspondences" in the late eighteenth and nineteenth centuries, it often seemed to me that the structural focus of Foucault gives us another fleshless skeleton, albeit a synchronic, rather than chronological, model. It can be difficult to distinguish Balzac from Leibniz, if one only considers the bare bones.

But if I have argued against Foucault's distinction between "correspondences" and "representations," his study was a major impetus for my own: the structural emphasis I have criticized called my attention to the problem of the relationship between the works of Swedenborg and those of French writers during the century following his death. I have also taken issue with one aspect of the work of another intellectual historian whose interpretations of Swedenborg, particularly his monograph on the doctrine of correspondences, have been of crucial importance for mine. Jonsson's emphasis on the continuing and overwhelming importance of seventeenth-century models for Swedenborg's work brings into focus the debts of this thinker to rationalist philosophy and to science, but tends to obscure the parallels and connections between the work of this well-travelled and well-read Swede and other, contemporaneous writers. Often despite his theological beliefs, Swedenborg shares significant common ground with other writers active in the mid-eighteenth century. In my chapter on Swedenborg, I have pointed to similarities between his work and that of Rousseau, a writer often cited along with the Swede in the last decades of the eighteenth century. The parallels between the work of Swedenborg and that of other writers, both contemporaneous and later, are often best characterized as "ideological." Swedenborg's later works display prominent utopian tendencies, as do the glosses of later writers—with the difference that some of his later interpreters conceived of the means to bring about a utopian transformation of society in terms that were far more practical and overtly political than the Swedish writer had been able to imagine.

I found, in fact, that French interpretations of Swedenborgianism and the doctrine of correspondences were inseparable from political dreams and aspirations. Desires, in other words, color even the most apparently impersonal and objective concept of literary and linguistic structure. This is perhaps most obvious in the *flâneur* narratives of Balzac and Baudelaire, in which the city becomes a kind of hallucinatory landscape for the solitary wanderer and observer, who only imagines his detachment. But it is no less an important factor in the work of a minor writer such as Constant/ Lévi. In fact, I have argued, it was precisely the disguised political and social aspirations of this persecuted and prosecuted figure that led him, in his *Dogme et rituel de la haute magie*, to focus on the ritualistic and performative aspects of language. The spells in the second volume of this work are designed to empower the initiated writer or performer, to break him out of the isolation of the small rooms and small circles of readers and admirers he moved among. If they failed to work (or, at least, work very well) for Constant/Lévi, the model he provided proved very fruitful for poets who read him, especially Mallarmé.

Like those of Baudelaire, Constant/Lévi's interpretations of Sweden-borg and his doctrine of correspondences were more concerned with the way in which language functions than with sectarian beliefs or orthodoxy. In Baudelaire's prose, the word *correspondances* almost always appears in connection with a discussion of the effect of a work of art or poem. Constant/Lévi's spells take this concern one step further, for although he was perhaps even less a linguist than he was a trained philosopher or historian, the strange mixture of cabalistic ruminations and politics that character-izes his work led him to conceive of language as a system that might, under controlled circumstances, perform certain functions. Separated and living alone in rented rooms in Paris, Constant/Lévi was far from imagin-ing the performative potential of language in terms such as those of J. L. Austin, whose linguistic performances rely on contractual relationships among at least two people, not the least important of which is marriage. Constant/Lévi's spells, in contrast, are designed either to bring the isolated circumstances of the solitary individual into immediate alignment with the stars or to allow him to shatter the rigid and alienating order of the world merely through the uttering of a few words.

What was it Constant/Lévi meant when he wrote in 1848 that he was giving up politics? Certainly, there is ample evidence in his published works after this date to suggest that he continued to oppose any regime in power. But it also seems that he renounced more than overt statements concerning his beliefs, for the increasing isolation of his existence, as well as the focus on the empowerment of the solitary individual in his writings, suggest that he also left behind a belief in collectivist politics, except under the most extraordinary—and perhaps violent—of circumstances. Con-stant/Lévi's works enjoyed a certain underground reputation in late-nine-teenth-century France, among poets, it is true, but also among those searching for new forms of oppositional politics, especially anarchists. This is not a point I can make with any kind of completeness, since the connec-tions among anarchist politics and fin-de-siècle aestheticism are only be-ginning to be explored, but I would like to suggest that the texts of Con-stant/Lévi may well prove to be of key importance for the understanding of interrelationships among language and politics at this time. What I will say here is that this writer's focus on linguistic rituals and performances suggests the impossibility of understanding how a writer's notions of language come into being apart from the contexts in which they arise, including his or her social and political beliefs and desires. Although Swedenborg is occasionally cited in the works of minor French poets in the late nineteenth century, there is little to link his work directly to that of the most important of them, Mallarmé. If there is a connection, it goes through the texts of Constant/Lévi, which Mallarmé read and even seems to quote—at least indirectly—in several important texts. Recall, for example, Constant/Lévi's discussions of the relation of the magus to the stars in *Dogme et rituel de la haute magie.* Or his evocation of a new, esoteric, book, which presents striking similarities to Mallarmé's project for an all-inclusive Book whose pages might be manipulated at will by a creative reader.

Mid-nineteenth-century French writers turned to Swedenborgianism, as well as a panoply of other religious and esoteric doctrines, in order to create their own idiosyncratic world-embracing systems, systems that, in many cases, were intended to represent and carry on political agendas outlawed during the Second Empire. In the work of some of these writers—Baudelaire, for example, or, to an even greater extent, Constant/Lévi—these systems were allied with a concept of language as a system capable of producing certain effects, at times merely aesthetic, but at others fusing aestheticism and violence. By the end of the Second Empire, Swedenborgianism had become one distant ancestor among others of a theory of language that was to prove of crucial importance in the poetics of Mallarmé and the linguistics of Saussure.

Both Mallarmé and Saussure—like Foucault—tend to emphasize the distance between concepts of linguistic structure and their context. By looking back at the reception of Swedenborg and the transformations of his doctrine of correspondences and the word *correspondances* in nineteenth-century France, we are reminded of the importance of the contexts of writers who transmitted and transformed esoteric doctrines and accompanying theories of language at this time. We are also reminded that theories of language, like words themselves, perform certain kinds of work, sometimes (but not always) in accordance with the wishes and desires of their users or even inventors. By the late nineteenth century, one of the tasks some writers imagined language might perform had to do with the radical transformation—apart from collective social action or democratic politics—of the social world as a whole. But this was by no means the only conceivable kind of work a linguistic system might perform. In my interpretations of Balzac and Baudelaire, I also argued that the notion of a totality these writers associated with the work of Swedenborg, as well as other philosophical and scientific writers, carried with it a sense of loss and nostalgia. Imagining the world and language as a system, then, also allowed writers to mourn.

This aspect of Swedenborgianism is perhaps most evident in a text by a writer who is, to my knowledge, never cited as an interpreter of Swedenborg, although he pays at least as much attention to the role and function of language as any nineteenth-century writer. The novelist Flaubert's account, in his very late and unfinished novel, *Bouvard et Pécuchet*, of the two protagonists' involvement with Swedenborgianism links these doctrines to both politics and an aesthetics that eschews all political involvement.

At their farm in the provinces, the protagonists of Bouvard et Pécuchet experience at second hand a sense of excitement at the revolution of 1848 and of disappointment and disillusionment following the coup d'état of 1851. During the years preceding the revolution, they undertake a number of projects designed to make of their farm an enterprise run according to completely rational and scientific principles. On every occasion, however, the gap between theory and practice causes their projects to founder, much like the utopian schemes of social reformers in faraway Paris. After 1851, they abandon experiments in the natural world for investigations into the supernatural, turning first to Mesmerism and animal magnetism, then to Swedenborgianism, and finally to Catholicism in their search for principles which would guarantee the stability of the social order and their place within it. Bouvard et Pécuchet represents a kind of ironic Encyclopédie, attesting to the popularization and trivialization of the science and philosophy of the Enlightenment. The short summary of Swedenborgianism shows how, by the 1870s, this process has rendered the doctrines of Swedenborg as preposterous-seeming as the utopian ideologies with which they had often been associated.

One night, after Bouvard and Pécuchet had been surprised by the visit of a spiritualist who explains that "le spiritisme pose en dogme l'amélioration fatale de notre espèce," and that the dead inhabit astral worlds, the more skeptical Bouvard comes upon his friend Pécuchet at the window, contemplating the stars:

Swedenborg y a fait de grands voyages. Car, en moins d'un an, il a exploré Vénus, Mars, Saturne et vingt-trois Jupiter. De plus, il a vu à Londres Jésus-Christ, il a vu saint Paul, il a vu saint Jean, il a vu Moïse, et, en 1736[14], il a même vu le jugement dernier.
Aussi nous donne-t-il des descriptions du ciel.
On y trouve des fleurs, des palais, des marchés et des églises absolument comme chez nous.

*Les anges, hommes autrefois, couchent leurs pensées sur des feuil-
lets, devisent des choses du ménage ou bien de matières spirituelles, et
les emplois ecclésiastiques appartiennent à ceux qui, dans leur vie terres-
tre, ont cultivé l'Ecriture sainte.*

*Quant à l'enfer, il est plein d'une odeur nauséabonde, avec des ca-
hutes, des tas d'immondices, des fondrières, des personnes mal habillées.*

*Et Pécuchet s'abîmait l'intellect pour comprendre ce qu'il y a de
beau dans ces révélations. Elles parurent à Bouvard le délire d'un imbé-
cile. (195–96)*

*For Flaubert, as for Baudelaire, Swedenborgianism represented a
kind of secularized theology inferior to Catholicism because, like the theories of nineteenth-century reformers, it failed to achieve a viable synthesis
of science and theology: what was left from Swedenborgianism and utopian schemes to find an absolute order underlying nature and society was
the concept of language as a system. Flaubert's obsession with style and
his fetishization of "le mot juste" cannot be traced back to Swedenborgianism, and if Balzac and Baudelaire discuss Swedenborgianism and language together, it is to show how, by mid-century, all that remains of
Swedenborg's elaborate descriptions of invisible other worlds is a sense of
the fictionality of all ideologies and of the role of language in generating
artificial paradises which can be identified—according to the whim of the
reader—with utopian societies, the pleasures of sex and food, or the little
worlds evoked by novels and poems. The angelic apparatus of Swedenborg's later works serves, in the works of Balzac, Baudelaire, and Flaubert,
to point up the hollowing out of language and to justify writers' desires to
distinguish their works from those of others whom they imagined as inferior—perhaps as gullible and tasteless as Bouvard and Pécuchet.*

*Yet to read this passage in Flaubert's novel as merely condemnatory
is to overlook the elements of compassion and admiration in its portrayal
of the two main characters and their apparently naive beliefs. For it is
precisely their gullibility that enables them to act and feel in ways that
the language of the narrator can only treat ironically. And while it affirms
this gap, Flaubert's text—like those of Balzac and Baudelaire—also
mourns for the loss it entails.*

*One can read Bouvard and Pécuchet as caricatures of writers whose
works never entered—and probably never will enter—the French literary
canon, many of whom were interested in marginal movements such as
Swedenborgianism or Mesmerism. As we saw in the chapters on Constant/
Lévi and other French interpreters of Swedenborgianism, these doctrines
gave outsiders—distinguished from Parisian bourgeois writers by their
provincial or working-class origins, as well as education and talent—a*

sense of their right to speak out on issues that concerned them. Among these writers, Swedenborgianism was very much associated with the search for a voice, the clamoring for political enfranchisement.

In its portrayal of its two main characters, Flaubert's last novel represents this quest as both noble and futile. His emphasis on textuality and the representation of the world as a network of written signs, however, is less tolerant. By the end of the Second Empire, the notion of a totality that had allowed Balzac and some of his protagonists to imagine themselves as capable of understanding, representing, and perhaps controlling the whole of French society had been reduced to the dimensions of a single literary text. The miroir concentrique *reflected the faces of a clown or two—or nothing.*

Appendix:
Baudelaire's "Correspondances" and
Constant/Lévi's "Les correspondances

Baudelaire: "Correspondances"

La Nature est un temple où de vivants piliers
Laissent parfois sortir de confuses paroles;
L'homme y passe à travers des forêts de symboles
Qui l'observent avec des regards familiers.

Comme de longs échos qui de loin se confondent
Dans une ténébreuse et profonde unité,
Vaste comme la nuit et comme la clarté,
Les parfums, les couleurs et les sons se répondent.

Il est des parfums frais comme des chairs d'enfants,
Doux comme les hautbois, verts comme les prairies,
—Et d'autres, corrompus, riches et triomphants,

Ayant l'expansion des choses infinies,
Comme l'ambre, le musc, le benjoin et l'encens,
Qui chantent les transports de l'esprit et des sens.

Alphonse-Louis Constant / Eliphas Lévi: "Les correspondances"

Le sentiment des harmonies extérieures
fait des poètes.
L'intelligence des harmonies intérieures
fait des prophètes.

Quand succombent nos sens débiles
Aux enchantements du sommeil.

Le pinceau des songes immobiles
Présente à l'âme un faux réveil.
Alors nos vagues fantaisies
De formes au hasard choisies
Colorent leur égarement:
Toute idée enfante une image,
Et les formes sont un langage
Que nous nous parlons en dormant.

Le rêve est le miroir de l'âme;
Ses élans planent sur les airs,
Ses désirs s'allument en flamme,
Ses chagrins la chargent de fers;
La terreur dont elle est la proie
Se change en monstre qui la broie
De ses hideux embrassements;
Et ses espérances chéries
S'étendent en ombres fleuries
Sur des paysages charmants.

Par une secrète harmonie,
La terre ainsi répond aux cieux,
Et l'instinct sacré du génie
Voit leur lien mystérieux.
Notre vie est un plus long rêve,
Et ce que la mort nous enlève
Trouve au ciel sa réalité.
En dormant nous rêvons la vie,
Mais la veille, au temps asservie,
N'est qu'un rêve d'éternité.

Formé de visibles paroles,
Ce monde est le songe de Dieu;
Son verbe en choisit les symboles,
L'esprit les remplit de son feu.
C'est cette écriture vivante,
D'amour, de gloire et d'épouvante,
Que pour nous Jésus retrouva;
Car toute science cachée
N'est qu'une lettre détachée
Du nom sacré de Jéhova.

C'est là que lisent les prophètes;
Et ceux dont les yeux sont ouverts
Sont d'eux-mêmes les interprètes

De l'énigme de l'univers;
Les astres, serviteurs mystiques,
Tracent en signes elliptiques
Le mot que le Seigneur écrit;
Et la terre, à sa voix naissante,
N'est qu'une cire obéissante
Sous le cachet de son esprit.

Tout signe exprime une pensée,
Et toute forme dans les cieux
Est une figure tracée
Par le penseur mystérieux,
Depuis l'herbe de la campagne
Jusqu'au cèdre de la montagne,
De l'aigle jusqu'au moucheron,
Depuis l'éléphant, masse informe,
Et la baleine, plus énorme,
Jusqu'à l'invisible ciron.

Comme les soleils dans l'espace
Indiquent leur route aux soleils,
Comme le jour qui brille et passe
Promet aux cieux des jours pareils;
Ainsi, par un calcul possible,
L'invisible est dans le visible,
Le passé prédit l'avenir;
Et, dans Nineve confondue,
La prophétie inattendue
N'est que la voix d'un souvenir.

Rien n'est muet dans la nature
Pour qui sait en suivre les lois:
Les astres ont une écriture,
Les fleurs des champs ont une voix,
Verbe éclatante dans les nuits sombres,
Mots rigoureux comme des nombres,
Voix dont tout bruit n'est qu'un écho,
Et qui fait mouvoir tous les êtres,
Comme jadis le cri des prêtres
Faisait tressaillir Jérico.

Passez, passez, sans rien comprendre,
Vain troupeau d'aveugles penseurs!
Le néant dort pour vous attendre
Auprès des chimères ses soeurs.

Mais, dans l'éternelle pensée,
Votre route est déjà tracée,
Et tous vos systèmes obscurs
Rehaussent d'une ombre effrayante
Cette inscription flamboyante
Que les rois lisent sur les murs.

Mais que l'âme simple et fidèle,
En attendant l'agneau vainqueur,
Ecoute, active sentimelle,
Le Verbe de Dieu dans son coeur:
Car toute pensée extatique
Est comme une onde sympathique,
Où se réflète l'univers:
Et l'âme, à soi-même attentive,
Comme le pêcheur sur la rive
Peut contempler les cieux ouverts.

Notes

Introduction

1. The occasion for Valéry's essay was the publication of E. Söderlindh's French translation of Lamm's *Swedenborg*. Söderlindh's work appeared in 1936; a German translation of Lamm's intellectual biography, which was published in Swedish in 1915, had come out in 1922. Unfortunately, the biography has never been translated into English.

Lamm's biography of Swedenborg was followed by the publication, three years later, of a much broader study of eighteenth-century Swedish writers entitled *Upplysningstidens romantik, The Romanticism of the Enlightenment*. This work, which also contains a chapter on Swedenborg, develops the thesis that had informed his biography, that the turn to religious matters in the lives and works of some eighteenth-century writers represents a "preromantic" tendency in eighteenth-century intellectual life. For Lamm, the defeat of King Charles XII and the return of Swedish prisoners of war from Russia, where, he argues, pietism had helped them to withstand the trials of their imprisonment, were key events that turned some Swedish writers away from what one might characterize as the optimistic tendency of Enlightenment culture.

Lamm seems to have come to the study of Swedenborg and eighteenth-century literature from an early interest in Strindberg, not at that time a reputable subject in Swedish literary studies. Strindberg, as was well known at the time Lamm was writing, had portrayed himself as having undergone a personal crisis not unlike that of Swedenborg, and, in fact, Strindberg often cited Swedenborg as a kind of predecessor or model in his works written after the mid-1890s. But Swedenborg was more than a religious model or influence for Strindberg, for the later writer refers to him in his autobiographical fiction, *Inferno*, as a scientist and a theosopher. Strindberg's interpretation of Swedenborg may well have led Lamm to search for the unity of Swedenborg's thought and to emphasize, in his study, the works written in the late 1730s and early 1740s that seem to combine elements of what, in the twentieth century, have come to seem two separate approaches to knowledge and experience. But Lamm's biography also shows an admirable command of European literary and intellectual history, and his work on Swedenborg and eighteenth-century literature presents parallels to French intellectual histories,

261

such as Daniel Mornet, *Les origines intellectuelles de la révolution française*; Paul Hazard, *The European Mind*; and, especially, Henri Brémond, *Histoire du sentiment religieux en France*. Inge Jonsson has pointed to the limitations of Lamm's method, which he shares with many intellectual and literary historians of the first decades of this century and which often views intellectual developments in terms of vague "tendencies," described from above and with little reference to specific texts. Characterizing Swedenborg's work after 1745 as preromantic tells us more about ourselves, individuals who have undergone a "dissociation of sensibility," than about Swedenborg or his work. On Lamm, see Ingvar Andersson, *Martin Lamm*.

2. No documentary evidence concerning Oegger's birth or death has been unearthed to date. See chapter 3, note 11.

3. On the tangled strands of the development of linguistics and language theory in the late eighteenth and nineteenth centuries, see above all Hans Aarsleff, *The Study of Language in England, 1780–1860* and *From Locke to Saussure*. On the importance of contemporary theories of language for poets at this time, see M. H. Abrams, *Natural Supernaturalism*, which emphasizes the importance of individual places and particular languages for poets. In his *Ferdinand de Saussure*, Jonathan Culler emphasizes the parallels and debt of Saussure to eighteenth-century language theory.

For a lucid discussion of the relationship of the particularist language theory of Herder to nationalism, see F. M. Barnard, *Herder's Social and Political Thought*, especially chapter 3, section 1: "Language and Political Association." (55–62) Barnard writes:

> But if language is capable of arousing a sense of identity within a community, it will, in doing so, simultaneously give rise to the community's consciousness of difference from those speaking another language. This, Herder feels, is as it should be. For diversity is the fundamental characteristic of the universal order. The world must be a world of many nationalities. Diversity, not uniformity is the design of the Almighty. Emperor Joseph II is taken to task for ignoring what patently is a law of Nature and a decree of God: "Truly, just as God tolerates all languages of this world, so too should a ruler tolerate, nay, treasure, the diverse languages of his subject nations."
>
> A *Volk*, on this theory, then, is a natural division of the human race, endowed with its own language, which it must preserve as its most distinctive and sacred possession. Language is as much the embodiment of a *Volk*'s "soul" or character, as it is the expression of an individual's unique personality. By forsaking it, a *Volk* destroys its "self" for language and the national consciousness to which it gives rise are inseparably joined. Intermixture with other nationalities, therefore, is to be avoided. The situation most congenial to the preservation of the natural order of things is that analogous to the growth of a plant rooted in the soil. If all nations re-

mained where they were originally "planted," one could look upon the world as a garden of diverse national plants, each flowering according to its own nature and development. (58–59)

4. For an overview of utopian theories in the west, see Manuel and Manuel, *Utopian Thought in the Western World*, especially part 1, "The Ancient and Medieval Wellsprings," 31–114.

5. For a history of the concept in western Marxism, see Jay, *Marxism and Totality*.

6. For an explicit discussion of this concept, see chapter 9 of *Marxism and Literature*, "Structures of Feeling," 128–35. For Williams, linking the notion of structure with emotions undercuts the tendency to reify experience inherent in many theories of human experience. He writes:

> Yet the actual alternative to the received and produced fixed forms is not silence: not the absence, the unconscious, which bourgeois culture has mythicized. It is a kind of feeling and thinking which is indeed social and material, but each in an embryonic phase before it can become fully articulate and defined exchange. Its relations with the already articulate and defined are then exceptionally complex. (*Marxism and Form*, 131)

William's term has reminded me to look for the many, often half-articulated, meanings of the words "correspondences" and *correspondances*, which writers often link both to explicit political agendas and to the resolution of contradictions in the most intimate aspects of their lives.

I have also drawn on many of Williams's earlier works, however, particularly his explorations of both the meanings of "culture" and particular cultures as they developed historically, especially his *Culture and Society* and *The Country and the City*.

7. The subtitle for Viatte's chapter, "Les Swedenborgiens," in *Les sources occultes* reads: "Swedenborg: sa vie; son caractère placide; rien d'un enthousiaste." (72) Viatte's depiction of Swedenborg's career as a visionary is characteristic of his view of Swedenborg and Swedenborgianism:

> A partir de 1736, des tentations l'assaillirent sous la forme de rêves symboliques. "Il voyait des spectres épouvantables qui, bien que sans vie, se démenaient dans leurs chaînes. Tantôt il se trouvait couché sur une montagne, suspendu au-dessus d'un abîme, et sans force propre qui pût l'empêcher d'y tomber. Tantôt il se sentait attaqué par des animaux furieux; une foix c'était un serpent, qui se transforma bientôt en chien." Enfin, un beau jour de l'année 1745, une voix l'avertit, au milieu de son repas, de ne pas manger tant; la nuit suivante, le Christ lui apparut; dès lors, ses hallucinations s'harmonisèrent en un système invariable, revêtirent le caractère d'une certitude; et, se croyant le Messie d'une foi nouvelle, il

s'attribua le devoir de la faire connaître aux hommes. Il prend la plume, pour ne plus la quitter; aux dix-huit volumes des *Arcanes célestes*, il en ajoute quantité d'autres; heureusement qu'il se répète, car son fatras ne rend pas la besogne agréable aux commentateurs, et l'on se demande avec stupeur comment il peut susciter des enthousiasmes! (74)

8. See Sjödén, *Swedenborg en France*, and "Remarques sur le swedenborgisme balzacien."

9. Even the illuminating studies of Auguste Viatte fall into this category. See also Jacques Borel, *Balzac et le mysticisme swedenborgien*; Robert Kirven, "Swedenborg and the Revolt against Deism"; and, for a panorama of illuminist and occult doctrines in France at the turn of the eighteenth century, Brian Juden, *Traditions orphiques et tendances mystiques dans le romantisme français*.

10. See Jonsson, *Swedenborgs korrespondenslära*, especially 21–27; and the English summary, 394.

11. See Jonsson, *Swedenborgs skapelsedrama*, *Swedenborgs korrespondenslära*, and the survey of Swedenborg's life and works in English, *Emanuel Swedenborg*, especially 13.

12. Jonsson, for example, suggests that the impressive array of citations from Greek, Latin, and patristic literature one sometimes finds in Swedenborg's scientific treatises can be traced back to handbooks, rather than the almost impossibly extensive reading they might imply. He notes that one such passage in Swedenborg's *Oeconomia* seems to be lifted outright and without attribution to Scipion Dupleix's *Corps de philosophie*, but other such summaries also seem to have been of importance for Swedenborg's overviews of contemporary science and philosophy.

13. Eighteenth- and early-nineteenth-century writers, as well as their publics, seemed well aware of the parallels between Mesmerism and Swedenborgianism. The connections are emphasized as early as the 1780s in the letters of the marquis de Thomé and of the Stockholm Exegetical and Philanthropical Society to the Strasbourg Société des amis réunis. In 1847, a certain George Bush published a book entitled *Mesmer and Swedenborg; or, The Relation of the Developments of Mesmerism to the Doctrines and Disclosures of Swedenborg.* An awareness and interest in the similarity of the two traditions also informs the studies of Frank Podmore, *Modern Spiritualism* and *Mesmerism and Christian Science*, both written from the perspective of Christian Science. None of these studies, however, addresses the issue of the relationship of the imaginary structures of the work of Mesmer and his followers and the theories of language associated with that of Swedenborg and Swedenborgianism. That Freud came to his discovery of a "talking cure" through experiments in hypnosis makes the subject a compelling one.

14. In a work published by Masonic Publishing in New York in 1870, for example, Samuel Beswick argues that Swedenborg had been initiated into a lodge at Lund in 1706 when he was eighteen (17–18), and that in 1737 he visited a lodge in

Paris, where he and several members were arrested in December of that year. (44) One of Beswick's sources, however, was the unreliable Pernety, whose lodge at Avignon developed a rite that seems to have had little to do with Swedenborg's doctrines but was anxious to claim his work as a source, probably to legitimate their activities. Pernety apparently had claimed that Swedenborg was first initiated into an English lodge called Emanuel Lodge, Number 6, at London.

There would be nothing very unusual about Swedenborg's joining a masonic lodge—if in fact he did so. My own view is that the rituals and symbolism of freemasonry and their general cultural diffusion did play a role in Swedenborg's intellectual and religious development, that he drew on them in order to construct his own imaginative order—with mythological or religious roots stretching back at least as far as that of the masons—but that these myths gave him a language to describe and encourage a certain kind of individual development.

15. See Darnton, *The Literary Underground of the Old Regime*.

16. For critical discussions of the limits of Habermas's concept of the "public sphere," see Calhoun, ed. *Habermas and the Public Sphere*, and Nathans, "Habermas's 'Public Sphere' in the Age of the French Revolution."

17. I discuss Constant/Lévi's life and works in chapter 1. Other discussions include Chacornac, *Eliphas Lévi*; Bowman's preface to his anthology, *Eliphas Lévi, visionnaire romantique*, 5–61; McIntosh, *Eliphas Lévi and the French Occult Revival*; Williams, *Eliphas Lévi*; and Buisset, *Eliphas Lévi*.

18. See William H. Sewell, *Work and Revolution in France: The Language of Labor from the Old Regime to 1848*.

19. Suggestive recent studies of the culture of freemasonry and its relationship to the evolution of democratic cultures in the eighteenth century include Margaret Jacob, *The Radical Enlightenment* and *Living the Enlightenment*; and Mary Ann Clawson, *Constructing Brotherhood*. In *Fictions of Freemasonry*, Scott Abbott discusses how aspects of these cultures and their fictions entered German literary tradition.

20. See Sjödén, *Swedenborg en France* for the history of Swedenborgian proselytizers in France.

21. Barbey d'Aurévilly's remarks occur in the context of an argument that *Les fleurs du mal* is a profoundly moral work, despite the emphasis on evil in the title and in individual poems:

> Nous ne pouvons ni ne voulons rien citer du recueil de poésies en question, et voici pourquoi: une pièce citée n'aurait que sa valeur individuelle, et il ne faut pas s'y méprendre, dans le livre de M. Baudelaire, chaque poésie a, de plus que la réussite des détails ou la fortune de la pensée, *une valeur très importante d'ensemble et de situation* qu'il ne faut pas lui faire perdre, en la détachant. Les artistes qui voient les lignes sous le luxe

et l'efflorescence de la couleur percevront très bien qu'il y a ici *une architecture secrète*, un plan calculé par le poète, méditatif et volontaire.

22. *The Symbolist Movement*, 12. Balakian's studies of symbolism and surrealism all emphasize the parallels between the aesthetics of these movements and a mystical tradition which would include Swedenborgianism. Following Jean Pommier's argument in *La mystique de Baudelaire*, she argues that Baudelaire's sonnet "Correspondances" is a pivotal work in the transmission and transformation of this tradition, but that it was the poet's distortion of "natural" correspondences that proved to be most important for later writers.

23. See especially his *Illuminations*, his essays on Baudelaire, and the unfinished *Passagen-Werk*.

24. See Schorske, *Fin-de-Siècle Vienna*.

25. See Jean Starobinski, "Sur l'histoire des fluides imaginaires"; and Henri Ellenberger, *The Discovery of the Unconscious*.

Chapter One

1. In chapter 1 of *Swedenborgs korrespondenslära* [*Swedenborg's Doctrine of Correspondences*], Inge Jonsson traces the word back to a Middle Latin term, *correspondentia*, used as a rhetorical term in Robert de Basevorn's *Forma praedicandi* from 1322. (19) The earliest record of the word in French occurs in Jean de Meung's *Les remonstrances ou la complainte de Nature à l'Alchymiste errant*, where it refers to the parallel or harmony—it is difficult not to use the term "correspondence" here—between heavenly movement and the state of affairs on earth. (20) The word also occurs in Francis Bacon's *On the Advancement of Learning* (20), but the most important, perhaps the only, source of the term for Swedenborg was, Jonsson argues, the work of Malebranche and his translators. (24–25) See chapter 1, "Begreppet och ordet" ["The Concept and the Word"], 17–25. See also the English summary of the study as a whole, 394–417, especially 394.

2. Oddly enough, commentaries on Baudelaire that refer to Constant's "Les correspondances" almost always characterize the latter work as allegorical in the tradition of discursive romantic poems that some readers and writers believe to espouse a particular religious or ideological point of view. See Jonathan Culler's excellent summary of this interpretation in "Intertextuality and Interpretation: Baudelaire's 'Correspondances,'" a summary that, following a deconstructive path, shows the inadequacy of this view. From any perspective, however, the "romantic-allegorical" interpretation of "Les correspondances" is highly problematic, since, as we shall see, Constant never seems to have believed in or even have studied systematically any religious or political doctrine—except, perhaps, Catholic theology, which he came to loathe.

The literature on allegory is enormous. I have found most useful works that emphasize the ideological functions of the tradition, especially Angus Fletcher's *Allegory: The Theory of a Symbolic Mode*, and Walter Benjamin's early *Der Begriff der Kunstkritik in der deutschen Romantik*. Later, in his most famous essay on Baudelaire, Benjamin's discussion of *correspondances* as both echoing the jolting anonymity of the city crowds and arousing a fantasy of a harmonious and natural world of childhood, echoes the early discussion, while tying concepts of allegory to mid-nineteenth-century French society and politics. I shall argue in this chapter that Constant's use of the word *correspondances* is similarly bound up with transformations of experience that are laden with political dreams and agendas.

3. My reading of the poem owes much to Jonathan Culler's masterful synthesis in "Intertextuality and Interpretation."

4. In *La mystique de Baudelaire*, Jean Pommier drew a distinction between what he saw as the "vertical correspondences" of the opening quatrain and the "horizontal correspondences" suggested by the rest of the poem. His reading has served as a model for many others that have situated Baudelaire as a transitional figure whose work incorporates romantic elements, as well as foreshadowing a later symbolist aesthetic. In addition to Culler, see Raymond, *De Baudelaire au surréalisme*, and Balakian, especially *The Literary Origins of Surrealism*, chapter 3, "Baudelaire and the Break with Tradition," 45–61; and *The Symbolist Movement*, chapters 2, "Swedenborgism and the Romanticists," 12–28, and 3, "Baudelaire," 29–53.

5. See, for example, Culler, "Intertextuality and Interpretation," 120, and Pichois's commentary to Baudelaire's sonnet in Baudelaire, *Oeuvres complètes*, 1:840.

6. In *Work and Revolution in France*, William H. Sewell argues that the language of prerevolutionary corporatism played a key role in the construction of language and rituals that fostered class consciousness and action in mid-century Paris. See also Maurice Agulhon's *1848*, which surveys the general context, while emphasizing the importance of elements of the cultures of the Enlightenment and 1789 for the events of 1848.

7. Bowman's very useful survey and anthology, *Eliphas Lévi: visionnaire romantique*, focuses—despite its name—on the life and work of Constant/Lévi before his apparent abjuration of politics and turn to magic. In doing so, however, he fills a gap in the scholarship, for most studies of Constant/Lévi emphasize his later production.

8. Although Constant/Lévi published a brief autobiographical sketch entitled "Confession de l'auteur," the most important account of his life is by his friend, Paul Chacornac. It serves as the basis for all subsequent lives, which add little or nothing to the information he provides concerning Constant/Lévi's *life*. Subsequent biographies focus on the relationship of Constant/Lévi's work to the contexts of nineteenth-century culture and literature or the esoteric tradition. Works empha-

sizing the first include Bowman, *Eliphas Lévi*, Williams, and McIntosh. Buisset focuses on esoteric tradition.

9. Chacornac notes that if the subject matter of the book was Flora Tristan's, the form was Constant's. See also Sandra Dijkstra, *Flora Tristan: Pioneer Feminist and Socialist*, especially 56–57.

10. The note occurs at the beginning of chapter 13, "La nécromancie," in book 1, *Dogme*, of *Dogme et rituel de la haute magie*. Constant/Lévi writes:

> Nous avons dit que dans la lumière astrale se conservent les images des personnes et des choses. C'est aussi dans cette lumière qu'on peut évoquer les formes de ceux qui ne sont plus dans notre monde, et c'est par son moyen que s'accomplissent les mystères aussi contestés que réels de la nécromancie.
>
> Les cabalistes qui ont parlé du monde des esprits ont simplement raconté ce qu'ils ont vu dans leurs évocations.
>
> Eliphas Lévi Zahed (1), qui écrit ce livre, a évoqué, et il a vu.
>
> (1) Ces noms hébreux, traduits en français, sont Alphonse Louis Constant. (260)

If the note emphasizes the continuity between the two names and identities, Constant/Lévi probably placed it in a chapter in the body of the text, rather than in the introduction, in order to keep it from eyes that might take offense. It is, however, one of many "clues" scattered throughout these volumes that suggest that the author's occult interests, as well as his apparent change of name and orientation, represent a continuation of the political and social beliefs that had landed him in prison.

11. Cited in Buisset, 172–73.

12. Buisset calls the collection a "recueil de chansons." (83)

13. Constant/Lévi, *Histoire de la magie*, 411. Balzac emphasizes the similarity of aspects of the work of Leibniz and Swedenborg throughout *La comédie humaine*. In his very early preface to a version of *Les Chouans*, for example, he compares the consciousness of the author, who in many respects appears to be a forerunner of the protagonist of *Louis Lambert*, one of Balzac's novels most influenced by Swedenborgianism, to a Leibnizean concentric mirror: "Cette âme était enfin, selon la magnifique expression de Leibniz, *un miroir concentrique de l'univers*." (8:1675) And one sweeping sentence near the beginning of the Avant-propos to the novel cycle, written much later, in 1842, includes both men in a catalogue of authors whose works underwrite Balzac's systematic portrayal of contemporary society:

> En relisant les oeuvres si extraordinaires des écrivains mystiques qui se sont occupés des sciences dans leurs relations avec l'infini, tels que

Swedenborg, Saint-Martin, etc., et les écrits des plus beaux génies en histoire naturelle, tels que Leibniz, Buffon, Charles Bonnet, etc., on trouve dans les monades de Leibniz, dans les molécules organiques de Buffon, dans la force végétatrice de Needham, dans l'*emboîtement* des parties similaires de Charles Bonnet, assez hardi pour écrire en 1760: L'animal végète comme la plante; on trouve, dis-je, les rudiments de la belle loi du *soi pour soi* sur laquelle repose l'*unité de composition*. (1:8–9)

The implications of Balzac's development of a concept of novelistic totality in relation to a diverse array of models are discussed in chapter 4 below.

14. On the general context of French political theory in the late eighteenth and early nineteenth centuries, see Charlton's useful survey, "Religious and Political Thought," and Reardon, *Liberalism and Tradition: Aspects of Catholic Thought in Nineteenth-Century France*. See also the studies of Leroy, and Manuel. On Bonald, see Reardon, 43–53. On Maistre, see Lively and Reardón, 20–42. On the Idéologues, see Welch.

Concerning the differences between Bonald and Maistre in their views of language and emanation, Lively cautions:

Bonald and Lamennais (in his early writings) put forward boldly the idea that national traditions embody the primitive revelations of God. While Maistre was never so explicit, he was just as sure that widely held traditional beliefs were in some sense the voice of God. The idea was not novel; Hooker, Bossuet, Burke are just the most well known in a long line of writers who expounded it. And in England, France, and Germany at this time there were many who were defending old institutions and beliefs against the attacks of the Benthamites, the republicans, the writers of the *Aufklärung* on the grounds that any idea of political form which had survived for long must be presumed to perform some practical function in the community. (15)

On Maistre's theory of language, Lively continues:

This same fixed view of knowledge as revelation dominated his view of language. Like other romantic writers, he built a mystique of language, which subserved nationalist ends; and, like other romantic writers, he reserved a special scorn for those eighteenth-century thinkers, such as Condillac, who had been concerned with the philosophic improvement of language. In his view, language could not be created a priori or perfected by the wit of man or philosopher. Far from philosophy being the instrument by which language could be refined and improved, it had a dead and stultifying influence. In the formation of languages, the primitive were the creative ages, and the civilized and scientific the most sterile. This again was because the primitives had been given language, like the knowledge of which it was the sinews, directly by God. Particular languages might have been born in recorded history, but they were simply modifications and reformations of older tongues. The archetypal language itself emerged, like Minerva, fully formed from the mind of God.

Knowledge and language were then for Maistre the revelations of God, felt most perfectly by man before his corruption, but still glimpsed in the traditions and prejudices of modern man. Yet, despite this nostalgia for a Golden Age, he was willing to talk at times as though men, or rather *righteous* men, had not lost entirely the primitive instinct for truth. (18)

Lively's summary of Maistre's theory of language, which also holds true in a general sense for Bonald, suggests why these writers and some of their readers may have associated their ideas with the work of Swedenborg, for in *Heaven and Hell*, as I shall point out in chapter 2, Swedenborg had also written of the doctrine of correspondences as an original language emanating from God whose significance had been lost in corrupt times. There are, however, important differences. Throughout his work, scientific and visionary, Swedenborg emphasizes the individual's ability and obligation to choose and choose wisely. *Heaven and Hell* describes a third, intermediate, world in which the spirits of the recently dead are free to go on improving themselves until they are fit for heaven—or to do the opposite, if that is their desire. Angels in the separate spheres of heaven marry and raise children (although these are adopted orphans). The implications and contours of Swedenborg's parallel worlds and the theory of language that allowed him to describe, as well as to see or believe he saw them, are intimately bound up with Enlightenment beliefs in progress, privacy, and individualism that are fundamentally alien to the work of Bonald and Maistre. On the other hand, the Idéologues would have found his theological beliefs utterly foreign, while agreeing that the existence of an ideal language that pointed the way to an ideal social order was certainly not evident at the beginning of the nineteenth century.

15. On this subject, see above all the studies of Bowman. See also the surveys of Viatte and Bénichou.

16. The work was published under the aegis of the prolific fraud, abbé Migne, the subject of a recent monograph by R. Howard Bloch.

17. The opening of "La mort du poète" reproduces that of the fifteenth *légende* of the earlier work, "Le poète mourant":

Il y avait donc en ce temps-là un jeune homme qui, de bonne heure, avait écouté dans son âme l'écho des harmonies universelles.

Or, cette musique intérieure avait distrait son attention de toutes les choses de la vie mortelle, parce qu'il vivait dans une société encore sans harmonie.

Enfant, il était le jouet des autres enfants, qui le prenaient pour un idiot; jeune homme, il trouva à peine une main pour serrer sa main, un cœur pour reposer son cœur.

> Ses jours passaient dans un long silence et dans une profonde rê-
> verie; il contemplait avec d'étranges extases le ciel, les eaux, les arbres, les
> campagnes verdoyantes; puis ses regards devenaient fixes, des magnifi-
> cences intérieures se déployaient dans sa pensée et l'emportaient encore
> sur le spectacle de la nature. Des larmes alors coulaient à son insu le long
> de ses joues pâles d'émotion, et si l'on venait lui parler, il n'entendait pas.
> (95)

The earlier version, however, states unambiguously that the young man is visited
by Christ, while in the later the identity of the stranger is undetermined. And in
the earlier, there are no references to Swedenborg or the cabala.

18. *Erdgeister* appear to Faust at the beginning of *Faust* 2, where they com-
fort and refresh him. In *Faust* 1, however, the *Erdgeist* sign appears to the protagonist in his study. On the relationship of the *Erdgeist* sign that appears at the beginning of Goethe's work to theories of language and interpretation, see Neil Flax,
"The Presence of the Sign in Goethe's *Faust*," esp. 187–88.

19. In his *Le livre de Mallarmé*, the Mallarmé scholar, Jacques Scherer has
attempted to synthesize what the poet had to say about his project to construct a
total Book from the cryptic comments in published essays and the fragments of a
manuscript. See Scherer, *Le Livre de Mallarmé*, especially 7–154.
   It is difficult to pin down Mallarmé's slippery comments on the subject to any
one context, since he draws on and subverts a dizzying array of discourses. One
paragraph, however, does stand out as evoking the context of both Constant/Lévi's
and Swedenborg's work. It contains the only use of the *correspondances* I have
found in Mallarmé's prose (and as the concordance of Pierre Guiraud shows, there
are none in his verse):

> Le livre, expansion totale de la lettre, doit d'elle tirer, directement,
> une mobilité et spacieux, par correspondances, instituer un jeu, on ne
> sait, qui confirme la fiction. ("Le livre, instrument spirituel," in *Oeuvres*,
> 296)

20. Much has been written on the subject of the possible doctrinal influence
of contemporary occult theory, including the work of Constant/Lévi, on Mallarmé's
aesthetics. We have seen, however, how difficult it is to trace *any* doctrine back
through the works of Constant/Lévi, which, like the canonized literary works they
are often said to have "influenced," use these doctrines to construct fictions and
textual worlds of their own.
   A more promising point of departure would be to consider parallels between
both the theories of language and the situations of the two men. The writings of
the two men evince a palpable tension between interior and exterior worlds, suggesting that for both the poet and the *mage* eclectic theories of a universal language or Book linking a room with the stars allowed them to imagine a way out of
a painful isolation.

If references to interiors with windows and to inaccessible but beckoning skies and stars are scattered throughout Mallarmé's work, nowhere, I think, are the parallels between his thematic universe and that of Constant/Lévi suggested more clearly than in the sequence of four sonnets that opens with "Quand l'ombre menaça de la fatale loi" and which also contains the famous "sonnet en yx," in which the gleam of pearl-like nails evokes the distant presence—or absence—of the stars. While realizing that any attempt to characterize these two supremely complex and difficult sonnets in a note of this length is bound to omit more than it includes, I cite them both here:

> Quand l'ombre menaça de la fatale loi
> Tel vieux rêve, désir et mal de mes vertèbres,
> Affligé de périr sous les plafonds funèbres
> Il a ployé son aile indubitable en moi.
>
> Luxe, ô salle d'ébène où, pour séduire un roi
> Se tordent dans leur mort des guirlandes célèbres,
> Vous n'êtes qu'un orgueil menti par les ténèbres
> Aux yeux du solitaire ébloui de sa foi.
>
> Oui, je sais qu'au lointain de cette nuit, la Terre
> Jette d'un grand éclat l'insolite mystère,
> Sous les siècles hideux qui l'obscurcissent moins.
>
> L'espace à soi pareil qu'il s'accroisse ou se nie
> Roule dans cet ennui des feux vils pour témoins
> Que s'est d'un astre en fête allumé le génie.
>
>
> Ses purs ongles très-haut dédiant leur onyx,
> L'angoisse, ce minuit, soutient, lampadophore,
> Maint rêve vespéral brûlé par le Phénix
> Qui ne recueille pas de cinéraire amphore
>
> Sur les crédences, au salon vide: nul ptyx
> Aboli bibelot d'inanité sonore,
> (Car le Maître est allé puiser des pleurs au Styx
> Avec ce seul objet dont le Néant s'honore.)
>
> Mais proche la croisée au nord vacante, un or
> Agonise selon peut-être le décor
> Des licornes ruant du feu contre une nixe.
>
> Elle, défunte nue en le miroir, encor
> Que, dans l'oubli fermé par le cadre, se fixe
> De scintillations sitôt le septuor.

21. Buisset, 202.

22. Waite writes:

> In a multitude of statements and in the spirit of the text throughout, it is certain that the *Histoire de la magie* offers "negation of dogma" on its absolute side. We obtain a continual insight into free sub-surface opinions, ill concealed under external conformity to the Church, and we get also useful sidelights on the vanity of the author's sham submissions. (Preface to the English translation, *A History of Magic*, 13)

Waite's preface emphasizes the inaccuracies and inconsistencies in Constant/Lévi's account, but admits a polemical purpose:

> Throughout all my later literary life I have sought to make it plain, as the result of antecedent years spent in occult research, that the occult sciences—in all their general understanding—are paths of danger when they are not paths of simple make-believe and imposture. (5)

23. In his introduction to *Transcendental Magic*, Waite characterizes Constant/Lévi's beliefs after 1851 as a kind of "transcendentalised Imperialism," (10) and justifies his omission of the first preface in the following terms:

> I have judged it the wiser course to leave out the preliminary essay which was prefixed to the second edition of the DOCTRINE AND RITUAL; its prophetic utterances upon the mission of Napoleon III have been stultified long since by subsequent events; it is devoid of any connection with the work which it precedes, and, representing as it does the later views of Lévi, it would be a source of confusion to the reader. (xx)

24. The passage occurs in the first scene in Faust's study, near the beginning of *Faust I*:

> Aber ach! schon fühl' ich, bei dem besten Willen,
> Befriedigung nicht mehr aus dem Busen quillen.
> Aber warum muß der Strom so bald versiegen,
> Und wir wieder im Durste liegen?
> Davon hab' ich so viel Erfahrung.
> Doch dieser Mangel läßt sich ersetzen:
> Wir lernen das Übererdische schätzen,
> Wir sehnen uns nach Offenbarung,
> Die nirgends würd'ger und schöner brennt
> Als in dem Neuen Testament.
> Mich drängt's, den Grundtext aufzuschlagen,
> Mit redlichem Gefühl einmal
> Das heilige Original
> In mein geliebtes Deutsch zu übertragen.
> [Er schlägt ein Volum auf und schickt sich an.]
> Geschrieben steht: "Im Anfang war das Wort!"
> Hier stock' ich schon! Wer hilft mir weiter fort?
> Ich kan das W o r t so hoch unmöglich schätzen,

Ich muß es anders übersetzen,
Wenn ich vom Geiste recht erleuchtet bin.
Geschrieben steht: Im Anfang war der S i n n.
Bedenke wohl die erste Zeile,
Daß deine Feder sich nicht übereile!
Ist es der S i n n, der alles wirkt und schafft?
Es sollte stehn: Im Anfang war die K r a f t!
Doch, auch indem ich dieses niederschreibe,
Schon warnt mich was, daß ich dabei nicht bleibe.
Mir hilft der Geist! Auf einmal seh' ich Rat
Und schreibe getrost: *Im Anfang war die T a t!* (*Faust I*, 1210–1237; in
    Goethe, 3:43–44; my emphasis)

But oh! though my resolve grows even stronger,
I feel contentment welling from my soul no longer.
Yet why must the flood so soon run dry,
And we be left again in thirst to lie?
I have had proof of it in such full measure.
Still, for this lack there's compensation:
The supernatural we learn to treasure,
We come to long for revelation,
Which nowhere burns so finely, so unflawed,
As in the Gospel of our Lord.
I feel an urge to reach
For the original, the sacred text, appealing
To simple honesty of feeling
To render it in my dear German speech.
    [He opens a tome and sets forth.]
"In the beginning was the Word"—thus runs the text.
Who helps me on? Already I'm perplexed!
I cannot grant the word such sovereign merit,
I must translate it in a different way
If I'm indeed illumined by the Spirit.
"In the beginning was the Sense." But stay!
Reflect on this first sentence well and truly
Lest the light pen be hurrying unduly!
Is sense in fact all action's spur and source?
It should read: "In the beginning was the Force!"
Yet as I write it down, some warning sense
Alerts me that it, too, will give offense.
The spirit speaks! And low the way is freed,
I calmly write: *"In the beginning was the Deed!."* (Arndt, tr., 30; my
    emphasis)

On the theological and hermeneutic contexts of these lines, see the commentaries
of Trunz (3:508–09) and Hamlin (313–14), and, for an interpretation that links

these issues to current theoretical debates, Neil M. Flax, "The Presence of the Sign in Goethe's *Faust*," especially 188–89.
Hamlin writes:

> Faust introduces the theme of Christian revelation as a valid analogue to his own intellectual concern. From Goethe's point of view this would not necessarily indicate the perspective of religion. Historically, Faust was a contemporary of Martin Luther, whose translation of the Bible into German (New Testament, 1524) included the familiar version of the opening verse of John which Faust begins with: "In the beginning was the Word" (*Im Anfang war das Wort*). Here Faust is, in effect, sharing in Luther's labor of translation, though he immediately transforms the text to accord with his own philosophy of life. Within the dramatic situation, the translation of scripture provides an ironic parallel to the appearance of Mephistopheles: both the devil in his guise as poodle and the text of the Gospel as Word of God provide instances of the incarnation of spirit, for which Christ himself is the essential model. Mephistopheles apparently recognizes this as competition and grows increasingly violent in his barking.
>
> Faust's sequence of terms for the Greek *logos* reflects the intellectual background to Romantic thought which Goethe himself participated in during the latter half of the eighteenth century. The rejection of "Word" for "Sense" corresponds to the rejection of traditional rhetorical views of language as mere form or artifice in favor of the sense, the meaning, the feeling which language represents. An analogue to this is provided by Faust himself in the scene from the Gretchen tragedy (composed before 1775), "Marthe's Garden," where Faust discusses religion and refuses to accept any name for God, asserting instead that "Feeling is all!" (line 3456). The alternative choice of term, "Force" (*Kraft*), would correspond to the basic view of life in the era of the German *Sturm und Drang* during the 1770s, which Goethe himself established in large measure through such works as *The Sorrows of Young Werther* and *Götz von Berlichingen*. The final choice of term, "Deed" (*Tat*), is clearly the most Faustian, the most valid for Goethe's drama as a whole, corresponding to the famous couplet in Faust's last monologue in Part II: "He only earns both freedom and existence / Who must reconquer them each day." (lines 11575–76) (See also the Lord's statement about the need for mankind to be active even if the devil must drive men to it, lines 340 ff.) *Logos* as Deed would also correspond to the philosophy of Idealism, as in Fichte's *Wissenschaftslehre* (1794), which argues that experience, consciousness, and even life itself begin when the self posits itself through action (*Tathandlung*). Thus, whether Faust himself is aware of any such implications, Goethe has here transformed the Biblical Word from the context of Luther and the historical Faust to the context of Romantic Idealism, the context in which Goethe was writing and the context to which his *Faust* was addressed. (313–14)

For Goethe, as for Constant/Lévi, action held a political dimension—although his initial enthusiasm for the French Revolution turned to distrust and disapproval. The French writer's interpretation was far less ambivalent and nuanced, for Constant/Lévi seems never entirely to have abandoned the leftist political beliefs of his youth.

That Constant/Lévi knew something about Goethe's *Faust* and the Faust legend in general is attested by the entry on Faust in his *Dictionnaire de la littérature chrétienne*. The generalness of the entry, however, suggests that it would be foolish to attribute the kind of philosophical and aesthetic background to Constant/Lévi's discussions of action and language that Hamlin evokes in his discussion of Goethe's work.

25. On the connections between anarchism and the work of Mallarmé and other Symbolists, see Joan U. Halperin's exploratory studies of Félix Fénéon, especially her *Félix Fénéon: Aesthete and Anarchist in Fin-de-Siècle Paris*.

26. On the relationship between Mesmerism and charisma, see especially Maria Tatar, *Spellbound*.

27. In his "Biographical Preface" to *Transcendental Magic*, Waite, for example, writes:

> He outlived the Franco-German war, and as he had exchanged Socialism for a sort of transcendentalised Imperialism, his political faith—at its value—must have been tried as much by the events which followed the siege of Paris as was his patriotic enthusiasm by the reverses which culminated at Sédan. (x)

28. *Les mystères de la Kabbale*. Paris: Nourry, 1920.

29. Waite writes:

> Readers of his History must be prepared for manifold inaccuracies, which are to be expected in a writer like Eliphas Lévi. Those who know anything of Egypt—the antiquities of its religion and literature—will have a bad experience with the chapter on Hermetic Magic; those who know Eastern religion on its deeper side will regard the discourse on Magic in India as title-deeds of all incompetence; while in respect of later Jewish theosophy I have had occasion in certain annotations to indicate that Lévi had no extensive knowledge off those Kabalistic texts on the importance of which he dwells so much and about which he claims to speak with full understanding. (Preface to the English translation, *A History of Magic*, 13)

In his introduction to his translation of *Transcendental Magic*, Waite takes Constant/Lévi to task for his scanty knowledge of the work of Guillaume Postel:

The French verb *parcourir* represents his method of study and not the verb *approfondir*. Let us take one typical case. There is no occult writer whom he cites with more satisfaction, and towards whom he exhibits more reverence, than William Postel, and of all Postel's books there is none which he mentions so often as the CLAVIS ABSCONDITORUM A CONSTITUTIONE MUNDI; yet he had read this minute treatise so carelessly that he missed a vital point concerning it, and apparently died unaware that the symbolic key prefixed to it was the work of the editor and not the work of Postel. (xiv)

30. See the studies by Abbott, Clawson, and Jacob.

31. On the invention of a Rosicrucian tradition, see Yates, *The Rosicrucian Enlightenment*.

32. The studies of Agulhon, Bowman, Charlton, and Manuel all emphasize the broader range of cultural influences and appeal at play in the formation and dissemination of French political thought, especially on the left, at this time.

33. See especially *Mesmerism*, chapter 5, "From Mesmer to Hugo," 127–59.

34. See also Frank Paul Bowman, "Illuminism, Utopia, Mythology," chapter 3 of *The French Romantics*, ed. D. G. Charlton, 2 vols. (Cambridge: Cambridge Univ. Press, 1984)1:76–112, especially 92–93.

Chapter Two

1. Inge Jonsson notes at least one instance in which the dizzying array of mythological references seems to be the result of Swedenborg's cribbing from Scipion Dupleix's handbook, *Corps de philosophie contenant la logique, la physique, la metaphysique, et l'éthique*. See *Swedenborgs korrespondenslära*, esp. 106–7 and 133–35.

2. There is, unfortunately, no biography of Swedenborg that takes into account recent scholarship on cultural, religious, and intellectual history. Although it is not accurate on all matters, Sigstedt's 1952 biography gives the best account of the cultural and historical contexts of Swedenborg's work, and is extremely useful for a non-Swede. See Jonsson's criticisms, especially "Köpenhamn–Amsterdam–Paris."

The best general intellectual biography is still Martin Lamm's *Swedenborg*, which is available in French and German translations. See also Jonsson's introductory survey, *Emanuel Swedenborg*, which not only summarizes Swedenborg's life, but also gives an overview of his intellectual work and its contexts, often providing important correctives to Lamm's very general and sometimes dated conclusions.

Tafel's *Documents Concerning the Life and Character of Emanuel Sweden-*

borg is an invaluable resource for anyone investigating the life and work of this protean individual.

This account of Swedenborg's life draws principally on the work of Sigstedt and Jonsson.

3. On Sweden during the early modern period, see Michael Roberts's studies: *Gustavus Adolphus: A History of Sweden, 1611–1631; The Swedish Imperial Experience, 1560–1718; The Age of Liberty: Sweden, 1719–1772;* and the essays in the collection he edited, *Sweden's Age of Greatness, 1632–1718.* The best survey of Swedish science during this period is Sten Lindroth's *Svensk lärdomshistoria,* vols. 2 and 3. For an overview in English of Swedish culture in the mid- and late eighteenth century, see Paul Britten Austin, *The Life and Songs of Carl Michael Bellman: Genius of the Swedish Rococo.*

4. The sole reference to Swedenborg in Jesper Swedberg's memoirs reads:

Min son *Emanuels* namn betyder, *Gud med oß.* At han alt jemt påminner sig Gudz närwarelse, och then noga, heliga och hemliga förening, som wi genom trona ståm vti med med wår gunstiga och nådiga Gud. Och wi med Honom och vti Honom. (239)

My son *Emanuel's* name means "God with us." That he may constantly remember the presence of God and the close, holy, and secret union, that binds us through faith with our bountiful and merciful God. And we with Him and in Him. (my translation)

Can one read the sentence following the comment on his son's name as an exhortation that a wayward child return to the ways of his father's religion? Such religious comments and exhortations are common in Jesper Swedberg's memoirs. The brevity and placement of the reference to Swedenborg, however, suggest distance and perhaps resentment, for Swedberg's youngest son, Jesper, is mentioned near the beginning of the chapter and at considerably greater length. Jesper Swedberg writes that he had sent this son to America and then called him home again to Sweden, where he was successful enough to pay his father 200 dalars a year. The comments on the younger Jesper are followed by the remark "Som ock alla andra öfriga barnen äro i landet mig til hugnat och glädie" (230) "As all my other children in the country please and gladden me." Was Swedenborg out of the country at the time the words were written? There is certainly a noticable gap between the references to the first and to the other two sons, which come at the very end of a long chapter. But if Jesper Swedberg's feelings for Swedenborg were less than purely affectionate, he harbored far more ill will towards his eldest son, Albrecht, who, he writes, was not really his son at all, but the child of a relative who had been mistakenly identified as his at birth.

5. On the subject of Swedenborg's Latin literary production, see Inge Jonsson, *Swedenborgs skapelsedrama, De cultu et amore Dei;* and Hans Helander's introduction to his edition of Swedenborg's *Festivus applausus.*

Notes   279

6. Lindroth writes:

> Swedenborgs Principia är en av de stora böckerna i svensk vet-
> enskapshistoria, i tankekraft har den få likar. Men den föll död till
> marken, just ingen här hemma eller ute i Europa brydde sig om den.
> Saken har sitt särskilda intresse, därför att Swedenborgs framställning av
> solsystemets uppkomst faktiskt öppnade en ny och fruktbar väg för forsk-
> ningen. Buffon i sin Histoire naturelle, senare Kant och Laplace med
> deras s. k. nebularhypotes framställde kosmologiska teorier, enligt vilka
> planeterna hade sitt ursprung i solen resp. en töcknig urnebulosa. Man
> har menat, att de kanske inspirerats av Swedenborg. Men det är föga
> troligt. (2:565)

> Swedenborg's *Principia* is one of the great books in Swedish intellec-
> tual history, in sheer intellectual power it has few equals. But it fell dead
> to the ground, scarcely anyone here at home or abroad in Europe paid
> any attention to it. The matter holds a particular interest, because
> Swedenborg's presentation of the origin of the solar system in fact
> pointed in a new and fruitful direction for research. Buffon in his *Histoire
> naturelle* and Kant and Laplace with their so-called nebular hypothesis
> presented cosmological theories according to which the planets origi-
> nated in the sun or a thick primeval haze. Some have argued that they
> may have been inspired by Swedenborg. But this is hardly likely. (my
> translation)

His discussion of Swedenborg's early scientific work emphasizes its debts to Descartes, as well as the Swedish engineer, Christopher Polhem, and gives a particularly fine summary of *Principia*. See his chapter, "Naturforskaren Swedenborg"
["Swedenborg the Scientist"], 2:555–66, especially 562–66.

7. For a recent assessment of the two men's work, see Jonsson, "I skaparens
spår—Swedenborg och Linné."

8. See, for example, Lindroth's chapter on Swedenborg's scientific work in
Svensk lärdomshistoria.

9. On the relationship of new forms of visual technology to ways of seeing in
eighteenth-century science and aesthetics, Barbara Maria Stafford, *Body Criticism*;
and Catherine Wilson, "Visual Surface and Visual Symbol." Wilson's concluding
comments on the impact of the microscope are suggestive of how the new technology may have informed Swedenborg's visions:

> In closing, I should like to return to Bachelard's assessment of the
> microscope. It was his view that the microscope constituted an actual
> impediment to knowledge in the seventeenth and eighteenth centuries
> because it revealed things which were beautiful but which could not lead
> to the acquisition of any new theoretical information, or which suggested

to observers theories of the wrong sort—for example, the theory that the world was a *plenum* filled with an infinity of tiny animals—and made a quantitative handling of phenomena seem impossible or unimportant. We have seen that there are indeed several senses in which people dreamed with the new images presented by the microscope. They dreamed in the sense that they could experience them only in a passive way, unable to put what they saw to further use. They dreamed as well in assigning them a central place in fanciful, premature, or conceptually unsound explanatory programs. They dreamed, finally, in spinning around the instrument a fine web of theological and moral significance, supposing it capable of mitigating the effects of sin or restoring a pure and uncorrupted commerce with the physical world. When researchers of the seventeenth century wanted to defend the theoretical relevance of the microscope by contrast with the purely recreational interest it aroused, they tended to point to the same example: the direct verification of the circulation of the blood in animals with diaphanous blood-vessels, such as fish and frogs. It would be a long time before anyone could see with this instrument anything which might help to make him, in the sense of Bacon and Descartes, a master and possessor of nature.

Nevertheless the microscope gave a sense to the notion of the interpretation of nature which neither the corpuscular philosophy of Descartes and Boyle nor the mathematical philosophy of Galileo and Newton was able to supply. . . . What the microscope did in revealing layer after layer of articulated structure was to restore the solidity and accessibility to the understanding of an otherwise atomized and mathematicized world. Even for those who were to a greater or lesser degree skeptical about the actual powers of the microscope, what Hume was later to call "hidden mechanism and secret structure of parts" were nevertheless irrevocably proposed as possible objects of experience. (106–07)

See also Svetlana Alpers's fine study of seventeenth-century Dutch art, *The Art of Describing*, for an exemplary discussion of how the new technologies were intertwined with ways of viewing and representing the world.

10. Jürgen Habermas, *Strukturwandel der Öffentlichkeit*.

11. See Jonsson, *Swedenborgs korrespondenslära*, Chapter 1, "Begreppet och ordet" ("The Concept and the Word"), 17–25, especially 23–25; and the English summary, 394.

12. See Jonsson, "Köpenhamn–Amsterdam–Paris."

13. In his autobiographical fiction, *Tjänstekvinnans son*, Strindberg writes of his initial impression of Swedenborg:

> Svedenborg tyckte han var fjoskig, och Thorilds brev till Per Tamm på Dagsnäs angick honom inte.
> Svedenborg och Thorild voro två yverborna svenskar, vilka i enslighetens land gripits av den sjukan, G r ö s s e n w a h n, som enslighet

medför, och som i Sverige just genom dess isolerade läge och på en vid-
sträckt yta utplanterade lilla folkmängd är ganska vanlig och ofta brutit
ut: i Gustav Adolfs kejsarplaner, Carl X:s europeiska stormaktsidéer, Carl
XII:s Attila projekt, Rudbecks Atlantica-mani, sist i Svedenborgs och Tho-
rilds himlastorms- och världsbrandsfantasier. (18:228)

He thought Swedenborg was simple, and Thorild's letters to Per
Tamm at Dagsnäs had nothing to say to him.

Swedenborg and Thorild were two frenzied Swedes, who in the land
of solitude had been seized by the illness that solitude brings, *Grössenwahn*, and that in Sweden, precisely because of its isolated situation and
tiny population spread out over a huge surface, is quite common and has
often broken out: in the imperial plans of Gustavus Adolphus, Charles X's
ideas of becoming a European great power, Charles XII's Attila project,
Rudbeck's Atlantica mania, and last in Swedenborg's and Thorild's fantasies of storming the heavens and burning down the world. (my translation)

These words seem uncannily prophetic when one considers that in the 1890s, while
living an extremely isolated existence in Paris, Strindberg, like the Swedes he describes so mockingly above, very anxious to "conquer" Europe, turned not only to
the work of Swedenborg, but also to the production of the kind of literary texts he
disapproved of in his youth. See Strindberg's account of this crisis and his new-
found interest in Swedenborg in his *Inferno*. Martin Lamm's interpretation of this
work and its significance for Strindberg's life and work has set a pattern for Swedish Strindberg scholarship. See especially Lamm, *August Strindberg*, part II, "Efter
omvändelsen," 243–440. For a more recent discussion of Strindberg's mystical
"crisis" in relation to mythological and psychological motifs in his work, see Göran
Stockenström, *Ismaël i öknen*.

14. See, for example, Margaret Goldsmith, *Franz Anton Mesmer*.

15. See Jonsson, "Köpenhamn–Amsterdam–Paris."

16. d 17 reste ifrån Hamburg, öfwer Elfwen til Buxtahude, hwarest en mil
sågs den charmantesta campagne jag sedt i Tyskland, passerade igenom
en stendig trägård, af äppel, peron, plommon, walnötz, castanie-träen,
sam[t] Lind och alm. (2)

17.   d 8 x 9
denna natten war den förnöjsamaste ibland alla, emedan jag såg
Regnum Jnnocentiae; såg nedanföre mig den skiönaste trägård, som ses
kunde, derpå hwart trä sattes hwita rosor efter hand, kom sedan vti en
long kammare, ther stodo hwita skiöna kiärl med miölck och bröd vti,
så appetitligit, at intet appetiteligare kunde förestellas, jag war i selskap
med ett fruentimmer, som jag intet mins serdeles, så gick jag tilbakars,
kom til mig ett litet wackert och oskyldigt barn, som sade mig at hon
det fruentimret har gådt bort, vtan at tagit afsked, bad mig köpa åt

henne en bok, som hon wille taga op, men wiste mig intet, waknade, vtom dess tychte jag tractera på min räkning en hoper vti ett hus el*ler* palais för sig sielft, der woro bekante; bl*and* dem RikzR*ådet* Lagerberg, tror Ehrenpreus och andra, s*om* alt war på min depence, tychte det kosta mig mycket, men tanckarne gingo fram och tilbakars, at det wore depence, ibland skiötte jag der intet om, ty jag merckte, at alt bestodes af den Herren, som hade de*n* egendom*en*, el*ler* wiste mig det. *War vti Regno Jnnocentiae, och at jag tracterade de andra och werldzliga vtan at se dem, om det betyder mitt arbete, at intet wara liksom med dem, fast jag tracterar dem dermed, eller något annat: barnet war sjelfwa innocentia, af det wardt jag ganska rörd, och önskade wara i ett sådant rike, der all inno[cen]ce wore: bekla[ga]de at jag wid wak[n]andet kom derifrån: hwad det fruentimbret war, som gick bort vtan afsked, wet jag intet hwad det wil säja.*

war dagen derpå el*ler* d 9, så klarsynt at jag såg läsa de*n* granna bibele*n* vta*n* minsta incom*m*oditet. (57)

18.   d 15 x 16 Juni, d 16 *war en söndag*

fördes mig repraesentatio*n* af mitt förra lefwerne, och huru sed*an* jag gick der afgrunder woro på alla sidor, och at jag wände om; då kom jag i en ganska härlig lund, besatt öfwer alt med skönast*e* fikona-trä i skiön wext och ordning, på en tychtes der wara qwar wissnad*e* fikon, lunden war med grafwar omsteng[d], doch intet de*n* sid*an* jag war; jag wille öfwe*r* en spong, som war högt jord och gräs på, men jag wågade mig intet för fahrlighete*n* skull; såg något stycke derifrån ett stort och ganska skiönt palais med flyglar, der wille jag taga logement tychte mig, at altid hafwa prospect af lunde*n* och grafwarne, ett fönster longt vt på flygeln war ock öpit; der jag tychte wille hafwa mitt rum. Betyder at om sönda*gen* jag skull*e* war*a* i det andeliga, s*om* betyde*r* de*n* härliga lunden, palais läre*r* wara min dessein af mitt arbete, som syftar åt lund*en*, dit jag ärnar dermed at se. (44)

19.   om morgon*en* syntes mig vti en vision den marcknad s*om* en dis-ting war vti min faders hus i upsala, i salen ofwanföre, vti ingånge*n* och elliest öfwer alt, *detta betyder det samma, så at det bör ske, så mycket wissare* (62)

20. Explicit references to ladders and stairs (versions of *trappa* and *stege*) occur in the entries for March 24–25 and April 7–8, 14–15, 15–16, and 21–22. (Klemming, 4, 14, 28, 29, 35; Wilkinson/Woofenden, 6, 19–20, 40, 41, 50) These references, however, form part of a geography of consciousness, that emphasizes up-and-down movements.

21.   Denna natten som []: sof] jag helt tranqvilt, kl: 3 a 4 om morg: waknade jag, och log waken, men som vti en vision, jag kunde se op och wara waken, enär jag wille, så at jag intet war anna[r]s än wakande,

doch i andanom, war en inwertes och kenbar öfwer hela kroppen glädie,
tychte alt på öfwerswinnerligit sett huru alt abouterade, flög likasom
op, och giömde sig vti ett oendeligt, som ett centrum, der war amor
ipse, och at derifrån extenderade sig omkring och så ned igen, således
per incomprehensibilem circulum, a centro, som war amor, omkring
och så dit igen, denna amor vti en dödelig kropp, hwaraf jag tå war full,
liknade then glädien, som en kysk man har då är [): han] är i werckelig
kiärlek och in ipso actu med sin maka, sådan amaenitas extrema war
suffunderad öfwer min hela kropp, och det lenge, hwilcket jag också
hela tiden tilförene, helst wid nest för än jag insomnade, och efter
sömnen 1/2 ja 1 tima; nu medan jag war i andanom, doch waken, ty jag
kunde lyfta op ögonen och wara waken, komma in igen vti det, så såg
och merckte jag, at den innerliga och werckeliga glädien kom dervtaf,
och at så mycket man kunde wara dervti, så mycken welfägnad hade
man, och så snart man kom vti en annan kiärlek som intet concentrerade sig dit, at man då strax war vtur wägen, som til någon kiärlek
til sig, eller som intet der concentrerade sig, då war man dervtur, kom
en liten köld öfwer mig, och en sort af liten rysning, som och at det
qwalde mig, hwaraf jag fant hwaraf mitt qwahl ibland har kommit, och
fant då hwaraf det stora qwahl kommer, enär anden bedröfwer en, och
at den på slutet stannar vti en ewig pina, och får helfwetet, enär man
owärdeligen vndfår Christum i nattwarden, ty anden är som plågar en
owärdighet då. i samma stånd som jag war, kom jag än diupare i andanom, och fast jag war waken, intet kunde regera mig sielf, vtan kom
som en öfwermechtig drift, at kasta mig på mitt ansichte, och taga
ehop henderne och bedia hwad tilförene, om min owärdighet, och med
diupeste ödmiukhet och wördnad bedia om nåd, at jag som den störste
Syndaren, får syndernes förlåtelse, då jag merckte och [): at] jag war i
det stånd, som natten näst för den sista, men widare intet kunde se,
emedan jag war waken; det vndrade jag, och så wistes mig i andanom,
at menniskia i detta tilstånd, är som en menniskia som wänder fötterne
op, och hufwudet ner; och kom för mig hwarföre Moses moste afkläda
sig sina skor, då han skulle gå til den helige; och at Christus twettade
Apostlarnes fötter, och swarade Petrum, at när fötterna äro twettade är
alt nog: *Sedan i andanom fant jag, at det som går ifrån sielfwa centro,
som är amor, är den helge ande, som repraesenteras igenom watn, ty
det nemdes och aqva eller unda*; i summa, enär man är i det stånd, at
hafwa ingen kiärlek, som concentrerar sig, hos sig sielft, vtan som concentrerar sig vti det allmenna besta, som repraesenterar här på jorden
seu mundo morali, den kierleken in spirituali, och den intet för sig
eller societetens skull, vtan för Christi skull, hwarest kierleken är och
centrum, då är man vti retta statu, Christus är finis ultimus, de andre
äro fines medii, de der directe föra dit. (19–21; my emphasis)

22. See Introduction, *The Animal Kingdom*, 1–15. Swedenborg's remarks on
the blood are representative of his argument as a whole:

In a word, the science of the blood includes all the sciences that treat of the substances of the world, and of the forces of nature. For this reason we find that man did not begin to exist till the kingdoms were completed; and that the world and nature concentrated themselves in him: in order that in the human microcosm the entire universe might be exhibited for contemplation from its last end to its first. (3)

23. 1. vti vngdomen och Gustavianska familien.
    2. vti Venedig om then skiöna Palais.
    3. vti Sverje om himelens hwita sky.
    4. vti Leipsig, om den som låg vti siudhett watn.
    5. om den som ramlade med keden ned i diupet.
    6. om konungen, som gaf i en torparestuga så dyrbart.
    7. om drengen som wille jag skulle resa bort.
    8. om mina förnöjligheter om nättren. (3)

24. "detta ansåg det jag då bracht til slut om formis organicis in genere." (53)

25.   Sades *Nicolaiter*, och *Nicolaus nicolai*, om det betyder mitt nya namn wet jag intet; det merckwerdigaste war det, at jag nu repraesenterade den inre menniskian, och som en annan än mig sjelf, som at jag helsade på mine tanckar, skremde dem, mine res memoriae, anklagade en annan, så at nu är wändt, at jag repraesenterar en som är emot en annan, eller inre menniskian, ty jag har bedt Gud, at jag intet motte wara min, vtan at Gud techtes låta mig blifwa sin. (30)

26. Nicolaus nicolai war en philosophe, som skickade hwart åhr til Augustus panes, först dettes, som jag fant min skyldighet at åter försona mig med wår Herre, emedan jag i andelige saker är ett stinckande as. (30)

27.   Så såg jag min fader, vti en annan habit, nestan rödachtigt, han kallade mig til sig, och tog mina armar, der jag hade halfarmar men manchetter frammanföre, han tog begge manchetterna fram och knytte dem med mina band, at jag hade manchetter, som betydde, at jag er intet ibland Presterskapet, vtan är och bör wara en civil betient. Sedan frågade han mig, huru jag tycker om den qvaestionen, at en konung har gifwit wid pass 30 lof, som woro inwigde til det andeliga ståndet, at gifta sig, och således ändra sitt stånd, jag swarade, at jag har tenckt och skrifwit något om sådant, men det har ingen rapport härtil, straxt derpå fant jag at swara, efter mitt samwete, at det intet bör tillåtas at byta om sitt stånd, hwarcken den eller den, til hwad han opgifwit sig, det sade han ock wara af samma mening, men jag sade har konungen resolveradt, så blir doch derwid, han sade sig skulle legga sitt votum skrifteligit, om de äro 50 så blir derefter, det jag observerade war merckwerdigt, at jag intet kallade honom min fahr, vtan min Bror, tenckte

derefter, huru det kom til, tychte at min fahr war död, och denne, som
är min fahr, moste således wara min Bror. (12–13)

28. "jag ännu intet är klädd och beredd som sig bör." (44)

29. "om jag skulle admitteras vti societeten, derest min fader war." (46)

30. Surely the most significant passage, already quoted, describes a dreamed
or imagined encounter with Jesper Swedberg, in which the older man, who in his
memoirs rails against decorative clothing, approves his son's fancy apparel. See
Wilkinson/Woofenden 18 and Klemming 12–13. Several other passages in the journal evoke the writer's anxieties concerning correct apparel in more general terms.
See, for example, Wilkinson/Woofenden 6–7, 63, 67, 79, and 87; and Klemming 5,
44, 47, 55, and 60–61.

31. "6. om konungen, som gaf i en torparestuga så dyrbart." (3)

32. See Hans Helander, Introduction, Emanuel Swedenborg, *Festivus applausus*.

33.   Vti Harderwik, som war wid ankomsten i England, sof jag allenast
några timar, och då syntes mig mycket, som lärer angå mitt arbete här,
det war d 4 x 5 Maj; efter Engelska stylen; 1 huru som jag förlorade en
zedel, och den som fant den fick derföre allenast 9 styfwer: som ock en
annan, som hittat en sådan zedel, och den köptes för allenast 9 styfwer;
och sade jag på skemt, at det war pietasteri: förmodeligen huru man är
fatt i England, en dehl redligit, en dehl oredeligit 2. wore som vndrade
på mine kopparstycken, som woro wel giorde, och wille se mitt concept,
som om jag kunde så concipera dem som de woro giorde. lärer betyda
at mitt arbete winner approbation, och de tro at jag intet kunnat giöra
det. 3. kom mig til handa ett litet bref, som jag betalte före 9 styfwer,
enär jag öpnade det låg invti en stor bok med rent papper, och mitt vti
monga skiöna desseiner, det öfriga war rent papper; der sått ett fruen-
timber på wenstra handen; som sig flyttade på högra, och blädde i
boken, ock desseiner kommo fram, jag tychte det wara meningen af
brefwet, at jag skulle i England låta rita en hop sådana deseiner eller
mönster: fruentimbret hade en ganska bred gorge, och på begge
sidorne ända ned hel bar, hudet war gläntzande som glaserad, och på
tummen war en miniaturmålni[n]g; som lärer betyda, at jag med Gudz
hielp, lärer i England vtföra en hop wackra desseiner i mitt arbete; och
at sedan speculation wender sig ad priora, som förr warit in posterioribus, som omskiftni[n]g af rummet synes betyda. 4. tychtes jag wara
befalt at gå med Bergenstierna på en commission, hwartil penningar
ordinerades, tychte det wara bortom sicilien, med hwilcken commission
jag war hel nöjd: men tychte doch at man kommer der at achta sig för
scorpioner: lärer betyda något som jag sedan lärer få i commissis sedan

mitt arbete blifwer ferdigt, om kanske jag kommer at werckstella det på
någon annan ort: och kanske vti någon annan sak. (41)

34. It was notably the subject of a long poem in Swedish by the seventeenth-
century poet and polymath, Georg Stiernhielm (1598–1672). His *Hercules*, completed in 1658, portrays the dilemma of Hercules, confronted with a choice between pleasure and virtue, embodied as two women, Fru Lusta and Fru Dygd.

35. On the subject of the relationship of Baillet's account to others and to the
supposedly lost original, see Cole, *The Olympian Dreams and Youthful Rebellion of
René Descartes*, especially part 1, "The Surviving Evidence on Descartes's Lost Little Notebook," 19–48.

36. For an overview of negative accounts of the dreams, see Cole, especially 6–
11 and 41–48.

37. See, for example, the discussions of Cole and Melzer, "Descartes' Dreams
and Freud's Failure."

38. See Cole, especially chapter 8, 149–70.

39. Male figures in many of the entries in the *Journal of Dreams* are described
as attempting to lure the writer into the enjoyment of pleasures that more often
than not are unspecified. Throughout the second part of the diary, individuals
change shape, sex, and identity, sometimes quite innocuously, sometimes not.
Jesper Swedberg, for example, appears to become the writer's brother. (April 6–7;
Klemming, 13; Wilkinson/Woofenden, 18) In several entries, however, an individual
appears to change sex in a sexually charged situation. One of the scenes most
suggestive of homosexuality occurs at the very end of the diary:

d 11 x 12 [Maj?]
— tychtes med Öhlreick wara med 2 fruentimmer han lade sig, och
som jag tychte efter åt warit hos ett fruen[tim]mer: han decouvr[er]ade
det, det kom mig in, som jag berettade, at jag ock legat hos ett och min
fader såg det, men gick förbi, och sade intet ord derom.
— Jag gick ifrån Öhlreick och i wägen war diupt watn, men på sidan
war ganska litet, en gång, dit gick jag på sidan, tychte mig intet böra gå i
diupa wattnet.
— tychte at en racquet slog lös opöfwer mig, som sprider en hop
gnistor af wacker eld: kiärlek til det höga. kanske. (63)
[May?] 11–13 (sic)
It seemed to me that I was with Oelreich and two women; he laid
[sic] down; and afterwards it seemed he had been with a woman. He
admitted it. It occurred to me, as I also stated, that I also had lain with
one, and my father saw it, but went past, and said not a word about it.
I walked away from Oelreich and on the way there was deep water,

but at the side there was very little. I therefore took the path at the side
and thought to myself that I ought not to go into the deep water.
It seemed that a rocket burst over me spreading a number of spar-
kles of lovely fire. Love for what is high, perhaps. (90)

But if this scene represents the women as no more than go-betweens in an un-
acknowledged sexual transaction between men, in *The Journal of Dreams* the bor-
derline between homosexual and homosocial desire is often more ambiguous.

40. See Darnton, *Mesmerism and the End of the Enlightenment in France,*
especially chapters 2, 3, and 4 (47–125).

41. See especially "Politics and Patricide in Freud's *Interpretation of Dreams,*"
in *Fin-de-Siècle Vienna,* 181–207.

42. Variations on "represent" or "representation" occur 19 times in the Swedish text, on pages 5, 8, 20, 25 (twice), 26, 30 (twice), 37, 38 (twice), 42, 43, 44, 48,
54 (twice), 55, 62.

43. For Pitkin, the distinction between the two German words, *vertreten* and
darstellen serves as a point of departure for a discussion of "representation" that
takes into account its relationship to human activity:

> If we attempt to penetrate beyond the formalities of representation
> to its substantive content, two directions of inquiry are open to us. We
> may ask what a representative does, what constitutes the activity of repre-
> senting. Or we may ask what a representative is, what he must be like in
> order to represent. The distinction may be expressed by contrasting the
> two German words, *vertreten*, to act for another, and *darstellen*, to stand
> for another. These two further senses of, or questions about, representa-
> tion are often intertwined, but their implications and consequences are
> very different; so they are best considered separately. (59)

Her words, which lead into a complex discussion of the nuances of "representation"
and its cognates, point beyond my discussion of Swedenborg here, but they suggest
the importance of looking beyond textual sources in understanding Swedenborg's
use of the term "represent." Its appearances in the journal of 1743–44 suggest that,
for Swedenborg, "representation" was intimately bound up with his everyday life
and his attempts to span very different worlds.

44.   5. kom vti en magnifique kammare, och talte med en fruentim*m*er,
som war hoffmesterinna; hon wille beretta mig något, då kom drott-
ningen in och gick derigenom i en anna*n* kam*m*are, tychte warit den
sam*m*a som repraesenterade wår successor, jag gick vt, ty jag war ganska gement klädd . . . (5)

45. Sedan i andanom fant jag, at det som går ifrån sielfwa centro, som är amor, är den helge ande, som repraesenteras igenom watn, ty det nemdes och aqva eller unda. (20–21)

46.   Om morgonen då jag waknade kom åter på mig en sådan swimning eller deliqvium, som jag hade för 6 eller 7 åhr sedan i Amsterdam, då jag begynte oecon:[omiam] Regni anim:[alis] men mycket subtilare, så at jag syntes wara när döden, kom enär jag såg liuset, kastade mig på mitt ansichte, gick doch småningom öfwer, emedan små sömner betogo mig, så at detta deliqvium var inre och diupare, men strax gick öfwer, *betyder som då at mitt hufwud städas och renssas werkeligen ifrån det, som hindra skola dessa tanckar, som ock förra gången skedde, emedan det gaf mig penetration, helst vti pennan,* som ock nu repraesenterades mig at jag syntes skrifwa en fijn styl. (62)

47.   Sades *Nicolaiter,* och *Nicolaus nicolai,* om det betyder mitt nya namn wet jag intet; det merckwerdigaste war det, at jag nu *repraesenterade* den inre menniskian, och som en annan än mig sjelf, som at jag helsade på mine tanckar, skremde dem, mine res memoriae, anklagade en annan, så at nu är wändt, at jag repraesenterar en som är emot en annan, eller inre menniskian, ty jag har bedt Gud, at jag intet motte wara min, vtan at Gud techtes låta mig blifwa sin. (30)

48.   The Latin title was *De coelo et ejus mirabilibus, et de inferno ex auditis et visis.*

49.   For recent discussions of the evolution of ideas of the afterlife in relation to earthly political beliefs, see Le Goff, *The Birth of Purgatory;* and McDannell and Lang, *Heaven: A History.*

50.   On Swedenborg's reception in the work of William Blake, see Paley, "A New Heaven is Begun." See also Blake's marginalia in his editions of *Heaven and Hell, Divine Love and Divine Wisdom,* and *Divine Providence,* in *The Poetry and Prose of William Blake,* 590–600. Blake's comments, at the beginning of the marginalia to *Divine Love and Divine Wisdom* undercut the emphasis on quiet contemplation in Swedenborg's work, for Blake argues that evil and suffering are intrinsic to human activity and knowing. (591)

51.   See Jean Starobinski, *Jean-Jacques Rousseau: la transparence et l'obstacle;* and Judith Shklar, *Men and Citizens.*

52.   On the early reception of Swedenborg in England and France, see Clarke Garrett, *Respectable Folly* and "Swedenborg and the Mystical Enlightenment in Late Eighteenth-Century England"; and Morton D. Paley, "A New Heaven is Begun."

53.   On the worldwide diffusion of Swedenborgianism, see Inge Jonsson and Olle Hjern, *Swedenborg.*

54. On the relation of Kant's satire on Swedenborg to his own intellectual development, see Ernst Cassirer, *Kant's Life and Thought*, 77–86.

55. An invaluable source is the collection of works by Mesmer published in *Le magnétisme animal*. For an overview of Mesmer's career, see Goldsmith; Darnton's *Mesmerism* provides information about the therapeutic practices of Mesmer and his followers.

56. On Rousseau's inquiry into the origin of languages, see especially Starobinski's *Présentation* to his edition of Rousseau's *Essai sur l'origine des langues*.

Chapter Three

1. Viatte's *Victor Hugo et les illuminés de son temps* is both the last and the most humorous of his surveys of late-eighteenth- and early-nineteenth-century occultism in French culture.

2. Sjödén gives no little information concerning Moët's life, and I have been unable to locate any other sources.

3. On the subject of Bernard and his circle, see Viatte, "Les Swedenborgiens en France de 1820 à 1830," and Sjödén, 74–83.

4. The recent studies of Margaret Jacob and Mary Ann Clawson have emphasized the role of masonic rituals in constructing small, often proto-democratic, communities that were limited in scope and inclusiveness. The relation of these rituals to contemporary fiction is emphasized in Scott Abbott's study of masonic imagery and themes in German-language novels from the eighteenth through the twentieth centuries.

5. See Beswick, especially 17–18.

6. On the history of Mesmerism, see Margaret Goldsmith's underrated biography. See also the early partisan history by Deleuze.

7. Interest in Mesmerism and Swedenborgianism was widespread in Swedish court circles in the 1780s. On this milieu and the development of the Stockholm Exegetical and Philanthropic Society, see Johannisson. On the exchange with the Strasbourg Société des amis réunis, see Sjödén, 44–55.

8. Commentators cannot even agree on the spelling of this individual's name. Of the author of the *Abrégé*, Sjödén writes:

> Cet *Abrégé* aurait été préparé par Daillant Delatouche, admirateur nancéen de Swedenborg, qui devait par la suite s'engager dans le spiritisme, s'il faut en croire les sources swedenborgiennes. Nous ne savons pas grand'chose sur lui, sinon qu'il était membre correspondant de la

Société Exégétique et Philanthropique, comme Pernety, le Marquis de Thomé, le traducteur Moët et le magnétiseur Montravel. (51)

9. On this milieu, see Garrett and Paley.

10. See F. Piet, *Mémoires sur la vie et les ouvrages d'Edouard Richer.*

11. On Rousseau's understanding of the origins of language and its relation to eighteenth-century language theory, see Starobinski's introduction to his 1990 edition of the *Essai sur l'origine des langues.* Useful surveys of this field also include Fano, Land, and Stam.

12. The only account of Oegger's life and work I have found is the chapter, "Oegger and the Language of Nature," in Kenneth Walter Cameron's *Young Emerson's Transcendental Vision.* Cameron notes that Oegger "was born probably during the last decade of the eighteenth century at Bitche, not far from Metz," and that he published under a variety of names in both French and German. (295) Cameron speculates that he may have died soon after 1853, since there is no "further evidence of activity or of publication" after that date, when he published a book entitled *Cinq lettres sur une réforme générale.* (298)

13. See Burke's *Popular Culture in Early Modern Europe*; Bakhtin's most important work on "voice" in nineteenth-century literature is *Problems of Dostoevsky's Poetics.*

Chapter Four

1. See Philippe Bertault, *Balzac et la religion*; and Ernst Robert Curtius, *Balzac.* A number of more recent studies have focused on the fantastic elements of Balzac's text from the perspectives of the intellectual and aesthetic structures of the work. See especially Per Nykrog, *La pensée de Balzac dans la Comédie humaine*; and Martin Kanes, *Balzac's Comedy of Words.*

Nineteenth-century readers and writers were well aware of the fantastic elements in Balzac's works, and even, as David Bellos points out, saw him at times predominantly as a visionary writer. See David Bellos, *Balzac Criticism in France.* Until the publication of Tzvetan Todorov's *Introduction à la littérature fantastique,* twentieth-century French literary history and criticism tended to view the two tendencies in terms of an opposition in which the fantastic narratives played a clearly subordinate role, serving mainly to shore up the Catholic aspects of the novel system as a whole.

Some twentieth-century German critics, however, have insisted on the integral role of the *Etudes philosophiques* in *La comédie humaine,* seeing these early narratives in Hegelian terms as an essential moment in Balzac's representation of contemporary society. In his *Philosophy of the Novel,* for example, Georg Lukacs argued that Balzac's characters are motivated by a single demonic passion; later essays emphasized the parallels between the "spiritual" themes of some of Balzac's

CRINAN
BOATYARD
LTD.

(Incorporating Skipness Engineering)

Crinan Argyll
Scotland PA31 8SW
Tel: (01546) 830232
Fax: (01546) 830281

Dear Mr. Cloves,

Many thanks for your payment & invoice 44215
for which I enclose a receipt.

I'm also enclosing a statement for your
information, along with a copy of invoice
44053, in case it slipped the net.

Thanks once again.

Yours sincerely

Becky Park

novels and Marx's notion of a superstructure. Many of Walter Benjamin's remarks on the role of the *flâneur* in the work of Baudelaire and his contemporaries also apply to Balzac (See "On Some Motifs in Baudelaire," *Illuminations*, 155–200); and Benjamin's insights were developed by Theodor Adorno in his essay, "Balzac-Lektüre." Erich Auerbach's famous characterization of the style of *Le père Goriot* as "atmospheric realism" seems to belong to this tradition. See "In the Hôtel de la Mole," in *Mimesis*, 454–92, especially 468–82.

2. See chapter 1, note 14, on Bonald and Maistre.

3. For surveys of the literature on supernatural themes in Balzac's work, see above all the commentaries on the novels included in the section of *La comédie humaine* called *Les études philosophiques*. (vols. 10 and 11) See also Pauline Bernheim, *Balzac und Swedenborg*; Madeleine [Ambrière-]Fargeaud, *Balzac et la recherche de l'Absolu* and "Madame Balzac, son mysticisme, et ses enfants"; Jacques Borel, *Séraphîta et le mysticisme balzacien*; Henri Evans, *Louis Lambert et la philosophie de Balzac*; Pierre Laubriet, *L'intelligence de l'art chez Balzac*; and K. E. Sjödén, "Remarques sur le *swedenborgisme* balzacien."

4. See [Ambrière-]Fargeaud, "Madame Balzac, son mysticisme, et ses enfants."

5. *La comédie humaine*, 11:773. An additional work, *Oeuvres philosophiques et minérologiques*, is mentioned separately (11:767). The list of works bound is cited in [Ambrière-]Fargeaud, "Madame Balzac, son mysticisme, et ses enfants," 30.

6. Benjamin's scattered remarks on the aura are suggestive, but contradictory. The most extended attempt at definition occurs in "The Work of Art in an Age of Mechanical Reproduction," and ties the concept to one's time-bound presence in natural surroundings:

> If, while resting on a summer afternoon, you follow with your eyes a mountain range on the horizon or a branch which casts its shadow over you, you experience the aura of those mountains, of that branch. This image makes it easy to comprehend the social bases of the contemporary decay of the aura. It rests on two circumstances, both of which are related to the increasing significance of the masses in contemporary life. Namely, the desire of contemporary masses to bring things "closer" spatially and humanly, which is just as ardent as their bent toward overcoming the uniqueness of every reality by accepting its reproduction. Every day the urge grows stronger to get hold of an object at very close range by way of its likeness, its reproduction. (*Illuminations*, 222–23)

But if, for Benjamin, reproductions most often destroy the distance necessary for the perception of an object's "aura," they also seem to evoke a kind of echo or aura of the sacred distance that the critic sees as constituting an experience that is fundamentally opposed to mass produced or reproduced objects.

7. Wellek argues that religiosity and a penchant for symbolism are common features of European romantic literature. Thus, Balzac's "Swedenborgianism" allows the critic to situate his work—albeit obliquely—in this context.

8. In the passage in question, Faust not only goes to extraordinary lengths to avoid a direct answer, but also suggests a kind of alternative to conventional Christianity:

MARGARETE. . . .
    Glaubst du an Gott?
FAUST.   Mein Liebchen, wer darf sagen:
    Ich glaub' an Gott?
    Magst Priester oder Weise fragen,
    Und ihr Antwort scheint nur Spott
    Über den Frager zu sein.
MARGARETE.   So glaubst du nicht?
FAUST. Mißhör mich nicht, du holdes Angesicht!
    Wer darf ihn nennen?
    Und wer bekennen:
    Ich glaub' ihn.
    Wer empfinden,
    Und sich unterwinden
    Zu sagen: ich glaub' ihn nicht?
    Der Allumfasser,
    Der Allerhalter,
    Faßt und erhält er nicht
    Dich, mich, sich selbst?
    Wölbt sich der Himmel nicht dadroben?
    Liegt die Erde nicht hierunten fest?
    Und steigen freundlich blickend
    Ewige Sterne nicht herauf?
    Schau' ich nicht Aug' in Auge dir,
    Und drängt nicht alles
    Nach Haupt und Herzen dir,
    Und webt in ewigem Geheimnis
    Unsichtbar sichtbar neben dir?
    Erfüll davon dein Herz, so groß es ist,
    Und wenn du ganz in dem Gefühle selig bist,
    Nenn es dann, wie du willst,
    Nenn's Glück! Herz! Liebe! Gott!
    Ich habe keinen Namen
    Dafür! Gefühl ist alles;
    Name ist Schall und Rauch,
    Umnebelnd Himmelsglut.
MARGARETE: Das ist alles recht schön und gut;
    Ungefähr sagt das der Pfarrer auch,

Nur mit ein bißchen andern Worten. (*Faust*, 3426–61; Trunz,
109–10)

————

MARGARETE. . . .
   Do you believe in God?
FAUST.   My dear one, who may say:
   I believe in God?
   Ask all your sages, clerical or lay,
   And their reply appears but sport
   Made of the questioner.
MARGARETE.   So you don't believe?
FAUST. Do not mishear me, dear my heart,
   For who may name Him
   And go proclaiming:
   Yes, I believe in him?
   Who search his heart
   And dare say for his part:
   No, I believe him not?
   The all-comprising,
   The all-sustaining,
   Does he comprise, sustain not
   You, me, himself?
   Are not the vaulted heavens hung on high?
   Is earth not anchored here below?
   And do with kindly gaze
   Eternal stars not rise aloft?
   Join I not eye to eye with thee,
   Does all not surge
   Into thy head and heart,
   And in perpetual mystery
   Unseenly visible weave beside thee?
   Till full your heart, all it will hold, with this,
   And when you're all suffused and lost in bliss,
   Then call it what you will,
   Call it fulfillment! Heart! Love! God!
   I have no name for it!
   Feeling is all;
   Name is but sound and fume
   Befogging heaven's blaze.
MARGARETE. All well and good; the turn of phrase
   Is something different, but I presume
   What the parson says means much the same. (*Faust*, 3424–61;
Arndt and Hamlin, 84–85)

9. See *La comédie humaine* 8:1668, esp. n. 1.

10. On the history of the text, see the commentary to *Louis Lambert* in the Pléiade edition (11:1470–92). See also Marcel Bouteron and Jean Pommier's edition of the novel.

11. The *Oxford Latin Dictionary* gives thirteen meanings for *species*, including those that emphasize sight and spectacle (1–4), mere appearances (5–7), artistic representations or figures (8), appearances of the supernatural (9), a class or species (10), the designation of a legal situation or property (11–12), or a Platonic archetype or essence (13). Balzac's *Spécialité* also draws together notions of knowledge as based on a particular kind of penetrating vision capable of seizing essences and the taxonomic sense of species fundamental to natural history.

A passage from M. M. Slaughter's fine study, *Universal Languages and Scientific Taxonomy in the Seventeenth Century*, suggests both Balzac's debt to taxonomy and universal language theory and the implications of the term *species* for science and the novel. For Slaughter, the word allowed writers to endow the natural world with a comforting sense of familiarity, to impose the structures of the contemporary family on natural phenomena. It was, she argues, a dream, and a narcissistic one at that:

> All dreams contain selected images, and this one was no exception. It took as its image the natural, biological, genealogical order. It is not insignificant that taxonomic concepts and constructs take as their point of departure the most primitive and basic form of order that we have, the order of the family. The word *genus* comes from a word originally related to the family, "what something derives from"; *species* is related to a verb meaning "to see" or "spy out." The genealogical order is something given by the mysterious processes of procreation, of life; it is something confirmed by what we see around us in our first most familiar, familial world. Through the genus we are given our reality, our essence, our nature. Through the external, visible features of mother's eyes and father's chin, (genetic) nature is known and confirmed. The genealogical family is our first (and perhaps our last) intimation of connection, relation and order.
> The epistemic structure of taxonomy built upon this image is a tie that binds man to nature. In that bond lie comfort, protection and reassurance. The language which was built upon that episteme was the means by which men tried to subjugate nature to the cozy, known confines of the family circle. As men know their natures by virtue of their genealogy, who they are really and certainly, and as they state it by virtue of their names; so by language created on a genealogical, taxonomic model could they know, name, and state the reality of nature, of the world literally beyond them. It was a happy dream, which, like all dreams had finally to come to an end. (185–86)

12. The brief exchange between two characters in *Ursule Mirouët* points to the economic overtones of Mesmerist and Swedenborgian themes:

"Croyez-vous aux revenants? dit Zélie au curé.
"Croyez-vous aux revenus? répondit le prêtre en souriant. (3:976)

But the economic implications of supernatural themes had been emphasized as early as *La peau de chagrin*, in which the magic skin can provide its owner with the fulfillment of a very limited number of wishes, shrinking with every satisfied desire. Both *Louis Lambert* and *Séraphîta*, moreover, emphasize the dangers of unlimited desires.

This aspect of the *Etudes philosophiques* has been most suggestively explored by the Marxist critic, Georg Lukacs, and other German critics who have followed the general tendency of his interpretations, such as Walter Benjamin, Theodor Adorno, and, in a very general sense, Erich Auerbach in his essay on Balzac in "In the Hôtel de la Mole," in *Mimesis*, 454–92.

13. This early preface, "Introduction par Félix Davin aux 'Etudes de moeurs au XIXe siècle,'" was probably inspired, if not written, by Balzac himself. See the "Introduction," in *La comédie humaine* 1:1145–72, and Anne-Marie Meininger's *Présentation*, 1:1143–44.

14. See Piet's biography of Richer and chapter 3 above.

15. In his introduction to *Séraphîta* in the Pléiade edition of *La comédie humaine*, Henri Gautier argues: "Si la vie de Swedenborg racontée par le pasteur Becker ne pose pas beaucoup de questions, la source en étant le 'Discours préliminaire" de l'*Abrégé des ouvrages d'Em. Swedenborg* par Daillant de la Touche, le résumé de sa doctrine est depuis longtemps contesté par les spécialistes." (11:703) But if, as Pauline Bernheim argues, in *Balzac und Swedenborg*, the wording of Balzac's narrative follows the *Abrégé* closely, it is by no means certain that this is his only or major source.

See also Sandel, "Eulogium"; and "Remarques de M. de Thomé," in Benedict Chastanier, *Tableau analytique et raisonné de la doctrine céleste*, 244–52; and Benedict Chastanier, *Tableau analytique et raisonné de la doctrine céleste*.

16. See Balzac, "La dissertation sur l'homme."

17. Possible sources for Balzac's interpretation include: Jacques Matter's *Histoire critique du gnosticisme* (1828); Goethe's work on natural history; and Madame de Staël's expositions of German *Naturphilosophie* and religious thought. The reference to Mme de Staël at the beginning of *Louis Lambert* suggests that she did play an important role in "translating" aspects of German culture for Balzac and other French writers in the early nineteenth century. See her *De l'Allemagne*. The correspondence between Mme Hanska and Balzac, moreover, points to the awareness of both letter writers of the parallels between Balzac's narratives of the early 1830s and German Romantic literature and philosophy.

18. One of the aspects of Swedenborg's doctrines which the afterworld found especially interesting was the notion that angels possess sexual organs and engage in sexual relations in heaven. His *Conjugial Love* or *Delitiae Sapientiae de Amore*

Conjugiali; post quas sequuntur voluptates insaniae de Amore Scortatorio was one
of the more popular titles. The work, however, focuses on the details of marriage in
heaven, a state which parallels the institution on earth.

19. See Per Nykrog, *La pensée de Balzac dans La comédie humaine.*

20. On the genesis of the text, see the commentary to the novel in the Pléiade
edition, 10:1221–25.

21. See "On Some Motifs in Baudelaire," *Illuminations*, 155–200; and the un-
completed *Passagen-Werk.*

22. I have explored the subject of the relationship of the representation of the
occult and the daguerreotype in *Le cousin Pons* to various definitions of the word
"ideology." See Wilkinson, *"Le cousin Pons* and the Invention of Ideology."

23. For a more focused discussion of the implication of the body metaphors in
L'envers de l'histoire contemporaine, see Wilkinson, "Embodying the Crowd."

Chapter Five

1. Source studies that attempt to trace Baudelaire's aesthetics back to
Swedenborgianism, eighteenth-century esotericism and illuminism, or the mystical
tradition in general include Anne-Marie Amiot, *Baudelaire et l'illumisme*; Paul Arnold, *Esotérisme de Baudelaire*; and Marc Eigeldinger, *Le platonisme de Baudelaire.* On the virtues and pitfalls of this approach, see Lloyd James Austin, *L'univers poétique de Baudelaire*; and Anna Balakian, *The Literary Origins of
Surrealism*, chapter 3, "Baudelaire and the Break with Tradition," 45–61; and *The
Symbolist Movement*, chapter 2, "Swedenborgism and the Romanticists," 12–28,
and chapter 3, "Baudelaire," 29–53.

It was Jean Pommier's interpretation of the sonnet in *La mystique de Baudelaire* that turned the interpretation of the poem and its title away from origins to
questions of rhetoric and structure. His view that the first quatrain of the sonnet
evokes "vertical correspondences" that are subsequently undermined in the remaining quatrain and sestet, which sketch out "horizontal correspondences," has
served as the point of departure for many subsequent interpretations of the poem.

Walter Benjamin's famous comments on Baudelaire's *correspondances* seem
quite independent of the French interpretations of the poem. Taking another sonnet, "A une passante," as his point of departure, Benjamin argues that Baudelaire's
correspondances represent a response to the jarring and fragmentary experience of
the city streets and crowds, an attempt to evoke a unified and harmonious experience that might be remembered as part of one's childhood. See Marshall Berman's
All That Is Solid Melts into Air, especially chapter 3, "Baudelaire: Modernism in the
Streets," 131–71, and T. J. Clark, *The Absolute Bourgeois*, especially chapter 5,
"Delacroix and Baudelaire," 124–77, for suggestive explorations of Benjamin's often

cryptic comments on the relationship of aesthetic structures to the transformation of the city in the nineteenth and twentieth centuries.

2. Bourdieu's arguments that modernism is often elitist and conservative often seem targeted against later artists and writers, but many of his criticisms might be applied to those of Baudelaire and his generation.

3. See chapter 1 of *Image of the People*, "On the Social History of Art," 9–20. In his preface to the new editions of this and its companion volume, *The Absolute Bourgeois*, Clark reflects on his intentions in writing about artists in 1848 and the years immediately following:

> They [these studies] wished to establish what happened to art when it became involved, however tangentially, in a process of revolution and counter-revolution: in other words, when it lost its normal place in the machinery of social control and was obliged for a while to seek out other spaces for representation—other publics, other subjects, other idioms, other means of production. As my Jamesian title was meant to imply, one could hardly have expected the story, in an order already irredeemably capitalist, to be other than one of failure to find such space. (*Image of the People*, 6; *The Absolute Bourgeois*, 6)

4. On the history of this text, see Baudelaire, *Oeuvres complètes* 1:1413–17.

5. On the history of this text, see Baudelaire, *Oeuvres complètes* 1:1358–68.

6. On the widespread association of wine and revolutionary crowds, see Susanna Barrows, *Distorting Mirrors*, especially chapter 2, "Metaphors of Fear: Women and Alcoholics," 43–72.

7. On the history of this text, see Baudelaire, *Oeuvres complètes* 2:1138–41.

8. Both Martin Lamm and Inge Jonsson emphasize Swedenborg's debts to other sources, rather than to the literature of the cabala. In his overview of Swedenborg's life and work, *Emanuel Swedenborg*, Jonsson comments:

> How familiar Swedenborg was with the rabbinic tradition and the Cabala is uncertain, but one can find numerous examples of an extremely negative attitude on his part: almost concurrently with the explication of Genesis 28:14 he anathematized all philosophy (with the exception of his own works!) in *Diarium spirituale*, and included in philosophy "fables and silly stories, especially such as have formerly and do still distinguish the Rabbinical writers, which are innumerable." Statements of this nature should make us extremely cautious about attributing any influence on Swedenborg by the Cabala, for example, which has not seldom been done. (168)

One might, however, view the question of "influence" considerably more broadly. In his study of the origins and evolution of Swedenborg's doctrine of correspondences,

Swedenborgs korrespondenslära, Jonsson emphasizes the importance of Leibniz for Swedenborg's theory of language.

9. Noted in Robert T. Cargo's concordance to *Les petits poèmes en prose.*

10. Benjamin's most famous remarks on Baudelaire and the role of *correspondances* in his work occur in a rich, complex, and contradictory essay entitled "On Some Motifs in Baudelaire," where the German critic comments:

> Disregarding the scholarly literature on the *correspondances* (the common property of the mystics; Baudelaire encountered them in Fourier's writings), Proust no longer fusses about the artistic variations on the situation which are supplied by synaesthesia. The important thing is that the *correspondances* record a concept of experience which includes ritual elements. Only by appropriating these elements was Baudelaire able to fathom the full meaning of the breakdown which he, a modern man, was witnessing. Only in this way was he able to recognize in it the challenge meant for him alone, a challenge which he incorporated in the *Fleurs du mal.* If there really is a secret architecture in the book—and many speculations have been devoted to it—the cycle of poems that opens the volume probably is devoted to something irretrievably lost. (*Illuminations,* 181)

Benjamin cites the sonnet "Correspondances" and goes on to note:

> What Baudelaire meant by *correspondances* may be described as an experience which seeks to establish itself in crisis-proof form. This is possible only within the realm of the ritual. If it transcends this realm, it presents itself as the beautiful. In the beautiful the ritual value of art appears. (*Illuminations,* 182)

But the essay as a whole emphasizes that both the word and the concept of "crisis-proof experience" it may evoke are inseparable from the jarring world of the city and its crowd and the technology of mechanical reproduction that both disseminated Baudelaire's poetry and influenced his readers' perceptions of the world and its texts.

11. Baudelaire, *Oeuvres complètes* 1:841–42. See also Robert T. Cargo's concordance to *Les petits poèmes en prose,* which, as noted above, also records the use of *correspondant* in the prose poem, "Le chien et le flacon."

12. Johnson notes that commentators have often disapproved of the way in which the prose poem appears to "translate" the vague references in the verse poem to an otherworldly voyage into the details of a trip as it might be undertaken—or sold—in the nineteenth century. She comments:

What the sonnet *Correspondances* calls the "transports of spirit and sense" are here literalized, making the metaphorical voyage (etymologically, *metaphor* literally means "transport") into a business trip. The prose poem thus reveals that "poeticity" has its own economy, that the equating of signifier with signified, of the lady with the land, functions in the same way as the equating of wage with labor, or of product with price. (35)

For Johnson, however, neither text is primary or definitive; in her deconstructive reading, meaning circulates between the two, necessarily incomplete and unsatisfactory, versions. Furthermore, the notion of *correspondances* plays an important role in conjuring up the idea of an impossible totality:

> Baudelaire, however, refers to the notion of correspondences not only so as "to speak like the mystics" but also so as to speak like—and comment on—another Baudelaire, the Baudelaire who wrote a sonnet called *Correspondances*. In that sonnet, the word *comme* (like)—used seven times in fourteen lines—acts as a kind of "Archimedes' fulcrum" to lift up the "ténébreuse et profonde unité" ("deep, dark unity") of the world. . . . This ironic proliferation of likenesses does not render comparison impossible, but it does put in question the validity of taking comparison as a sign of the ultimate unity of the world. (33)

13. Recent deconstructive readings have emphasized the element of oscillation in Baudelaire's work, arguing that all of his texts necessarily and ambiguously deflect the reader's quest for meaning onto other texts. In a masterful reading of "Correspondances," for example, Jonathan Culler writes concerning the poem's second quatrain:

> Baudelaire's scenario in this quatrain presents two activities: living pillars "laissent parfois de confuses paroles" and forests of symbols observe man with "des regards familiers." What is striking, in the intertextual context, is how each of these two formulations and the combination of the two transform the clarity of individual sources into an indeterminate rhetoricity. Some precursors declare that all nature speaks; others have it silently signify; but Baudelaire first raises doubts about whether nature engages in wilful speech or whether something like confused words simply emerge, as pillars *"laissent* parfois *sortir"*; Baudelaire then presents symbols that instead of signifying, being read, or bearing meaning, as the sources would lead one to expect, *observe* the passer-by. They do not even fix one with an "oeil lumineux" as in Hugo, so as to make it clear that one should attend to them. Rather they install the passer-by with the familiar modern condition of seeing people in crowds whom one does not exactly recognize but who look at one in a way that seems to betoken familiarity, leading one to wonder: Do I know them? Do they know me? (123)

For another, earlier, reading of intertextual oscillations in Baudelaire's texts, see Barbara Johnson, "Poetry and Its Double: Two *Invitations au voyage*."

Absent in these deconstructive readings is a discussion of the possible political or social implications of the linguistic movements they describe. The readings of Walter Benjamin, which tie *correspondances* to the evocation of utopia, might serve as a supplement to deconstructive interpretations.

Conclusion

1. The date is incorrect; Swedenborg has 1757.

Works Cited

Aarsleff, Hans. *The Study of Language in England, 1780–1860.* 1967. Minneapolis: Univ. of Minnesota Press, 1983.

Aarsleff, Hans. *From Locke to Saussure: Essays on the Study of Language and Intellectual History.* Minneapolis: Univ. of Minnesota Press, 1982.

Abbott, Scott. *Fictions of Freemasonry: Freemasonry and the German Novel.* Detroit: Wayne State Univ. Press, 1991.

Abrams, M. H. *The Mirror and the Lamp: Romantic Theory and the Critical Tradition.* New York: Oxford Univ. Press, 1953.

Abrams, M. H. *Natural Supernaturalism: Tradition and Revolution in Romantic Literature.* New York: Norton, 1971.

Adorno, Theodor. "Balzac Lektüre." *Noten zur Literatur.* suhrkamp taschenbuch wissenschaft 355. Frankfurt am Main: Suhrkamp, 1981. 139–57.

Agulhon, Maurice. *1848, ou, L'apprentissage de la République, 1848–1852.* 2nd edition. Paris: Seuil, 1992.

Agulhon, Maurice. *The Republican Experiment, 1848–1852.* Trans. of *1848, ou, L'apprentissage de la république, 1848–1852.* Trans. Janet Lloyd. Vol. 2 of *The Cambridge History of Modern France.* Cambridge and New York: Cambridge Univ. Press, 1983.

Albouy, P. *La création mythologique chez Hugo.* Paris: Corti, 1963.

Allen, James Smith. *Popular French Romanticism: Authors, Readers, and Books in the Nineteenth Century.* Syracuse: Syracuse University Press, 1981.

Alpers, Svetlana. *The Art of Describing: Dutch Art in the Seventeenth Century.* Chicago: Univ. of Chicago Press, 1983.

[Ambrière-]Fargeaud, Madeleine. "Madame Balzac, son mysticisme, et ses enfants." *L'Année balzacienne* (1965): 3–33.

[Ambrière-]Fargeaud, Madeleine. *Balzac et la recherche de l'Absolu.* Paris: Hachette, 1968.

301

Amiot, Anne-Marie. *Baudelaire et l'illuminisme*. Paris: Nizet, 1982.

Andersson, Ingvar. *Martin Lamm*. Stockholm: Norstedt, 1950.

Arndt, Walter, trans. *Faust: A Tragedy*. By Johann Wolfgang von Goethe. Ed. Cyrus Hamlin. New York: Norton, 1976.

Arnold, Paul. *Esotérisme de Baudelaire*. Paris: Vrin, 1972.

Auerbach, Erich. *Mimesis: The Representation of Reality in Western Literature*. Trans. Willard R. Trask. Princeton, N.J.: Princeton Univ. Press, 1968.

Austin, Lloyd James. *L'univers poétique de Baudelaire: Symbolisme et Symbolique*. Paris: Mercure de France, 1956.

Austin, Paul Britten. *The Life and Songs of Carl Michael Bellman: Genius of the Swedish Rococo*. Malmö: Allhem, 1967.

Baillet, Adrien. *La vie de monsieur Descartes*. 2 vols. New York and London: Garland Press, 1987.

Bakhtin, Mikhail. *Problems of Dostoevsky's Poetics*. Ed. and trans. Caryl Emerson. Intro. Wayne C. Booth. Minneapolis: Univ. of Minnesota Press, 1984.

Bakhtin, Mikhail. *Rabelais and His World*. Trans. Helene Iswolsky. Cambridge, Mass.: MIT Press, 1968.

Balakian, Anna. *Literary Origins of Surrealism: A New Mysticism in French Poetry*. New York: New York Univ. Press, 1947.

Balakian, Anna. *Surrealism: The Road to the Absolute*. New York: Noonday Press, 1959.

Balakian, Anna. *The Symbolist Movement: A Critical Appraisal*. New York: New York Univ. Press, 1977.

Balzac, Honoré de. *La comédie humaine*. Ed. Pierre-Georges Castex et al. 12 vols. Editions de la Pléiade. Paris: Gallimard, 1975–81.

Balzac, Honoré de. *Louis Lambert*. Ed. Marcel Bouteron and Jean Pommier. Paris: Corti, 1954.

Balzac, Honoré de. "Lettre à Charles Nodier sur son article intitulé: 'De la Palingénésie humaine et de la résurrection." In *Oeuvres diverses* II. Vol. 39 of Balzac, *Oeuvres complètes*. Ed. Marcel Bouteron and Henri Lognon. Paris: Conard, 1940.

Balzac, Honoré de. *Lettres à Madame Hanska*. Ed. Roger Pierrot. 4 vols. Paris: Bibliophiles de l'originale, 1967.

Barbey d'Aurévilly, Jules. *"Les fleurs du mal* par M. Charles Baudelaire." Charles Baudelaire. *Oeuvres complètes*. Ed. Claude Pichois. 2 vols. Editions de la Pléiade. Paris: Gallimard, 1975–76. 1:1191–96.

Bardèche, Maurice. *Balzac romancier*. Paris: Plon, 1940.

Bardèche, Maurice. *Balzac*. Paris: Julliard, 1980.

Barnard, F. M. *Herder's Social and Political Thought*. Oxford: Clarendon Press, 1965.

Barrows, Susanna. *Distorting Mirrors: Visions of the Crowd in Late Nineteenth-Century France*. New Haven: Yale Univ. Press, 1981.

Barruel, Abbé Augustin. *Mémoires pour servir à l'histoire du jacobinisme*. 5 vols. Hamburg: P. Fauche, 1789–1799.

Baudelaire, Charles. *Oeuvres complètes*. Ed. Claude Pichois. 2 vols. Editions de la Pléiade. Paris: Gallimard, 1975–76.

Baudelaire, Charles. *Correspondance*. Ed. Claude Pichois and Jean Ziegler. 2 vols. Editions de la Pléiade. Paris: Gallimard, 1973.

Bec, Annie. "Les traditions ésotériques en France de la Révolution à la Restauration." *Manuel d'histoire littéraire de la France*. Editions sociales, 1972. 4: 275–301.

Béguin, Albert. *Balzac visionnaire*. Genève: A. Skira, 1946.

Béguin, Albert. *L'âme romantique et le rêve: Essai sur le romantisme allemand et la poésie française*. Paris: Corti, 1946.

Bellos, David. *Balzac Criticism in France: The Making of a Reputation*. Oxford: Clarendon Press, 1976.

Bénichou, Paul. *Le sacre de l'écrivain, 1750–1830*. Paris: Corti, 1973.

Benjamin, Walter. *Illuminations*. Ed. Hannah Arendt. Trans. Harry Zohn. New York: Schocken, 1970.

Benjamin, Walter. *Charles Baudelaire: A Lyric Poet in the Age of High Capitalism*. Trans. Harry Zohn. London: NLB, 1973.

Benjamin, Walter. *Der Begriff der Kunstkritik in der deutschen Romantik. Gesammelte Schriften* 1:1:7–122.

Benjamin, Walter. *Charles Baudelaire: Ein Lyriker im Zeitalter des Hochkapitalismus. Gesammelte Schriften* 1:2:509–690.

Benjamin, Walter. *Das Passagen-Werk*. Vol. 5 of *Gesammelte Schriften*. Ed. Rolf Tiedemann. Frankfurt am Main: Suhrkamp, 1982.

Benz, Ernst. *Swedenborg in Deutschland. F. C. Oetingers und Immanuel Kants Auseinandersetzung mit der Person und Lehre Emanuel Swedenborg*. Frankfurt am Main: V. Klostermann, 1947.

Bergquist, Lars. *Swedenborgs drömbok: glädjen och det stora kvalet*. Stockholm: Norstedt, 1988.

Berman, Marshall. *All That Is Solid Melts into Air: The Experience of Modernity.* New York: Simon and Schuster, 1982.

Bernheim, Pauline. *Balzac und Swedenborg. Einfluss der Mystik Swedenborgs und Saint-Martins auf die Romandichtung Balzacs.* Romanische Studien 16. Berlin: Emil Ebering, 1916.

Bernheimer, Charles. Introduction. *In Dora's Case: Freud–Hysteria–Feminism.* 2nd edition. New York: Columbia Univ. Press, 1990. 1–18.

Bernheimer, Charles and Claire Kahane, ed. *In Dora's Case: Freud–Hysteria–Feminism.* 2nd edition. New York: Columbia Univ. Press, 1990.

Bertault, Philippe. *Balzac et la religion.* Paris: Boivin,, 1942.

Beswick, Samuel. *Swedenborg Rite and the Great Masonic Leaders of the Eighteenth Century.* New York: Masonic Publishing, 1870.

Bloch, R. Howard. *God's Plagiarist: Being an Account of the Fabulous Industry and Irregular Commerce of the abbé Migne.* Chicago: Univ. of Chicago Press, 1994.

Borel, Jacques. *Séraphîta et le mysticisme balzacien.* Paris: J. Corti, 1967.

Borst, A. *Der Turmbau von Babel.* Stuttgart, 1957–63.

Bourdieu, Pierre. *Distinction: A Social Critique of the Judgement of Taste.* Trans. Richard Nice. Cambridge: Harvard Univ. Press, 1984.

Bowman, Frank Paul. Préface. *Eliphas Lévi, visionnaire romantique.* Paris: Presses universitaires de France, 1969. 5–61.

Bowman, Frank Paul. "Occultism and the Language of Poetry." *New York Literary Forum* 4 (1980): 51–64.

Bowman, Frank Paul. "Illuminism, Utopia, Mythology." Chapter 3 of *The French Romantics.* Ed. D. G. Charlton. 2 vols. Cambridge: Cambridge Univ. Press, 1984. 1:76–112.

Brémond, Henri. *Histoire du sentiment religieux en France depuis la fin des guerres de religion jusqu'à nos jours.* 12 vols. Paris: Blond et Gay, 1929–38.

Buisset, Christiane. *Eliphas Lévi: sa vie, son oeuvre, ses pensées.* Paris: G. Trédaniel, 1984.

Burke, Peter. *Popular Culture in Early Modern Europe.* New York: New York Univ. Press, 1978.

Bush, George. *Mesmer and Swedenborg; or, The Relation of the Developments of Mesmerism to the Doctrines and Disclosures of Swedenborg.* New York: John Allen, 1847.

Busst, A. J. L. "The Image of the Androgyne in the Nineteenth Century." Ed. Ian Fletcher. *Romantic Mythologies*. London: Routledge and Kegan Paul, 1967.

Cahagnet, Louis Alphonse. *Magnétisme: Arcanes de la vie future dévoilés, où l'existence, la forme, les occupations de l'âme après la séparation du corps sont prouvées par plusieurs années d'expériences au moyen de huit somnambules extatiques qui ont eu quatre-vingts perceptions de trente-six personnes de diverses conditions décédées à différentes époques, leur signalement, conversations, renseignements, preuves irrécusables de leur existence au monde spirituel*. Paris: Chez l'auteur, 1848.

Cahagnet, Louis Alphonse. *Abrégé des Merveilles du ciel et de l'enfer d'Emmanuel Swedenborg avec annotations et observations*. Paris: Germer-Baillière, 1854.

Calhoun, Craig, ed. *Habermas and the Public Sphere*. Cambridge, Mass.: MIT Press, 1992.

Cameron, Kenneth Walter. "Oegger and the Language of Nature." *Young Emerson's Transcendental Vision: An Exposition of his World View with an Analysis of the Structure, Backgrounds, and Meaning of Nature*. Hartford: Transcendental Books, 1971. 295–302.

Cargo, Robert T. *Concordance to Baudelaire's* Les fleurs du mal. Chapel Hill: Univ. of North Carolina Press, 1965.

Cargo, Robert T. *Concordance to Baudelaire's* Petits poèmes en prose. University, Alabama: Univ. of Alabama Press, 1971.

Cassirer, Ernst. *Kant's Life and Thought*. Trans. James Haden. Yale Univ. Press, 1981.

Certeau, Michel de. *La Fable mystique, xvie-xviie siècle*. Paris: Gallimard, 1982.

Chacornac, Paul. *Eliphas Lévi: Rénovateur de l'occultisme en France (1810– 1875)*. Paris: Chacornac Frères, 1926.

Chambefort, Edouard. *Essai sur Swedenborg et ses idées eschatologiques*. Strasbourg: G. Silbermann, 1859.

Chambers, Ross. *Spirite de Théophile Gautier: une lecture*. Archives des lettres modernes, 153. Paris: Minard, 1974.

Chambers, Ross. *Mélancolie et opposition: Les débuts du modernisme en France*. Paris: Corti, 1987.

Chanut, Hector-Pierre. *Inventaire succinct des escrits qui se sont trouvez dans les coffres de Mons. Descartes après son décedz à Stockholm en Feb. 1650*. René Descartes. *Oeuvres de Descartes*. Ed. Charles Adam. 13 vols. Paris: J. Vrin and Le Cerf (vols. 10 and 11), 1908–57. 10:5–12.

Charlton, Donald Geoffrey. *Secular Religions in France, 1815–1870*. London: Oxford Univ. Press, 1963.

Charlton, Donald Geoffrey. "Religious and Political Thought." Chapter 2 of *The French Romantics*. Ed. D. G. Charlton. 2 vols. Cambridge: Cambridge Univ. Press, 1984. 1:53–75.

Chartier, Roger. *The Cultural Origins of the French Revolution*. Tr. Lydia G. Cochrane. Durham: Duke Univ. Press, 1991.

Chastanier, Bénédict. *Tableau analytique et raisonné de la doctrine céleste de l'Eglise de la Nouvelle Jérusalem; ou Précis des oeuvres théologiques d'Emanuel de Swedenborg*. London: The Author, 1786.

Chateaubriand, René de. *Mémoires d'outre-tombe*. Ed. Pierre Clarac. 3 vols. Paris: Livre de poche, 1973.

Clark, T. J. *Image of the People: Gustave Courbet and the 1848 Revolution*. London, 1973. Princeton: Princeton Univ. Press, 1982.

Clark, T. J. *The Absolute Bourgeois: Artists and Politics in France, 1848–1851*. London, 1973. Princeton: Princeton Univ. Press, 1982.

Clawson, Mary Ann. *Constructing Brotherhood: Class, Gender and Fraternalism*. Princeton: Princeton Univ. Press, 1989.

Cole, John R. *The Olympian Dreams and Youthful Rebellion of René Descartes*. Urbana and Chicago: Univ. of Illinois Press, 1992.

Constant, Alphonse-Louis. "Confession de l'auteur." *L'assomption de la femme ou le livre de l'amour*. Paris: Le Gallois, 1841. iii-xxviii.

Constant, Alphonse-Louis. *Les trois harmonies: chansons et poésies*. Paris: Fellens et Dufour, 1845.

Constant, Alphonse-Louis. *Le livre des larmes, ou Le Christ consolateur: essai de conciliation entre l'Eglise catholique et la philosophie moderne*. Paris: Paulier, 1845.

Constant, Alphonse-Louis. *La dernier incarnation: légendes évangéliques du XIXe siècle*. Paris: Librairie Sociétaire, 1846.

Constant, Alphonse-Louis. *Le testament de la liberté*. 1848. Geneva: Slatkine Reprints, 1980.

Constant, Alphonse-Louis. *Dictionnaire de la littérature chrétienne*. Vol. 7 of *La nouvelle encyclopédie théologique*. Ed. J.-P. Migne. Paris: J.-P. Migne, 1851.

Constant, Alphonse-Louis. [Eliphas Lévi.] *Histoire de la magie, avec une exposition claire et précise de ses procédés, de ses rites et de ses mystères*. Paris: G. Baillière, 1860.

Constant, Alphonse-Louis. [Eliphas Lévi.] *Dogme et rituel de la haute magie*. 2nd edition. 2 vols. Paris: Baillière, 1861.

Constant, Alphonse-Louis. [Eliphas Lévi]. *La science des esprits: révélation du dogme secret des kabbalistes, esprit occulte des Evangiles, appréciation des doctrines et des phénomènes spirites.* Paris: Baillière, 1885.

Constant, Alphonse-Louis. [Eliphas Lévi.] *Les mystères de la Kabbale.* Paris: Nourry, 1920.

Constant, Alphonse-Louis. *The Mysteries of Magic: A Digest of the Writings of Eliphas Lévi.* Ed. Arthur Edward Waite. London: Redway, 1886. Secaucus, N. J.: University Books, 1974.

Culler, Jonathan. *Ferdinand de Saussure.* New York: Penguin Modern Masters, 1977.

Culler, Jonathan. "Intertextuality and Interpretation: Baudelaire's 'Correspondances.'" *Nineteenth-Century French Poetry: Introductions to Close Reading.* Ed. Christopher Prendergast. Cambridge: Cambridge Univ. Press, 1990. 118–37.

Curtius, Ernst. Robert. *Balzac.* Bonn: F. Cohen, 1923.

[Daillant de la Touche]. *Abrégé des ouvrages d'Em. Swedenborg, contenant la doctrine de la nouvelle JERUSALEM-CELESTE, précédé d'un discours où l'on examine la vie de l'auteur, le genre de ses écrits, et leur rapport au temps présent.* Stockholm and Strasbourg: Treuttel, 1788.

Darnton, Robert. *Mesmerism and the End of the Enlightenment in France.* Cambridge: Harvard Univ. Press, 1968.

Darnton, Robert. *The Literary Underground of the Old Regime.* Cambridge: Harvard Univ. Press, 1982.

David, M.-V. *Le débat sur les écritures et l'hiéroglyphe aux XVII et XVIIIe siècles.* Paris, 1965.

Deleuze, J.-P.-F. *Histoire critique du magnétisme animal.* 2 vols. Paris: Mame, 1813.

Descartes, René. *Oeuvres de Descartes.* Ed. Charles Adam. 13 vols. Paris: J. Vrin and Le Cerf (vols. 10 and 11), 1908–57.

Dijkstra, Sandra Kanter. *Flora Tristan: Pioneer Feminist and Socialist.* Berkeley: Center for Socialist History, 1984.

Dupuis, Charles-François. *Origine de tous les cultes, ou Religion universelle.* 4 vols. Paris: Agasse, an III.

Eigeldinger, Marc. *Le platonisme de Baudelaire.* Neuchâtel, 1952.

Eisenstein, Elizabeth. *The Printing Press as an Agent of Change: Communication and Cultural Transformations in Early Modern Europe.* 2 vols. Cambridge: Cambridge Univ. Press, 1979–80.

Ellenberger, Henri. *The Discovery of the Unconscious: The History and Evolution of Dynamic Psychiatry.* New York: Basic Books, 1970.

Erdan, Alexandre. (Alexandre André Jacob). *La France mistique [sic]: Tablau [sic] des excentricités religieuses de ce tems* [sic]. 2 vols. Paris: Coulon-Pineau, n. d.

Erdan, Alexandre. *Congrès linguistique: Les révolutionnaires de l'A–B–C.* Paris: Coulon-Pineau, n. d.

Evans, Henri. *Louis Lambert et la philosophie de Balzac.* Paris: J. Corti, 1951.

Fano, Giorgio. *The Origins and Nature of Language.* Trans. Susan Petrilli. Bloomington and Indianapolis: Indiana Univ. Press, 1992.

Ferran, André. *L'esthétique de Baudelaire.* Paris: Hachette, 1933.

Flaubert, Gustave. *Bouvard et Pécuchet.* Vol. 5 of *Oeuvres complètes de Gustave Flaubert.* Ed. Société des études littéraires françaises. Paris: Club de l'honnête homme, 1971.

Flax, Neil M. "The Presence of the Sign in Goethe's *Faust.*" *PMLA* 98:2 (March 1983):183–203.

Fletcher, Angus. *Allegory: The Theory of a Symbolic Mode.* Ithaca: Cornell Univ. Press, 1964.

Forgame, M. *De l'influence de l'esprit philosophique et de celle des sociétés secrètes sur le XVIII et le XIX siècle.* Paris: Dentu, 1858.

Foucault, Michel. *Les mots et les choses.* Paris: Gallimard, 1965.

Franck, Adolphe. *La kabbale ou la philosophie des Hébreux.* Paris: Hachette, 1843.

Frank, Manfred. *Was ist Neostrukturalismus?* Frankfurt: Suhrkamp, 1984.

Frank, Manfred. *What is Neostructuralism?* Trans. Sabine Wilke and Richard Gray. Theory and History of Literature, 45. Minneapolis: Univ. of Minnesota Press, 1989.

Garrett, Clarke. *Respectable Folly: Millenarians and the French Revolution in France and England.* Baltimore: The Johns Hopkins Univ. Press, 1975.

Garrett, Clarke. "Swedenborg and the Mystical Enlightenment in Late Eighteenth-Century England." *Journal of the History of Ideas* (1984): 67–81.

Genette, Gérard. *Mimologiques, voyage en Cratylie.* Paris: Seuil, 1976.

Goethe, Johann Wolfgang von. *Faust.* Vol. 3 of *Werke.* Hamburger Ausgabe. Ed. E. Trunz. Munich: C. H. Beck, 1976.

Goethe, Johann Wolfgang von. *Faust: A Tragedy.* Trans. Walter Arndt. Ed. Cyrus Hamlin. New York: Norton, 1976.

Goldsmith, Margaret. *Franz Anton Mesmer: The History of an Idea.* London: Arthur Barker, 1934.

Grégoire, Abbé Henri Baptiste. *Histoire des sectes religieuses qui depuis le commencement du siècle dernier jusqu'à l'époque actuelle, sont nées, se sont modifiées, se sont éteintes dans les quatres parties du monde.* 6 vols. Paris: Baudouin frères, 1828–45.

Guiraud, Pierre. *Index du vocabulaire du symbolisme.* vol. 1–3, 5, 7. Paris: C. Klincksieck, 1953.

Guyon, Bernard. *La pensée politique et sociale de Balzac.* Paris: A. Colin, 1947.

Habermas, Jürgen. *Strukturwandel der Öffentlichkeit: Untersuchungen zu einer Kategorie der bürgerlichen Gesellschaft.* Neuwied: H. Luchterhand, 1962.

Habermas, Jürgen. *The Structural Transformation of the Public Sphere: An Inquiry into a Category of Bourgeois Society.* Tr. Thomas Burger with the assistance of Frederick Lawrence. Cambridge, MA: MIT Press, 1989.

Halperin, Joan U. *Félix Fénéon and the Language of Art Criticism.* Ann Arbor, Mich.: UMI Research Press, 1980.

Halperin, Joan U. *Félix Fénéon: Aesthete and Anarchist in Fin-de-Siècle Paris.* New Haven: Yale Univ. Press, 1988.

Hamlin, Cyrus, ed. *Faust: A Tragedy.* By Johann Wolfgang von Goethe. Trans. Walter Arndt. New York: Norton, 1976.

Hazard, Paul. *The European Mind, 1680–1715.* Trans. J. Lewis May. Cleveland: World Publishing, 1964.

Heinrichs, Michael. *Emanuel Swedenborg. Eine kritische Darstellung der Rezeption des schwedischen Visionärs im 18. und 19. Jahrhundert.* Frankfurt am Main: Peter D. Lang, 1979.

Helander, Hans. Introduction. Emanuel Swedenborg. *Festivus applausus in Caroli XII in Pomeraniam suam adventum.* Studia Latina Upsaliensis 17. Stockholm: Almqvist and Wiksell, 1985. 9–50.

Hindmarsh, Robert. Preface. *An Hieroglyphic Key to Natural and Spiritual Mysteries by Way of Representations and Correspondences.* By Emanuel Swedenborg. Ed. and trans. Robert Hindmarsh. 1792. London: Thomas Goyder, 1826. iii–x.

Hindmarsh, Robert. *A Compendium of the Chief Doctrines of the True Christian Religion. Manchester, 1816.*

Hindmarsh, Robert. *Abrégé des principaux points de doctrine de la Vraie Religion Chrétienne d'après les écrits de Swedenborg.* 1820; Saint-Amand: Librairie de la Nouvelle Jérusalem, 1862.

Hunt, Lynn Avery. *Politics, Culture, and Class in the French Revolution*. Berkeley: Univ. of California Press, 1984.

Irwin, John T. *American Hieroglyphics: The Symbol of the Egyptian Hieroglyphics in the American Renaissance*. New Haven: Yale Univ. Press, 1980.

Jacob, Margaret. *The Radical Enlightenment: Pantheism, Freemasons, Republicans*. London: Allen and Unwin, 1981.

Jacob, Margaret. *Living the Enlightenment: Freemasonry and Politics in Eighteenth-Century Europe*. New York: Oxford Univ. Press, 1991.

Jay, Martin. *Marxism and Totality: The Adventures of a Concept from Lukacs to Habermas*. Berkeley: Univ. of California Press, 1984.

Johannisson, Karin. *Magnetisörernas tid. Den animala magnetismen i Sverige*. [*Mesmerism in Sweden*]. Lychnos Bibliotek. Stockholm: Almqvist & Wiksell, 1974.

Johnson, Barbara. "Poetry and Its Double: Two *Invitations au voyage.*" *The Critical Difference: Essays in the Contemporary Rhetoric of Reading*. Baltimore: Johns Hopkins Univ. Press, 1980. 23–51.

Johnson, Barbara. *Défigurations du langage poétique: la seconde révolution baudelairienne*. Paris: Flammarion, 1979.

Jonsson, Inge. Introduction. Jesper Swedberg. *Levernesbeskrivning*. Selections. Ed. Inge Jonsson. Stockholm: Natur och Kultur, 1960. 5–13.

Jonsson, Inge. "Köpenhamn–Amsterdam–Paris: Swedenborgs resa 1736–1738." *Lychnos* 1967–68. 30–76.

Jonsson, Inge. *Swedenborgs skapelsedrama De Cultu et Amore Dei. En studie av motiv och intellektuell miljö*. [*Swedenborg's Drama of Creation:* On the Worship and Love of God: *Themes and Intellectual Background*]. Stockholm: Natur och kultur, 1961.

Jonsson, Inge. *Swedenborgs korrespondenslära*. [*Swedenborg's Doctrine of Correspondences*]. Stockholm Studies in History of Literature 10. Stockholm: Almqvist & Wiksell, 1969.

Jonsson, Inge. *Emanuel Swedenborg*. Trans. Catherine Djurklou. New York: Twayne, 1971.

Jonsson, Inge and Hjern, Olle. *Swedenborg: sökaren i naturens och andens världar: hans verk och efterföljd*. Stockholm: Proprius, 1976.

Jonsson, Inge. "I skaparens spar—Swedenborg och Linné." *Upplysning och romantik, 1718–1830*. Vol. 2 of *Den svenska litteraturen*. Ed. Lars Lönnroth and Sven Delblanc. Stockholm: Bonnier Alba, 1988. 48–76.

Juden, Brian. *Traditions orphiques et tendances mystiques dans le romantisme français*. Paris: Klincksieck, 1971.

Kanes, Martin. *Balzac's Comedy of Words*. Princeton: Princeton Univ. Press, 1975.

Kaplan, Fred. *Dickens and Mesmerism: The Hidden Springs of Fiction*. Princeton: Princeton Univ. Press, 1975.

Kirven, Robert. "Emanuel Swedenborg and the Revolt Against Deism." Diss. Brandeis University, 1965.

Knowlson, James. *Universal Language Schemes in England and France, 1600–1800*. Toronto and Buffalo: Univ. of Toronto Press, 1975.

Lamm, Martin. *Swedenborg. En studie öfver hans utveckling till mystiker och andeskadare*. Stockholm: Hugo Geber, 1915.

Lamm, Martin. *Swedenborg*. Trans. E. Söderlindh. Paris: Stock, 1936.

Lamm, Martin. *Swedenborg: Eine Studie über seine Entwicklung zum Mystiker und Geisterseher*. Trans. Ilse Meyer-Lüne. Leipzig: Meiner, 1922.

Lamm, Martin. *Upplysningstidens romantik: Den mystiskt sentimentala strömningen i svensk litteratur*. Stockholm: Hugo Geber, 1918.

Lamm, Martin. *August Strindberg*. 1948. Stockholm: Aldus Series. Bonniers, 1968.

Land, Stephen K. *From Signs to Propositions: The Concept of Form in Eighteenth-Century Semantic Theory*. London: Longman, 1974.

Laubriet, Pierre. *L'intelligence de l'art chez Balzac*. Paris: Didier, 1958.

Le Couteulz de Canteleu, Jean-Baptiste-Emmanuel-Hector. *Les sectes secrètes, politiques et religieuses, essai sur leur histoire depuis les temps les plus reculés jusqu'à la Révolution française*. Paris: Didier, 1863.

Le Goff, Jacques. *The Birth of Purgatory*. Tr. Arthur Goldhammer. Chicago: Univ. of Chicago Press, 1984.

Leibniz, Gottfried Wilhelm. *Cartesii cogitationes privatae. Oeuvres inédites de Descartes*. Ed. Alexandre Foucher de Careil. 2 vols. Paris: Auguste Durand, 1859. 1:2–17.

Leibniz, Gottfried Wilhelm. *Cartesii cogitationes privatae*. René Descartes. *Oeuvres de Descartes*. Ed. Charles Adam. 13 vols. Paris: J. Vrin and Le Cerf (vols. 10 and 11), 1908–57. 10:211–19.

Lenhammar, Harry. *Tolerans och bekännelsetvång. Studier i den svenska swedenborgianismen, 1765–1795*. [*Tolerance and Doctrinal Unity: A Study in Swedish Swedenborgianism, 1765–1795*]. Studia historico-ecclesiastica Upsaliensia, 11. Stockholm: Almqvist & Wiksell, 1966.

"Lettre sur la seule explication satisfaisante des phénomènes du magnétisme animal et du somnambulisme." Stockholm, 1787.

"Briefe über die Phénomene des thierischen Magnetismus und Somnam-
bulismus." *Der Teutsche Merkur*, Nov. 1787.

Sendschreiben über d. thierischen Magnetismus. Trans. K. Sprengel. Halle,
1788.

Lindroth, Sten. *Svensk lärdomshistoria.* [Swedish Intellectual History]. 3 vols.
Stockholm: Norstedts, 1975–77.

Linné, Carl von. *Nemesis divina.* Ed. Elis Malmström and Telemak Fredbärj. Stockholm: Bonnier, 1968.

Lively, Jack. Introduction. *The Works of Joseph de Maistre.* Ed. Jack Lively. New
York: Macmillan, 1965. 1–45.

Lokke, Kari. *Gérard de Nerval: The Poet as Social Visionary.* Lexington, KY: French
Forum, 1987.

Luchet, Jean-Pierre-Louis de la Roche du Maine. *Essai sur la secte des illuminés.*
Paris, 1789; Paris: Santus, 1792.

Maistre, Joseph de. *Les soirées de Saint-Petersbourg, ou, Entretiens sur le gouver-
nement temporel de la providence.* 1821; Paris: La Colombe, 1960.

Maistre, Joseph de. *The Works of Joseph de Maistre.* Ed. and trans. Jack Lively. New
York: Macmillan; London: Collier-Macmillan, 1965.

Mallarmé, Stéphane. *Oeuvres.* Ed. Yves-Alain Faivre. Paris: Garnier, 1985.

Manuel, Frank. *The Prophets of Paris.* Cambridge: Harvard Univ. Press, 1962.

Manuel, Frank and Fritzie P. Manuel. *Utopian Thought in the Western World.* Cambridge: Harvard Belknap Press, 1979.

Marx, Karl. *The Eighteenth Brumaire of Louis Bonaparte. The Marx-Engels
Reader.* Ed. Robert C. Tucker. New York: Norton, 1972. 436–525.

Matter, Jacques. *Histoire critique du gnosticisme et de son influence sur les sectes
religieuses et philosophiques des six premiers siècles de l'ère chrétienne.* 2
vols. Paris: F.-G. Levrault, 1828.

Matter, Jacques. *Saint-Martin, le philosophe inconnu: Sa vie et ses écrits, son maître
Martinez et leurs groupes, d'après des documents inédits.* Paris: Didier, 1862.

Matter, Jacques. *Emanuel de Swedenborg: Sa vie, ses écrits et sa doctrine.* Paris:
Didier, 1863.

May, Gita. *Diderot et Baudelaire, critiques d'art.* Genève: Droz, 1957.

McDannell, Colleen and Bernard Lang. *Heaven: A History.* New Haven: Yale Univ.
Press, 1988.

McIntosh, Christopher. *Eliphas Lévi and the French Occult Revival*. London: Rider, 1972.

Melzer, Françoise. "Descartes' Dreams and Freud's Failure, or The Politics of Originality." *The Trials of Psychoanalysis*. Chicago: Univ. of Chicago Press, 1988. 81–102.

Mesmer, F.-A. *Le magnétisme animal*. Ed. Robert Amadou, Frank A. Pattie and Jean Vinchon. Paris: Payot, 1971.

Michaud, Guy, ed. *La doctrine symboliste: documents*. Paris: Nizet, 1947.

Michaud, Guy. *Message poétique du symbolisme*. 3 vols. Paris: Nizet, 1947.

Mornet, Daniel. *Les origines intellectuelles de la révolution française (1715–1787)*. 4th edition. Paris: Armand Colin, 1947.

Nathans, Benjamin. "Habermas's 'Public Sphere' in the Era of the French Revolution." *French Historical Review* 16:3 (1990): 620–44.

Nerval, Gérard de. *Oeuvres*. Ed. Albert Béguin and Jean Richer. 2 vols. Paris: Pléiade, 1956.

Nykrog, Per. *La pensée de Balzac dans la Comédie humaine: Esquisse de quelques concepts-clé*. Copenhagen: Munksgaard, 1965.

Oegger, Guillaume. *Le vrai Messie, ou l'Ancien et le Nouveau Testaments examinés d'après les principes de la langue de la nature*. Paris: F. Locquin, 1829.

Oegger, Guillaume. *Essai d'un dictionnaire de la langue de la nature, ou Explication de huit cents images hiéroglyphiques*. Paris: Delaunay-Levavasseur, 1831.

Oegger, Guillaume. *Rapports inattendus établis entre le monde matériel et le monde spirituel, par la découverte de la langue de la nature, ou Transition de Guillaume Oegger*. Paris: Heideloff et Campé, 1834.

Oxford Latin Dictionary. Ed. P. G. W. Glare. Oxford: Clarendon Press, 1976.

Ozment, Steven E. *Mysticism and Dissent: Religious Ideology and Social Protest in the Sixteenth Century*. New Haven: Yale Univ. Press, 1973.

Ozouf, Mona. *La fête révolutionnaire, 1789–1799*. Paris: Gallimard, 1976.

Ozouf, Mona. *Festivals and the French Revolution*. Tr. Alan Sheridan. Cambridge, Mass.: Harvard Univ. Press, 1988.

Paley, Morton D. "A New Heaven is Begun: Blake and Swedenborgianism." *Blake and Swedenborg: Opposition is True Friendship: The Sources of William Blake's Arts in the Writings of Emanuel Swedenborg*. New York: Swedenborg Foundation, 1985. 15–34.

Pernety, Dom Antoine-Joseph. *Les fables égyptiennes et grecques dévoilées et ré-*

duites en même principe, avec une explication des hiéroglyphes et de la guerre de Troye. Paris: Baucche, 1758.

Pernety, Antoine-Joseph. *Les fables égyptiennes et grecques: dévoilées et réduites au même principe: avec une explication des hiéroglyphes et de la guerre de Troye*. Paris: La table d'éméraude, c. 1982.

Pernety, Antoine-Joseph, trans. *Les merveilles du ciel et de l'enfer et des terres planétaires et astrales d'après le témoignage de ses yeux et de ses oreilles*. Berlin: G. J. Decker, 1782.

Pernety, Antoine-Joseph. *Dictionnaire mytho-hermétique*. Paris, 1787.

Piet, F. *Mémoires sur la vie et les ouvrages d'Edouard Richer*. Nantes: Mellinet; Paris: Denn, 1836.

Pitkin, Hanna Fenichel. *The Concept of Representation*. Berkeley: Univ. of California Press, 1967.

Podmore, Frank. *Modern Spiritualism: A History and a Criticism*. London: Methuen, 1902.

Podmore, Frank. *Mesmerism and Christian Science: A Short History of Mental Healing*. London: Methuen, 1909.

Poe, Edgar Allan. "Mesmeric Revelation." *The Complete Tales and Poems of Edgar Allan Poe*. Intro. Hervey Allen. New York: Modern Library, 1938. 88–95.

Pommier, Jean. *La mystique de Baudelaire*. Paris: Les Belles Lettres, 1932.

Pommier, Jean. "Deux moments dans la genèse de *Louis Lambert*." *L'année balzacienne* 1960: 87–107.

Quilligan, Maureen. *The Language of Allegory: Defining the Genre*. Ithaca: Cornell Univ. Press, 1979.

Reardon, Bernard. *Liberalism and Tradition: Aspects of Catholic Thought in Nineteenth-Century France*. Cambridge: Cambridge Univ. Press, 1975.

Richer, Edouard. *De la Nouvelle-Jérusalem*. 8 vols. Paris: Treuttel et Wurtz, 1834–35.

Richer, Edouard. *Oeuvres littéraires*. Ed. Camille Mellinet. 7 vols. Nantes: C. Mellinet, 1838.

Riffaterre, Hermine. *L'orphisme dans la poésie romantique*. Paris: Nizet, 1970.

Robb, Graham. *Baudelaire, lecteur de Balzac*. Paris: Corti, 1988.

Roberts, Michael. *Gustavus Adolphus: A History of Sweden, 1611–1631*. 2 vols. London: Longman, 1953–58.

Roberts, Michael, ed. *Sweden's Age of Greatness, 1632–1718*. New York: St. Martin's Press, 1973.

Roberts, Michael. *The Swedish Imperial Experience, 1560-1718*. Cambridge: Cambridge Univ. Press, 1979.

Roberts, Michael. *The Age of Liberty: Sweden, 1719-1772*. Cambridge: Cambridge Univ. Press, 1986.

Roos, Jacques. *Aspects littéraires du mysticisme philosophique et l'influence de Boehme et de Swedenborg au début du romantisme: William Blake, Novalis, Ballanche*. Strasbourg: P. H. Heitz, 1951.

Rousseau, Jean-Jacques. *Oeuvres complètes*. Ed. Bernard Gagnebin, Marcel Raymond, et al. 4 vols. Bibliothèque de la Pléiade. Paris: Gallimard, 1959-69.

Rousseau, Jean-Jacques. *Essai sur l'origine des langues, où il est parlé de la mélodie et de l'imitation musicale*. Ed. Jean Starobinski. Editions folio. Paris: Gallimard, 1990.

Sahlberg, Oskar. *Baudelaire und seine Muse auf dem Weg zur Revolution*. Frankfurt am Main: Suhrkamp, 1980.

"Sandels' Eulogium on Emanuel Swedenborg." *Documents Concerning Swedenborg*. Ed. and trans. Rudolf L. Tafel. 2 vols. London: Swedenborg Society, 1875-77. 1:11-29.

Scherer, Jacques. *L'expression littéraire dans l'oeuvre de Mallarmé*. Paris: E. Droz, 1947.

Scherer, Jacques. *Le livre de Mallarmé: premières recherches sur les documents inédits*. Paris: Gallimard, 1957.

Schorske, Carl E. *Fin-de-Siècle Vienna: Politics and Culture*. New York: Knopf, 1980.

Sewell, William H. *Work and Revolution in France: The Language of Labor from the Old Regime to 1848*. Cambridge: Cambridge Univ. Press, 1980.

Shklar, Judith. *Men and Citizens: A Study of Rousseau's Social Theory*. London: Cambridge Univ. Press, 1969.

Sigstedt, Cyriel Odhner. *The Swedenborg Epic: The Life and Works of Emanuel Swedenborg*. New York: Bookman Associates, 1952.

Sjödén, K. E. "Remarques sur le *swedenborgisme* balzacien." *L'Année balzacienne* (1966): 34-45.

Sjödén, Karl-Erik. *Swedenborg en France*. Stockholm Studies in History of Literature, 27. Stockholm: Almqvist & Wiksell, 1985.

Slaughter, M. M. *Universal Languages and Scientific Taxonomy in the Seventeenth Century*. Cambridge: Cambridge Univ. Press, 1982.

Smith, Olivia. *The Politics of Language, 1791-1819*. Oxford: Clarendon, 1984.

Stafford, Barbara Maria. *Body Criticism: Imagining the Unseen in Enlightenment Art and Medicine*. Cambridge: MIT Press, 1991.

Stam, James H. *Inquiries into the Origin of Language: The Fate of a Question*. New York: Harper and Row, 1976.

Stamelman, Richard. "Under the Sign of Saturn: Allegories of Mourning and Melancholy in Charles Baudelaire." Chapter 2 of *Lost beyond Telling: Representations of Death and Loss in Modern French Poetry*. Ithaca: Cornell University Press, 1990. 49–69.

Starobinski, Jean. *Jean-Jacques Rousseau: la transparence et l'obstacle*. Paris: Gallimard, 1971.

Starobinski, Jean. "Sur l'histoire des fluides imaginaires." *L'oeil vivant II: La relation critique*. Paris: Gallimard, 1971. 196–213.

Starobinski, Jean. *Présentation. Jean-Jacques Rousseau. Essai sur l'origine des langues, où il est parlé de la mélodie et de l'imitation musicale*. Ed. Jean Starobinski. Editions folio. Paris: Gallimard, 1990. 9–54.

Stiernhielm, Georg. *Hercules, och Bröllopsbeswärs Ihugkommelse*. Ed. Adolf Noreen. Uppsala: Edv. Berling, 1910.

Stockenström, Göran. *Ismael i öknen: Strindberg som mystiker*. Acta Universitatis Upsaliensis: historia litterarum, 5. Stockholm: Almqvist & Wiksell, 1972.

Strindberg, August. *Tjänstekvinnans son*. Vols. 18 and 19 of *Samlade skrifter*. Ed. John Landqvist. 55 vols. Stockholm: Bonniers, 1912–1919.

Strindberg, August. *Inferno* and *From an Occult Diary*. Trans. Mary Sandbach. Harmondsworth: Penguin, 1979.

Swedberg, Jesper. *Jesper Swedbergs lefwernes beskrifning*. Ed. Gunnar Wetterberg. 2 vols. Publications of the New Society of Letters at Lund. Lund: Gleerup, 1941.

Swedenborg, Emanuel. *Festivus applausus in Caroli XII in Pomeraniam suam adventum*. Ed. Hans Helander. Studia Latina Upsaliensis 17. Stockholm: Almqvist and Wiksell, 1985. 9–50.

Swedenborg, Emanuel. *The Economy of the Animal Kingdom Considered Anatomically, Physically, and Philosophically*. Trans. Augustus Clissold. 2 vols. Swedenborg Scientific Association, 1955.

Swedenborg, Emanuel. *Clavis hieroglyphica Arcanorum Naturalium & Spiritualium per viam Repræsentationum et Correspondententiarum*. London: Robert Hindmarsh, 1784.

Swedenborg, Emanuel. *An Hieroglyphic Key to Natural and Spiritual Mysteries by Way of Representations and Correspondences*. Ed. and trans. Robert Hindmarsh. 1792. London: Thomas Goyder, 1826.

Swedenborg, Emanuel. *La clef hiéroglyphique des arcanes naturels et spirituels par voie des représentations et des correspondances*. Trans. Lino de Zaroa. Paris: Dupont, 1843.

Swedenborg, Emanuel. *Swedenborgs Drömmar 1744, jemte andra hans anteckningar*. Ed. G. E. Klemming. Stockholm: 1859.

Swedenborg, Emanuel. *Swedenborgs drömmar: Emanuel Swedenborgs dagbok, 1743–1744*. Ed. Knut Barr. Stockholm: Norstedts, 1924.

Swedenborg, Emanuel. *Drömboken: Journalanteckningar, 1743–44*. Ed. Per Erik Wahlund. Stockholm: Wahlström & Widstrand, 1952.

Swedenborg, Emanuel. *Swedenborg's Journal of Dreams, 1743–1744*. Ed. G. E. Klemming. Trans. J. J. G. Wilkinson. Trans. ed. William Ross Woffenden. New York: Swedenborg Foundation, 1977.

Swedenborg, Emanuel. *Arcana coelestia: The Heavenly Arcana Contained in the Holy Scriptures or Word of the Lord Unfolded, Beginning with the Book of Genesis together with Wonderful Things Seen in the World of Spirits and the Heaven of Angels*. Ed. John Faulkner Potts. 12 vols. with an index. New York: American Swedenborg Printing and Publishing Society, 1909–10.

Swedenborg, Emanuel. *De coelo et ejus mirabilibus, et de inferno ex auditis et visis*. London: J. Lewis, 1758.

Swedenborg, Emanuel. *Heaven and its Wonders and Hell from Things Seen and Heard*. Standard Edition. Trans. J. C. Ager. New York: Swedenborg Foundation, 1952.

Swedenborg, Emanuel. *Les merveilles du ciel et de l'enfer et des terres planétaires et astrales*. Trans. Pernety, Antoine-Joseph. Berlin: G. J. Decker, 1782.

Swedenborg, Emanuel. *Du ciel et de ses merveilles, et de l'enfer, d'après ce qui a été entendu et vu*. Trans. J.-P. Moët. Brussels: J. Maubach, 1819.

Swedenborg, Emanuel. *Du ciel et de ses merveilles, et de l'enfer, d'après ce qui a été entendu et vu*. Trans. J.-F.-E. Le Boys des Guays (sur l'édition princeps). Saint-Amand (Cher): Porte, 1850.

Swedenborg, Emanuel. *Abrégé des Merveilles du ciel et de l'enfer d'Emmanuel Swedenborg avec annotations et observations*. Ed. L.-A. Cahagnet. Paris: Germer-Baillière, 1854.

Swedenborg, Emanuel. *Delitiae Sapientiae de Amore Conjugiali; post quas sequuntur voluptates insaniae de amore scortatorio*. Amsterdam, 1768.

Swedenborg, Emanuel. *The Delights of Wisdom pertaining to Conjugial Love, after Which Follow the Pleasures of Insanity pertaining to Scortatory Love*. Trans. Samuel M. Warren. Rev. Louis H. Tafel. New York: Swedenborg Foundation, 1828.

Tafel, Rudolf L, ed. *Documents concerning the Life and Character of Emanuel Swedenborg.* 2 vols. London: Swedenborg Society, 1875–77.

Tatar, Maria. *Spellbound: Studies on Mesmerism and Literature.* Princeton: Princeton Univ. Press, 1978.

Thompson, E. P. *The Making of the English Working Class.* London: Gollancz, 1963.

Todorov, Tzvetan. *Introduction à la littérature fantastique.* Paris: Editions du Seuil, 1970.

Todorov, Tzvetan. *Théories du symbole.* Paris: Editions du Seuil, 1977.

Todorov, Tzvetan. *Theories of the Symbol.* Trans. Catherine Porter. Ithaca: Cornell Univ. Press, 1982.

Valéry, Paul. "Svedenborg." *Oeuvres.* Ed. Jean Hytier. 2 vols. Editions de la Pléiade. Paris: Gallimard, 1957–60. 1:867–83.

Van Dusen, Wilson. *The Presence of Other Worlds: The Psychological/Spiritual Findings of Emanuel Swedenborg.* New York: Harper and Row, 1975.

Van Dusen, Wilson. *Swedenborg's Journal of Dreams, 1743–44.* New York: Swedenborg Foundation, 1986.

Viatte, Auguste, *Les sources occultes du romantisme. Illuminisme—Théosophie, 1770–1820.* 2 vols. Paris: Honoré Champion, 1928.

Viatte, Auguste. "Les Swedenborgiens en France de 1820 à 1830." *Revue de littérature comparée* (1931): 416–443.

Viatte, Auguste. *Victor Hugo et les illuminés de son temps.* Montreal: Les éditions de l'arbre, 1942.

Waite, Arthur Edward. "Biographical Preface." *Transcendental Magic: Its Doctrine and Ritual.* By Eliphas Lévi. London: William Rider and Son, 1923. v–xx.

Waite, Arthur Edward. Preface to the English Translation. *The History of Magic.* By Eliphas Lévi (Alphonse-Louis Constant). Trans. Arthur Edward Waite. London: Rider, 1971. 5–14.

Welch, Cheryl. *Liberty and Utility: The French Idéologues and the Transformation of Liberalism.* New York: Columbia Univ. Press, 1984.

Wellek, René. "The Concept of Romanticism in Literary History." *Concepts of Criticism.* Ed. Stephen G. Nichols. New Haven: Yale Univ. Press, 1963. 128–98.

Wilkinson, Lynn R. "Embodying the Crowd: Balzac's *L'Envers de l'histoire contemporaine* and the Languages of Class Consciousness." *Symposium* 43:2 (Summer 1989): 127–37.

Wilkinson, Lynn R. *"Le cousin Pons* and the Invention of Ideology." *PMLA* 107:2 (March 1992): 274–89.

Williams, Raymond. *Culture and Society, 1780–1950.* 2nd edition. New York: Columbia Univ. Press, 1983.

Williams, Raymond. *The Country and the City.* New York: Oxford Univ. Press, 1973.

Williams, Raymond. *Marxism and Literature.* New York: Oxford Univ. Press, 1977.

Williams, Thomas A. *Eliphas Lévi: Master of Occultism.* University, Alabama: Univ. of Alabama Press, 1975.

Woofenden, William Ross. Preface. *Swedenborg's Journal of Dreams.* Trans. J. J. G. Wilkinson. Ed. Woofenden. New York: Swedenborg Foundation, 1977. i–iv.

Wilson, Catherine. "Visual Surface and Visual Symbol: The Microscope and the Occult in Early Modern Science." *Journal of the History of Ideas.* 49: 1(1988): 85–108.

Yates, Frances. *The Rosicrucian Enlightenment.* Boston: Routledge and Kegan Paul, 1972.

Yates, Frances. *The Art of Memory.* Chicago: Univ. of Chicago Press, 1966.

Zaroa, Lino de, trans. *La clef hiéroglyphique des arcanes naturels et spirituels par voie des représentations et des correspondances.* Paris: Dupont, 1843.

Index

Index

Cahagnet, Louis-Alphonse, 49, 107, 109–
112, 119, 142, 143
Arcanes de la vie future, 109–112
Calhoun, Craig, 7n (265)
Caligula (emperor), 23, 39
Cameron, Kenneth Walter, 127n (290)
Cargo, Robert T., 238n (298), 240n (298)
Cassirer, Ernst, 104n (289)
Catholic Church, xi, xii, 3, 21, 26, 38, 121,
137, 209, 210
Catholicism, 27, 47, 114, 115, 119, 124,
126, 135, 137, 142, 149, 189, 195,
196, 254, 255
Cazotte, Jacques, 139
Chacornac, Paul, 7n (265), 21n (267), 22n
(268)
Chambefort, Edouard
*Essai sur Swedenborg et ses idées escha-
tologiques*, 136
Champfleury (Jules Husson or Fleury), 220,
221, 223
Chanut, Pierre Hector, sieur de Bisches, 83
Charcot, Jean-Martin, 111
Charles X of Sweden, 67n (281)
Charles XII of Sweden, 1n (261), 58, 60,
67n (281), 77, 79–81, 89
Charlton, Donald Geoffrey, 26n (269), 50n
(277), 53n (277), 112
Chasles, Philarète, 170
Chastanier, Bénédict, 121, 123
*Tableau analytique et raisonné de la
doctrine céleste de la Nouvelle
Eglise*, 121–123, 170, 175, 175n
(295)
Chateaubriand, François René de, 27,
123
Mémoires d'outre-tombe, 123
Chinese writing, viewed as a hieroglyphic
language, 44
Chouan Rebellion, 156, 211, 212
Christ, 75, 76, 165, 166, 254
Clark, T. J., 218n (296), 220
Clawson, Mary Ann, 8n (265), 48n (277),
117n (289)
Cole, John R., 84n (286)
Collections, art, 17, 190, 202, 204
Communism, 210, 211, 213
Comte, Auguste, 137
Condillac, Etienne de, 26n (269), 105
Confucius, 165

Constant, Alphonse-Louis. *See* Constant/
Lévi
Constant, Benjamin, 133
Constant/Lévi (Alphonse-Louis Constant,
a.k.a. Eliphas Lévi), 2, 7, 10, 19–54,
55, 70, 107–109, 111, 142, 143, 219–
221, 237, 240, 247, 251–253, 255
Life, 21–24
on correspondences, 24–31
political and religious beliefs, 24, 38
on anarchism, 38, 39
an "emperor-worshiper"?, 45
possible authorship of *L'émancipation de
la femme*, 22
and literature
and Baudelaire, 19–21, 51, 52
admirer of the tradition of French revolutionary songs, 24
on novel reading, 27
works on magic, complexity of, 50
and popular culture 50–54

WORKS

"Allégorie," 27
"L'Anti-Caligula," 23, 39
La Bible de la liberté, 7, 22, 52
"Caligula," 23, 39
La clef des grands mystères, 31, 36, 37
"Les correspondances" (poem), 10, 20, 21,
24–28, 30, 32, 47, 48, 50, 219
and Baudelaire's "Correspondances,"
19–21, 219–220
La dernière incarnation, 30
Dictionnaire de la littérature chrétienne,
27–29, 30, 32, 37n (267)
"Allégorie" (entry), 27
"Les mystiques" (entry), 27
Dogme et rituel de la haute magie, 23,
27, 31–37, 40, 252, 253
introduction to 1856 edition, 35
preface to 1861 edition, 36, 37–40
and the notion of the Book, 35
engravings in, 40
L'histoire de la magie, 25, 27, 31, 36, 37,
40–49
two possible conclusions, 46
Le livre des larmes, 22, 27, 28
"La mort du poëte," 30–31, 50

328 *Index*